DETENTION UNDER THE IMMIGRATION ACTS

Law and Practice

GRAHAM DENHOLM
RORY DUNLOP

Consultant Editor
LISA GIOVANNETTI QC

OXFORD
UNIVERSITY PRESS

OXFORD

UNIVERSITY PRESS

Great Clarendon Street, Oxford, OX2 6DP,
United Kingdom,

Oxford University Press is a department of the University of Oxford.
It furthers the University's objective of excellence in research, scholarship,
and education by publishing worldwide. Oxford is a registered trade mark of
Oxford University Press in the UK and in certain other countries

Published in the United States of America by Oxford University Press
198 Madison Avenue, New York, NY 10016, United States of America

British Library Cataloguing in Publication Data

Data available

Library of Congress Control Number: 2014950939
ISBN 978–0–19–871413–2

Printed and bound by
Lightning Source UK Ltd

DETENTION UNDER THE IMMIGRATION ACTS

FOREWORD

The authors of this important book are to be congratulated for having exposed a gap in the literature on immigration law and having plugged it so successfully. As they point out in their introduction, no book to date has explored comprehensively all aspects of the law of immigration detention. There are now many aspects which need to be considered by those who advise immigrants and by Government. The law has become increasingly complex as domestic legislation covers more ground and EU law and Strasbourg jurisprudence has more to say on the subject. This complexity continues to generate large amounts of case-law. This book impressively explains, interprets, and analyses the legislation and the case-law in a clear way which will be invaluable to the intelligent lay person, practitioners, and judges alike.

In *Hardial Singh,* Woolf J famously set out some principles as to the limits of the Secretary of State's power to detain immigrants pending deportation. In the past 30 years, these principles have been refined and amplified in a plethora of case-law which this book analyses in detail and with great skill. The law in this area has become very complicated and in some respects difficult to apply. This book illuminates some of the problems and offers some solutions. Where the authors think that the reasoning of the judges could be improved, they say so tactfully and gently. There is much food for thought here, particularly for the judges!

There is much else of value. The discussion on the difference between 'imprisonment' under the common law and 'deprivation of liberty' under Article 5 of the ECHR is excellent and important. So too is the discussion about the distinction between the existence and exercise of the power to detain.

There is a penetrating exploration of the common law requirement that discretionary powers of detention must be exercised in accordance with established principles of public law; and of the different kinds of public law errors that may be material to a decision to detain. These issues are not theoretical or esoteric: they have real practical relevance. This book should provide considerable assistance in their resolution. It also contains valuable discussion on a number of procedural issues as well as on damages, including damages for unlawful detention.

The law in this area is moving very fast. Parliament continues to legislate and case-law abounds. The authors themselves note that the book does not consider the amendments made by the Immigration Act 2014 because, at the time of writing, they had not yet come into force. A new edition will, therefore, be necessary very soon.

I have no doubt that this book will be an essential addition to the library of anyone who practises in the field of the law of immigration. The authors have done a great service to all such practitioners. I commend the book most warmly.

The Rt Hon Lord Dyson,
Master of the Rolls
July 2014

PREFACE

This is, as we note in the introduction, the first attempt to provide a comprehensive textbook on the law and practice of immigration detention. We hope it will be of use to practitioners in this field (both novice and expert) and to judges called upon to grapple with cases that can raise issues of great legal and factual difficulty. We also hope that the book might find a wider readership amongst lay people with a professional interest in the topic—e.g. those working in voluntary organizations, government agencies, academia, and beyond.

There are many people we would like to thank, not all of whom can be mentioned in this preface. First, we would like to thank Oxford University Press for publishing a book that we believe is much needed but which, given the subject matter and price, is unlikely to earn them a large profit. Secondly, we would like to thank Lisa Giovannetti QC, our editor. Lisa gave up time from her extremely busy practice to read and edit our work. In her characteristically modest, generous, and polite manner she has suggested many helpful and insightful changes to content and structure. Thirdly, we would like to thank Lord Dyson, Master of the Rolls, for writing the foreword. We consider ourselves very fortunate to have an introduction from the judge that has most influenced the case-law in this field.

Rory would like to thank the people that helped him. Catherine Dobson provided excellent first drafts of the chapters on the definition of detention and other international law. She is a first rate academic and a first rate lawyer and we were very lucky to have her help. Andrew Deakin was very generous in taking time off from his impressive practice to help with the chapter on the EEA Regulations. Tom Tabori was extraordinarily helpful—volunteering himself without being asked and doing a large amount of very helpful work in relation to the case-law of the European Court of Human Rights. Rowena Moffatt, a very talented barrister and academic, produced an excellent first draft of the chapter on principles of EU law. Rory is also very grateful to Cathryn Costello, who holds the Andrew W. Mellon University Lectureship in International Human Rights and Refugee Law at the Refugee Studies Centre, Oxford, and Professor Elspeth Guild of Kingsley Napley for taking the time to read drafts of the EU law chapter. Each of them is a pre-eminent expert in the field and we were very lucky to have their contributions. Finally, Rory would like to thank his chambers, 39 Essex Street, and his wife, Lika, for supporting his decision to take six months out of his practice to write this book.

Graham would like to thank the following people. Catherine Robinson provided an excellent first draft of the chapter on the Detained Fast Track, an area of practice in which she has great experience and expertise. Pressure of space meant that some of her work did not survive the final edit. Greg Ó Ceallaigh gave up a great deal of time in the midst of a very busy period to contribute excellent drafts of the material on places and conditions of detention. Ben Bundock provided invaluable research on habeas corpus. Discussions over the years with valued colleagues, in particular David Chirico and Tim Buley, have informed many parts of this work. We were also very fortunate to have input from three pre-eminent solicitors in this field: Jane Ryan and Jed Pennington of Bhatt Murphy Solicitors and James Elliott of Wilson Solicitors LLP gave generously of their time in reviewing the chapters on damages, unsuitability for detention, and bail respectively. Finally, Graham is immensely grateful to his partner, Janette, for her unstinting support throughout this project.

We have attempted in this book to state the law as it was on 16 June 2014.[1]

---

[1] Save in one respect: we have included reference in Chapters 13 and 15 to the important decision of the Administrative Court in *Detention Action v Secretary of State for the Home Department* [2014] EWHC 2245 (Admin) and [2014] EWHC 2525 (Admin).

TABLE OF CONTENTS

CONTENTS

Contents

PART V LOCATIONS AND CONDITIONS OF DETENTION

PART VI REMEDIES AGAINST DETENTION

18. Statutory Powers to Release and Grant Bail

19. Litigating Unlawful Detention

20. Damages

TABLE OF CASES

COURT OF JUSTICE OF THE EUROPEAN UNION

UNITED NATIONS HUMAN RIGHTS COMMITTEE

TABLE OF STATUTES

TABLE OF SECONDARY LEGISLATION

ENFORCEMENT INSTRUCTIONS AND GUIDANCE LIST

LIST OF ABBREVIATIONS

AD	assistant director
AI(ToC)A 2004	Asylum and Immigration (Treatment of Claimants, etc.) Act 2004
AVR	assisted voluntary return
Bail Guidance	Presidential Guidance Note No 1 of 2012, Bail Guidance for Judges Presiding over Immigration and Asylum Hearings
BCIA 2009	Borders, Citizenship and Immigration Act 2009
CA 2004	Children Act 2004
CAAMHS	Child and Adult Mental Health Services
CAFCASS	Children and Family Court Advisory and Support Service
CAT	Council of Europe Convention on Action against Trafficking in Human Beings
CC	Immigration Enforcement Criminal Casework
CCD	UK Border Agency Criminal Casework Directorate
CFR	Charter of Fundamental Rights of the European Union
CIO	chief immigration officer
Citizens Directive	Directive 2004/38/EC
CJEU	Court of Justice of the European Union
CPR	Civil Procedure Rules
DCR 2001	Detention Centre Rules 2001, SI 2001/238
DEPMU	Home Office Detainee Escorting and Population Management Unit
DFT	Detained Fast Track
DNSA	Detained Non-Suspensive Appeals
DSOs	Detention Service Orders
EA 2010	Equality Act 2010
ECHR	European Convention on Human Rights
ECtHR	European Court of Human Rights
EEA Regulations	Immigration (European Economic Area) Regulations 2006, SI 2006/1003
EIG	Enforcement Instructions and Guidance
ERS	early release scheme
FNOs	foreign national offenders
FRP	Family Returns Process
FWF	family welfare form
FTT	First-tier Tribunal (Immigration and Asylum Chamber)
FTT Procedure Rules	Asylum and Immigration Tribunal (Procedure) Rules 2005, SI 2005/230
HRA	Human Rights Act 1998
HRC	United Nations Human Rights Committee
IA 1971	Immigration Act 1971

IA 2014	Immigration Act 2014
IAA 1999	Immigration and Asylum Act 1999
IAC Practice Directions	The Senior President's Practice Directions, Immigration and Asylum Chambers of the First-tier Tribunal and the Upper Tribunal of 10 February 2010
IAN 2006	Immigration Asylum and Nationality Act 2006
ICCPR	International Covenant on Civil and Political Rights (1966)
IDIs	Immigration Directorate Instructions
IFRP	Independent Family Returns Panel
IO	immigration officer
IRC	Immigration Removal Centre
JP	justice of the peace
LACS	local authority children's services
MAPPA	Multi Agency Public Protection Arrangements
MHA 1983	Mental Health Act 1983
MHCS	Mental Health Casework Section
NIAA 2002	Nationality, Immigration and Asylum Act 2002
NOMS	National Offender Management Service
NRM	National Referral Mechanism
OASYS	Offender Assessment System
OCC	Office of the Children's Champion
OEM	Operational Enforcement Manual
PCT	primary care trust
PNC	police national computer
PSIs	Prison Service Instructions
PSOs	Prison Service Orders
RDs	removal directions
Refugee Convention	The Convention relating to the Status of Refugees (1951) as amended and added to by its Protocol (1967)
RSC	Rules of Supreme Court
SCI RDs	Self check-in removal directions
SIAC	The Special Immigration Appeals Commission
SIACA 1997	Special Immigration Appeals Commission Act 1997
SIAC Procedure Rules	Special Immigration Appeals Commission (Procedure) Rules 2003
SLA	Service Level Agreement
TA	temporary admission
TR	temporary release
UDHR	Universal Declaration of Human Rights 1948
UKBA 2007	UK Borders Act 2007
UKBA	UK Border Agency
UKHTC	UK Human Trafficking Centre
UNCAT	United Nations Convention Against Torture, Inhuman and Degrading Treatment or Punishment 1984
UNCRC	United Nations Convention on the Rights of the Child 1989
UNHCR	UN High Commissioner for Refugees
UT	Upper Tribunal
YOTs	Youth Offending Teams

PART I

INTRODUCTION

1

THE SCOPE OF THE BOOK

A. The Purpose of the Book

In December 1983, Woolf J (as he then was) declared that there were implicit **1.01** limits on the Secretary of State's power to detain immigrants pending deportation.[1] These limits, known as the *'Hardial Singh* principles', have subsequently been applied in over 230 reported judgments. Several times as many cases have been settled—in the nine months from 1 July 2012 to 31 March 2013, for example, the Home Office paid out £4 million in compensation to persons detained under immigration powers.[2] The vast amount of case-law in this area has obliged the courts to consider and refine the common law, not just the *Hardial Singh* principles themselves but other areas too, such as the law of legitimate expectation and the tort of false imprisonment.

Despite the fast growth in litigation in this area, no book to date has explored **1.02** comprehensively and in detail all aspects of the law of immigration detention. The aim of this book is to fill that gap. It is intended to assist experts and novices alike. The established law is summarized in a comprehensive and (it is hoped) readable way. Where there are unresolved issues, the arguments on either side are set out with analysis by the authors. The book takes no position on the vexed political debates about the use of administrative powers of detention in the immigration context.

---

[1]   *R (Hardial Singh) v Governor of Durham Prison* [1984] 1 WLR 704.
[2]   Response to Freedom of Information Act request made on behalf of the authors, dated 28 August 2013, stating: 'Since July 2012 we have been reporting internally on compensation payments, including ex-gratia payments for unlawful detention claims. From 1 July 2012 until 31 March 2013 we paid £4,089,342 and from 1st April 2013 until May 2013 we paid £509,750.'

B. Overview of the Different Parts of the Book

1.03 The following Parts of the book are structured as follows:

(1) Part II—The definitions of detention and imprisonment;
(2) Part III—Liability to detention;
(3) Part IV—Limitations on the power to detain;
(4) Part V—Locations and conditions of detention;
(5) Part VI—Remedies against detention.

1.04 To succeed in a claim for unlawful detention, a claimant must first prove that they were detained. The onus then passes on to the defendant to prove that the detention was lawful.

1.05 Part II is concerned with what a claimant must prove—i.e. imprisonment (if the claim is in tort); or 'deprivation of liberty' (if the claim is under Article 5 of the European Convention on Human Rights ('ECHR')).

1.06 Chapter 2 looks at the respective definitions of 'imprisonment' and 'deprivation of liberty'. The two concepts are not synonymous.[3] It is possible that someone may have been deprived of their liberty, for the purposes of Article 5, without having suffered 'imprisonment' under the common law.[4] The reverse is also true—i.e. someone may be 'imprisoned' for the purposes of the tort, even though they have not been 'deprived of their liberty' under Article 5 of the ECHR. For example, in the case of *Austin v Commissioner of Police of the Metropolis* the Court of Appeal held that the claimants were 'imprisoned' for the purposes of the tort of false imprisonment even though there had been no deprivation of liberty within the meaning of Article 5(1).[5]

1.07 Chapter 3 applies the concepts of 'imprisonment' and 'deprivation of liberty' to situations where there might be dispute about whether a claimant had been detained. Specifically, it focuses on the following three questions:

(1) Can temporary admission, or a restriction order, or bail ever amount to a deprivation of liberty and/or imprisonment?
(2) When will the treatment of an individual by border control officers amount to a deprivation of liberty and/or imprisonment?

---

[3] See *HL v United Kingdom* (2004) 40 EHRR 761 at [90].
[4] *HL v United Kingdom* (2004) 40 EHRR 761 at [90].
[5] *Austin v Commissioner of Police of the Metropolis* [2008] AC 600 at [87]. See also the analysis of Tugendhat J at first instance—*Austin v Commissioner of Police of the Metropolis* [2005] EWHC 480 (QB) at [45] and [71].

(3) When will stopping and questioning an individual about their immigration status away from ports of entry amount to a deprivation of liberty and/or imprisonment?

Parts III and IV explore the two matters which the defendant must prove in order to establish that detention under immigration powers was lawful: **1.08**

(1) the detainee was/is 'liable to detention'—i.e. there was a statutory provision which makes/made provision for their detention;[6] and

(2) the use of detention was/is lawful in all the circumstances—i.e. detention did not and does not offend against any of the relevant legal principles.

The distinction between (1) and (2) has been described, by the House of Lords in *R (Khadir) v Secretary of State for the Home Department*,[7] as a distinction between the 'existence' of a power to detain and the 'exercise' of the power to detain. On the analysis in *Khadir*,[8] the power to detain an illegal alien pending deportation 'exists' so long as the Secretary of State remains 'intent on' deporting them and there is 'some prospect'[9] of achieving this, even if it would not, in all the circumstances, be lawful to exercise that power. If those conditions are fulfilled, the power of detention pending deportation will continue to exist until the subject of that power arrives at the final destination to which they were to be deported.[10] **1.09**

This distinction between the 'existence' and the 'exercise' of the power to detain is perhaps best illustrated by an example. Consider the position of X, an illegal **1.10**

---

[6] If there was, in the past, a Royal prerogative to detain aliens, that power has long been supplanted and replaced by statute—see *R (Soblen) v Governor of Brixton Prison* [1963] 2 QB 243 at 300–301 per Lord Denning and *R (Alvi) v the Secretary of State for the Home Department* [2012] UKSC 33; [2012] 1 WLR 2208 at [27]–[31] per Lord Hope.

[7] [2005] UKHL 39; [2006] 1 AC 207 at [33].

[8] However, the power to detain lapses if the person to be deported succeeds on appeal and the time limit for the Secretary of State to appeal lapses—*R (Gomes) v Secretary of State for the Home Department* [2014] EWHC 1169 (Admin). See paragraphs 7.07 and 7.09.

[9] *R (Khadir) v Secretary of State for the Home Department* [2005] UKHL 39; [2006] 1 AC 207 at [32] per Lord Brown. The House of Lords was forced to add the gloss that there be 'some prospect' of removal, in order to be consistent with the Privy Council's decision in *Tan Te Lam v Superintendent of Tai A Chau Detention Centre* [1997] AC 97. In *Tan Te Lam*, an appeal from the Court of Appeal of Hong Kong, the Privy Council had found that there was no power to detain Vietnamese boat people because there was no prospect of their being returned to Vietnam in light of the position of the Vietnamese authorities on such returns. As Lord Brown suggested in *Khadir* at [33], *Tan Te Lam* is probably best viewed now as an application of the *Hardial Singh* principles—i.e. detention was unreasonable, and hence unlawful, because there was no real prospect of removal *within a reasonable period of time*. Certainly, since *Khadir*, the courts have tended to accept that there was 'some prospect' of removal even when there have been significant obstacles to removal that might never be overcome, see e.g. *R (MS, AR & FW) v Secretary of State for the Home Department* [2009] EWCA Civ 1310; [2010] INLR 489 at [27], [44], and [51]. The authors are not aware of any reported case, other than *Tan Te Lam*, where it has been successfully argued that there was no prospect of removal and hence no power to detain.

[10] *R (Salimi) v Secretary of State for the Home Department & Independent Police Complaints Commission* [2012] EWCA Civ 422 at [15].

entrant from country Y. Assume that there is some prospect of removal to 'Y' but that it is unlikely to happen for many years. Assume that X poses no risk of absconding and no risk to the public. On the analysis in *Khadir*, there 'exists' a power[11] to detain X but it would be unlawful to 'exercise' that power.[12]

1.11   Some authorities have questioned whether, post-*Anisminic*,[13] a legitimate distinction can be drawn between the 'existence' and the 'exercise' of the power to detain.[14] However, those authorities are concerned with liability for false imprisonment and/or unlawful detention, where the distinction between condition (1) and condition (2) in paragraph 1.08 is unimportant—those who commit public law errors in exercising a statutory power to detain have committed the same tort, and the same human rights violation, as those who had no statutory power to detain in the first place.[15] There are, nonetheless, at least in theory, some contexts where the distinction between the existence and exercise of the power to detain is or could be helpful.[16] For example, there is an important distinction, in practice, between being granted temporary admission and being granted leave to remain. Those with temporary admission may have many more restrictions imposed on their liberty.[17] Only persons who are 'liable to detention' may be subject to temporary admission.[18] Thus, it can be very important to determine whether there exists a power to detain someone, even in circumstances where there is no prospect of that power being exercised.[19]

---

[11]   The relevant provision is paragraph 16(2) of Schedule 2 to the Immigration Act 1971. See paragraph 7.03.

[12]   Because it would breach the third *Hardial Singh* principle—see paragraphs 8.49–8.75. For the sake of completeness risk to the public is referred to in this example but see the discussion at paragraph 8.70 as to whether risk to the public is a relevant factor in detention for the purposes of removal, as opposed to detention for the purposes of deportation.

[13]   In *Anisminic Ltd v Foreign Compensation Commission* [1969] 2 AC 147 the House of Lords held that decisions which are vitiated by public law errors are 'outside the jurisdiction' of decision makers.

[14]   In *ID v Secretary of State for the Home Department* [2005] EWCA Civ 38; [2006] 1 WLR 1003 at [111] Brooke LJ suggested that an immigration officer who failed to have regard to a material consideration when exercising his powers of detention will have had 'no power' to detain that person because that is 'what the doctrine of ultra vires is all about'. In *R (Lumba & Mighty) v Secretary of State for the Home Department* [2011] UKSC 12; [2012] 1 AC 245 at [188] Lord Walker suggested that the 'wide general principle of not deviating from the statutory purpose is of such fundamental importance that it can be seen as going to the existence of the power, rather than merely to its exercise'. If that were right then the first *Hardial Singh* principle would be something that went to the existence, rather than the exercise of the power to detain.

[15]   *R (Francis) v Secretary of State for the Home Department* [2014] EWCA Civ 718 at [43].

[16]   *R (Francis) v Secretary of State for the Home Department* [2014] EWCA Civ 718 at [42]–[43].

[17]   See *R (MS, AR & FW) v Secretary of State for the Home Department* [2009] EWCA Civ 1310; [2010] INLR 489 at [2] where Sedley LJ vividly describes persons subject to temporary admission as existing in a 'half-world'. In theory, the conditions attached to temporary admission may be capable of amounting to deprivation of liberty for the purposes of Article 5 ECHR and/or imprisonment for the purposes of the tort of false imprisonment—see paragraphs 3.04–3.07.

[18]   See paragraph 21 of Schedule 2 to the Immigration Act 1971.

[19]   *R (Francis) v Secretary of State for the Home Department* [2014] EWCA Civ 718 at [43].

In any event, whether one uses the terminology of 'existence' and 'exercise' or not, **1.12** it is convenient, for the purposes of this book, to have separate analyses of:

(1) the particular statutory provisions in the Immigration Acts which authorize detention; and
(2) the general principles which the courts have established as to how such statutory provisions should be exercised.

Part III of this book is concerned with the analysis of paragraph 1.08(1)—what **1.13** the House of Lords in *Khadir* would call the 'existence' of the statutory power to detain for immigration purposes. In the words of the Immigration Acts, Part III is concerned with who is 'liable to detention'. It examines the statutory provisions from which all powers of immigration detention stem as they define who is 'liable to detention'.[20] Chapter 4 examines each of the statutory sources of the power to detain in turn. It does not consider the amendments to be made by the Immigration Act 2014 because, at the time of writing, those had not yet come into force. Chapters 5 to 7 look at the question of who is liable to detention from the perspective of the individual. Three categories of persons, separated according to their immigration status, are examined in turn. In each case, the chapter looks at when they may be liable to detention under immigration powers. Chapter 5 is concerned with British nationals. There is no statutory power to remove or deport a British national so it is debatable when, if ever, a British national may be detained under immigration powers. Chapter 5 examines some situations where a British national might arguably be liable to detention under the Immigration Acts—e.g. where there is doubt about their British nationality. Chapter 6 looks at the situation of persons who are covered by the Immigration (European Economic Area) Regulations 2006. Chapter 7 is concerned with everyone else. It looks in turn at each of the situations where an alien may be liable to detention, i.e.:

(1) because their immigration status is being examined;
(2) because they may be removable;
(3) because they may be deportable;
(4) because someone in their family falls within one of the three categories above.

Part IV of this book is concerned with the analysis of paragraph 1.08(2)—what the **1.14** House of Lords in *Khadir* would call the 'exercise' of that power. In other words, it examines the limitations which have been imposed on the power of immigration detention by the 'justice of the common law'[21] or international instruments. In other words, Part IV considers the restrictions on statutory powers of detention

---

[20] Section 67 of the Nationality, Immigration and Asylum Act 2002 provides that someone is liable to detention, even if they cannot be detained because of difficulties in removing them. See paragraphs 1.08–1.12 for a discussion of 'liability' to detention and the distinction between the existence and the exercise of the power to detain.

[21] *Secretary of State for the Home Department v Abdi; Khalaf v Secretary of State for the Home Department* [2011] EWCA Civ 242 at [7].

which are not explicit on the face of the statute but are inferred by the courts to be Parliament's intention.[22]

1.15   Chapter 8 looks at the most well established of the limitations on immigration detention—i.e. the *Hardial Singh* principles. It starts with the original judgment in *R (Hardial Singh) v Governor of Durham Prison*[23] and then looks at how that judgment has been interpreted in subsequent cases. It examines in detail the various issues which the courts have considered when applying those principles.

1.16   Chapter 9 explores another kind of common law limitation on immigration detention: the requirement that discretionary[24] powers of detention must be exercised in accordance with established principles of public law. It examines the different kinds of public law errors that may be relevant in this context, and considers the Supreme Court's approach to whether or not an error of law is 'material' to a decision to detain.

1.17   Administrative powers of immigration detention in the United Kingdom are widely drawn, and the detailed regulation of their exercise is largely by way of published policy. Chapters 10 to 13 examine key provisions of the Secretary of State's published policies on immigration detention, focussing in particular on the circumstances in which a breach of, or a failure to properly apply or have regard to, a policy, might render detention unlawful. Chapter 10 looks at the general principles in the Secretary of State's policy on immigration detention. Chapter 11 examines particular categories of alien who are generally considered unsuitable for detention and usually only detained in exceptional circumstances. Chapter 12 considers the detention of unaccompanied children and families with children. Chapter 13 looks at the Secretary of State's policies in relation to the Detained Fast Track.

1.18   Chapters 14 to 16 are concerned with the limitations imposed by international law. Chapter 14 explores when EU law may limit the Secretary of State's powers of detention. Chapter 15 examines the limitations which come from the ECHR, in particular Articles 3, 5, and 8. We argue that Article 5 is potentially more helpful to claimants than has so far been recognized. Chapter 16 considers the effect of other international instruments on the power to detain.

1.19   Part V is concerned with the location and conditions of immigration detention. It looks at where a person may be detained under immigration powers, and the regulation of places of detention.

---

[22] *R (Francis) v Secretary of State for the Home Department* [2014] EWCA Civ 718 at [45].
[23] [1984] 1 WLR 704.
[24] Most immigration detention is 'discretionary'. However, on the current state of the authorities, detention under paragraph 2(1) of Schedule 3 to IA 1971 is mandatory because it provides that someone recommended for deportation 'shall be detained' unless the Secretary of State directs otherwise—see paragraphs 9.02 to 9.06.

Part VI of the book is concerned with the remedies against detention. Chapter **1.20** 18 considers the different methods by which a detainee might secure their release without establishing before the courts that their detention was unlawful. Chapter 19 examines the different ways in which a claim that detention was unlawful might be litigated, and looks at a number of issues of particular relevance to practitioners in this field. Chapter 20 considers the courts' approach to damages for false imprisonment and/or breach of Articles 3, 5, and 8 of the ECHR. We suggest that a breach of Article 5 should generally sound in substantial damages, even when only nominal damages are available at common law. Appendix I provides summaries of a number of decisions of the domestic courts on the quantum of damages for false imprisonment as a result of unlawful detention under the Immigration Acts and more broadly.

Part II

DETENTION

2

DEFINITIONS OF DETENTION

A. False Imprisonment

Imprisonment, for the purposes of the common law tort of false imprisonment, **2.01** consists in the total restraint of another's freedom of movement from a particular place.[1] The following five propositions can be distilled from the case-law on false imprisonment.

(1) Defined area

Imprisonment requires confinement within a defined area.[2] It requires something **2.02** more than partial obstruction or merely loss of the freedom to be able to go where one pleases and includes the notion of restraint.[3] Thus if one person obstructs the passage of another in a particular direction but leaves him at liberty to stay where he is or to go in any other direction, he does not thereby imprison him.[4]

(2) No need for a prison

It is not necessary for confinement to be in a prison: any restraint within defined **2.03** bounds which is a restraint in fact may be an imprisonment.[5]

---

[1] *Collins v Wilcock* [1984] 1 WLR 1172, p 1178; *Bird v Jones* (1845) 7 AB 742, p 746; *Meering v Grahame-White Aviation Co. Ltd* [1918–19] All ER Rep Ext 1490, p 1507.

[2] *Bird v Jones* (1845) 7 AB 742, pp 745, 748, 751.

[3] *Bird v Jones* (1845) 7 AB 742, p 745.

[4] *Bird v Jones* (1845) 7 AB 742, p 751.

[5] *Meering v Grahame-White Aviation Co* [1918–19] All ER Rep Ext 1490, p 1507.

(3) No minimum time period

2.04 Any total restraint of the liberty of the person, for however short a time, will amount to an imprisonment.[6] In *Hunter v Johnson*[7] the court held that the after-school detention of a child for 45 minutes amounted to false imprisonment and in *Collins v Wilcock*,[8] the period of time for which a person was detained to be questioned by the police amounted to false imprisonment. In *Kuchenmister v Home Office*[9] the court held that the wrongful detention of a foreign national at the immigration hall for a period of two hours and 30 minutes amounted to false imprisonment.

(4) No need for coercion

2.05 There is no requirement for physical coercion to be used: all that is necessary is for one person to compel another to stay in a given place against his will.[10]

(5) No need for awareness

2.06 It is not necessary for a person to be aware that he has been imprisoned at the time that it took place: 'a person could be imprisoned without his knowing it. I think a person can be imprisoned while he is asleep, while he is in a state of drunkenness, while he is unconscious and while he is a lunatic.'[11]

B. Deprivation of Liberty—Article 5—General Principles

2.07 Article 5 of the European Convention on Human Rights ('ECHR')[12] protects the liberty and security of the person against arbitrary interference. It is concerned with liberty in its classic sense, that is to say the physical liberty of the person.[13] It provides that no one shall be deprived of their liberty, save in certain defined circumstances. There is no definition of 'deprivation of liberty' in the ECHR itself. The European Court of Human Rights ('ECtHR') has developed its own case-law on what amounts to a deprivation of liberty. A deprivation of liberty for the purposes of Article 5 is an autonomous concept. The ECtHR does not consider

---

[6] *Bird v Jones* (1845) 7 AB 742, p 751.
[7] (1884) 13 ABD 225.
[8] [1984] 1 WLR 1172.
[9] [1958] 1 QB 496.
[10] *Bird v Jones* (1845) 7 AB 742, p 751; *Meering v Grahame-White Aviation Co* [1918–19] All ER Rep Ext 1490, p 1507; *Collins v Wilcock* [1984] 1 WLR 1172, p 1180.
[11] *Meering v Grahame-White Aviation Co* [1918–19] All ER Rep Ext 1490, p 1507, per Atkin LJ; *Murray v Ministry of Defence* [1988] 2 All ER 521 and *R (L) v Bournewood Community and Mental Health NHS Trust* [1999] 1 AC 458, p 495.
[12] See paragraphs 15.07–15.65.
[13] *Engel v The Netherlands (No 1)* (1979–80) 1 EHRR 647 at [58]; *Guzzardi v Italy* Series A No 39 (1981) 3 EHRR 333 at [92].

itself bound by the conclusions of domestic courts as to whether a factual situation amounts to a deprivation of liberty.[14]

The ECtHR has drawn a distinction between a deprivation of liberty and a restriction on freedom of movement.[15] This distinction is 'merely one of degree or intensity and not one of nature or substance'.[16] Deciding on which side of the line a situation should fall 'sometimes proves to be no easy task in that some borderline cases are a matter of pure opinion'.[17] **2.08**

The closest that the ECtHR has come to defining what amounts to a 'deprivation of liberty' are the so-called *Engel*[18] or *Guzzardi*[19] criteria—i.e.: **2.09**

> In order to determine whether someone has been 'deprived of his liberty' within the meaning of Article 5, the starting point must be his concrete situation and account must be taken of a whole range of criteria such as the type, duration, effects and manner of implementation of the measure in question.

In *Guzzardi* the ECtHR emphasized that the nature or type of restriction will not be determinative.[20] **2.10**

Thus, the test for a deprivation of liberty is more fluid and less certain than the test for imprisonment under the common law. For example, under the common law, any complete restraint on movement is imprisonment, no matter how short. By contrast, under the *Engel* criteria, the duration of the restraint is one factor to be weighed along with others in determining whether there has been a deprivation of liberty. Being held in an airport transit zone, for example, will only amount to a deprivation of liberty after a certain period of time has passed.[21] **2.11**

---

[14] *Guzzardi v Italy* Series A No 39 (1981) 3 EHRR 333 at [92]; *HL v United Kingdom* (2004) 40 EHRR 761 at [90]; *HM v Switzerland* (2002) 38 EHRR 314 at [30] and [48]; *Creangă v Romania* (2013) 56 EHRR 11 at [92].

[15] *Engel & Ors v The Netherlands (No 1)* (1979–80) 1 EHRR 47 at [58]–[59].

[16] *Guzzardi v Italy* (1981) 3 EHRR 333 at [92]–[93]; *Rantsev v Cyprus and Russia* Application Number 25965/04 (7 January 2010) at [314]; *Stanev v Bulgaria* [GC] Application Number 36760/06 (17 January 2012) at [115].

[17] *Guzzardi v Italy* (1981) 3 EHRR 333 at [93].

[18] *Engel & Ors v The Netherlands (No 1)* (1979–80) 1 EHRR 647 at [59].

[19] *Guzzardi v Italy* (1981) 3 EHRR 333 at [92].

[20] (1981) 3 EHRR 333 at [95].

[21] See paragraphs 3.13–3.15.

3

DISPUTED DETENTION

A. Introduction

3.01 This chapter looks at situations where the fact of detention may be in dispute and focuses on three questions:

(1) Can temporary admission, or a restriction order, or bail ever amount to a deprivation of liberty and/or imprisonment?
(2) When will the treatment of an individual by border control officers amount to a deprivation of liberty and/or imprisonment?
(3) When will stopping and questioning an individual about their immigration status away from ports of entry amount to a deprivation of liberty and/or imprisonment?

B. Bail, Temporary Admission, and Restriction Orders

3.02 There are various alternatives to detention which may restrict a person's liberty significantly—e.g. bail, temporary admission, and restriction orders.[1] Each of these measures may be subject to conditions. Temporary admission and restriction orders may require residence at a certain location.[2] That residence requirement may be enforced by electronic monitoring of whether the person is in their house at certain times of day.[3] Bail may be subject to even more onerous conditions, including curfews and bans on leaving a defined geographical area, etc.

---

[1] See paragraphs 4.06, 4.08, 4.10, 4.14, 4.19, and 4.26.
[2] See paragraphs 4.06 and 4.08.
[3] Section 36 of the Asylum and Immigration (Treatment of Claimants) Act 2004.

The question arises—can these alternatives to detention ever amount to a depriva- **3.03** tion of liberty for the purposes of Article 5 of the European Convention on Human Rights ('ECHR') and/or imprisonment at common law?

(1) Deprivation of liberty

Temporary admission, restriction orders and bail with a curfew of 14 hours or **3.04** less are unlikely to be 'deprivations of liberty' for the purposes of Article 5 of the ECHR. The case-law in relation to control orders suggests that a curfew of 18 hours or more will amount to a deprivation of liberty, but 14 hours or less will probably not.[4] There is no rule that a curfew of 14 hours or less is not a deprivation of liberty but it is unlikely to be found to be so. Lord Bingham said, in *Secretary of State for the Home Department v E*,[5] that the court should focus on the extent to which the person is 'actually confined' and that other restrictions 'were not irrelevant, but they could not of themselves effect a deprivation of liberty if the core element of confinement, to which other restrictions (important as they may be in some cases) are ancillary, is insufficiently stringent'. In the grey area between 14-hour and 18-hour curfews, it is necessary to consider all the individual circumstances, in particular the effect of the measures imposed on the subject.[6]

(2) False imprisonment

It is at least arguable that temporary admission, restriction orders, and bail may **3.05** amount to 'imprisonment' for the purposes of the tort in at least two situations.

First, there is a reasonably strong argument that a measure which requires someone **3.06** to be in a specified address for certain defined hours of the day is 'imprisonment' for the purposes of the tort. The case-law on false imprisonment suggests that any confinement within a defined area will be an imprisonment, even it is for a relatively short period of time.[7] If that is correct, then if someone were to be granted temporary admission, with a requirement that they reside at a certain address for certain hours a day,[8] they would be 'imprisoned' for the purposes of the tort. The onus would then be on the Secretary of State to demonstrate that the imprisonment was lawful. If the person in question were not liable to detention, they would have been falsely imprisoned.

---

[4] See *Secretary of State for the Home Department v JJ and Ors* [2007] UKHL 45; [2007] 3 WLR 642; see also *Secretary of State for the Home Department v E and Anr* [2007] UKHL 47; [2007] 3 WLR 720; *Secretary of State for the Home Department v AF* [2007] UKHL 46; [2007] 3 WLR 681.

[5] [2008] AC 499 at [11].

[6] See *Secretary of State for the Home Department v AP* [2010] UKSC 24; [2010] 3 WLR 51 at [20].

[7] See paragraph 2.04.

[8] In our view, a mere residence restriction, without more, will not constitute imprisonment as it does not require the subject to be in a particular place at any particular time.

3.07   This argument has not been tested and it is not clear it would succeed. The case-law which defines 'imprisonment' for the purposes of the tort is old and long pre-dates the case-law of the House of Lords in relation to curfews, control orders, and Article 5.[9]

3.08   Secondly, it is arguable that anyone who is required, as a condition of their bail, not to leave a defined geographical area, has suffered 'imprisonment' for the purposes of the tort. In *Bird v Jones*,[10] Coleridge J said that 'a prison may have its boundary large or narrow, visible and tangible, or, though real, still in the conception only'. This has been interpreted by some American courts as meaning that there is no maximum area of confinement. *Allen v Fromme*[11] is sometimes cited for the proposition that confinement to an entire city could amount to imprisonment. If that is right, anyone who has been subject to bail which unlawfully imposed a condition they not leave a certain geographical area (e.g. a town or part of a town) will have an action for false imprisonment. It is not clear that this argument would succeed. On any normal interpretation of the word 'imprisonment', it would not include confinement to a city.

C. Treatment on Arrival

(1) Questioning in a room

3.09   Keeping an individual in a room for a period of time for questioning may amount to a deprivation of liberty for the purposes of Article 5 of the ECHR.[12] In *Salayev v Azerbaijan*[13] the European Court of Human Rights ('ECtHR') held that the applicant had been deprived of his liberty, having been kept at a police station after voluntarily attending for questioning.[14] In reaching this conclusion, the ECtHR noted that:

> although the applicant was not handcuffed, placed in a locked cell or otherwise physically restrained after entering the [police station], it appears that he had no opportunity to contact members of his family or lawyer of his own choosing.[15]

---

[9]   See paragraph 3.04.
[10]   (1845) 7 AB 742, p. 744.
[11]   141 App Div 362 (1910).
[12]   *Salayev v Azerbaijan* Application Number 40900/05 (9 November 2010) at [43]; *Osypenko v Ukraine* Application Number 4634/04 (9 November 2010) at [51]–[65]; *Aliyev (Farhad) v Azerbaijan* Application Number 37138/06 (9 November 2010) at [163].
[13]   Application Number 40900/05 (9 November 2010).
[14]   Application Number 40900/05 (9 November 2010) at [43].
[15]   Application Number 40900/05 (9 November 2010) at [42].

Being kept in a room for questioning may also constitute imprisonment, for the **3.10** purposes of the tort of false imprisonment, even if it is only for a short time.[16] However, it will not be imprisonment if the person attends voluntarily. In *R (Shaw and Anr) v Secretary of State for the Home Department*,[17] the claimant's attendance for interview was construed to be voluntary even though it was a condition of her grant of temporary admission that she attend.

(2) Restriction to a holding area

Restricting an individual to an area of an airport or port terminal for a period of **3.11** time is likely to amount to 'imprisonment' and may also constitute a deprivation of liberty.

(a) The tort

In *Kuchenmister v Home Office*[18] the court held that the wrongful detention of a **3.12** foreign national at the immigration hall for a period of two hours and 30 minutes amounted to false imprisonment. A foreign national had been transferring flights in the UK. Upon arrival, he was detained by immigration officials and prevented from crossing the airport to board his next flight. The court held that as the immigration officials had restricted his liberty to a greater degree than they were entitled to, the claimant was entitled to regard that restriction as false imprisonment and was entitled to damages.

(b) The ECHR

By contrast, holding aliens in the transit zone of an airport, while their applica- **3.13** tions are considered, will not normally amount to a deprivation of liberty for the purposes of Article 5 of the ECHR unless it is prolonged excessively.[19]

In *Amuur v France*,[20] the detention of asylum seekers in the airport transit zone **3.14** of Paris-Orly Airport for 20 days was held to be a deprivation of their liberty.[21] The ECtHR noted that, although the applicants were for the greater part left to their own devices, they were placed under strict and constant police surveillance and provided with no legal and social assistance. Moreover, neither the length nor necessity of the confinement was reviewed by the

---

[16] See paragraph 2.04.
[17] [2013] EWHC 42 (Admin) at [6]–[11], [41].
[18] [1958] 1 QB 496.
[19] *Amuur v France* (1996) 22 EHRR 533 at [43]; *Shamsa v Poland* Application Numbers 45355/99 and 45357/99 (27 November 2003); *Riad and Idiab v Belgium* Application Numbers 2978/03 and 29810/03 (24 January 2008).
[20] *Amuur v France* (1996) 22 EHRR 533.
[21] *Amuur v France* (1996) 22 EHRR 533 at [49].

court.[22] The same conclusion was reached in *Shamsa v Poland*[23] and *Riad and Idiab v Belgium*.[24]

3.15 However, the ECtHR distinguished *Amuur* in *Mahdid and Haddar v Austria*[25] and found no deprivation of liberty. In *Mahdid and Haddar*, the applicants' asylum request was decided within three days. During that period, they had been offered lodging in a special transit zone where beds and food were provided. Having refused this, they had been left to their own devices, and were free to correspond with third parties without interference from the authorities.

D. Stopping and Questioning

3.16 An immigration officer can stop and question someone away from any port of entry so long as he possesses information which 'causes him to enquire whether the person being examined is a British citizen and, if not. . . whether he should be given leave and on what conditions'.[26] Such stopping and questioning may amount to a deprivation of liberty for the purposes of Article 5 and imprisonment at common law.

(1) The ECHR

3.17 The ECtHR has held in a number of cases that the period of time during which a person is stopped and searched by the police may amount to a deprivation of liberty.[27] This can be the case even where the period of time during which an individual is stopped is of short duration.[28] What is critical is the existence of an element of coercion.[29] It is therefore very likely where a person is compelled to stop and answer questions in circumstances where they object to doing so, that the period of time for which they are stopped will amount to a deprivation of liberty for the purposes of Article 5.

---

[22] *Amuur v France* (1996) 22 EHRR 533 at [45].
[23] *Shamsa v Poland* Application Numbers 45355/99 and 45357/99 (27 November 2003).
[24] *Riad and Idiab v Belgium* Application Numbers 2978/03 and 29810/03 (24 January 2008) at [47].
[25] Application Number 74762/01 (8 December 2005).
[26] Immigration Act 1971, paragraph 2 of Schedule 2; *Singh v Hammond* [1987] 1 WLR 283, [1987] 1 All ER 829.
[27] *Foka v Turkey* Application Number 28940/95 (24 June 2008) at [77]–[79]; *Gillan and Quinton v United Kingdom* (2010) 50 EHRR 45 at [57]; *Shimovolos v Russia* Application Number 30194/09 (21 June 2011) at [50]; *Brega and Ors v Moldova* Application Number 61485/08 (23 November 2010) at [43].
[28] The Court has even found that an individual was deprived of his liberty when stopped by police for a period of only eight minutes: in *Brega and Ors v Moldova* Application Number 61485/08 (23 November 2010) at [43].
[29] *Gillan and Quinton v United Kingdom* (2010) 50 EHRR 45 at [57]; *Foka v Turkey* Application Number 28940/95 (24 June 2008) at [78].

(2) The tort

A similar approach is adopted by the common law. Any restraint within defined   **3.18**
bounds, for however short a period, may be an imprisonment.[30] There is no requirement for physical coercion to be used; all that is necessary is for one person to
compel another to stay in a given place against his will.[31]

---

[30] See paragraph 2.04.
[31] See paragraph 2.05.

PART III

LIABILITY TO DETENTION

4

STATUTORY SOURCES

A. Introduction

The Immigration Acts[1] provide powers of detention for the following purposes: **4.01**

(1) in order to examine immigration status;

(2) in order to facilitate removal;[2] and

(3) in order to facilitate deportation.[3]

These powers of detention come from the following statutory sources: **4.02**

(1) the Immigration Act 1971 ('IA 1971');[4]

(2) the Immigration and Asylum Act 1999 ('IAA 1999');

(3) the Nationality, Immigration and Asylum Act 2002 ('NIAA 2002');

---

[1] 'The Immigration Acts' are defined by section 61(2) of the UK Borders Act 2007. They do not include the Extradition Act 2003 and connected legislation, which is more closely connected to criminal law than immigration law and is outside the scope of this book. As a result, extradition is not included as a purpose of detention under the Immigration Acts.

[2] 'Removal', in the context of this chapter, refers to administrative removal for breach of immigration laws, as opposed to deportation.

[3] 'Deportation', in the context of this chapter, refers to expulsion under section 3(5) and (6) of the Immigration Act 1971—i.e. where the Secretary of State has decided it would be conducive to the public good to remove someone from the UK, e.g. because they have committed a criminal offence, or where, on a person being convicted of an offence, the sentencing court has made a recommendation that the person be deported.

[4] Save where otherwise set out, all references to the Immigration Act 1971 are to the Immigration Act 1971 as amended.

(4) the Immigration (European Economic Area) Regulations 2006 ('the EEA Regulations');[5] and

(5) the UK Borders Act 2007 ('UKBA 2007').

4.03 At the time of writing, the Immigration Act 2014 ('IA 2014') has just received Royal Assent. Sections 1 and 5 of IA 2014 propose an amendment to section 10 of IAA 1999 and paragraph 16 of Schedule 2 to IA 1971. Neither amendment has yet come into force and there is no timetable for when they will commence so they are not considered further in this chapter.

B. The Immigration Act 1971

(1) Schedule 2

4.04 Section 4 and Schedule 2 to IA 1971 give immigration officers the power to authorize detention for examination purposes in the following circumstances:

(1) to examine whether someone, who has arrived in the UK by ship or aircraft, requires leave to enter;[6]

(2) to examine whether someone, who has arrived in the UK by ship or aircraft and who requires leave to enter, should be given or refused such leave;[7]

(3) to examine whether someone, who has arrived in the UK with leave to enter granted to him before his arrival, should have his leave cancelled;[8] and

(4) for the further examination, for up to 12 hours, of someone who was previously examined, on embarking or seeking to embark in the United Kingdom, and who was given notice in writing requiring him to attend for further examination.[9]

4.05 Section 4 and Schedule 2 to IA 1971 also give immigration officers the power to authorize detention for removal purposes. That power exists where there are reasonable grounds for suspecting that the person is someone in respect of whom removal directions may be given because:

(1) they have been refused leave to enter;[10]

(2) they are an illegal entrant;[11]

(3) they are a member of the family of someone who falls within (1) or (2) of this list;[12] or

---

[5] The EEA Regulations are not an Immigration Act but they are a portal to detention powers under the Immigration Acts—see paragraphs 6.04–6.14.

[6] Paragraphs 2(1)(a) and (b) and 16(1) of Schedule 2 to IA 1971.

[7] Paragraphs 2(1)(c) and 16(1) of Schedule 2 to IA 1971.

[8] Paragraphs 2A and 16(1A) of Schedule 2 to IA 1971.

[9] Paragraphs 3(1A) and 16(1B) of Schedule 2 to IA 1971.

[10] Paragraphs 8, 10 and 16(2) of Schedule 2 to IA 1971.

[11] Paragraphs 9, 10 and 16(2) of Schedule 2 to the IA 1971.

[12] Paragraphs 10A and 16(2) of Schedule 2 to IA 1971. The power to give removal directions to Y on the basis that Y is a member of X's family can only be exercised where removal directions are

(4) they are a member of a ship or aircraft or Channel Tunnel train's crew who has stayed beyond the time permitted or is reasonably suspected by an immigration officer of intending to do so.[13]

Paragraphs 21–22 of Schedule 2 to IA 1971 and, where an appeal is pending, paragraph 29 of Schedule 2 to IA 1971, provide alternatives to detention in the situations described at paragraphs 4.04–4.05:[14]   **4.06**

(1) the person may be temporarily admitted to the United Kingdom, under the written authority of an immigration officer, and made subject to restrictions as to residence, employment and occupation;[15] and
(2) if the person has been detained, and the special provisions in relation to national security do not apply,[16] they may, in general,[17] be released on bail by an immigration officer not below the rank of chief immigration officer or by the First Tier Tribunal.[18]

(2) Schedule 3

Sections 3(5)–(6), 5 and Schedule 3 to IA 1971 provide powers to detain for deportation purposes. A person will be liable to detention under these powers if: **4.07**

(1) a court has recommended their deportation;[19]

---

given to X as well. However, Y may be detained before removal directions have been given either to X or Y, so long as there are reasonable grounds for suspecting that X and Y are persons in respect of whom such directions may be given.

[13] Paragraphs 12–14 and 16(2) of Schedule 2 to the IA 1971. See also the Channel Tunnel (International Arrangements) Order 1993, SI 1993/1813, Schedule 4, paragraph 1(11)(n) and (p). Members of such crews may be given leave of short duration or they may be allowed to enter the United Kingdom without leave for a short period (see section 8 of IA 1971).

[14] Neither temporary admission nor bail is available to anyone detained for further examination, of up to 12 hours, after previously having been examined, on embarking or seeking to embark in the United Kingdom, and being given notice in writing requiring him to attend for further examination—see paragraphs 21(1) and 22(1) of Schedule 2 to IA 1971.

[15] Paragraph 21(1) of Schedule 2 to IA 1971.

[16] Where detention has been certified as being necessary in the interests of national security, or where the detainee has been detained following a decision to refuse leave to enter on national security grounds, or where a decision has been taken to deport on national security grounds, the only body that may grant bail is the Special Immigration Appeals Commission (section 3(2) of and Schedule 3 to the Special Immigration Appeals Commission Act 1997 ('SIACA 1997')). See paragraphs 18.110–18.126.

[17] Bail is not available to anyone detained pending examination and/or a decision on whether to refuse leave to enter, unless seven days have elapsed since his arrival in the United Kingdom—see paragraph 22(1B) of Schedule 2 to IA 1971.

[18] Paragraph 22(1A) of Schedule 2 to IA 1971. In addition, if they have an appeal pending, they may be released on bail by a police officer not below the rank of inspector—see section 29(2) of IA 1971.

[19] Paragraph 2(1) of Schedule 3 to IA 1971. This provides for a mandatory power of detention— i.e. any person recommended for deportation 'shall be detained' unless the Secretary of State directs otherwise. The distinction between the mandatory powers of detention—under paragraph 2(1) and the corresponding element of paragraph 2(3) of Schedule 3 to IA 1971—and other powers of

(2) a notice has been[20] properly served[21] of a decision to make a deportation order against them[22] and the Secretary of State has authorized detention;[23] and

(3) where a deportation order is in force[24] against them and the Secretary of State has authorized detention.[25]

4.08 Paragraphs 2(4A)–(6) and (in relation to bail, where an appeal is pending) 3 of Schedule 3 to IA 1971 provide alternatives to detention where someone is liable to detention for one of the three reasons identified in paragraph 4.07:

(1) the person may be released by the Secretary of State subject to restrictions as to residence, employment and occupation;[26] and

(2) if the person has been detained, and the special provisions in relation to national security do not apply,[27] he may be released on bail by an immigration officer not below the rank of chief immigration officer or by the First Tier Tribunal.[28]

C. The Immigration and Asylum Act 1999

4.09 Section 10(7) of IAA 1999 supplements the powers of immigration officers, under IA 1971, to authorize detention for the purposes of removal. In particular, it provides a power for immigration officers to authorize detention where there

---

detention is significant when the Secretary of State has made a material error of public law—see paragraphs 9.02–9.06.

[20] The first arrest may take place before the notice of decision has been served so long as it is ready to be served at the time of arrest—see paragraph 2(4) of Schedule 3 to IA 1971 and paragraph 17 of Schedule 2 to IA 1971.

[21] 'Properly served' here means that the notice was served in accordance with the Immigration (Notices) Regulations 2003, SI 2003/568.

[22] See paragraphs 7.01 and 7.08–7.09 for a discussion of the persons against whom deportation orders can be made.

[23] Paragraph 2(2) of Schedule 3 to IA 1971.

[24] A deportation order is only 'in force' when it has been served on the detainee—*R (S) v Secretary of State for the Home Department* [2011] EWHC 2120 (Admin) at [151]–[159]. However, the first arrest may take place before the deportation order has been served so long as it is ready to be served at the time of arrest—see paragraph 2(4) of Schedule 3 to IA 1971 and paragraph 17 of Schedule 2 to IA 1971.

[25] Paragraph 2(3) of Schedule 3 to IA 1971.

[26] Paragraph 2(5)–(6) of Schedule 3 to IA 1971.

[27] Where detention has been certified as being necessary in the interests of national security, or where the detainee has been detained following a decision to refuse leave to enter on national security grounds, or where a decision has been taken to deport on national security grounds, the only body that may grant bail is the Special Immigration Appeals Commission (section 3(2) of and Schedule 3 to SIACA 1997). See paragraphs 18.40–18.42.

[28] Paragraph 2(4A) of Schedule 3 to IA 1971 and paragraphs 22(1A) and 29 of Schedule 2 to IA 1971. Where an appeal is pending, such that the power to grant bail arises under paragraph 29, it may also be exercised by a police officer not below the rank of inspector.

are reasonable grounds for suspecting that the person in question may be given removal directions because:

(1) they only have limited leave to enter or remain and have not observed a condition attached to that leave;[29]

(2) they have overstayed—i.e. stayed beyond the limits of their leave to enter or remain;[30]

(3) they used deception in seeking (whether successfully or not) leave to remain;[31]

(4) their indefinite leave to remain has been revoked under section 76(3) of NIAA 2002 because they have ceased to be a refugee;[32] or

(5) they are a member of the family of someone within categories (1) to (4).[33]

The same alternatives to detention are available as to someone detained under **4.10** Schedule 2 to IA 1971—i.e. temporary admission and bail.[34]

D. The Nationality Immigration and Asylum Act 2002

The NIAA 2002 gives the Secretary of State powers to detain pending examina- **4.11** tion and removal. The power to authorize detention need not be exercised by the Secretary of State but may be exercised by one of her officials under Carltona[35] principles.

In particular, section 62(2) of NIAA 2002 makes provision for the Secretary of **4.12** State to authorize detention for the purposes of examination in the following circumstances:

(1) to examine someone who is seeking leave to enter the United Kingdom and has:
    (a) made a claim for asylum;[36]

---

[29] Section 10(1)(a) and 10(7) of IAA 1999. Note that such directions cannot be given if the person concerned has made an application for leave to remain in accordance with the Immigration (Regularisation Period for Overstayers) Regulations 2000: see section 10(2) of IAA 1999.

[30] Section 10(1)(a) and 10(7) of IAA 1999.

[31] Section 10(1)(b) and 10(7) of IAA 1999.

[32] Section 10(1)(ba) and 10(7) of IAA 1999.

[33] Section 10(1)(c) and 10(7) of IAA 1999. Note that removal directions may not be given to a family member unless (a) the Secretary of State has given that family member notice of the intention to remove him (section 10(3) of IAA 1999); and (b) directions have been given for the removal of the person to whose family he belongs (section 10(1)(c) of IAA 1999). Such notice may not be given if the person, whose removal under section 10(1)(a) or (b) of the IAA 1999 is the cause of the proposed removal direction, has left the United Kingdom more than eight weeks previously (section 10(4) of IAA 1999).

[34] Section 10(7) of IAA 1999. See paragraph 4.06 for the alternatives to detention under Schedule 2 to IA 1971.

[35] *Carltona Ltd v Commissioners of Works* [1943] 2 All ER 560.

[36] See section 62(2)(a) of NIAA 2002, section 3A(7)–(8) of IA 1971, and Article 2(2)(a) of the Immigration (Leave to Enter) Order 2001, SI 2001/2590.

(b) made a claim that it would be contrary to the Human Rights Convention for them to be removed from, or required to leave, the United Kingdom;[37] or

(c) sought leave to enter outside the immigration rules;[38] and

(2) for so long as it may take to make a decision on whether to grant leave to enter to a person referred to in (1).

4.13 Section 62(1)–(2) of NIAA 2002 also makes provision for the Secretary of State to authorize detention for the purposes of removal in the following circumstances:

(1) where the Secretary of State has reasonable grounds to suspect[39] that she may set removal directions[40] for the person in question because:

(a) they have been refused leave to enter;[41]

(b) they are an illegal entrant;[42]

(c) they are a member of the family of someone within (a) or (b) above;[43] or

(d) they are a member of a ship or aircraft or Channel Tunnel train's crew who has stayed beyond the time permitted or is reasonably suspected by an immigration officer of intending to do so;[44] or

---

[37] See section 3A(7)–(8) of IA 1971 and Article 2(2)(b) of the Immigration (Leave to Enter) Order 2001, SI 2001/2590.

[38] See section 3A(7)–(8) of IA 1971 and Article 2(3) of the Immigration (Leave to Enter) Order 2001, SI 2001/2590.

[39] See section 62(1)(a) and (7) of NIAA 2002.

[40] Removal directions must be given by an immigration officer, rather than the Secretary of State, unless (a) it would not be practicable or effective to direct the captain or the owners or agents of the ship or aircraft, on which the person in question arrived, to remove him; (b) more than two months have passed since the person in question was refused leave to enter, and no notice of the intention to set removal direction was given, in the meantime, to the owners or agents of the ship or aircraft on which the person in question arrived; or (c) the person in question seeks leave to enter the United Kingdom and has made an asylum or human rights claim or sought leave to enter outside the immigration rules. See section 3A(7)–(8) of and paragraphs 8–10 of Schedule 2 to IA 1971, section 62(c)–(d) of NIAA 2002 and Article 2 of the Immigration (Leave to Enter) Order 2001, SI 2001/2590.

[41] See section 62(1)(a) and (7) of and paragraphs 8 and 10 of Schedule 2 to NIAA 2002; and section 62(2)(c)–(d) of NIAA 2002, section 3A of IA 1971, and Article 2 of the Immigration (Leave to Enter) Order 2001, SI 2001/2590. See footnote 40 as to who may be subject to removal directions by the Secretary of State, as opposed to an immigration officer.

[42] See section 62(1)(a) and (7) of and paragraphs 9 and 10 of Schedule 2 to NIAA 2002. See footnote 40 as to who may be subject to removal directions by the Secretary of State, as opposed to an immigration officer.

[43] See section 62(1)(a) and (7) of and paragraph 10A of Schedule 2 to NIAA 2002. See footnote 40 as to who may be subject to removal directions by the Secretary of State, as opposed to an immigration officer. The power to give removal directions to Y on the basis that Y is a member of X's family can only be exercised where removal directions are given to X as well. However, Y may be detained before removal directions have been given either to X or Y, where the Secretary of State has reasonable grounds for suspecting that he may make removal directions against X and Y (section 62(7) of NIAA 2002).

[44] See section 62(1)(a) and (7) of NIAA 2002 and paragraphs 14 and 16(2) of Schedule 2 to the IA 1971. See also the Channel Tunnel (International Arrangements) Order 1993, SI 1993/1813, Sch. 4, para. 1(11)(n) and (p). Members of such crews may be given leave of short duration or they may be allowed to enter the United Kingdom without leave for a short period (see section 8 of IA

(2) removal directions have been set by the Secretary of State for one of the reasons identified at (1)(a)–(d).[45]

The same alternatives to detention are available as to someone detained under **4.14** Schedule 2 to IA 1971—i.e. temporary admission and bail.[46] Section 71(1)–(3) of NIAA 2002 provide for the detention of anyone who:

(1) has made an asylum claim at a time when they had leave to enter or remain in the United Kingdom;

(2) was granted temporary admission subject to a restriction as to residence, reporting or occupation; and

(3) failed to comply with that restriction.

E. The Immigration (European Economic Area) Regulations 2006

The EEA Regulations (SI 2006/1003) were introduced to give effect, in domestic **4.15** law, to Directive 2004/38/EC.[47] The EEA Regulations set out when powers of detention, under the Immigration Acts, may be used in relation to certain persons with rights under EU law.[48]

First, the EEA Regulations provide that the powers of immigration officers (under **4.16** section 4 and paragraphs 2 and 16(1) of Schedule 2 to IA 1971) to authorize detention for examination purposes[49] apply in relation to:

(1) EEA nationals claiming a right of admission under the EEA Regulations, where there is reason to believe they may fall to be excluded on grounds of public policy, public security or public health and/or that they are subject to a deportation or exclusion order;[50] and

(2) other persons claiming a right of admission under the EEA Regulations, who are not themselves EEA nationals.[51]

1971). See footnote 40 as to who may be subject to removal directions by the Secretary of State, as opposed to an immigration officer.

[45] See section 62(1)(b) and (7) of NIAA 2002.

[46] Section 62(3) of NIAA 2002. See paragraph 4.06 for the alternatives to detention under Schedule 2 to IA 1971.

[47] Directive 2004/38/EC of the European Parliament and the Council of 29 April 2004 on the rights of citizens of the Union and their family members to move and reside freely within the territory of the Member States.

[48] See Chapter 6 for more details on the EEA Regulations.

[49] See paragraph 4.04.

[50] See regulations 19(1) and (1A) and 22(1)(b) and (2) of the EEA Regulations 2006.

[51] I.e. family members of an EEA national, family members who have retained a right of residence, persons who have derivative rights of residence and persons with permanent rights of residence under regulation 15 of the EEA Regulations 2006—see regulation 22(1)(a) and (2) of the EEA Regulations 2006.

4.17 Secondly, the EEA Regulations provide for a power to authorize detention for removal purposes where:

(1) a decision has been taken to refuse the person admission under the EEA Regulations;[52] or

(2) a decision has been taken to remove the person in question on the grounds that they do not have a right to reside under the EEA Regulations.[53]

4.18 Finally, the EEA Regulations provide for a power to authorize detention for deportation purposes, where:

(1) there are reasonable grounds for suspecting that the person in question may be removed under Regulation 21 of the EEA Regulations on grounds of public policy, public security or public health;[54]

(2) a decision has been taken to remove someone under Regulation 21 of the EEA Regulations on grounds of public policy, public security or public health;[55] or

(3) the person in question has entered in breach of a deportation order or exclusion order.[56]

4.19 With one exception, the EEA Regulations provide that the alternatives to detention available under IA 1971[57] should be available to anyone liable to detention under the EEA Regulations.[58] The exception is where someone is liable to detention because there are reasonable grounds for suspecting that he may be removed on grounds of public policy, public security, or public health. The EEA Regulations do not provide for a power to grant temporary admission or a restriction order or bail in regard to such a person. Regulation 24(1) of the EEA Regulations simply says that paragraphs 17 and 18 of Schedule 2 to IA 1971 are to apply to such a person. It does not say that the provisions in relation to temporary admission, restriction orders, or bail in Schedule 2 to IA 1971 should apply. This is anomalous and may well have been a slip by the draftsman—it is extraordinary that there is a power for executive detention, with no power to apply for bail.

4.20 Regulation 24(6) of the EEA Regulations provides that those who are to be expelled from the United Kingdom—whether on grounds that they have no right of residence, or on the grounds of public policy, public security, or public health—should

---

[52] Regulation 23(1) of the EEA Regulations.

[53] See regulation 24(2) of the EEA Regulations. The powers of detention under section 10(7) of the IAA 1999 are deemed to apply in this situation.

[54] See regulations 24(1) and 19(3)(b) of the EEA Regulations.

[55] See regulation 24(3) of the EEA Regulations. The powers of detention under section 5 of and Schedule 3 to the IA 1971 are deemed to apply in this situation.

[56] See regulation 24(4) of the EEA Regulations. The powers of detention under Schedule 2 to the IA 1971 are deemed to apply in this situation.

[57] See paragraphs 4.06 and 4.08.

[58] See regulations 22(2), 23(2), and 24(2)–(4) of the EEA Regulations.

generally (subject to certain exceptions)[59] be 'allowed' one month to leave the United Kingdom voluntarily, beginning on the date when they are notified of the decision to expel them.[60]

F. The UK Borders Act 2007

Section 2(1) of UKBA 2007 gives an immigration officer the power to detain an **4.21** individual for three hours if the officer thinks that the individual may be liable to arrest under certain constable powers or is subject to a warrant for arrest. Section 2(1) is not discussed further because it is better viewed as detention under criminal powers rather than under immigration powers—in effect it transfers the detention powers of a police constable to an immigration officer for three hours.

Section 36(1)(a) of UKBA 2007 gives the Secretary of State a power to detain per- **4.22** sons who have served a period of imprisonment while she considers whether section 32(5) of UKBA 2007 applies to them. Section 32(5) of UKBA 2007 requires the Secretary of State to make a deportation order in respect of a 'foreign criminal'[61] unless one of the exceptions specified in section 33 of UKBA 2007 applies, e.g. expulsion would breach their rights under the ECHR.

Section 36(1)(a) of UKBA 2007 thus extends the power of the Secretary of State **4.23** to authorize detention for deportation purposes. Prior to the coming into force of UKBA 2007, the Secretary of State could only detain, for deportation purposes, where either:

(1) the court had recommended deportation;
(2) the Secretary of State had made a decision to make a deportation order; or
(3) a deportation order was in force.

Now the Secretary of State can detain a foreign national prisoner, who has served **4.24** the custodial part of their sentence, while she makes up her mind about whether to deport them. Where someone is liable to detention under this provision, the

---

[59] The exceptions are (a) where there is a 'duly substantiated case of urgency', (b) where the person is detained pursuant to the sentence or order of a court, (c) where the person entered the United Kingdom in breach of a deportation order or exclusion order, (d) where a decision has been taken to remove him on the grounds that he has ceased to have a derivative right of residence, and (e) where the person does not have a right of derivative residence as a result of a decision to remove on the grounds of public policy, public security or public health. See regulation 21(6)–(7) of the EEA Regulations 2006.
[60] See paragraph 6.33 for a discussion of the effect of this provision.
[61] Defined under section 32(1)–(3) of UKBA 2007 to be someone who is not a British citizen and who has been convicted of an offence for which he received a sentence of imprisonment and either (1) the sentence was for at least 12 months imprisonment; or (2) the offence was specified by order of the Secretary of State under section 72(4)(a) of NIAA 2002 as being a serious criminal offence.

alternatives to detention provided for by Schedule 3 to IA 1971 are available—i.e. restriction orders and bail.[62]

4.25 Section 36(1)(b) of UKBA 2007 also allows for a power of detention where the Secretary of State thinks that section 32(5) applies. In practice, this provision is seldom relied on for long, if at all, because the Secretary of State tends to make the deportation order immediately after deciding that section 32(5) applies. Once a deportation order has been made in accordance with section 32(5), section 36(2) provides that the Secretary of State '*shall* exercise the power of detention under paragraph 2(3) of Schedule 3 to the Immigration Act 1971 . . . unless in the circumstances the Secretary of State thinks it inappropriate' (our emphasis).[63]

G. Immigration, Asylum and Nationality Act 2006

4.26 An amended version of section 47 of the Immigration Asylum and Nationality Act ('IAN 2006') came into force on 8 May 2013. It permits the Secretary of State to give removal directions at the same time as making a 'pre-removal decision'—i.e. a decision not to grant someone further leave to remain or to take away his existing leave to enter or remain.[64] It allows the Secretary of State to set removal directions even though the person still has leave.[65] Section 47(3) of IAN 2006 allows for the detention of a person if there are reasonable grounds for suspecting that they are a person in respect of whom such directions may be given and provides for the same alternatives to detention as are available under Schedule 2 to IA 1971.[66]

---

[62] See section 36(4)–(5) of UKBA 2007.
[63] See paragraphs 9.02–9.06 for a discussion of the effect of this mandatory wording on the lawfulness of detention.
[64] See section 47(1A) of IAN 2006. 'Taking away' leave means either revoking leave or varying it so that there is no more leave.
[65] They will have leave either because their original leave has not yet expired or because it has been extended under sections 3C–D of IA 1971 pending an appeal. That is why the decision is called a 'pre-removal decision'.
[66] See paragraph 4.06.

5

BRITISH CITIZENS

A. Introduction

If someone claims to be a British citizen, the onus of proof is on them.[1] The stand- **5.01**
ard of proof is the balance of probabilities.[2] The production of a genuine British
passport describing the holder as a British citizen is usually sufficient to prove
British citizenship.[3] In such a situation, the onus passes to the Secretary of State
to prove that the person in question is not, in fact, a British citizen, for example
because:

(1) the passport was not issued to them;[4] or
(2) they used fraud, false representation or concealment in order to obtain the
passport.[5]

This chapter is not concerned with those who merely appear to be British citizens **5.02**
but who are not, for example because of the reasons set out in paragraph 5.01(1)
and (2). Such persons will be liable to detention for one of the reasons considered
in paragraphs 7.06–7.08. This chapter is concerned with people who genuinely are

---

[1] Section 3(8) of Immigration Act 1971 ('IA 1971') and *R v Secretary of State for the Home Department,
ex p Bamgbose* [1990] Imm AR 135.
[2] *Beckett (Anthony Donovan) v Secretary of State for the Home Department* [2008] EWHC 2002
(Admin) at [2].
[3] Section 3(9) of IA 1971.
[4] See *R (Parvaz Akhtar) v Secretary of State for the Home Department* [1981] QB 46; and *R (Obi) v
Home Secretary* [1997] 1 WLR 1498.
[5] See *R (Kadria) v Secretary of State for the Home Department* [2010] EWHC 3405 (Admin) at
[19]–[33]. Note that British citizenship obtained by fraud, false representation or concealment is not
always a 'nullity'. It depends on the nature, quality, and extent of the fraud, deception, or concealment.

British citizens. There are at least three situations,[6] set out in this chapter, in which a British citizen may, arguably, be liable to detention under the Immigration Acts:

(1) on arrival in the UK;
(2) where the immigration officer or Secretary of State has a reasonable suspicion that the person is not a British citizen but is either:
   (a) someone who may be removed; or
   (b) someone who may be deported; and
(3) where the person is to be deprived of their British citizenship.

B. Examination on Arrival

5.03 When a British citizen has arrived in the United Kingdom by ship or aircraft, he may be detained under the authority of an immigration officer for so long as it may take to examine whether or not he is, in fact, a British citizen.[7] This need not happen at the point of arrival. An immigration officer can stop and question someone away from any port of entry so long as he possesses information which 'causes him to inquire whether the person being examined is a British citizen'.[8] A person shall prove that they are a British citizen if they have a passport describing themselves as a British citizen.[9]

C. Suspicion that Expellable

5.04 British citizens cannot lawfully be removed[10] or deported[11] from the United Kingdom.[12] If someone faced with removal or deportation alleges that they are a British citizen, they can bring an application for judicial review of the proposed expulsion and the High Court will determine whether they are a British citizen as a question of precedent fact.[13] The court will not defer to the Secretary of State's

---

[6] We have not included the situation where British citizens are detained under section 2(1) of the UK Borders Act 2007 ('UKBA 2007')—i.e. because the immigration officer thinks they may be liable to arrest or subject to an arrest warrant—as that provision is better analysed in a textbook on criminal law than a textbook on immigration detention.

[7] See paragraph 2(1)(a) and 16(1) of Schedule 2 to the IA 1971. As noted at paragraph 5.01, the burden of proof rests on the person asserting British citizenship to prove that they are, in fact, a British citizen (see section 3(8) of IA 1971).

[8] IA 1971, paragraph 2 of Schedule 2; *Singh v Hammond* [1987] 1 WLR 283; [1987] 1 All ER 829.

[9] Section 3(9) of IA 1971. See paragraph 5.01.

[10] See section 10(1) of Immigration and Asylum Act 1999 ('IAA 1999'): a person must not be a British citizen in order to be liable to administrative removal from the United Kingdom.

[11] See section 3(5)–(6) of IA 1971: a person must not be a British citizen in order to be liable to deportation.

[12] A British citizen can be extradited to face criminal charges in another country but that is outside the scope of this book.

[13] *R (Lim) v Secretary of State for the Home Department* [2007] EWCA Civ 773; [2008] INLR 60 at [19] and [25].

judgment and will hear live evidence, if necessary.[14] An out of country appeal to the First Tier Tribunal will not be an adequate alternative remedy.[15]

However, that does not necessarily mean that British citizens cannot be detained **5.05** pending removal or deportation from the United Kingdom.

(1) Removal

Immigration officers and the Secretary of State may authorize the detention of **5.06** someone if there are 'reasonable grounds for suspecting' that they are someone in respect of whom removal directions may be served.[16] A reasonable suspicion may be based on a mistake of fact, so long as that mistake is honest and reasonable, although it cannot be based on a mistake of law.[17] As a result, a British citizen will be liable to detention under immigration powers if the detaining official honestly and reasonably believes that he is not a British citizen but someone who could be removed. Even if a court finds, subsequently, that the detainee was actually a British citizen, that will not, in itself, render the past detention unlawful. If there were reasonable grounds for the suspicions held at the time of detention, detention will have been lawful.[18]

(2) Deportation

It is arguable that British citizens, who have served a sentence of imprisonment, **5.07** are liable to detention, at the expiry of that sentence, while the Secretary of State decides whether they can be subject to automatic deportation.[19] This submission was made by Treasury Counsel in *R (Rashid Hussein) v Secretary of State for the Home Department*.[20] Nicol J said that this would be a 'dramatic extension of the law' but declined to rule on the issue. The words of the statute tend to support the Treasury Counsel's submission—the only precondition for the exercise of the power of detention under section 36(1) of UKBA 2007 is that the person has served a sentence of imprisonment.

---

[14] *Beckett (Anthony Donovan) v Secretary of State for the Home Department* [2008] EWHC 2002 (Admin) at [3].
[15] *R (Lim) v Secretary of State for the Home Department* [2007] EWCA Civ 773; [2008] INLR 60 at [19].
[16] Paragraph 16(2) of Schedule 2 to IA 1971, section 10 of IAA 1999 and section 62 of NIAA 2002.
[17] See *Walker v Lovell* [1975] 1 WLR 1141 *per* Lord Diplock at p 1151 E–F.
[18] See *R (AA) v Secretary of State for the Home Department* [2012] EWCA Civ 1383 at [40], where Arden LJ held that the detention power under paragraph 16(2) of Schedule 2 to IA 1971 was exercisable 'whenever the Secretary of State forms a view that there are reasonable grounds for a suspicion' that the person may be removed. It is not necessary for the Secretary of State also to show that her suspicions were correct. See also paragraph 5.01 on when a passport will prove nationality.
[19] I.e. deportation under section 32(5) of UKBA 2007—the provision which requires the deportation of 'foreign criminals' unless one of the exceptions in section 33 of UKBA 2007 apply.
[20] [2009] EWHC 2492 (Admin) at [44].

5.08 In practice, it will seldom be lawful to exercise the power, even if it exists. If a British citizen is sentenced to imprisonment, the Secretary of State should, in most situations, have realized that they are British, and therefore not susceptible to automatic deportation,[21] before they have come to the end of their criminal sentence. In theory, however, there remains a possibility that such a power may lawfully be exercised, for example where the Secretary of State has reasonable doubts as to the criminal's true identity and they do not hold a valid British passport.

D. Deprivation of British Citizenship

5.09 It is arguable that the Secretary of State and immigration officers may authorize the detention of a British citizen where there are reasonable grounds for suspecting that he will be deprived of his British citizenship[22] and then be removed. The power of detention under paragraph 16(1) of Schedule 2 to IA 1971 exists whenever there are reasonable grounds for suspecting that the detainee is 'someone in respect of whom removal directions may be given'. It is arguable that this power arises even if the person in question cannot yet be subject to removal directions because he has not yet been deprived of his British citizenship. In *R (Khan) v Secretary of State*,[23] 'a person in respect of whom [removal directions] may be given' was held to include persons who could not yet, at the time of detention, be subject to removal directions. The context was different, however, as it concerned the detention of illegal entrants who claimed asylum, rather than British citizens.

5.10 However, we suggest that, given the importance of the right to liberty and the aversion of the courts to using immigration powers to detain British citizens,[24] paragraph 16(1) should be construed narrowly and limited to persons reasonably suspected of not being British citizens. If that is correct, British citizens are not liable to detention under immigration powers, when they have proved their nationality, even if they are likely to be deprived of their nationality in the near future.[25]

---

[21] I.e. deportation under section 32(5) of UKBA 2007.

[22] Under section 40(2)–(3) of the British Nationality Act 1981.

[23] [1995] Imm AR 348.

[24] See *R (Rashid Hussein) v Secretary of State for the Home Department* [2009] EWHC 2492 (Admin) at [44] per Nicol J, discussed at paragraph 5.07.

[25] See *R (Parvaz Akhtar) v Secretary of State for the Home Department* [1981] QB 46 at pp. 51–52 where Templeman LJ held that a certificate of naturalization obtained on the false basis that a parent was British would be effective until the certificate holder was deprived of their British citizenship. In the meantime, the certificate holder could not be treated as an illegal entrant. See also *R (Naheed Ejaz) v Secretary of State for the Home Department* [1994] QB 496. These authorities support our view that the powers of detention available only against non-British citizens should not be used against persons with British citizenship unless and until they are deprived of that citizenship.

In any event, a person who is to be deprived of his British citizenship because the **5.11** Secretary of State considers this 'conducive to the public good' is more likely to be deported than removed. In that situation, the Secretary of State would usually deprive the person of their citizenship first and then make a deportation order.[26] In other words, detention is most likely to occur under deportation detention powers, after the person has already been deprived of their citizenship.

[26] See *GI v Secretary of State for the Home Department* [2012] EWCA Civ 867 at [13].

6

EEA REGULATIONS

A. Introduction

6.01 In this introduction, we explore two connected questions:

(1) What is the origin and purpose of the EEA Regulations? and

(2) Why is there a chapter in this book on the EEA Regulations?

(1) Origin and purpose

6.02 The Immigration (European Economic Area) Regulations 2006, SI 2006/1003 ('the EEA Regulations') were enacted to implement Directive 2004/38/EC ('the Citizens Directive').[1] The EEA Regulations have periodically been amended to reflect relevant case-law of the Court of Justice of the European Union ('CJEU'). The EEA Regulations should be interpreted, as far as possible, so as to be compatible with EU law obligations, in particular the Citizens Directive.[2] This is a 'broad and far-reaching' requirement which does not require ambiguity and permits departure from the literal meaning of words. The only limits are that the interpretation should 'go with the grain of the legislation' and be compatible with its 'underlying thrust' and that it cannot require courts to make decisions for which they are not equipped. If and in so far as the EEA Regulations cannot be interpreted compatibly with EU law obligations, they should be ignored and direct effect should be given to rights under the Citizens Directive.[3]

---

[1] To give it its full title, Directive 2004/38/EC of the European Parliament and the Council of 29th April 2004 on the right of citizens of the Union and their family members to move and reside freely within the territory of the Member States.

[2] *Marleasing SA v La Comercial Internacional de Alimentación SA* (Case C-106/89) [1990] ECR I-4135 at [37]–[38].

[3] *R (Owusu) v Secretary of State for the Home Department* [2009] EWHC 593 (Admin) at [9].

This chapter falls within a Part of the book that is concerned with liability to **6.03** detention—in other words, with the powers of statutory detention which exist in the relevant statutory provisions. Part IV examines when it may be lawful to exercise those powers. The distinction between the existence and exercise of the power to detain was drawn up in the context of domestic statutes.[4] It is more difficult to apply when the statutory provisions are intended to implement EU law. For example, if there is a power of detention under the EEA Regulations, which has no equivalent in the Citizens Directive or EU law more generally, it might be said that the power to detain does not 'exist' at all. Alternatively, it might be said that the power exists, because it is provided for by a statutory instrument, but EU law makes it unlawful to exercise that power. For the sake of clarity, we have adopted the latter approach. In this chapter we analyse all the powers of detention which are provided for by the EEA Regulations. Where we think there is doubt as to the applicability or interpretation of the Regulations, we have flagged that up. However, it is in Chapter 14 of Part IV, that we examine in more detail when EU law might make it unlawful to exercise a power under the EEA Regulations.

(2) Why a chapter on the EEA Regulations?

The Immigration Acts are defined by section 61(2) of the UK Borders Act 2007 **6.04** ('UKBA 2007') as an exhaustive list of statutes concerning immigration. That list does not include the EEA Regulations. Why, then, is there a chapter on the EEA Regulations in the Part of a book that concerns liability to detention under the Immigration Acts?

The reason is that someone with rights under the EEA Regulations is only liable to **6.05** detention under the Immigration Acts, when they meet the requisite criteria under the EEA Regulations. This becomes clear when one understands how the EEA Regulations inter-relate with the Immigration Acts. The EEA Regulations contain certain provisions concerning detention.[5] These provisions operate as a portal to the powers of detention under the Immigration Acts—if the criteria in these provisions are fulfilled, someone with rights under the EEA Regulations is 'to be treated as if' they were liable to detention under the Immigration Acts.

The implication of this portal mechanism is that if someone with rights under **6.06** the EEA Regulations does not meet the criteria for detention under the EEA Regulations, they are not liable to detention under the Immigration Acts. In other words, if someone with rights under the EEA Regulations cannot be detained via the portal of the EEA Regulations, they cannot be detained under immigration powers at all. If it were otherwise, the portal detention provisions in the EEA Regulations (i.e. the provisions which provide that certain categories of EEA rights holders should be 'treated as if' they were liable to detention under the Immigration

---

[4] See paragraph 1.09.
[5] Regulations 22–24 of the EEA Regulations.

Acts) would be otiose. The portal detention provisions in the EEA Regulations assume that the persons in question are not otherwise liable to detention under the Immigration Acts.

6.07 It follows that there is only a power, under the Immigration Acts, to detain someone with rights under the EEA Regulations if they meet the criteria for detention under the EEA Regulations.

6.08 This analysis has been disputed by the Secretary of State. The claimant in *R (Nouazli) v Secretary of State for the Home Department*[6] was a family member of an EEA national who had committed criminal offences and whom the Secretary of State wished to deport. The Secretary of State submitted that she had a choice as to whether to detain the claimant under regulation 24(1) of the EEA Regulations or section 36(1) of UKBA 2007. The High Court did not find it necessary to determine this issue.

6.09 The Court of Appeal said that EEA nationals cannot be detained pending deportation or removed otherwise than in accordance with the EEA Regulations.[7] However, their reasoning appears to be based on the assumption that section 36(1) of UKBA 2007 does not go further than regulation 24(1) of the EEA Regulations—i.e. that the power of detention under section 36(1) of UKBA 2007 only exists where deportation would be compatible with the EU rights of the detainee. That assumption is questionable. The power of detention under section 36(1)(a) of UKBA 2007 exists where the Secretary of State is merely *considering* whether to deport. In theory, at least, if section 36(1)(a) applied to a foreign national prisoner with EEA rights, their liability to detention would extend beyond the circumstances identified in regulation 24(1) of the EEA Regulations. They would be liable to detention, even in the absence of reasonable grounds for suspecting that they may be removed, where the Secretary of State had not yet completed her consideration of the case.

6.10 A better line of reasoning was employed by the Court of Appeal in Northern Ireland in *Bassey v Secretary of State for the Home Department*.[8] The claimant in that case was a Nigerian national who entered the United Kingdom by deception—i.e. on a visitor's visa when he intended to stay indefinitely. If it were not for his rights under EU law, he would have been liable to detention as an illegal entrant. However, he had a right to reside in the United Kingdom for at least three months under EU law by reason of his Irish daughter. The Court of Appeal held that the claimant's EU rights had primacy and the Secretary of State had no power to detain him as an illegal entrant. We suggest that this judgment was correct. If it were otherwise, EEA nationals and their family members would lose the protection against detention afforded by the Citizens Directive and the EEA Regulations.

---

[6] [2013] EWCA Civ 1608.
[7] [2013] EWCA Civ 1608 at [17].
[8] [2011] NICA 67.

Indeed, the analysis proposed at paragraph 6.10 is more consistent with EU law. **6.11**
The CJEU has held that Member States may not restrict someone's right to freedom of movement under EU law save where there is an express derogating provision in EU law.[9] It is not enough that there is a domestic law which might (absent
EU law) authorize their detention for immigration purposes. The detention provisions in the EEA Regulations are intended to give effect to the provisions of EU law
which authorize a derogation from the right to freedom of movement. If someone
does not qualify for detention under the EEA Regulations, that is because there
is no provision in EU law to justify the derogation from their right to freedom of
movement.

It follows that, where a detainee may have rights under EU law, the first questions **6.12**
to be asked are:

(1) Do they have rights under the EEA Regulations? and
(2) If so, is there a power to detain them under the EEA Regulations?

If the answer to (1) is 'yes', and the answer to (2) is 'no', their detention will be **6.13**
unlawful. If the answer to each question is 'yes', it does not follow that their detention is lawful, only that there is a power to detain them. That power must be exercised lawfully. The limitations on the lawful exercise of that power are considered
in Part IV. Of particular importance, in this area, is Chapter 14 which examines
the limitations that EU law imposes on the use of powers of detention.

The remainder of this chapter answers the two questions at 6.12. Section B analyses **6.14**
who has rights under the EEA Regulations. Section C considers when the EEA
Regulations treat persons with rights under the EEA Regulations as liable to detention under the Immigration Acts.

B. EEA Rights Holders

The EEA Regulations are concerned with two categories of person: **6.15**

(1) EEA nationals; and
(2) third country nationals with a right (or claimed right) of residence.

Each category is considered in turn below. **6.16**

(1) EEA nationals

The EEA Regulations define 'EEA national' as a 'national of an EEA State who **6.17**
is not also a British citizen'.[10] The 'EEA States' are defined as Norway, Iceland,

---

[9] *Salah Oulane v Minister voor Vreemdelingenzaken en Integratie*, Case C-215/03 at [41].
[10] See regulation 2(1) of the EEA Regulations.

Lichtenstein and Switzerland and all the EU Member States other than the United Kingdom.[11] Although British citizens are not EEA nationals for the purposes of the EEA Regulations, their family members are treated as the family members of EEA nationals in certain circumstances.[12] As well as being EEA nationals, citizens of the Republic of Ireland enjoy special protections against deportation (and therefore detention).[13]

(2) Third country nationals

6.18 Third country nationals may have a right of residence under the EEA Regulations in the following circumstances:

(1) They are the family member of an EEA national, who is either:
    (a) in their first three months of admission to the United Kingdom; or
    (b) a 'qualified person';

(2) They were the family member of an EEA national and they have now obtained an independent right of residence—either a 'retained right of residence' or a 'permanent right of residence';

(3) They have a derivative right of residence.

(a) Family members

6.19 Save for certain exceptions in the case of students,[14] an EEA national's family member is:[15]

(1) their spouse or civil partner.[16] This does not include marriages of convenience;[17] nor does it include the spouse of an EEA national where either of them

---

[11] See regulation 2(1) of the EEA Regulations.

[12] See regulation 9 of the EEA Regulations for the precise circumstances. In broad summary, a British citizen's family member will be treated as an EEA national's family member where the British citizen is or was residing in 'an EEA State'. If the family member is a spouse or civil partner, they need to have been living in that EEA State. This Regulation was designed to give effect to the judgment in *Surinder Singh* (Case C-370/90) although it is arguable that it does not go far enough and, for example, does not cover the situation where a British citizen is exercising Community rights by providing services in another EEA State while residing in the United Kingdom—see *Carpenter v Secretary of State for the Home Department*: Case C-60/00 [2003] QB 416.

[13] See section 7 of the Immigration Act 1971 ('IA 1971'); Chapter 15.9 of the Secretary of State's Enforcement Instructions and Guidance; and *'European Economic Area (EEA) Foreign National Offender (FNO) Cases'* in the Secretary of State's Modernised Guidance.

[14] See paragraph 6.21.

[15] Regulation 7(1) of the EEA Regulations.

[16] See regulation 7(1)(a) of the EEA Regulations.

[17] See the definition of 'spouse' in regulation 2(1) of the EEA Regulations. A marriage of convenience has been construed to be one where the marriage was entered into without the intention of matrimonial cohabitation and for the primary reason of securing admission to the country (*Papajorgji (EEA spouse – marriage of convenience) Greece* [2012] UKUT 00038(IAC) at [14] and [30]). There is no burden on an individual to prove that their marriage is not one of convenience unless the circumstances known to the decision maker give reasonable ground for suspecting that this was the case (*Papajorgji* at [27]).

has a spouse, civil partner or durable partner already present in the United Kingdom.[18]

(2) their or their spouse's/civil partner's direct descendants under the age of 21.[19] 'Direct descendant' includes children and grandchildren to the nth generation but not nephews, nieces etc.[20] European case-law suggests that 'direct descendant' may also extend to step-children.[21]

(3) their or their spouse's/civil partner's dependant direct descendants.[22] The test for 'dependency' is whether the descendant needed the support of the family member/spouse to meet essential needs in their state of origin. It does not depend on whether the descendant could support themselves by taking up paid employment.[23]

(4) their or their spouse's/civil partner's dependant direct relatives in an ascending line.[24] This includes parents, grandparents and any more remote ancestors in a direct line[25] and is likely to include step-parents and adoptive parents.

(5) an 'extended family member' who has been issued with the appropriate EEA permit, registration certificate, or residence card[26] and who continues to comply with the requirements of regulation 8 of the EEA Regulations.[27]

Regulation 8 of the EEA Regulations defines 'extended family members' as persons who are not family members of the EEA national and who fall into one of the categories below:[28] **6.20**

(1) A relative of an EEA national or their spouse/civil partner who is dependent on the EEA national or is a part of their household and who:
   (a) resides in a country other than the United Kingdom;[29]
   (b) once resided in a country other than the United Kingdom and is now accompanying the EEA national to the United Kingdom or wishes to join them there;[30] or

---

[18] Regulation 2(1) of the EEA Regulations.
[19] See regulation 7(1)(b)(i) of the EEA Regulations.
[20] See *PG and VG (EEA 'direct descendants' includes grandchildren) Portugal* [2007] UKAIT 00019.
[21] *Ayaz v Land Baden-Wurttemburg* [2004] All ER (D) 188 (ECJ).
[22] See regulation 7(1)(b)(ii) of the EEA Regulations.
[23] See *SM (India)* [2009] EWCA Civ 1426.
[24] See regulation 7(1)(c) of the EEA Regulations.
[25] See *PG and VG (EEA 'direct descendants' includes grandchildren) Portugal* [2007] UKAIT 00019 at [4].
[26] Where the EEA national is a student, the extended family member will only be treated as a family member if the EEA family permit, registration certificate or residence card was issued under regulations 12(2), 16(5), or 17(4) respectively—see regulation 7(3)–(4) of the EEA Regulations.
[27] See regulation 7(3) of the EEA Regulations.
[28] See regulation 8(1) of the EEA Regulations.
[29] See regulation 8(2)(a) of the EEA Regulations.
[30] See regulation 8(2)(b) of the EEA Regulations.

   (c) once resided in a country other than the United Kingdom and has now joined the EEA national or their spouse/civil partner in the United Kingdom and remains dependant on the EEA national and/or a member of the EEA national's household.[31]

(2) A relative of an EEA national or their spouse/civil partner who, on 'serious health grounds',[32] strictly requires the personal care of the EEA national or their spouse/civil partner.[33]

(3) A relative of an EEA national who would meet the requirements in the immigration rules (other than those relating to entry clearance) for Indefinite Leave to Enter or Remain in the United Kingdom as a dependant relative of the EEA national if the EEA national were a person present and settled in the United Kingdom.[34]

(4) A partner of an EEA national who can prove themselves to be in a 'durable relationship'.[35]

6.21 Where the EEA national is a student—and is not also a jobseeker, worker, self-employed person or self-sufficient person[36]—the definition of family member is the same as for any other category of EEA national for the first three months after their admission to the United Kingdom.[37] However, when those three months have passed, the situation changes in two respects:

---

[31] See regulation 8(2)(c) of the EEA Regulations.

[32] 'Serious health grounds' need to go significantly beyond ordinary ill health—see *TR (Reg 8(3) EEA Regs 2006)* [2008] UKAIT 00004. There must be a need for daily personal care.

[33] Regulation 8(3) of the EEA Regulations.

[34] Regulation 8(4) of the EEA Regulations.

[35] Regulation 8(5) of the EEA Regulations. 'Durable relationship' is not defined in the EEA Regulations. The Secretary of State's guidance suggests that a the following conditions should normally be satisfied before a relationship can be considered durable—(1) The parties have been living together in a relationship akin to marriage which has subsisted for two years or more; (2) The parties intend to live together permanently; (3) The parties are not involved in a consanguineous relationship with one another (i.e. they are not blood relatives who would not be allowed to marry as this would constitute incest); and (4) Any previous marriage (or similar relationship) by either party has permanently broken down (see Chapter 5 of the European Casework Instructions). The guidance suggests that parties should satisfy a number of conditions before they will be considered to be in a durable relationship (i.e. the parties will have been living together in a relationship akin to marriage for two years or more). These conditions are not, however, mandatory and each case must be assessed in the round (see *YB (EEA Reg 17(4)—proper approach) Ivory Coast* [2008] UKAIT 00062). Each case falls to be assessed on its facts. An applicant will only have a right of appeal against a refusal to issue a relevant permit under the EEA Regulations if they can produce sufficient evidence to satisfy the Secretary of State that they are in a relationship with an EEA national—see regulation 26 of the EEA Regulations.

[36] Regulation 7(2)(b) makes clear that where an EEA national is both a student and a qualified person for another reason—i.e. a jobseeker, worker, self-employed person or self-sufficient person—the usual principles apply for determining who is their family member.

[37] Although see footnote 26 on what kinds of permit, certificate or card are necessary for an extended family member where the EEA national is a student.

(1) The dependent direct relatives in the ascending line of the EEA national student or their spouse or civil partner are no longer to be treated as family members;[38]

(2) The direct descendants of the student and/or their spouse or civil partner are not to be treated as family members unless they are dependent children of the student or their spouse or civil partner.[39]

(b) Former family members

Someone who was a family member of an EEA national will have an independent right of residence: **6.22**

(1) if they have retained their right of residence;[40] or

(2) they have obtained a permanent right of residence.[41]

(c) Derivative right of residence

Regulation 15A of the EEA Regulations provides for a 'derivative right of residence'. It is intended to implement various judgments of the CJEU.[42] It covers the situation of third country nationals who need to be given a right to reside because an EEA national depends on them. The criteria for having a derivative right to reside are that the person ('P') is not 'exempt'[43] and falls into one of certain categories, i.e.:[44] **6.23**

(3) P is the primary carer of an EEA national who is under the age of 18, residing in the United Kingdom as a self-sufficient person, and who would be unable to remain in the United Kingdom if P had to leave.[45]

(4) P is the child of an EEA national, resided in the United Kingdom when P's EEA national parent was residing in the United Kingdom as a worker, is

---

[38] See regulation 7(2) of the EEA Regulations.

[39] See regulation 7(2)(a) of the EEA Regulations.

[40] See regulation 10 of the EEA Regulations.

[41] See regulation 15 of the EEA Regulations.

[42] I.e. Cases C-200/02 *Kunqian (Catherine Zhu) and Man (Lavette Chen) v Secretary of State for the Home Department*; C-310/08 *Nimco (Hassan Ibrahim) v London Borough of Harrow and Secretary of State for the Home Department*; C-480/08 *Teixeira (Maria) v London Borough of Lambeth and Secretary of State for the Home Department*; and C-34/09 *Zambrano* [2011] All ER (EC) 491 (see the Explanatory Notes to The Immigration (European Economic Area) (Amendment) Regulations 2012, SI 2012/1547 and The Immigration (European Economic Area) (Amendment) (No. 2) Regulations 2012, SI 2012/2560).

[43] An 'Exempt person' is defined in regulation 15A(6) as (i) those who have the right to reside in the United Kingdom under any provision of the EEA Regulations save for regulation 15A; (ii) those who have a right of abode by virtue of section 2 of IA 1971; (iii) those to whom section 8 of IA 1971 (or any order made under section 8(2)) applies; or (iv) those who have indefinite leave to enter or remain.

[44] Regulation 15A(1) and 15A(6)(c) of the EEA Regulations.

[45] Regulation 15A(2) of the EEA Regulations.

in education in the United Kingdom, and was in education when the EEA national parent resided in the United Kingdom as a worker.[46]

(5) P is the primary carer of someone satisfying regulation 15A(3) of the EEA Regulations and the child would be unable to continue to be educated in the United Kingdom if P were required to leave.[47]

(6) P is the primary carer of a British citizen, the British citizen is residing in the United Kingdom, and that British citizen would be unable to reside in the United Kingdom or another EEA State if that person was required to leave.[48]

(7) P is under 18 years old, their carer is entitled to a derivative right of residence under one of the provisions just listed but P does not have leave to enter or remain in the United Kingdom and requiring P to leave the United Kingdom would prevent P's primary carer from residing in the United Kingdom.[49]

6.24 P will be regarded as a primary carer if P is a direct relative or legal guardian of that person and is the person with primary responsibility for that person's care or shares responsibility for care equally (with someone who is not an excepted person).[50]

C. Liability to Detention

6.25 The EEA Regulations governing immigration detention are examined by reference to each of the categories of person with rights under the EEA Regulations.

(1) EEA Nationals

6.26 On arrival, an EEA national will be liable to detention if there is reason to believe that they may be refused admission to the United Kingdom on one of the following grounds:[51]

(1) their exclusion is justified on grounds of public policy, public security, or public health in accordance with regulation 21 of the EEA Regulations;[52]

(2) they are subject to a deportation or exclusion order;[53] or

---

[46] Regulation 15A(3) of the EEA Regulations. In *Ahmed (Amos; Zambrano; reg 15A(3)(c) 2006 EEA Regs)* [2013] UKUT 00089 (IAC), the Upper Tribunal held that the requirement that P's entry into education overlaps with residence of the parent as a worker is not consistent with Article 12 of Regulation 1612/68 (now Article 10 of Regulation 492/2011) and is not consistent with the rights identified by the CJEU in *Teixeira (Maria) v London Borough of Lambeth* (C 480/08) and *Secretary of State for Work and Pensions v Czop and Punakova* (Joined Cases C-147/11 and C-148/11).

[47] Regulation 15A(4) of the EEA Regulations.

[48] Regulation 15A(5) of the EEA Regulations.

[49] Regulation 15A(2) of the EEA Regulations.

[50] Regulation 15A(7) of the EEA Regulations.

[51] See regulation 22(1)(b) of the EEA Regulations.

[52] See regulation 19(1) and 22(1)(b) of the EEA Regulations.

[53] See regulation 19(1A) and 22(1)(b) of the EEA Regulations.

(3) their admission would lead to the abuse of a right to reside in accordance with regulation 21B(1) of the EEA Regulations.[54]

6.27 If there is reason to believe that the EEA national falls into one of the categories set out in paragraph 6.26, they are to be treated as if they were an ordinary alien seeking leave to enter.[55] As a result, they are liable to detention pending a decision on whether to refuse them admission.

6.28 An EEA national, who is already in the United Kingdom, will be liable to detention, pending removal, in the following circumstances.

6.29 First, they will be liable to detention if they have been refused admission.[56] If the EEA national produces a valid national identity card, or passport from an EEA State, they may only be refused admission in two situations:

(1) their exclusion is justified on grounds of public policy, public security, or public health;[57] or
(2) they entered in breach of a deportation or exclusion order.[58]

6.30 Secondly, an EEA national is liable to detention where there are reasonable grounds for suspecting[59] that they may be removed on grounds of public policy, public security, or public health in accordance with regulation 21 of the EEA Regulations. This power to detain exists unless and until the Secretary of State takes a decision on removal. Because 'reasonable grounds' are required, this power of detention requires some analysis of the prospects of removal. The likelihood of removal needs to be assessed by reference to the relevant principles. If removal is to be based on public security or public policy:

(1) the relevant decision must comply with the principle of proportionality;[60]
(2) the decision must be based exclusively on the personal conduct of the person concerned;[61]

---

[54] See the discussion at paragraphs 14.23–14.25 as to whether the Citizens Directive allows an EEA national to be detained on the basis of an abuse of rights.

[55] See regulation 22(2) of the EEA Regulations.

[56] See regulation 23(1) of the EEA Regulations.

[57] See regulation 19(1) of the EEA Regulations.

[58] See regulation 19(1A) of the EEA Regulations.

[59] See regulation 24(1) of the EEA Regulations. In the criminal context, a reasonable suspicion may be one that is based on an honest and reasonable mistake of fact but it cannot be based on a mistake of law—see *Walker v Lovell* [1975] 1 WLR 1141 *per* Lord Diplock at p. 1151 E–F. Applying those principles to this context, if an immigration officer detains an EEA rights holder under regulation 24(1) of the EEA Regulations in the mistaken belief that they are removable, they will only have a defence to a claim of unlawful detention or false imprisonment if their mistake was one of fact rather than law. It may be difficult to discern whether a mistake was one of fact or law but if the immigration officer failed to apply the correct threshold, in deciding whether removal would be possible, that would be an error of law.

[60] Regulation 21(5)(a) of the EEA Regulations.

[61] Regulation 21(5)(b) of the EEA Regulations.

(3) the personal conduct of the person concerned must represent a genuine 'present'[62] and sufficiently serious threat affecting one of the fundamental interests of society.[63] The prospective conduct relied on must be 'prohibited' by law (though it need not necessarily be strictly criminal in nature);[64]

(4) matters isolated from the particulars of the case or which relate to general prevention cannot justify the decision;[65]

(5) a person's previous criminal convictions cannot *in themselves* justify a relevant decision;[66] and

(6) certain considerations, such as the age, health, length of residence, etc. must be taken into account.[67]

6.31   There are also strict conditions which must be fulfilled before an EEA national or family member may be removed on grounds of public health.[68]

6.32   Where the person in question has a permanent right of residence, removal can only be on *serious*[69] grounds of public policy or public security, not on grounds of public health.[70] Where the person in question has resided in the United Kingdom for a continuous period of at least 10 years prior to the relevant decision[71] and/or where the person in question is under the age of 18, the threshold is even higher

---

[62]   A threat will be 'present' only if it subsists at the date of the relevant hearing and it is imperative that a decision maker grapple with this issue when making a relevant decision—*BF (Portugal) v Secretary of State for the Home Department* [2009] EWCA Civ 923.

[63]   Regulation 21(5)(c) of the EEA Regulations.

[64]   *GW (EEA Regulation 21 'fundamental interests')* [2009] UKAIT 00050 (in which the AIT allowed an appeal by a right wing Dutch politician against a refusal to admit him to the United Kingdom).

[65]   Regulation 21(5)(d) of the EEA Regulations.

[66]   Regulation 21(5)(e) of the EEA Regulations. Of course, previous criminal convictions can be relevant to an assessment of the likelihood of further offending—see *Nazli v Stadt Nurnberg* (Case C-340/97) [2000] ECR I-957 at [58].

[67]   See regulation 21(6) for the full list of mandatory considerations.

[68]   See regulation 21(7) of the EEA Regulations. In short, the disease must have occurred within the first three months of arrival in the United Kingdom and reached a certain defined level of dangerousness.

[69]   In the absence of European Community guidance on the point domestic courts are entitled to determine whether the 'seriousness' threshold has been reached having due regard to the seriousness ascribed to relevant conduct under domestic law—see *R (Bulale) v Secretary of State for the Home Department* [2008] EWCA Civ 806.

[70]   See regulations 19(3)(b) and 21(3) of the EEA Regulations.

[71]   Whether or not residence has been continuous for a period of 10 years prior to the relevant decision is a question of fact to be calculated by counting backwards from the decision. Periods of absence and imprisonment are capable of breaking the period of continuity, even if the person lived continuously in the member state for 10 years prior to the absence or imprisonment (*Secretary of State for the Home Department v MG* [2014] EUECJ C-400/12). On the other hand, neither periods of absence nor time spent in prison automatically disqualify a person from this highest level of protection. The Tribunal must make a qualitative assessment of the degree of integration and the nature and consequences of the gaps in lawful residence in the host Member State—see *Land Baden Württemberg v Panagiotis Tsakouridis* [2010] C-145/09; *Secretary of State for the Home Department v FV (Italy)* [2012] EWCA Civ 1199.

still[72]—subject to one exception,[73] a decision to remove can only be taken on *imperative* grounds of public security.[74]

Thirdly, an EEA national is liable to detention, pending removal, if a decision has **6.33** been made to remove under regulation 19(3)(a)–(c) of the EEA Regulations[75]—i.e. on grounds that they do not have or have ceased to have a right to reside under the EEA Regulations; or on grounds of public policy, public security, or public health, or abuse of rights in accordance with regulations 21 or 21B of the EEA Regulations.[76] In such a situation, they should be allowed one month, after notification of the decision to remove, to leave the United Kingdom voluntarily, save in cases of 'duly substantiated urgency' or where they are detained pursuant to a sentence or order of the court.[77] In the meantime, they will still be liable to detention but it may be unlawful to exercise the power of detention if it prevents them from being able to return voluntarily and none of the exceptions apply.

Fourthly and finally, an EEA national is liable to detention if they entered the **6.34** United Kingdom in breach of a deportation or exclusion order.[78] Such a person is treated as an illegal entrant and liable to detention pending removal.[79]

(2) Third country nationals

Third country nationals with rights under the EEA Regulations are liable to deten- **6.35** tion in all of the circumstances set out at paragraphs 6.25–6.34. In addition, they are liable to detention in the following circumstances.

First, when a third country national claims a right of admission on arrival, they **6.36** are liable to detention as if they were seeking leave to enter, pending a decision on whether to refuse them admission.[80] Unlike with EEA nationals, the detaining official does not need to have reason to believe that the third country national may be refused admission.[81] However, if the person in question is able to produce a valid

---

[72] Regulation 21(4)(b) of the EEA Regulations.

[73] The exception is where the person to be removed is a minor and the decision to remove is necessary in their best interests—see regulation 21(4) of the EEA Regulations. In this situation, the usual principles set out in the earlier parts of paragraphs 6.30–6.32 apply.

[74] 'Imperative grounds' are qualitatively different to 'serious grounds' and require an '. . . actual risk to public security, so compelling that it justifies the exceptional course of removing someone who. . . has become 'integrated' by 'many years' residence in the host state'—see *Secretary of State for the Home Department v FV (Italy)* [2012] EWCA Civ 1199.

[75] See regulations 19(3)(a)–(c) and 24(2)–(3) of the EEA Regulations. Such persons are liable to detention as if they were ordinary aliens who have been subject to decisions to remove or deport— see paragraphs 7.06–7.09.

[76] See regulation 24(3) of the EEA Regulations.

[77] See regulation 24(6) of the EEA Regulations.

[78] See regulation 24(4) of the EEA Regulations.

[79] See regulation 24(4) of the EEA Regulations.

[80] Compare regulation 22(1)(a) of the EEA Regulations.

[81] Compare regulation 22(1)(a) and 22(1)(b) of the EEA Regulations.

passport and either (i) an EEA family permit, (ii) a residence card, (iii) a derivative residence card, or (iv) a permanent residence card,[82] they must be admitted unless they fall within certain narrow exceptions.[83] Even if they are not able to produce the requisite documents, they must be given 'every reasonable opportunity' to obtain such a document, or have it brought to them within a reasonable period of time, or to prove their right of admission by other means, before they are refused admission.[84] Detention which would prevent them having such an opportunity is likely to be unlawful.[85]

6.37 Secondly, third country nationals may be refused admission in a wider range of circumstances. Unlike an EEA national, they may be refused admission if:

(1) they fail to produce an EEA family permit, residence card, derivative residence card or a permanent residence card,[86] even after having been given every reasonable opportunity to obtain one or have it brought to them, and cannot prove their status as an EEA rights holder by other means;[87]

(2) they are not accompanying or joining the EEA national on whom they base their EEA rights;[88] or

(3) the EEA national on whom they base their EEA rights does not have a right to reside in the United Kingdom under the EEA Regulations.[89]

6.38 Thirdly, third country nationals, whose claim under the EEA Regulations is or was based on a derived right of residence, do not have the one month grace period to leave the United Kingdom after a decision has been made to remove them.[90]

6.39 At the time of writing, there is a case pending before the CJEU as to the lawfulness of the EEA Regulations on the admission of third country nationals.[91] In the EEA Regulations, 'residence cards' refers to residence cards issued by the UK authorities. Residence cards issued by other Member States will not guarantee entry into the United Kingdom.[92] Indeed, the UK has issued an instruction to carriers to discourage them from transporting third country nationals to the United Kingdom on the basis of residence cards issued by other states.[93] In the Advocate General's

---

[82] See paragraph 6.39 as to the meaning of 'residence card'.

[83] See regulation 11(2) of the EEA Regulations. The exceptions are where their exclusion is justified on grounds of public policy, public security, or public health, or where they are subject to a deportation or exclusion order—see regulation 19(1) and 19(1A) of the EEA Regulations.

[84] See regulation 11(4) of the EEA Regulations.

[85] Although it is probably correct to say that they remain liable to detention until they prove their EEA right to admission.

[86] See paragraph 6.39 as to the meaning of 'residence card'.

[87] See regulation 11(2)–(4) and 23(1) of the EEA Regulations.

[88] See regulation 19(2)(a) and 23(1) of the EEA Regulations.

[89] See regulation 19(2)(b) and 23(1) of the EEA Regulations.

[90] See regulation 24(7) of the EEA Regulations.

[91] *McCarthy v Secretary of State for the Home Department*, Case C-202/13.

[92] See regulation 2 of the EEA Regulations.

[93] *McCarthy v Secretary of State for the Home Department*, Case C-202/13, Opinion of Advocate General Szpunar of 20 May 2014 at [26].

opinion, the UK's refusal to recognize residence cards issued by other member states is unlawful.[94] If the CJEU agrees, it may be necessary, under *Marleasing* principles,[95] to interpret 'residence cards' in the EEA Regulations as 'residence cards issued by any EU Member State'. In any event, a residence card issued by another Member State should generally be sufficient to prove a right of admission for the purposes of the EEA Regulations.

---

[94] *McCarthy v Secretary of State for the Home Department*, Case C-202/13, Opinion of Advocate General Szpunar of 20 May 2014.

[95] See paragraph 6.02.

7

EVERYONE ELSE

A. Introduction

7.01   This chapter is concerned with everyone else—i.e. those who are not British citizens and have no rights under the Immigration (European Economic Area) Regulations 2006, SI 2006/1003 ('the EEA Regulations').[1] For present purposes it is helpful to call such persons 'ordinary aliens'. The situations in which they may be liable to detention are diverse and, in many cases, overlapping. In cases where there are several powers to detain, it may be important to identify which power is being used as it may affect whether or not it is lawful to 'exercise' the power to detain. At the end of this chapter, we consider some special cases—i.e. the crew of ships, aircraft and Channel Tunnel trains, and members of the armed services. This chapter was written at a time when the amendments made by the Immigration Act 2014 ('IA 2014') had not yet come into force. Those amendments will, *inter alia*, make unaccompanied children a special case who can only be detained when certain statutory criteria are fulfilled.[2]

---

[1] This chapter is not concerned with members of diplomatic missions. They are effectively in the same position as British citizens in relation to detention because they are not subject to the provisions of IA 1971 which relate to non-British citizens (see section 8(3) of IA 1971).

[2] Section 5 of IA 2014.

B. Arrival

With very limited exceptions,[3] aliens may not enter[4] the United Kingdom unless **7.02**
they have been given leave to enter.[5] Leave to enter will often be granted or refused
in the country of departure.[6]

(1) No leave to enter

Ordinary aliens who arrive in the United Kingdom without leave to enter are liable **7.03**
to detention in a number of circumstances which can overlap:

(1) If they arrive by ship or aircraft, they are liable to detention until a decision is
made by an immigration officer on whether to grant them leave to enter and,
if so, for what period and on what conditions.[7]

(2) If they are, or are reasonably believed to be, illegal entrants, they are liable to detention until they are removed from the United Kingdom.[8] 'Illegal
entrants' are persons who enter or seek to enter[9] the United Kingdom in
breach of a deportation order, or the Immigration Rules, or by means which
include deception.[10] This includes aliens who pass through immigration control without being granted leave to enter or temporary admission—e.g. aliens
who enter or seek to enter the United Kingdom clandestinely (e.g. concealed
in the back of a lorry). It even includes aliens who pass through immigration
control without being granted leave to enter or temporary admission because
of a mistake of the immigration officer.[11]

(3) If they seek leave to enter and make an asylum or human rights claim, or
a claim for leave to enter outside the Immigration Rules, they are liable to

---

[3] The members of the crew of a ship or aircraft or Channel Tunnel train may be allowed to enter
the United Kingdom without leave for short periods in certain situations—see section 8(1) of the
Immigration Act 1971 ('IA 1971'). See also the Channel Tunnel (International Arrangements)
Order 1993, SI 1993/1813, Schedule 4, paragraph 1(4).

[4] In immigration law, an important distinction is drawn between entering the United Kingdom
and arriving in the United Kingdom. A person is deemed not to have entered the United Kingdom if
they arrive by ship or aircraft and either: (a) they have not yet passed through immigration control;
or (b) they have passed through immigration control and were either detained, or granted temporary admission, or released while liable to such detention—see section 11(1) of IA 1971.

[5] Section 3(1)(a) of IA 1971.

[6] See section 3A of IA 1971 and the Immigration (Leave to Enter and Remain) Order 2000, SI
2000/1161.

[7] See paragraph 2(1)(c)(ii)–(iii) and 16(1) of Schedule 2 to IA 1971.

[8] See paragraphs 9 and 16(2) of Schedule 2 to IA 1971.

[9] Disembarkation is not to be equated with entry. An alien with a false passport who disembarks
and claims asylum before he has left the designated area is not an illegal entrant if he does not rely on
the false passport to make his asylum claim (see *R v Naillie* [1992] 1 WLR 1099).

[10] See section 33 of IA 1971.

[11] *R (Mokuolu (Catherine)) v Secretary of State for the Home Department* [1989] Imm AR 51.

detention until the Secretary of State makes a decision on whether to grant them leave to enter.[12]

(2) Arriving with leave to enter

7.04 Ordinary aliens who arrive in the United Kingdom by ship or aircraft, with leave to enter granted before their arrival, are liable to detention while an immigration officer examines whether their leave to enter is still in force.[13]

7.05 In addition, ordinary aliens are liable to detention if they have been served with a notice suspending their leave to enter[14] while an immigration officer examines whether:

(1) there has been such a change of circumstances, since their leave to enter was given, that it should be cancelled;[15]

(2) their leave was obtained as a result of false information or failure to disclose material facts;[16]

(3) there are medical grounds on which that leave should be cancelled;[17]

(4) leave derived from an entry clearance should be cancelled because the purpose of the arrival is different to the purpose specified in the entry clearance;[18] or

(5) it would be conducive to the public good for the leave to be cancelled.[19]

C. Removal

7.06 Ordinary aliens are liable to detention, pending a decision on whether to set removal directions and pending removal in pursuance of such directions,[20] if there are reasonable grounds for suspecting that they fall within one of the following categories:

---

[12] See section 62(2)(a) of the Nationality, Immigration and Asylum Act 2002 ('NIAA 2002'), section 3A(7)–(8) of IA 1971, and Article 2(2)(a)–(b) and 2(3) of the Immigration (Leave to Enter) Order 2001, SI 2001/2590.

[13] See paragraph 2(1)(c)(i) and 16(1) of Schedule 2 to IA 1971.

[14] See paragraphs 2A(7) and 16(1A) of Schedule 2 to IA 1971. Detention can continue until the examination is complete and a decision made as to whether to cancel the leave to enter: see paragraph 16(1A)(b) of Schedule 2 to IA 1971.

[15] See paragraph 2A(2)(a) of Schedule 2 to IA 1971.

[16] See paragraph 2A(2)(b) of Schedule 2 to IA 1971.

[17] See paragraph 2A(2)(c) of Schedule 2 to IA 1971.

[18] Paragraph 2A(2A) of Schedule 2 to IA 1971.

[19] Paragraph 2A(3) of Schedule 2 to IA 1971.

[20] Paragraph 16(2)(a) and (b) of Schedule 2 to IA 1971.

(1) they have been refused leave to enter;[21]

(2) they are an illegal entrant;[22]

(3) they only have limited leave to enter or remain and have not observed a condition attached to that leave;[23]

(4) they have overstayed—i.e. stayed beyond the limits of their leave to enter or remain;[24]

(5) they used deception in seeking (whether successfully or not) leave to remain;[25]

(6) their indefinite leave to remain has been revoked under section 76(3) of the NIAA 2002 because they have ceased to be a refugee;[26]

(7) they made an asylum claim at a time when they had leave to enter or remain in the United Kingdom and were made subject to a restriction as to residence, reporting, or occupation with which they failed to comply;[27] or

(8) a pre-removal decision has been made in relation to them—i.e. a decision not to grant them further leave to remain or to take away their existing leave to enter or remain.[28]

However, the Administrative Court held in *R (Gomes) v Secretary of State for the* **7.07** *Home Department*,[29] that the power of detention lapses, if the detainee succeeds in an appeal against removal and no appeal is brought by the Secretary of State within the time limit. This is considered further at paragraph 7.09.

---

[21] Paragraphs 8, 10 and 16(2) of Schedule 2 to IA 1971 and sections 62(1)(a)–(b) and (7) of NIAA 2002 which make provision for detention of such persons under the authority of an immigration officer and the Secretary of State respectively.

[22] Paragraphs 9, 10 and 16(2) of Schedule 2 to the IA 1971 and sections 62(1)(a)–(b) and (7) of NIAA 2002. See paragraph 7.03(2) for the definition of illegal entrant.

[23] Section 10(1)(a) and 10(7) of Immigration and Asylum Act 1999 ('IAA 1999'). Such directions cannot be given if the person concerned has made an application for leave to remain: see s. 10(2) of IAA 1999. Note that these provisions are due to be replaced when section 1 of IA 2014 comes into force. It appears that, when they are so replaced, persons who do not comply with a condition of their leave to enter or remain will not be liable to removal unless or until their leave is cancelled.

[24] Section 10(1)(a) and 10(7) of IAA 1999. An overstayer cannot be made subject to removal directions if they have made a valid application for further leave to remain: see section 10(2) of IAA 1999. See also paragraphs 12–14 and 16(2) of Schedule 2 to the IA 1971 for members of a ship or aircraft's crew who overstay. Note that these provisions are due to be replaced when section 1 of IA 2014 comes into force. However, those without the required leave will still be liable to removal under the new section 10(1) of IAA 1999, after section 1 of IA 2014 comes into force.

[25] Section 10(1)(b) and 10(7) of IAA 1999. Note that these provisions are due to be replaced when section 1 of IA 2014 comes into force. It appears that, when they are so replaced, persons who used deception in seeking leave to remain will not be liable to removal if their leave is still valid.

[26] Section 10(1)(ba) and 10(7) of IAA 1999.

[27] Section 71(1)–(3) of NIAA 2002.

[28] Section 47(1), (1A) and (3) of the Immigration Asylum and Nationality Act ('IAN 2006'). 'Taking away' leave here means either revoking leave or varying it so that there is no leave.

[29] [2014] EWHC 1169 (Admin) at [72].

D. Deportation

7.08 Ordinary aliens are liable to detention for deportation purposes in the following circumstances:

(1) if they have been recommended for deportation by a court, they are liable to detention pending the making of a deportation order;[30]

(2) if they have served a period of imprisonment they may be detained pending a decision on whether they fall for automatic deportation and, where the Secretary of State considers that they do, pending the making of a deportation order;[31]

(3) if they have been[32] properly served[33] with notice of a decision to make a deportation order against them, they may be detained under the authority[34] of the Secretary of State pending the making of a deportation order;[35] and

(4) if there is a deportation order in force[36] against them, they may be detained under the authority of the Secretary of State pending deportation.[37]

7.09 In *R (Gomes) v Secretary of State for the Home Department*[38] the Deputy High Court Judge held that the power of detention under paragraph 2(2) of Schedule 3 to IA 1971 (i.e. detention pending the making of a deportation order) lapses, if the detainee succeeds in an appeal against the decision to make a deportation order and no appeal is brought by the Secretary of State within the statutory time limit. In other words, someone who falls within paragraph 7.08(3) ceases to be liable to detention if they successfully appeal the deportation decision and the Secretary of State is out of time to appeal. Once the appeal had been allowed, the judge reasoned, the power to detain remained extant only for so long as the appeal remained 'pending' within the meaning of section 104 of NIAA 2002.[39] On this logic, if

---

[30] Paragraph 2(1) of Schedule 3 to IA 1971.

[31] Section 36(1) of the UK Borders Act 2007 ('UKBA 2007'). See paragraphs 4.21–4.25.

[32] The person may be arrested before the notice of decision to make a deportation has been served so long as the arresting officer has the notice of decision with him to serve—see paragraph 2(4) of Schedule 3 to IA 1971 and paragraph 17 of Schedule 2 to IA 1971.

[33] 'Properly served' here means that the notice was served in accordance with the Immigration (Notices) Regulations 2003, SI 2003/568.

[34] It is questionable whether the Secretary of State's authority must be in the form of an initial authority for detention (an 'ICD 0257 document') or whether a detention review will suffice—see *R (Qader) v Secretary of State for the Home Department* [2010] EWHC 2486 (Admin), which was quashed by consent.

[35] Paragraph 2(2) of Schedule 3 to IA 1971.

[36] A deportation order is only 'in force' when it has been served on the detainee—*R (S) v Secretary of State for the Home Department* [2011] 2120 (Admin) at [151]–[159]. However, the first arrest may take place before the deportation order has been served so long as it is ready to be served at the time of arrest—see paragraph 2(4) of Schedule 3 to IA 1971 and paragraph 17 of Schedule 2 to IA 1971.

[37] Paragraph 2(3) of Schedule 3 to IA 1971.

[38] [2014] EWHC 1169 (Admin) at [66]-[73].

[39] See at [72].

permission to appeal further is granted out of time (with the effect that the appeal is again 'pending' within the meaning of the 2002 Act) the power to detain revives. It should also be noted that the appeals regime in Part V of NIAA 2002 will be extensively changed when Part 2 of the Immigration Act 2014 comes into force.

E. Family Members

An alien may also be liable to detention because of their family connection to someone being considered for removal or deportation. In particular, the following are liable to detention: **7.10**

(1) a person (X) is liable to detention if there are reasonable grounds for suspecting that they may be subject to removal directions because they are a member of the family of another person (Y) who falls within paragraphs 7.06(1)–(6).[40] If Y falls within paragraphs 7.06(3)–(4) and has left the United Kingdom more than eight weeks previously, there is no power to make removal directions against X.[41]

(2) anyone who has been served[42] with notice of a decision to make a deportation order against them[43] on the grounds that they are a member of the family of someone who is or has been ordered to be deported;

(3) anyone against whom a deportation order has been made[44] on the grounds that they are a member of the family of someone who is or has been ordered to be deported.

Section 5(4) of IA 1971 defines who belongs to the family of someone who is to be deported—i.e.: **7.11**

(1) a wife[45] or husband or civil partner of the person to be deported; and

---

[40] Paragraph 10A of Schedule 2 to IA 1971, section 10(1)(c) of IAA 1999, and section 62(3) of NIAA 2002. Note that section 10(1)(c) of IAA 1999 is due to be replaced by a new version of section 10 of IAA 1999 when section 1 of IA 2014 comes into force. This new version of section 10 of IAA 1999 will impose various conditions that need to be complied with before someone may be removed on the basis of being the family member of someone subject to administrative removal.

[41] Section 10(3)–(4) of IA 1999.

[42] 'Properly served' here means that the notice was served in accordance with the Immigration (Notices) Regulations 2003, SI 2003/568.

[43] Note that the power to deport someone on the basis of their family membership alone is limited in time. On the one hand, if the principal of the family is a 'foreign criminal' who is to be deported under the automatic deportation provisions of UKBA 2007, his family members cannot be made the subject of a deportation order after the end of the relevant period of eight weeks. If no appeal is brought by the foreign criminal, this eight week period begins when an appeal can no longer be brought. If an appeal is brought, this eight week period begins when his appeal is no longer pending within the meaning of of section 104 of NIAA 2002 (see section 37 of UKBA 2007). On the other hand, if the principal of the family is not to be deported under the automatic deportation provisions of UKBA 2007, his family members cannot be made the subject of a deportation order if more than eight weeks have elapsed since the principal left the United Kingdom after the making of the deportation order against him (see section 5(3) of IA 1971).

[44] Paragraph 2(3) of Schedule 3 to IA 1971.

[45] Section 5(4) of IA 1971 provides that where a deportee has more than one wife, each is to be regarded as a family member.

(2) a child,[46] under the age of 18, of the person to be deported and/or his spouse or civil partner.

7.12 Although section 5(4) of IA 1971 is only concerned with 'family' in the context of deportation, 'family' should be construed in the same way in the context of administrative removal.[47]

F. Special Cases

7.13 The crew of ships, aircraft, and Channel Tunnel trains may be given limited leave to enter requiring them to leave in a particular ship, aircraft, or train.[48] Alternatively, they may be permitted to enter the United Kingdom without leave for a specified period of time if certain conditions are fulfilled.[49] In either case, they are liable to detention if they stay beyond the permitted time and/or if they are reasonably suspected by an immigration officer of intending to do so.[50]

7.14 Special provision is made for aliens who fall within one of the following categories:

(1) they are subject, as members of the home forces, to service law;[51]
(2) they are a member of a force from one of a specified list of countries and they are undergoing, or about to undergo training, with the home forces;[52] or
(3) they are serving or posted for service in the United Kingdom as a member of certain other categories of force.[53]

7.15 Such persons can only be detained under immigration powers in the following circumstances:

(1) the circumstances in which a British citizen might be detained;[54] or
(2) under the powers relating to deportation.[55]

---

[46] Section 5(4) of IA 1971 provides that a legally adopted child shall be treated as the child of the adopter; a child that has been adopted but is not legally adopted may be treated as the child of the adopter; an illegitimate child shall be regarded as the child of the mother.

[47] See *Ahmad & Ors v Secretary of State for the Home Department* [2012] UKUT 267 (IAC); [2013] Imm AR 1; [2013] INLR 102.

[48] See paragraphs 12–13 of Schedule 2 to IA 1971. See also the Channel Tunnel (International Arrangements) Order 1993, SI 1993/1813, Schedule 4, paragraph 1(11)(n) and (p).

[49] See section 8(1) of IA 1971. See also the Channel Tunnel (International Arrangements) Order 1993, SI 1993/1813, Schedule 4, paragraph 1(4).

[50] Paragraphs 14(2) and 16(2) of Schedule 2 to IA 1971. See also the Channel Tunnel (International Arrangements) Order 1993, SI 1993/1813, Schedule 4, paragraph 1(11)(n) and (p).

[51] See section 8(4)(a) of IA 1971.

[52] See section 8(4)(b) of IA 1971.

[53] See section 8(4)(c) of IA 1971.

[54] See Chapter 5.

[55] See paragraph 7.08.

PART IV

LIMITATIONS ON THE POWER TO DETAIN

8

HARDIAL SINGH

A. Origin and Development

In *R (Hardial Singh) v Governor of Durham Prison*,[1] Woolf J (as he then was) held **8.01** that the power to detain, under paragraphs 2(2) and 2(3) of Schedule 3 to the Immigration Act 1971 ('IA 1971'), was subject to implicit limitations, which he described as follows:

> First of all, it can only authorise detention if the individual is being detained in one case pending the making of a deportation order and, in the other case, pending his removal. It cannot be used for any other purpose. Secondly, as the power is given in order to enable the machinery of deportation to be carried out, I regard the power of detention as being impliedly limited to a period which is reasonably necessary for that purpose. The period which is reasonable will depend upon the circumstances of the particular case. What is more, if there is a situation where it is apparent to the Secretary of State that he is not going to be able to operate the machinery provided in the Act for removing persons who are intended to be deported within a reasonable period, it seems to me that it would be wrong for the Secretary of State to seek to exercise his power of detention.

> In addition, I would regard it as implicit that the Secretary of State should exercise all reasonable expedition to ensure that the steps are taken which will be necessary to ensure the removal of the individual within a reasonable time.

Those six sentences gave birth to 'the *Hardial Singh* principles', which have been **8.02** the subject of over 200 reported cases. In *R (I) v Secretary of State for the Home*

---

[1] [1984] 1 WLR 704; [1984] 1 All ER 983; [1983] Imm AR 198.

Department,[2] they were codified by Dyson LJ (as he then was) into four principles, each of which is explored in more detail in this chapter:

(1) The Secretary of State must intend to deport the person and can only use the power to detain for that purpose.
(2) The deportee may only be detained for a period that is reasonable in all the circumstances.
(3) If, before the expiry of the reasonable period, it becomes apparent that the Secretary of State will not be able to effect deportation within a reasonable period, he should not seek to exercise the power of detention.
(4) The Secretary of State should act with reasonable diligence and expedition to effect removal.

8.03 This distillation of the principles is often repeated and is faithful to the original text of Woolf J's judgment. However, it does not refer to the test, which has been derived from those principles and is frequently the key issue—i.e. whether, at a given point, there is (or was) a 'sufficient' prospect of removal within a reasonable period of time. This 'sufficient prospect' test was first formulated by Toulson LJ (as he then was) in *R (A) v Secretary of State for the Home Department,*[3] which post-dated *I*. Toulson LJ doubted whether the third *Hardial Singh* principle was distinct from, as opposed to being a facet of, the first and second. He suggested that the key question was whether there was a sufficient prospect of removal within a reasonable period of time. Neither party disagreed with his formulation. This test was later endorsed by Richards LJ in *R (MH) v Secretary of State for the Home Department.*[4] The 'sufficient prospect' test was not discussed by the Supreme Court in *Lumba & Mighty*. Instead, the four distinct principles identified by Dyson LJ in *I* were simply repeated. This was unfortunate as the 'sufficient prospect' test consolidates the second and third *Hardial Singh* principles and is easier than either to apply. The 'sufficient prospect' test is still good law, notwithstanding *Lumba & Mighty*.[5] It is just difficult to know how to fit it into the framework of four principles, which is now so entrenched in the case-law of *Hardial Singh*.

8.04 The authorities are divided on this issue: some have treated the 'sufficient prospect' test as embodying the second *Hardial Singh* principle;[6] others have considered the 'sufficient prospect' test when applying the third *Hardial Singh* principle;[7] and

---

[2] See *R (I) v Secretary of State for the Home Department* [2002] EWCA Civ 888; [2003] INLR 196 at [46].

[3] [2007] EWCA Civ 804, *per* Toulson LJ at [45].

[4] [2010] EWCA Civ 1112 *per* Richards LJ at [65].

[5] *R (Muqtaar) v Secretary of State for the Home Department* [2012] EWCA Civ 1270; [2013] 1 WLR 649, *per* Richards LJ at [37]–[38].

[6] *R (Mustafa Mohammed) v Secretary of State for the Home* [2014] EWHC 972 (Admin) at [22]–[23] and [62].

[7] *R (Shafiq-ur-Rehman) v Secretary of State for the Home Department* [2013] EWHC 1280 (Admin) at [28]–[29]; *AM v Secretary of State for the Home Department*, Unreported, 13 March 2012

others have simply avoided the issue by taking the second and third *Hardial Singh* principles together.[8] In this chapter, we consider the 'sufficient prospect' test in the sub-section that concerns the third *Hardial Singh* principle because the wording of each is so similar. However, as we discuss at paragraph 8.41, that leaves little, if any, distinct scope for the second *Hardial Singh* principle.

Although the case-law often distinguishes between breach of the *Hardial Singh* **8.05** principles and 'public law errors' which vitiate the legality of detention,[9] the *Hardial Singh* principles are, in their origin, a species of public law error:[10] the first *Hardial Singh* principle is an application of the general 'Padfield' principle that powers should be exercised consistently with their statutory purpose;[11] and the second to fourth principles derive from the duty to act reasonably in the *Wednesbury*[12] sense. Thus, the *Hardial Singh* principles are limitations which the 'justice of the common law'[13] has read into statutory powers of detention which appear, on their face, to be unfettered. Their origin lies in the presumption that Parliament did not intend the power of immigration detention to be unrestricted.[14]

Woolf J's observations in *Hardial Singh* were focused on the powers of detention **8.06** under paragraphs 2(2) and 2(3) of Schedule 3 to IA 1971—i.e. the powers of detention pending deportation, where no recommendation for deportation has been made. However, the same principles apply to detention under paragraph 16 of Schedule 2 to IA 1971—i.e. detention pending administrative removal.[15] The only modification necessary is to replace the word 'deportation' with 'administrative removal'. In *R (Francis) v Secretary of State for the Home Department*,[16] the Court of Appeal held that the *Hardial Singh* principles also apply to detention under paragraph 2(1) of Schedule 3 to IA 1971, even though the wording of that provision is

---

(Lawtel AC0131703) at [57]; *R (BXS) v Secretary of State for the Home Department* [2014] EWHC 737 (Admin) at [62].

[8] *R (Gomes) v Secretary of State for the Home Department* [2014] EWHC 1169 (Admin) at [97]. In *R (Muqtaar) v Secretary of State for the Home Department* [2012] EWCA Civ 1270; [2013] 1 WLR 649, at [36]–[38] Richards LJ stresses that the third *Hardial Singh* principle should be confined to its original formulation—i.e. whether it is 'apparent' that removal will not be possible within a reasonable period of time. However, he does not explain where the 'sufficient prospect' test, which he approves, is to fit within the four *Hardial Singh* principles.

[9] See e.g. *R (Francis) v Secretary of State for the Home Department* [2014] EWCA Civ 718 where the Court of Appeal held that detention under paragraph 2(1) of Schedule 3 to IA 1971 will be unlawful if it fails to comply with *Hardial Singh* principles but will not be unlawful if the Secretary of State has made a material public law error in failing to direct release.

[10] See *R (Lumba & Mighty) v Secretary of State for the Home Department* [2011] UKSC 12; [2012] 1 AC 245 at [30] *per* Lord Dyson.

[11] *Padfield v Minister of Agriculture, Fisheries and Food* [1968] AC 997, 1030B–D.

[12] *Associated Provincial Picture Houses Ltd v Wednesbury Corpn* [1948] 1 KB 22.

[13] *Secretary of State for the Home Department v Abdi; Khalaf v Secretary of State for the Home Department* [2011] EWCA Civ 242 at [7].

[14] *R (Francis) v Secretary of State for the Home Department* [2014] EWCA Civ 718 at [45].

[15] See *R (FM) v Secretary of State for the Home Department* [2011] EWCA Civ 807 at [25].

[16] [2014] EWCA Civ 718.

mandatory (i.e. 'he shall be detained', rather than 'he may be detained'). Before this judgment in *Francis*, there had been several inconsistent first instance decisions on this point.[17] At the time of writing, the Secretary of State is seeking leave to appeal *Francis* to the Supreme Court.

8.07 Modified versions of the *Hardial Singh* principles apply to detention pending a decision on whether to effect 'automatic deportation';[18] and detention pending examination.[19]

B. General Issues

8.08 There are several general questions, as to the *Hardial Singh* principles, which have been discussed in the case-law:

(1) Does a breach of any of the *Hardial Singh* principles render detention unlawful?

(2) In what order should the court consider the *Hardial Singh* principles?

(3) To what extent, if at all, should the court defer to the judgment of the Secretary of State?

(4) How should the court approach disputes of fact?

(5) On an appeal, should the Court of Appeal consider the application of *Hardial Singh* principles afresh?

(1) *Hardial Singh* and lawfulness

8.09 The *Hardial Singh* principles are not statutory rules, a breach of which gives rise to a right to damages and/or release.[20] They are not to be applied rigidly or mechanically.[21] It has been suggested that breach of the first three *Hardial Singh* principles will render detention unlawful, whereas breach of the fourth principle will only render detention unlawful where it causes detention to be longer than it would otherwise have been.[22] That is broadly correct, subject to two important qualifications, set out at paragraphs 8.10–8.14.

---

[17] *R (MI (Iraq) & AO (Iraq)) v Secretary of State for the Home Department* [2010] EWHC 764 (Admin); *Choy v Secretary of State for the Home Department* [2011] EWHC 365 (Admin); *R (BA) v Secretary of State for the Home Department* [2011] EWHC 2748 (Admin); *R (Solomon) v Secretary of State for the Home Department* [2011] EWHC 3075 (Admin).

[18] See paragraphs 8.97–8.98.

[19] See paragraphs 8.94–8.96.

[20] *R (Krasniqi) v Secretary of State for the Home Department* [2011] EWCA Civ 1549 at [12].

[21] *R (Lumba & Mighty) v Secretary of State for the Home Department* [2011] UKSC 12; [2012] 1 AC 245 at [115].

[22] See *R (Sino) v Secretary of State for the Home Department* [2011] EWHC 2249 (Admin) at [66]–[69].

First, the fact that one of the *Hardial Singh* principles may have been breached **8.10** in the *past* does not, in itself, mean that *present* detention is unlawful. A court is unlikely to order the release of anyone who poses a high risk of absconding if it is clear that their removal can take place in a very short period of time. If there were times, in the past, when that person should not have been detained (because there was an insufficient prospect of removal given all the relevant factors including the length of detention) or if their detention lasted longer than it should have done (e.g. because of an unreasonable lack of expedition on the part of the Secretary of State), they will have a good claim for damages for false imprisonment.[23] However, such historic failings will not, in themselves, require release from detention. That is not to say that the fact that detention breached the *Hardial Singh* principles in the past is irrelevant to the question of whether it breaches them in the present. On the contrary, it is usually highly relevant. The length of past detention is a very significant factor in the balance which must be struck if detention is to comply with the *Hardial Singh* principles—the longer past detention has been, the more certainty there must be that removal will take place and the shorter the time scale in which it must take place.[24] If detention has already been unreasonably long, the courts are likely to require a very high degree of certainty that removal may take place in a very short period of time if they are not to order release. However, the fact remains that even a finding that the second *Hardial Singh* principle was breached in the past will not necessitate an order for release. Thus, in *Hardial Singh* itself, Woolf J found a lack of expedition but did not order release because of the possibility of removal in a 'very short time indeed'.[25] Likewise, in *Abdi & Khalaf*,[26] Sedley LJ said that, even if past detention was unreasonable, it would not be appropriate to order release if a person will be deported within a reasonable period of time. Furthermore, in *Shafiq-ur-Rehman*,[27] the Deputy High Court Judge said: 'it cannot be said that a particular span of past detention makes continued detention unlawful if it is foreseeable that a person can be deported within a reasonable future period'.

Secondly, detention will not necessarily be unlawful from the instant it ceases to **8.11** comply with the *Hardial Singh* principles. The concept of reasonableness applies to the termination of detention as much as to the decision to detain.[28] As a result, if it becomes clear that a detainee cannot be removed within a reasonable period

---

[23] See Chapter 20.

[24] *R (MH) v Secretary of State for the Home Department* [2010] EWCA Civ 1112 at [64]–[66] and [68(v)].

[25] See *R (Hardial Singh) v Governor of Durham Prison* [1984] 1 WLR 704; [1984] 1 All ER 983; [1983] Imm AR 198 at [19] and [22].

[26] *Secretary of State for the Home Department v Abdi; Khalaf v Secretary of State for the Home Department* [2011] EWCA Civ 242 at [60].

[27] *R (Shafiq-ur-Rehman) v Secretary of State for the Home Department* [2013] EWHC 1280 (Admin) at [27].

[28] See *R (FM) v Secretary of State for the Home Department* [2011] EWCA Civ 807 at [64].

of time, the Secretary of State is not obliged to release them instantaneously. The Secretary of State is allowed a 'period of grace':

(1) to take stock of the change in circumstances;[29] and

(2) to make suitable arrangements for release.[30] If the detainee poses a risk of offending or absconding these arrangements may include tagging, notification of other agencies and the provision of accommodation that will minimize the risk of absconding. Even when there are no such risks, the Secretary of State may be allowed some time to identify suitable accommodation for them to be released to.[31]

8.12 The courts have been unwilling to specify how long such a grace period may be. In *R (Muqtaar) v Secretary of State for the Home Department*,[32] the majority of the Court of Appeal held that it was acceptable for the Secretary of State to take two weeks to respond to a judgment of the European Court of Human Rights ('ECtHR') by releasing the claimant, in part because there would have been many other detainees affected by the same judgment. Richards LJ said there was 'some force' in the Secretary of State's submission that she should not be obliged to react to changes in circumstances until the next monthly review under her policy.[33] Elias LJ, dissenting, said that the delay of two weeks displayed 'too cavalier an approach to the right to liberty'.[34] Lloyd LJ said he saw force in Elias LJ's point but found on the facts that two weeks was acceptable.[35]

8.13 The other authorities do not reveal any clear limits on the grace period:

(1) In *R (Wang) v Secretary of State for the Home Department*,[36] Mitting J found that continued detention would be unlawful but allowed the Secretary of State 48 hours to fit a tag to the claimant before he was released.

(2) In *R (I & Ors) v Secretary of State for the Home Department*,[37] a case involving the detention of a father with his four children, the Court of Appeal held that, following the institution of judicial review proceedings and the cancellation of removal directions on a Thursday, the decision to release Mr I and his children could 'and therefore should' have been taken and implemented by the following Monday.[38]

---

[29] See *R (FM) v Secretary of State for the Home Department* [2011] EWCA Civ 807 at [60]–[64] and *R (Bent) v Secretary of State for the Home Department* [2012] EWHC 4036 (Admin) at [106].

[30] See *R (FM) v Secretary of State for the Home Department* [2011] EWCA Civ 807 at [60]–[64].

[31] See *R (FM) v Secretary of State for the Home Department* [2011] EWCA Civ 807 at [60].

[32] [2012] EWCA Civ 1270 at [45] and [88] albeit, *per* Richards LJ 'with some hesitation'.

[33] *R (Muqtaar) v Secretary of State for the Home Department* [2012] EWCA Civ 1270 at [45]. See paragraph 8.14.

[34] *R (Muqtaar) v Secretary of State for the Home Department* [2012] EWCA Civ 1270 at [85].

[35] *R (Muqtaar) v Secretary of State for the Home Department* [2012] EWCA Civ 1270 at [88].

[36] [2009] EWHC 1578 (Admin) at [36].

[37] [2010] EWCA Civ 727.

[38] [2010] EWCA Civ 727 at [45].

(3) In *R (Rabbi) v Secretary of State for the Home Department*,[39] the Secretary of State took four days to release a claimant after receiving a Rule 39 indication from the European Court of Human Rights. Beatson J held that there had been no unlawfulness because it took four days for the Secretary of State to find an address to accommodate the claimant.

(4) In *Abdi & Khalaf*,[40] the Court of Appeal held that the Secretary of State should have appreciated the effect of a change of circumstances (a concession made by the Secretary of State in the course of an appeal in the light of a recent 'Country Guidance' decision) within a week and detention thereafter was unlawful.

(5) In *R (Bizimana) v Secretary of State for the Home Department*,[41] the Court of Appeal held that 'a couple of weeks' was a reasonable period of time to 'take stock and review matters'.

(6) In *R (LK (Somalia)) v Secretary of State for the Home Department*,[42] (which came between the first instance and Court of Appeal decisions in *Muqtaar*, and concerned the same ECtHR judgment) the Deputy High Court Judge allowed 24 days for the Secretary of State to take stock of the ECtHR's judgment, realise that the claimant would need to be released, and put in place the necessary monitoring arrangements. However, this aspect of the decision in *LK* should be approached with caution. Elias LJ granted permission to appeal to the Court of Appeal on the ground that it was arguable that the judge ought to have concluded that the Secretary of State should have dealt with MK's situation more speedily and released him more quickly. The appeal was subsequently withdrawn by agreement between the parties.

(7) In *R (Belkasim) v Secretary of State for the Home Department*,[43] Haddon-Cave J held that it was reasonable for the Secretary of State to take 26 days after a United Nations decision to impose a no-fly zone over Libya to release the Libyan claimant. However, Haddon-Cave J expressly accepted that the imposition of the no-fly zone was not the only catalyst for the decision to release so this cannot be read as a simple endorsement of a grace period of 26 days.

Like everything else in this field, the permissible grace period will depend on the **8.14** facts of the case.[44] The facts of the cases at paragraph 8.13 demonstrate how flexible the concept may be. We do not agree with the submission which Richards LJ appeared to favour in *Muqtaar*—i.e. that the Secretary of State should have until the date of the next detention review under the policy to take stock of a change

---

[39] [2010] EWHC 2074 (Admin) at [90].

[40] *Secretary of State for the Home Department v Abdi; Khalaf v Secretary of State for the Home Department* [2011] EWCA Civ 242 at [61].

[41] [2012] EWCA Civ 414 at [65].

[42] [2012] EWHC 1299 (Admin) at [62]–[64].

[43] [2012] EWHC 3109 (Admin) at [191].

[44] *R (Muqtaar) v Secretary of State for the Home Department* [2012] EWCA Civ 1270 at [45].

in circumstances.[45] It is not clear that Richards LJ was aware of the fact that the policy expressly requires ad hoc reviews if circumstances change.[46] Besides, the period before the next detention review may be as long as one month and the cases at paragraph 8.13 demonstrate that the courts have often expected the Secretary of State to appreciate a change of circumstances in significantly less than one month.

(2) Order of consideration

8.15 Lord Dyson in *Lumba* suggested that it was appropriate to begin with the third *Hardial Singh* principle, and that a 'convenient starting point is to determine whether, and if so when, there is a realistic prospect that deportation will take place'.[47] The Court of Appeal in *R (Khalid) v Secretary of State for the Home Department*[48] said that the *Hardial Singh* principles were best approached in the following order: first, third, fourth and second.

8.16 It is submitted that the most helpful order in which to address the relevant questions is as follows:

(1) Is current detention unlawful because:
  (a) detention is not being maintained for the statutory purpose; or
  (b) there is an insufficient prospect of removal/deportation within a reasonable period of time?
(2) Was past detention unlawful because:
  (a) detention was not being maintained for the statutory purpose;
  (b) at some point, or for some period, during the past detention, there ceased to be a sufficient prospect of removal/deportation within a reasonable period of time;
  (c) there was an unreasonable lack of expedition which caused detention to be longer than it otherwise would have been; or
  (d) the period of detention was too long?

8.17 In fact, it may not even be necessary to ask the question at (2)(d)—i.e. was the period of detention too long? It is hard to conceive of a situation where the answer to 2(d) is 'yes' without the answer to either 2(b) or 2(c) being 'yes' as well.[49] It is difficult to see how detention can be criticized as being too long if the Secretary of State acted with reasonable expedition throughout and there was, at all times, a sufficient prospect of removal within a reasonable period of time to make detention

---

[45] *R (Muqtaar) v Secretary of State for the Home Department* [2012] EWCA Civ 1270 at [45].
[46] EIG 55.8 'Additional reviews may also be necessary on an ad hoc basis, for example, where there is a change in circumstances relevant to the reasons for detention.'
[47] [2011] UKSC 12 at [103].
[48] [2012] EWCA Civ 1656 at [30].
[49] See paragraph 8.41.

reasonable, taking into account all relevant factors including the length of past detention.

(3) Deference to the Secretary of State

The Administrative Court is the judge of reasonableness in regard to the *Hardial Singh* principles. The usual *Wednesbury* principles do not apply and the court does not defer to the judgment of the Secretary of State on what is a reasonable period of time.[50] The court can take into account any facts that were known to the Secretary of State at the time, even if they did not feature in the reasons for detention provided by the Secretary of State at the material time.[51]   **8.18**

However, there may be incidental questions of fact which the court may recognize that the Secretary of State is better placed to decide than itself, and the court will take such account of her views on such matters 'as may seem proper'.[52] In practice this means that the courts will pay deference to the Secretary of State's views on matters where she has greater expertise than the court, for example the progress of diplomatic negotiations[53] or the attitude of other nations to accepting returnees.[54] The court will also make allowances for the way in which Government functions.[55]   **8.19**

(4) Disputes of fact

Although most challenges to immigration detention are brought by judicial review, disputes of fact can still be resolved by live evidence—there is no reason why disputed evidence cannot be tested by cross-examination in judicial review proceedings where the circumstances warrant this approach.[56] One such situation is where there is a 'substantial dispute of fact', for example where there is a direct conflict of evidence between the parties' accounts of a material event.[57] Either party may apply to cross-examine the other party's witness. Where no such application has   **8.20**

---

[50] See *R (A) v Secretary of State for the Home Department* [2007] EWCA Civ 804 at [60]–[62], [71]–[75].

[51] See *R (MS) v Secretary of State for the Home Department* [2011] EWCA Civ 938 at [49]; *R (Moussaoui) v Secretary of State for the Home Department* [2012] EWHC 126 (Admin) at [171]; *R (AAM) v Secretary of State for the Home Department* [2012] EWHC 2567 (QB) at [155].

[52] *R (A) v Secretary of State for the Home Department* [2007] EWCA Civ 804, *per* Toulson LJ at [62].

[53] See *HXA v The Home Office* [2010] EWHC 1177 (QB) at [67]–[72]; *R (Yegorov) v Secretary of State for the Home Department* [2011] EWHC 3358 (Admin), *per* Mitting J at [28].

[54] See *R (MH) v Secretary of State for the Home Department* [2010] EWCA Civ 1112 at [8].

[55] See *HXA v The Home Office* [2010] EWHC 1177 (QB) at [71].

[56] See *R (MH) v Secretary of State for the Home Department* [2009] EWHC 2506 (Admin) at [8]–[10]; *R (Khalid) v Secretary of State for the Home Department* [2012] EWCA Civ 1656 at [2]; *R (Davies) v Secretary of State for the Home Department* [2010] EWHC 2656 (Admin) at [3].

[57] See *R (MH) v Secretary of State for the Home Department* [2009] EWHC 2506 (Admin) at [8]–[10]. In that case, there was a conflict of evidence as to whether the claimant had cooperated with removal.

been made, the evidence in a witness statement should be treated with a 'measure of generosity'.[58]

8.21 The burden of proof is on the Secretary of State to justify detention[59] (although where the issue is not one of fact but reasonableness, it is inapt to talk of a burden of proof).[60] Gaps in evidence should be resolved in the detainee's favour.[61] The court may draw inferences against the Secretary of State where the Secretary of State fails to provide evidence she could reasonably be expected to provide[62] or fails to give full disclosure.[63]

8.22 What the court cannot do is apply hindsight. The lawfulness of past detention cannot be judged with hindsight.[64] In other words, the court cannot take into account matters that were not, and could not reasonably have been, known by the Secretary of State at the relevant time. The actions of a detainee after release, for example, are irrelevant.[65] The court has to put itself in the position of the decision maker at the relevant time[66] and consider the matter in light of the information available to the Secretary of State.[67]

8.23 The court's reluctance to apply hindsight should not be taken so far as to ignore matters of which the Secretary of State should have been aware. The Secretary of State cannot avoid liability by reference to her officials' notes on significant events, when those notes have not recorded events fairly and accurately. So, for example, where the Secretary of State's internal records give an account of non-cooperation that is disputed, the court should make its own findings as to the true level of non-cooperation rather than deferring to the Secretary of State's account.[68]

---

[58] See *R (MH) v Secretary of State for the Home Department* [2009] EWHC 2506 (Admin) at [10].

[59] See *R (Lumba & Mighty) v Secretary of State for the Home Department* [2011] UKSC 12; [2012] 1 AC 245 at [44].

[60] See *Saleh v Secretary of State for the Home Department* [2013] EWHC 61 (Admin) at [45]; *R (OM (Nigeria)) v Secretary of State for the Home Department* [2011] EWCA Civ 909 at [24].

[61] See *R (Azaroal) v Secretary of State for the Home Department* [2013] EWHC 1248 (Admin) at [59].

[62] See *R (Raki) v Secretary of State for the Home Department* [2011] EWHC 2421 (Admin) at [34].

[63] See *R (I & Ors) v Secretary of State for the Home Department* [2010] EWCA Civ 727 at [54]–[56]. See also paragraph 19.42.

[64] See *R (LK (Somalia)) v Secretary of State for the Home Department* [2012] EWHC 1299 (Admin) at [33]; *R (Alsaadon) v Secretary of State for the Home Department* [2013] EWHC 2184 (Admin) at [15]; *NS* [2013] CSOH 139 at [23].

[65] *NS (Palestine) v Secretary of State for the Home Department* [2013] CSOH 139 at [23].

[66] See *R (Anam) v Secretary of State for the Home Department* [2012] EWHC 1770 (Admin) at [82].

[67] *NS (Palestine) v Secretary of State for the Home Department* [2013] CSOH 139 at [23].

[68] See *R (MH) v Secretary of State for the Home Department* [2009] EWHC 2506 (Admin) at [8]–[10] and paragraphs 8.18–8.20. In *R (Belkasim) v Secretary of State for the Home Department* [2012] EWHC 3109 (Admin) at [185], Haddon-Cave J said, without reference to authority, that it was 'axiomatic' that the reasonableness of detention should be judged by reference to the risk that the detainee 'was reasonably thought to present at the time'. However, Haddon-Cave J appears to have assumed that the *Hardial Singh* principles were subject only to *Wednesbury* review (see

Likewise, we do not think that the Secretary of State can rely on the fact that the officials authorizing detention were, in fact, ignorant of matters of which they should have been aware. The Secretary of State may be given a short grace period to allow for information, held by a different department, to be passed on to, and absorbed by, the official authorizing detention but she cannot rely on such ignorance for long.[69]

(5) Appeals to the Court of Appeal

The authorities are divided as to what the approach of the Court of Appeal should be on an appeal against a judgment of the Administrative Court. Laws LJ held, in *AS (Sudan) v Secretary of State for the Home Department*,[70] that the Court of Appeal should reconsider the application of the *Hardial Singh* principles afresh as it is in just as good a position as the Administrative Court to decide on the relevant issues. However, more recent Court of Appeal authorities, in particular *R (Muqtaar) v Secretary of State for the Home Department*,[71] have suggested that this is wrong—the Court of Appeal should be slow to interfere with the judgment of the Administrative Court in relation to the *Hardial Singh* principles. The same has been said of appeals to the Court of Session against decisions of the Lord Ordinary.[72]   **8.24**

Muqtaar is more likely to be followed where the question is simply whether the judge at first instance erred. However, the approach in *AS (Sudan)* will still be appropriate where (like in *AS* itself):   **8.25**

(1) detention is ongoing and:
    (a) significant time has passed; or
    (b) the circumstances have changed; or
(2) new material has come to light since the first instance judgment.[73]

---

paragraph 184 of his judgment). This is inconsistent with well-established principle that the court forms its own view on whether the *Hardial Singh* principles have been breached—see paragraph 8.18.

[69] See *Secretary of State for the Home Department v Abdi; Khalaf v Secretary of State for the Home Department* [2011] EWCA Civ 242 at [61]; See also paragraphs 8.11 to 8.14.
[70] [2009] EWCA Civ 1518 at [7].
[71] [2012] EWCA Civ 1270 at [46]–[48].
[72] See *RN (Iraq) v Secretary of State for the Home Department* [2013] CSIH 11 at [9].
[73] See *R (M) v Secretary of State for the Home Department* [2008] EWCA Civ 307 at [19]; and *R (Lumba & Mighty) v Secretary of State for the Home Department* [2011] UKSC 12; [2012] 1 AC 245 at [145].

C. The First Principle

8.26 The first *Hardial Singh* principle, as summarized by Lord Dyson in *Lumba*, can be broken down into two inter-connected conditions:

(1) there must be an intention to deport; and
(2) detention must be for the purpose of deportation.

8.27 Both conditions must be fulfilled if the first *Hardial Singh* principle is to be complied with. At present, it is unclear whether a breach of the first *Hardial Singh* principle always renders detention unlawful, from the moment it occurs, or whether the Secretary of State may be allowed a short 'grace period' to effect release. In *FM*,[74] the Court of Appeal gave two reasons for finding that the Secretary of State should be allowed a grace period to effect release:

(1) In a case where removal directions might still be re-set, the Secretary of State should be allowed time to make arrangements that will allow her to keep track of the whereabouts of the detainee; and
(2) If the Secretary of State has assumed responsibility for the welfare of the detainee (for example because the detainee is a child) the Secretary of State should not be required to release the detainee without first ensuring they can survive outside detention.

8.28 Proposition (1) in the list at paragraph 8.27 does not conflict with the first *Hardial Singh* principle. In such a situation, the Secretary of State has not abandoned her intention to remove (even though she has accepted that removal cannot take place within a reasonable period of time). Furthermore, the purpose of the further detention is still to facilitate removal because it is to give the Secretary of State time to make arrangements that will allow her to keep track of the detainee after their release.

8.29 Proposition (2) in the list at paragraph 8.27 is more difficult to reconcile with the first *Hardial Singh* principle. In *FM* itself, the claimants were a mother and two young children. At one point, the mother had to be admitted to hospital, leaving the children behind in the detention centre. It is useful to consider whether the children's detention would have been unlawful if the Secretary of State had, at this point, abandoned her intention to remove the children. Would she have been obliged to let the children leave the detention centre without first ensuring that they would be taken care of? Or would it have been lawful to detain the children for a short period, while arrangements were made for their welfare? The second reason in *FM*, summarized at paragaph 8.27(2) implies that detention would have been lawful for a short period, while arrangements were made, even if there was no

---

[74] *R (FM) v Secretary of State for the Home Department* [2011] EWCA Civ 807 at [60].

intention to deport the children and the purpose of detention was to protect their welfare rather than to facilitate their removal. However, *FM* is not decisive on this issue because it was concerned with the second *Hardial Singh* principle, rather than the first, and, on the facts of the case, the Secretary of State had not abandoned her intention to deport the children. In any event, if there is a 'grace period' to be allowed, when detention ceases to comply with the first *Hardial Singh* principle, it must be relatively short. Prolonged detention for the purpose of protecting the detainee is not permissible.[75]

(1) Intention to deport

The first *Hardial Singh* principle requires an unconditional intention to deport. **8.30** *HXA v The Home Office*[76] is an example of a breach of this principle. HXA was a suspected terrorist detained by the Secretary of State pending deportation to Iraq. The Secretary of State only wished to deport HXA if he was to be detained on return to Iraq. The Secretary of State detained HXA while she examined whether she could ensure that HXA would be detained on return. Blake J held that HXA was not being detained for the 'sole and limited purpose of effecting his removal' but for the 'additional purpose' of investigating whether suitable arrangements could be made for his detention on return.[77] As a result, Blake J held that detention was not for the statutory purpose, and so was unlawful.

It would be a mistake to draw, from this case, the principle that no objective **8.31** other than that of effecting removal can be taken into account when deciding to detain under immigration powers. Protection of the public may be a purpose of immigration detention so long as there is also an intention to deport and detention does not make removal more difficult.[78] *HXA* is perhaps better analysed as a case where there was no intention to deport. Even though the Secretary of State had served notice of a decision to deport, she had not, in fact, made up her mind to as to whether she wished to deport HXA. Indeed, the Secretary of State actually opposed bail on the basis that HXA posed a risk of absconding to Iraq.[79]

(2) Purpose is deportation

The first *Hardial Singh* principle also requires that the purpose of detention **8.32** be deportation. It is not always straightforward to determine the purpose of detention.

---

[75] See paragraph 8.39.
[76] [2010] EWHC 1177 (QB).
[77] [2010] EWHC 1177 (QB) at [173].
[78] See paragraphs 8.36–8.38.
[79] [2010] EWHC 1177 (QB) at [21].

8.33 First, it may be difficult to ascertain the motives of the Secretary of State. The court will rely principally, if not exclusively, on the contemporaneous documentation to try to discern the purpose of detention. However, most of the comments and observations in detention reviews emanate from junior officials that are making recommendations, not from the senior official that authorizes detention. In *R (HE) v Secretary of State for the Home Department*,[80] the court held that it was only the motives of the senior authorizing official that mattered, not the motives of the junior officials that make proposals. The entries of senior officials in detention reviews will often be only a couple of sentences long and too formulaic to give much indication of their motives.

8.34 This difficulty arises acutely in non-cooperation cases.[81] On the one hand, the authorities are clear that detention cannot be used for the purpose of putting pressure on a detainee to leave voluntarily[82] or punishing a detainee for non-cooperation.[83] On the other hand, it is perfectly proper to detain someone while there is still a real possibility of their changing their mind,[84] particularly if every step is being taken in the meantime to persuade them to cooperate with removal or to circumvent their refusal to cooperate.[85] It will seldom be clear, from the contemporaneous documentation, on which side of the line a case may fall.

8.35 As a result, in this particular context, the first *Hardial Singh* principle seldom adds to the 'sufficient prospect' test—i.e. the detention of a non-cooperative detainee who cannot be removed without their cooperation ceases to be in accordance with the statutory purpose of detention at precisely the moment when there is no longer a sufficient prospect of removal within a reasonable period of time (either by persuading the detainee to change their mind or by circumventing their non-cooperation).

8.36 Secondly, the Secretary of State's motives may be mixed. The purpose of detention must be deportation but that does not mean that the only relevant factor, which the Secretary of State may take into account, is whether detention will make deportation more likely. The risk that the detainee may reoffend, if released, is also a relevant factor because protecting the public is part of the purpose of deportation.[86]

8.37 This principle was applied by Nicol J in *Mahajna (Raed Salah) v Secretary of State for the Home Department*.[87] Mr Mahajna, a strong supporter of the Palestinian cause,

---

[80] [2012] EWHC 3628 (Admin) at [25].

[81] See paragraphs 8.56–8.60.

[82] See *MI (Iraq) and AO (Iraq) v Secretary of State for the Home Department* [2010] EWHC 764 (Admin) at [52].

[83] See *R (Sino) v Secretary of State for the Home Department* [2011] EWHC 2249 (Admin); *R (Muaza) v Secretary of State for the Home Department* [2013] EWHC 3764 (Admin) at [79].

[84] See *R (IM (Nigeria)) v Secretary of State for the Home Department* [2013] EWCA Civ 1561 at [57]–[61].

[85] See *R (NAB) v Secretary of State for the Home Department* [2010] EWHC 3137 (Admin) at [76].

[86] *R (A) v Secretary of State for the Home Department* [2007] EWCA Civ 804, *per* Toulson LJ at [55], approved by Lord Dyson in *Lumba* at [107]–[110].

[87] [2011] EWHC 2481 (Admin).

was intending to go on a speaking tour of the United Kingdom. The Secretary of State considered that Mr Mahajna's speeches might lead to hatred and violence and decided to deport him for the public good. Mr Mahajna had a return ticket to Israel so he argued that detention was not being used for its proper purpose—i.e. to ensure his removal from the United Kingdom. He said he would have left anyway.[88] Nicol J found no breach of the first *Hardial Singh* principle. Nicol J said it was permissible for the Secretary of State to have regard to 'the public interest' (i.e. the public interest in preventing Mr Mahajna from speaking) when deciding whether to detain Mr Mahajna.[89] There was no analysis in the judgment of whether Mr Mahajna posed a risk of absconding or would have taken longer to leave the United Kingdom if he had not been detained.

8.38 In other words, reading *Lumba* and *Mahajna* together with *HXA*,[90] detention pending deportation will comply with the first *Hardial Singh* principle so long as it is for the good of the public in the United Kingdom, there is an intention to deport and detention is not prolonging the detainee's stay in the United Kingdom. The same is probably true of detention pending administrative removal.[91]

8.39 Although detention can properly be used to protect the public from a deportee, pending deportation, it cannot be used to protect the deportee from themselves except, perhaps, for a relatively short 'grace period' while the Secretary of State makes suitable arrangements for release.[92] As Cranston J put it in *AA (Nigeria) v Secretary of State for the Home Department*,[93] '[t]he use of immigration detention to protect a person from themselves, however laudable, is an improper purpose'. This principle has been assumed to be correct in subsequent cases,[94] especially where the risk of self-harm arises as a result of prolonged detention.[95]

D. The Second Principle

8.40 The second *Hardial Singh* principle is that detention may only be for a period of time that is reasonable in all the circumstances. Relevant circumstances are discussed at paragraphs 8.55–8.75. They include factors that require one to look backwards (e.g. the length of past detention) and factors that require one to look forwards (e.g. the obstacles to removal).

---

[88] See *Mahajna (Raed Salah) v Secretary of State for the Home Department* [2011] EWHC 2481 (Admin) at [26(i)].

[89] See *Mahajna (Raed Salah) v Secretary of State for the Home Department* [2011] EWHC 2481 (Admin) at [34]–[35].

[90] See paragraphs 8.30–8.31.

[91] See paragraph 8.06.

[92] *FM* at [6]; See paragraphs 8.11–8.14.

[93] [2010] EWHC 2265 (Admin) at [40].

[94] *R (OM) v Secretary of State for the Home Department* [2011] EWCA Civ 909 at [32].

[95] *R (BA) v Secretary of State for the Home Department* [2011] EWHC 2748 (Admin) at [153].

8.41 Toulson and Richards LJJ have suggested that the essential question to be determined is whether, at any particular point there was a sufficient prospect of removal within a reasonable period of time, having regard to all relevant factors including the length of past detention.[96] If this 'sufficient prospect' test is treated as a development of the third *Hardial Singh* principle, it leaves little, if any, distinct purpose for the second *Hardial Singh* principle. It is hard to envisage any situation where the period of detention could be said to be too long even though the Secretary of State acted with reasonable diligence throughout and there was, at all material times, a sufficient prospect of removal within a reasonable period of time.

8.42 Where a claimant is still detained at the time their case is heard, they are very unlikely to be able to secure release based on the length of their past detention alone. The lawfulness of their current detention, and the possibility of their securing release, will turn on whether there is a sufficient prospect of their being removed in a reasonable period of time. The length of their detention to date is a relevant factor but not a trump card. If they pose a risk of absconding and they can be removed within a very short period of time, the court will be extremely unlikely to order their release, no matter how long their past detention may have been.[97] The suggestion of Dyson LJ (as he then was) in *R (M) v Secretary of State for the Home Department*,[98] that 'there must come a time when, whatever the magnitude of the risks [of absconding or offending], *the period of detention*[99] can no longer be said to be reasonable' misses an important element from the equation—i.e. the prospect of removal within a reasonable period of time[100]—and could be misread as suggesting that length of detention alone might compel release regardless of prospects of removal. Lord Dyson rephrased this point in *Lumba*:[101] '(t)here must come a time when, however grave the risk of absconding and however grave the risk of serious offending, *it ceases to be lawful*[102] to detain a person pending deportation'. The later formulation is better. If one assumes that, at all times, deportation is never more than a possibility achievable (to a greater or lesser degree of certainty) in weeks or months, there will come a point when detention becomes unlawful no matter how great the risk of offending or absconding. However, that point is reached not simply because the period of detention is too long but because the period of detention is too long *when weighed against* the possibility of removal and the likely period of future detention. As a result, the point at which detention becomes unlawful is most easily identified by applying the 'sufficient prospect' test.[103]

---

[96] See paragraph 8.03.
[97] See paragraph 8.10.
[98] [2008] EWCA Civ 307 at [14].
[99] Emphasis added.
[100] Dyson LJ himself recognized this was an important factor.
[101] *R (Lumba & Mighty) v Secretary of State for the Home Department* [2011] UKSC 12; [2012] 1 AC 245 at [144].
[102] Emphasis added.
[103] See paragraph 8.03.

This explains why there are so few reported judgments where detention is said to be **8.43** unlawful by reason of the second *Hardial Singh* principle alone. The only reported judgment with such a finding was by Dyson LJ (as he then was) in *R (I) v Secretary of State for the Home Department*.[104] On the facts of that case, Dyson LJ found that there had been a breach of the second *Hardial Singh* principle, without considering the third *Hardial Singh* principle. The other member of the majority, Simon Brown LJ (as he then was), however found detention unlawful because of a breach of the third *Hardial Singh* principle. He asked himself whether 'it had become clear that the appellant's removal was not going to be possible within a reasonable period of time'.[105] Simon Brown LJ concluded that this had become clear by the date of the appeal hearing, having regard to the fact that detention had lasted for 16 months already, the risk of offending was low, and there was only a hope of deporting the appellant within the next few months.[106] What led Dyson LJ to find a breach of the second *Hardial Singh* principle was exactly what led Simon Brown LJ to find a breach of the third *Hardial Singh* principle—i.e. the length of past detention *when weighed against* the uncertainty and distance of removal. In other words, even this finding of a breach of the second *Hardial Singh* principle could be analysed as an application of the third *Hardial Singh* principle.

I is an example of a situation that arises in several *Hardial Singh* cases—someone is **8.44** detained pending the uncertain possibility of removal and they are kept in detention for a significant period of time even though the possibility of removal does not become any more likely. In such a case, there will come a point when the prospects of removal within a reasonable period of time cease to be 'sufficient' to justify continued detention. Describing this as a breach of the second *Hardial Singh* principle is really just another way of saying that one particular factor (i.e. the length of detention) was decisive in tipping the balance against detention.

The impotence of the second *Hardial Singh* principle, on its own, is no doubt the **8.45** reason why the Court of Appeal suggested in *R (Khalid) v Secretary of State for the Home Department*[107] that courts should only decide whether there has been a breach of the second *Hardial Singh* principle when they have considered whether there has been a breach of one of the other *Hardial Singh* principles. A finding that the second *Hardial Singh* principle has been breached—i.e. that detention has been longer than is reasonable in all the circumstances—is usually, if not invariably, a conclusion that one of the other *Hardial Singh* principles has been breached and caused detention to be too long. This is not what Dyson LJ had in mind, in *R (I) v Secretary of State for the Home Department*,[108] when he separated out the second and

---

104 [2002] EWCA Civ 888 at [57].
105 [2002] EWCA Civ 888 at [26].
106 [2002] EWCA Civ 888 at [38].
107 [2012] EWCA Civ 1656 at [30].
108 [2002] EWCA Civ 888 at [47].

third *Hardial Singh* principles saying they were 'conceptually distinct'. However, the third *Hardial Singh* principle has developed beyond its original formulation and, as a result, the original conceptual distinction has become blurred.[109]

8.46 When the limitations of the second *Hardial Singh* principle are properly understood, it is easier to chart a course between:

(1) the authorities which suggest that it is inappropriate and unhelpful to examine the length of detention permitted in other cases because each case turns on its own facts;[110] and

(2) the authorities which suggest that it is appropriate to have regard to the length of detention permitted in other cases because, otherwise, judgments on the appropriate period of time for detention would be 'at risk of being arbitrary, depending on the unguided intuition of the individual judge hearing any particular case'.[111]

8.47 Because there are so many relevant elements which determine what is a reasonable period, it is not helpful to focus exclusively on the length of detention in other cases. That is what some advocates have sought to do—relying on earlier judgments to submit that there is an outer limit on the maximum permissible period of immigration detention—a tariff beyond which there will be a breach of the second *Hardial Singh* principle, or a lower limit below which there is no prospect of establishing that detention is unlawful.[112] Irwin J described the notion of a tariff in this context as 'repugnant and wrong'.[113] The lawfulness of detention pending deportation cannot be judged on its duration alone. All the many relevant factors, set out at paragraph 8.55, must be taken into account. Two judgments of Mitting J[114] have been wrongly interpreted as setting a maximum of around two years detention for a criminal who has not committed a very serious offence and does not pose a risk to national security.[115] There is no such limit because the risk of re-offending is only one of the many

---

[109] See paragraphs 8.03–8.04 and 8.50–8.53.

[110] See *R (Davies) v Secretary of State for the Home Department* [2010] EWHC 2656 (Admin) at [45]; *R (NAB) v Secretary of State for the Home Department* [2010] EWHC 3137 (Admin) at [78]; *R (Shafiq-ur- Rehman) v Secretary of State for the Home Department* [2013] EWHC 1280 (Admin) at [12]; *R (Belkasim) v Secretary of State for the Home Department* [2012] EWHC 3109 (Admin) at [106]; *R (Khalid) v Secretary of State for the Home Department* [2012] EWHC 421 (Admin) at [53]; *R (Momoh) v Secretary of State for the Home Department* [2012] EWHC 3740 (Admin) at [29].

[111] See *R (Sino) v Secretary of State for the Home Department* [2011] EWHC 2249 (Admin) at [60]; *R (Moussaoui) v Secretary of State for the Home Department* [2012] EWHC 126 (Admin) at [156]; *R (LK (Somalia)) v Secretary of State for the Home Department* [2012] EWHC 1299 (Admin) at [33].

[112] See *R (NAB) v Secretary of State for the Home Department* [2010] EWHC 3137 (Admin) at [77] and *R (Sino) v Secretary of State for the Home Department* [2011] EWHC 2249 (Admin) at [57]; and *R (Shafiq-ur-Rehman) v Secretary of State for the Home Department* [2013] EWHC 1280 (Admin) at [12].

[113] See *R (NAB) v Secretary of State for the Home Department* [2010] EWHC 3137 (Admin) at [78]–[80].

[114] *R (Bashir) v Home Secretary* [2007] EWHC 3017 at [21]; and *R (Wang) v Home Secretary* [2009] EWHC 1578 at [27].

[115] *R (Sino) v Secretary of State for the Home Department* [2011] EWHC 2249 (Admin) at [59].

relevant factors, none of which is a 'trump card'.[116] Two detainees, A and B, may pose exactly the same risks of absconding and offending and may have been equally uncooperative in their removal. Nonetheless, it may be permissible to detain A for significantly longer than B because at all times there was a better reason for hoping that A could be deported. Furthermore, no matter how long detention has been, a court will not order release if deportation is likely to take place within an extremely short period of time.[117]

8.48 The only situation where comparison with the length of detention in other cases may be helpful is where all of the relevant factors are comparable. So, for instance, where the obstacles to removal are the same in two cases, and the risks of offending and absconding are comparable, it may be helpful to have regard to where earlier judgments have drawn the line. A common example is where the obstacle to removal is one that is generic to a particular country. In such cases, the court will carefully examine earlier judgments concerning the same country to see how other courts have assessed the prospects of removal. If the other relevant facts are comparable, judgments in earlier cases may assist in identifying whether detention was lawful and, if not, when it ceased to be.[118]

E. The Third Principle

8.49 As originally formulated by Woolf J, the third *Hardial Singh* principle was that detention should not continue if it was 'apparent' that removal would not be possible within a reasonable period of time. Lord Dyson has described this as a requirement that there be a 'realistic' prospect of removal within a reasonable period of time.[119] This is not to be conflated with the test in *Khadir*[120] for whether there is a power to detain—i.e. whether there is 'some prospect' of removal.[121] The *Khadir* test does not take into account *when* removal might take place. By contrast, the third *Hardial Singh* principle requires there to be a prospect of removal *within a reasonable period of time*. This distinction is very important because it is very difficult to establish that there is no prospect of removal at any point in the future.

---

[116] *Shafiq-ur-Rehman* at [27].

[117] See paragraph 8.10.

[118] See *R (Murad) v Secretary of State for the Home Department* [2012] EWHC 1112 (Admin) at [101]; *R (LK (Somalia)) v Secretary of State for the Home Department* [2012] EWHC 1299 (Admin) at [58]; *R (Mahmoud) v Secretary of State for the Home Department* [2012] EWHC 1834 (Admin) at [45]; *R (Alsaadon) v Secretary of State for the Home Department* [2013] EWHC 2184 (Admin) at [40].

[119] See *R (Lumba & Mighty) v Secretary of State for the Home Department* [2011] UKSC 12; [2012] 1 AC 245 at [103].

[120] *R (Khadir) v Secretary of State for the Home Department* [2005] UKHL 39; [2006] 1 AC 207 at [32]. See paragraph 1.09.

[121] In *BXS v Secretary of State for the Home Department* [2014] EWHC 737 (Admin) at [68], the Deputy High Court Judge rightly rejected the Secretary of State's submission that the third *Hardial Singh* principle was to be tested by asking whether there was 'some prospect of removal'.

Indeed, since *Khadir*, there is no reported case where a court has made such a finding. By contrast, there have been many cases where the court has found no prospect of removal within a reasonable period of time.

8.50 Even though some courts have suggested that it is important to keep to the original formulation of the third *Hardial Singh* principle[122]—i.e. whether it was 'apparent' that removal would not be possible within a reasonable period of time, much of the case-law has been concerned with a slightly different question—i.e. whether there was a 'sufficient'[123] (or, more ambiguously, a 'reasonable')[124] prospect of removal within a reasonable period of time. This may sound like the same test (and is often treated as being the same test) but it is not.

8.51 An example can demonstrate the difference. X has been detained under immigration powers, pending deportation, for a lengthy period. The only obstacle to X's deportation is the lack of a travel document. X's country is unpredictable in its grant of travel documents. There is, at all times, a low but nonetheless realistic chance that X might be granted a travel document at any time. If he is, he can be removed in a matter of days. Equally, X may never be granted a travel document. It is difficult to see when, if ever, Woolf J's original formulation of the third *Hardial Singh* principle would be breached—it is difficult to see when, if ever, it would become 'apparent' that removal will not be possible within a reasonable period of time. By contrast, there will definitely come a time when there is no longer a 'sufficient' prospect of removal within a reasonable period of time. After a certain period of detention, a low but realistic prospect of removal within a very short period of time will cease to be 'sufficient'. There would need to be more certainty that removal will take place in a reasonable period in order to justify continued detention.

8.52 This example demonstrates that detention may be unlawful under the 'sufficient prospect' test without being unlawful under the original formulation of the third *Hardial Singh* principle—i.e. even though it is not yet 'apparent' that removal will not be possible within a reasonable period of time. The converse is not true. If it is apparent that removal will not be possible within a reasonable period of time, then plainly there is not a sufficient prospect of removal within a reasonable period of time to justify continued detention. In other words, the 'sufficient prospect' test

---

[122] *Muqtaar* at [36] *per* Richards LJ; and *Shafiq-ur-Rehman* at [28] *per* Nicholas Paines QC. Ironically, having cautioned of the need to keep to the original wording of the third *Hardial Singh* principle, both Richards LJ and Paines QC went on to apply the 'sufficient prospect' test.

[123] See *R (A) v Secretary of State for the Home Department* [2007] EWCA Civ 804 at [45]; *R (MH) v Secretary of State for the Home Department* [2010] EWCA Civ 1112 at [64]–[66]; *R (Muqtaar) v Secretary of State for the Home Department* [2012] EWCA Civ 1270 at [37]–[38]; *NS* [2013] CSOH 139 at [16]; *R (Ismail) v Secretary of State for the Home Department* [2013] EWHC 3921 (Admin) at [16].

[124] *R (I) v Secretary of State for the Home Department* [2002] EWCA Civ 888 at [26]; *R (Othman) v SIAC, Secretary of State for the Home Department and the Governor of Long Lartin* [2012] EWHC 2349 (Admin) at [22]; *R (IM (Nigeria)) v Secretary of State for the Home Department* [2013] EWCA Civ 1561 at [53].

incorporates, and goes beyond, the original formulation of the third *Hardial Singh* principle.

The question of whether there is a 'sufficient' or 'reasonable' prospect of removal **8.53** within a reasonable period of time is the key issue in many, if not most, *Hardial Singh* cases. For present purposes, this question is treated as embodying the third *Hardial Singh* principle, as it has been developed and applied, although it could also be seen as a reformulation of the second *Hardial Singh* principle or an amalgamation of the second and third *Hardial Singh* principles.[125]

The third *Hardial Singh* principle is not concerned with unlawful removal—the **8.54** question is whether there is a sufficient prospect of *lawful* removal within a reasonable period of time.[126] The fact that the ECtHR is issuing Rule 39 indications on a 'fact-insensitive' basis to anyone who is threatened with removal to a particular country, does not, in itself, prevent lawful removal to that country. Removal of someone to such a country will be lawful unless and until they obtain a Rule 39 indication.[127]

Lord Dyson has provided a non-exhaustive list of the considerations which are **8.55** likely to be relevant when assessing what is a 'reasonable period of time':[128]

(1) the length of the detention to date;
(2) the nature of the obstacles in the path of deportation;
(3) the diligence, speed and effectiveness of the steps taken by the Secretary of State to surmount those obstacles;
(4) the conditions of detention;
(5) the effect of detention on the detainee and his family;
(6) the risk of absconding; and
(7) the risk of offending.

(1) The length of detention to date

In general, the longer a person has been detained, the sooner and more likely depor- **8.56** tation must be if continued detention is to be reasonable.[129] However, not all periods of past detention weigh equally. Past detention will not count significantly in a detainee's favour if it has been prolonged by abusive behaviour on the part of the detainee. So, for example, detention which has been prolonged by hopeless litigation brought by the detainee will be given 'minimal weight'.[130] Likewise, detention

---

[125] See paragraphs 8.03-8.04.
[126] See *HXA v The Home Office* [2010] EWHC 1177 (QB) at [65].
[127] See *R (AR (Somalia)) v Secretary of State for the Home Department* [2011] EWCA Civ 857.
[128] *R (I) v Secretary of State for the Home Department* [2002] EWCA Civ 888 at [46].
[129] See *R (MH) v Secretary of State for the Home Department* [2010] EWCA Civ at [68(v)] and *R (Mahmoud) v Secretary of State for the Home Department* [2012] EWHC 1834 (Admin) at [36].
[130] See *R (Lumba & Mighty) v Secretary of State for the Home Department* [2011] UKSC 12; [2012] 1 AC 245 at [120].

which has been prolonged by the detainee providing false and misleading information, giving rise to false hopes, will not weigh significantly in a detainee's favour.[131]

8.57 Lord Dyson made clear in *Lumba* that the refusal of voluntary return is not a form of abusive behaviour, to be equated with the use of hopeless litigation to thwart removal.[132] A refusal to return voluntarily may still be relevant if and in so far as it suggests a risk of absconding (an inference which cannot be drawn in every case).[133] However, that does not mean it can be of any relevance in itself. A refusal to return voluntarily is irrelevant if return is prevented by an obstacle for which the detainee is not responsible, or by litigation which is not abusive.[134] What is less clear is whether a refusal to return voluntarily is of any relevance, in itself, where there is no such obstacle. In *R (I) v Secretary of State for the Home Department*,[135] Dyson LJ (as he then was) said that 'the mere fact that a detained person refuses the offer of voluntary repatriation cannot make a reasonable period of detention which would otherwise be unreasonable'.[136] Although he did not speak for the majority in *I*, Dyson LJ's opinion was clear—a refusal of voluntary return was never of any relevance. The majority of the Court of Appeal disagreed in *R (A) v Secretary of State for the Home Department*[137] and Lord Dyson revisited the issue in *Lumba*. Lord Dyson's conclusion was that 'if the refusal of voluntary return has any relevance . . . even if a risk of absconding cannot be inferred from the refusal, it must be limited'.[138] This left the matter less clear—Lord Dyson held out the possibility that his comments in *I* might be wrong and that a refusal of voluntary return might have some, albeit limited, relevance. However, later courts have followed Lord Dyson's original approach in *I* and treated the refusal of voluntary return as a factor of no significance in itself.[139]

8.58 *Lumba* also left unclear the weight to be attached to detention which was prolonged by other forms of non-cooperation, i.e.:

(1) the pursuit of appeals or other forms of litigation which were not abusive; and

---

[131] See *R (Sino) v Secretary of State for the Home Department* [2011] EWHC 2249 (Admin) at [56]; *R (Amougou-Mbarga) v Secretary of State for the Home Department* [2011] EWHC 2249 (Admin) [2012] EWHC 1081 (Admin) at [41]; *R (Nourredine) v Secretary of State for the Home Department* [2012] EWHC 1707 (Admin) at [88].

[132] See *R (Lumba & Mighty) v Secretary of State for the Home Department* [2011] UKSC 12; [2012] 1 AC 245 at [123]–[128].

[133] See *R (Lumba & Mighty) v Secretary of State for the Home Department* [2011] UKSC 12; [2012] 1 AC 245 at [123].

[134] *Lumba* at [127].

[135] *R (I) v Secretary of State for the Home Department* [2003] INLR 196.

[136] *R (I) v Secretary of State for the Home Department* [2003] INLR 196 at [51].

[137] *R (A) v Secretary of State for the Home Department* [2007] EWCA Civ 804 at [54] and [67].

[138] See *R (Lumba & Mighty) v Secretary of State for the Home Department* [2011] UKSC 12; [2012] 1 AC 245 at [128].

[139] See *R (Khalid) v Secretary of State for the Home Department* [2012] EWHC 421 (Admin) at [62].

(2) a refusal to provide information or documents that are necessary in order to enforce deportation/removal.

In *Lumba*, Lord Dyson rejected the submission of the Secretary of State that **8.59** periods of detention taken up by appeals were to be discounted.[140] However, he said that a period of detention as a result of a meritorious appeal by the detainee should not necessarily be taken into account 'in its entirety' and that this issue was 'fact-sensitive'.[141] This could be read as suggesting that less weight should be given to periods of detention where the obstacle to removal was non-abusive litigation (the conclusion in *Abdi & Khalaf*,[142] a Court of Appeal judgment that preceded *Lumba*). However, it was significant that Lord Dyson held, on the facts of that case, that Mr Lumba's non-abusive appeals were 'irrelevant'.[143] The best analysis of this is that past detention which was prolonged by a non-abusive appeal is to be given full weight, unless it was conducted in an abusive manner. So, for example, if a detainee used deliberate delaying tactics to draw out an appeal which was not in itself abusive, the extra time they spent in detention as a result of those tactics would not count in their favour.

It is more difficult to determine how to assess detention which has been pro- **8.60** longed by the detainee refusing to provide information or documents necessary to facilitate deportation/removal. This is identified in *Lumba* as one of two types of non-cooperation (at [122]), but not examined in any detail. In principle, it is unclear why a detainee's refusal to provide the identifying information necessary to obtain an emergency travel document for his deportation should be treated any differently from the detainee's refusal to return voluntarily. Yet that is exactly what the courts have done. It has been held in several first instance judgments, which post-date *Lumba*, that a detainee's refusal to provide biographical data is a factor that weighs against them—they can be detained for longer before their detention becomes unreasonable.[144]

If there has been more than one period of past detention, interrupted by an inter- **8.61** val of liberty, the periods of past detention are to be aggregated unless the interval of liberty constituted an 'effective break' in the continuity of detention.[145]

---

[140] *Lumba* at [121].

[141] See *R (Lumba & Mighty) v Secretary of State for the Home Department* [2011] UKSC 12; [2012] 1 AC 245 at [121].

[142] *Secretary of State for the Home Department v Abdi; Khalaf v Secretary of State for the Home Department* [2011] EWCA Civ 242 at [44]–[46].

[143] See *R (Lumba & Mighty) v Secretary of State for the Home Department* [2011] UKSC 12; [2012] 1 AC 245 at [144].

[144] See *R (Sino) v Secretary of State for the Home Department* [2011] EWHC 2249 (Admin) at [56]; *R (Lamari) v Secretary of State for the Home Department* [2012] EWHC 1630 (Admin) at [105]; *R (HE) v Secretary of State for the Home Department* [2012] EWHC 3628 (Admin) at [30]; *R (Yegorov) v Secretary of State for the Home Department* [2011] EWHC 3358 (Admin); *R (Zergou) v Secretary of State for the Home Department* [2012] EWHC 4233 (Admin).

[145] *R (MC (Algeria)) v Secretary of State for the Home Department* [2010] EWCA Civ 347 at [34].

An interval of liberty will probably constitute an effective break where the claimant is only re-detained because of his own conduct. For example, in *R (MC (Algeria)) v Secretary of State for the Home Department*,[146] the claimant was released on bail after a period of immigration detention pending deportation. If he had abided by his bail conditions and not re-offended, he would not have been re-detained. As it was, he committed criminal offences very soon after being released and was re-detained and convicted. At the end of his criminal sentence he was detained under immigration powers. This second period of immigration detention was treated as a distinct period by the Court of Appeal. The length of the earlier period of immigration detention was not taken into account in his favour because there had been an 'effective break'. By contrast, in *NAB*,[147] Irwin J aggregated two periods of detention which were interrupted by just over a month of bail. Irwin J was apparently not referred to the judgment in *MC (Algeria)* but it is arguable that his conclusion was consistent with the principles in *MC (Algeria)*—in *NAB*, the interval of liberty was short and the claimant had not re-offended in the meantime or done anything which made his re-detention inevitable.[148] In *R (Badah) v Secretary of State for the Home Department*,[149] Singh J declined to add together two periods of detention that were separated by a gap of two years. However, he did say that the earlier detention was 'of some relevance and should lead to a greater sense of urgency even than would normally be the case in immigration detention'.

(2) Obstacles and diligence

8.62 It is characteristic of the fluid nature of the *Hardial Singh* principles that the Secretary of State's diligence in overcoming obstacles is both a principle in itself and a relevant factor in relation to other principles. There are, in general, three kinds of obstacle in the path of deportation:

(1) an obstacle within the control of the detainee—for example, the detainee has deliberately refused to provide information which is necessary in order to obtain an emergency travel document or refused to sign a disclaimer;

(2) an obstacle within the control of the Secretary of State—for example, the Secretary of State needs to take a decision on whether one of the exceptions to automatic deportation apply; and

---

146 [2010] EWCA Civ 347 at [34]–[37].
147 [2010] EWHC 3137 (Admin) at [15]–[19], [32], and [35]–[36].
148 There was a dispute as to whether the claimant had breached a condition as to curfew and residence, by moving home without first informing the authorities. Irwin J did not resolve this dispute. However, if there was a breach of conditions, it was relatively minor as there was no doubt that he informed the authorities of his change of residence at some point (even if later than he should have done) and that he complied with his reporting obligations.
149 [2014] EWHC 364 (Admin) at [59].

(3) an obstacle which is within the control of a third party—for example, test case litigation in Strasbourg or delays by the detainee's home authorities in providing the necessary travel documents.

If a detainee obstructs removal by refusing to cooperate, the Secretary of State is **8.63** not, at least initially, obliged to treat this as an insuperable obstacle. The Secretary of State is entitled to a reasonable period of time to see if the detainee will change his mind and cooperate.[150] Even where the detainee's refusal to cooperate involves a refusal to eat, the Secretary of State is entitled to wait and see if the detainee persists in his hunger strike.[151] However, the detainee must be released if and when it becomes clear that they are never going to provide the cooperation necessary for removal.[152] In *Sino*,[153] John Howell QC found that detention was unlawful from the outset because cooperation was necessary to effect removal and the Secretary of State had not established a realistic prospect of ever obtaining Mr Sino's cooperation. In other judgments, the courts have not questioned whether there was a realistic prospect of such cooperation from the outset of detention. Instead, they have assumed a reasonable prospect of cooperation notwithstanding the initial refusal to cooperate.[154] *Sino* is arguably closer to the approach of the ECtHR in some of their recent judgments, where they have held that it 'must have become clear quite soon' that removal would be impossible in light of the detainee's refusal to cooperate.[155]

By contrast, where the obstacle to removal is in the control of the Secretary of State, **8.64** it needs to be overcome relatively swiftly. Were it otherwise, the fourth *Hardial Singh* principle would be ineffective.[156] If the Secretary of State has shown a lack

---

[150] See *R (Yegorov) v Secretary of State for the Home Department* [2011] EWHC 3358 (Admin) at [28]; *R (BE) v Secretary of State for the Home Department* [2011] 690 (Admin) at [155].

[151] See *R (Mauza) v Secretary of State for the Home Department* [2013] EWHC 3764 (Admin) at [79].

[152] See *R (Sino) v Secretary of State for the Home Department* [2011] EWHC 2249 (Admin) at [56]; *R (Raki) v Secretary of State for the Home Department* [2011] EWHC 2421 (Admin) at [22]. The Deputy High Court Judge in *R (Kajuga) v Secretary of State for the Home Department* [2014] EWHC 426 (Admin) at [18] said that he 'did not entirely agree with the approach taken . . . in *Sino*' and that a non-cooperative detainee may be detained for 'a number of years, provided the Secretary of State makes real and continuous efforts to ascertain where the detainee has come from and should be deported to'. It is not clear which of the principles in *Sino* he was disagreeing with. *Kajuga* could be read as suggesting that a non-cooperative detainee may be detained so long as efforts are being made to discover their identity, even if there is no realistic prospect of their being removed within a reasonable period of time. Such a proposition would be inconsistent with binding domestic authority and several judgments of the ECtHR.

[153] [2011] EWHC 2249 (Admin) at [200].

[154] See *R (Yegorov) v Secretary of State for the Home Department* [2011] EWHC 3358 (Admin) at [28]; *R (BE) v Secretary of State for the Home Department* [2011] 690 (Admin) at [155].

[155] *Mikolenko v Estonia* Application number 10664/05 (8 October 2009) at [64]; *Massoud v Malta* Application number 24340/08 (27 July 2010) at [67]. But contrast *Tabassum v United Kingdom* Application number 2134/10 (24 January 2012) at [20]. See paragraph 15.58.

[156] See paragraph 8.76.

of diligence, speed or effectiveness in overcoming obstacles that only she can over-come, this may have the following effects:

(1) it may render some of the past detention unlawful; and

(2) it may shorten the limits for detention in the future—where the Secretary of State has not been diligent in the past, it is reasonable to require her to be correspondingly more diligent in the future.[157]

8.65 Where the obstacle to removal is something outside the control of the detainee or the Secretary of State, the court will expect a realistic evidence-based appraisal of how long it is likely to take to overcome. If the Secretary of State is to assert that removal can take place in a certain timescale, she should provide evidence to support her assertion.[158] However, it is not necessary for the Secretary of State to predict a date when removal will take place, or even to be certain that removal will be possible at all.[159] There can still be a sufficient prospect of removal within a reasonable period of time in circumstances where the Secretary of State is unclear whether and if so when removal will be possible.[160] The extent of the uncertainty is a factor in the balancing exercise.[161]

(3) Conditions and effect of detention

8.66 If a person's detention has caused or contributed to his suffering or illness then that is a factor which should be taken into account when assessing the reasonable-ness of detention. Where the impact is especially severe, this is a powerful fac-tor against detention to be balanced by some equally compelling factor the other way if detention is to be maintained.[162] The critical question in such cases will be whether there are facilities available to keep the illness under control and prevent suffering.[163] Thus, if a detainee is disabled and held in unsuitable conditions, that may tip the balance and render immigration detention unlawful.[164] However, a

---

[157] See *R (Sino) v Secretary of State for the Home Department* [2011] EWHC 2249 (Admin) at [67]–[69]; *R (Lamari) v Secretary of State for the Home Department* [2012] EWHC 1630 (Admin) at [113]–[114].

[158] See *R (MM (Somalia)) v Secretary of State for the Home Department* [2009] EWHC 2353 (Admin) at [34].

[159] See *R (MH) v Secretary of State for the Home Department* [2010] EWCA Civ 1112 at [65] and *R (Muqtaar) v Secretary of State for the Home Department* [2012] EWCA Civ 1270 at [38].

[160] See *R (MH) v Secretary of State for the Home Department* [2010] EWCA Civ 1112 at [65] and *R (Muqtaar) v Secretary of State for the Home Department* [2012] EWCA Civ 1270 at [38].

[161] See *R (MH) v Secretary of State for the Home Department* [2010] EWCA Civ 1112 at [65] and *R (Muqtaar) v Secretary of State for the Home Department* [2012] EWCA Civ 1270 at [38].

[162] *TN (Vietnam) & Ors v Secretary of State for the Home Department* [2010] EWHC 668 (Admin) at [55] (upheld on appeal as *MD (Angola) v Secretary of State for the Home Department* [2011] EWCA Civ 1238).

[163] See *R (M) v Secretary of State for the Home Department* [2008] EWCA Civ 307 at [39].

[164] See *R (BE) v Secretary of State for the Home Department* [2011] EWHC 690 (Admin) at [178]–[180].

single act of medical negligence in detention will not necessarily render detention unlawful.[165] Where the conditions of detention are particularly poor, they may even breach Article 3.[166] The effect on other family members also needs to be taken into account.[167] Where detention has an adverse effect on a child, that effect will need to be a primary consideration, albeit one that may be overcome by other factors.[168]

(4) Risk of absconding and offending

The risks of absconding and offending are 'are always of paramount importance' in assessing how long a period of detention is reasonable.[169] The greater the risks, the longer will be the period of detention that can be justified as reasonable in a given case. **8.67**

Risk of absconding is relevant because if a person absconds 'he will frustrate the deportation for which purpose he was detained in the first place'.[170] **8.68**

Risk of offending, if the person is not detained, is also a relevant factor, the strength of which will depend on the magnitude of the risk—both the likelihood of its occurring and the potential gravity of the consequences.[171] The purpose of deportation is to remove aliens whose continued presence would not be conducive to the public good, usually because they may commit a criminal offence. Detention pending deportation must have the same purpose: As a result, the public good and the risk of offending are relevant considerations when determining the reasonableness of detention pending deportation.[172] **8.69**

In *R (Polanco) v Secretary of State for the Home Department*,[173] the claimant argued that risk of offending was only relevant to detention pending deportation, not detention pending administrative removal, because the public good is not a central purpose of administrative removal. Although this argument appears to have been accepted by the Deputy High Court Judge in *Polanco*, it was later rejected by Sir Michael Harrison in *R (T) v Secretary of State for the Home Department*.[174] In our **8.70**

---

[165] See *R (MD (Angola)) v Secretary of State for the Home Department* [2011] EWCA Civ 1238 at [49], [51].

[166] See paragraphs 15.66–15.83.

[167] See *R (Lumba & Mighty) v Secretary of State for the Home Department* [2011] UKSC 12; [2012] 1 AC 245.

[168] See *R (Abdollahi) v Secretary of State for the Home Department* [2013] EWCA Civ 366 and section 55 of the Borders, Citizenship and Immigration Act 2009; See paragraph 15.90.

[169] See *R (Lumba & Mighty) v Secretary of State for the Home Department* [2011] UKSC 12; [2012] 1 AC 245 at [121].

[170] *R (Lumba & Mighty) v Secretary of State for the Home Department* [2011] UKSC 12; [2012] 1 AC 245 at [121].

[171] *R (A) v Secretary of State for the Home Department* [2007] EWCA Civ 804, *per* Toulson LJ at [55], approved by Lord Dyson in *Lumba* at [107].

[172] *R (A) v Secretary of State for the Home Department* [2007] EWCA Civ 804, *per* Toulson LJ at [55], approved by Lord Dyson in *Lumba* at [107].

[173] *R (Polanco) v Secretary of State for the Home Department* [2009] EWHC 826 at [24], *obiter*.

[174] *R (T) v Secretary of State for the Home Department* [2011] EWHC 370 at [50].

view, *T* is likely to be followed. Lord Dyson's conclusion, in *Lumba*, that the risk of offending was a relevant factor was not based solely on his analysis of the statutory purpose of deportation. Lord Dyson had a simpler way of reaching the same conclusion. He said that 'the period which is reasonable' (for detention pending deportation) depends on all the relevant circumstances and the risk of offending is an 'obviously relevant circumstance'.[175] The same can be said of detention pending administrative removal. When determining how long it is reasonable to detain someone pending administrative removal, the danger they pose to the public if released is 'obviously relevant'.

8.71   It has been suggested (in the obiter dicta of Court of Appeal judges) that, absent a risk of offending and/or absconding, the *Hardial Singh* principles will not permit detention.[176] If that were right, it would mean that *Hardial Singh* imposes a test of necessity not required by Article 5(1)(f) of the European Convention on Human Rights.[177] It is questionable whether these obiter dicta are correct. The House of Lords held in *R (Saadi) v Secretary of State for the Home Department*[178] that it may be reasonable to detain someone pending examination of their asylum claim, even if they pose no risk of absconding. Administrative convenience and the smooth operation of the system may justify detention for a short period. It is difficult to see why the same should not be true of detention pending removal, particularly when the House of Lords in *Saadi* said that 'analogous' principles apply to each kind of detention.[179] Moreover, the Secretary of State's policy allows for the detention of someone on the sole ground that their removal is 'imminent'.[180] The Court of Appeal in *FM* held that this policy was to be read as an application of *Hardial Singh* principles.[181] It seems likely, therefore, that, even in the absence of any risk of absconding or offending, the *Hardial Singh* principles do not prevent detention, pending removal, for very short periods. In any event, this may be a moot point, as in almost every case of enforced removal there is at least some risk of absconding.

8.72   It is for the court itself to form a view on the risks at the material time and the weight they attract. When considering the risk of offending, Probation Service/National Offender Management Service ('NOMS') assessments are usually treated with respect by the court. They are used throughout the criminal justice system and provide a process by which courts and officials are furnished with information in a consistent

---

[175]   *Lumba* at [108].
[176]   See *R (Abdollahi) v Secretary of State for the Home Department* [2013] EWCA Civ 366 at [28]; see also *R (A), per* Toulson LJ at Toulson at [53]: '[Counsel for the Secretary of State] accepted that if there was no risk of an individual absconding and no risk of him offending, in the ordinary way there would be no obvious reason for the Home Secretary to exercise his power of detention.'
[177]   See paragraph 15.16.
[178]   [2002] UKHL 41; [2002] 1 WLR 3131; [2002] 4 All ER 785 at [24]–[26].
[179]   [2002] UKHL 41; [2002] 1 WLR 3131; [2002] 4 All ER 785 at [26].
[180]   See paragraphs 10.08 and 10.09.
[181]   *R (FM) v Secretary of State for the Home Department* [2011] EWCA Civ 807 at [50].

way.[182] Independent evidence of risk from experts such as consultant forensic psychiatrists may also be of assistance to the court, particularly where official risk assessments are out of date or absent. Home Office detention policy includes detailed guidance on the approach case workers should take to assessing risk of offending and harm to the public.[183] Misbehaviour in detention has been held to be of limited relevance to the risk a detainee is likely to pose when at large.[184]

The court's view on absconding risk will necessarily be informed by the individual's past record of compliance with release conditions, any past absconding, any convictions the individual might have for failing to surrender or similar offences, as well as the individual's family and community ties. Home Office policy suggests any history of serious offending is indicative of a risk of absconding,[185] although it is not clear why this should be so in every case. It was observed in *Lumba* that risk of absconding may flow from a risk of offending: 'if a person re-offends there is a risk that he will abscond so as to evade arrest'.[186] It has been held that where a person's disability meant he would have been dependent on health services and benefits this would have made it likely that he would have to have been in contact with public services and thus traceable, albeit it did not follow that the Home Office would be aware of his whereabouts.[187]   **8.73**

Views on offending and absconding risk expressed by judges who have refused bail are 'relevant but not determinative'.[188] In assessing the weight to be attached to those bail decisions it is necessary to have regard to the extent and quality of the information which was available to the judges whose decisions are being considered.[189]   **8.74**

(5) Conclusion

None of these considerations is a 'trump card' which can justify indefinite immigration detention. Each must be balanced against the others.[190] The longer a person has been detained, the sooner and more likely deportation must be if detention is to be reasonable.[191] Even someone who poses a high risk of absconding and offending   **8.75**

[182]   *SM and FM v Secretary of State for the Home Department* [2011] EWHC 338 (Admin), *per* Beatson J at [83].
[183]   See the discussion in paragraphs 10.27–10.29 of the Secretary of State's obligation to seek risk assessments from NOMS in specified cases.
[184]   *R (BE) v Secretary of State for the Home Department* [2011] EWHC 690 (Admin) at [150].
[185]   Enforcement Instructions and Guidance ('EIG'), Chapter 55, Section 55.3A.
[186]   *R (Lumba & Mighty) v Secretary of State for the Home Department* [2011] UKSC 12; [2012] 1 AC 245, *per* Lord Dyson at [109].
[187]   *R (BE) v Secretary of State for the Home Department* [2011] EWHC 690 (Admin) at [144].
[188]   *R (Abdollahi) v Secretary of State for the Home Department* [2013] EWCA Civ 366, at [50].
[189]   *MA & TT v Secretary of State for the Home Department* [2010] EWHC 2350 at [15].
[190]   See *R (Shafiq-ur-Rehman) v Secretary of State for the Home Department* [2013] EWHC 1280 (Admin) at [27].
[191]   *R (MH) v Secretary of State for the Home Department* [2010] EWCA Civ 1112 at [64]–[66].

and frustrates deportation by his refusal to cooperate must be released eventually if they cannot be deported.

F. The Fourth Principle

8.76　The fourth *Hardial Singh* principle requires the Secretary of State to act with reasonable expedition to effect removal. In paragraph 12 of *Krasniqi*,[192] Carnwath LJ held that a breach of this principle will only render detention unlawful where:

(1) the lack of expedition is so serious as to amount to unreasonableness, as opposed to mere 'administrative failing'; and

(2) the lack of expedition caused detention to be longer than it otherwise would have been.[193]

8.77　This subsection deals with each of those conditions before turning to two other issues which have arisen in relation to the fourth *Hardial Singh* principle:

(3) Is the Secretary of State obliged to pursue different methods for effecting removal concurrently or may she attempt them sequentially? and

(4) Is the Secretary of State obliged to take preparatory steps towards deportation, prior to the start of immigration detention?

(1) Unreasonableness and administrative failing

8.78　There is no clear or sharp dividing line between administrative failing and unreasonableness. A survey of the case-law suggests that the line has been drawn in a wide variety of different places.

(1) In *Hardial Singh*, Woolf J found that the Secretary of State had not done all that he should have done as promptly as he should have done it, when there was a nine month period of inactivity (four months of which preceded Mr Singh entering into immigration detention).[194]

(2) In *R (Vovk) v Secretary of State for the Home Department*,[195] Calvert Smith J held that there had not been 'reasonable diligence and expedition' as a result of a delay of six weeks by the Secretary of State in making a decision as to deportation.

---

[192] [2011] EWCA Civ 1549.

[193] See *R (Krasniqi) v Secretary of State for the Home Department* [2011] EWCA Civ 1549 at [12].

[194] *R (Hardial Singh) v Governor of Durham Prison* [1984] 1 WLR 704; [1984] 1 All ER 983; [1983] Imm AR 198 at [19].

[195] [2006] EWHC 3386 (Admin) at [22].

(3) In *R (NAB) v Secretary of State for the Home Department*,[196] delay became unlawful after a year of taking no active steps to overcome a detainee's refusal to cooperate.

(4) In *R (OM) v Secretary of State for the Home Department*,[197] the Court of Appeal held that a delay of six months in responding to a 'fresh claim' was 'not a failure to act with reasonable diligence' or at least not a 'failure of sufficient seriousness as to render continued detention unreasonable'. However, this conclusion should be read in the light of the finding that the delay had 'only a minor effect overall'.

(5) In *R (Yegorov) v Secretary of State for the Home Department*,[198] Mitting J held that 10 months of the claimant's immigration detention had been unlawful because there were 10 months during which nothing was done to persuade a non-cooperative detainee to change his mind or to circumvent his non-cooperation.

(6) In *R (Moussaoui) v Secretary of State for the Home Department*,[199] Lindblom J held that a four month period where there was a 'lack of obvious momentum' was not 'unacceptable'.

(7) In *Reuter (Hans), Application for Judicial Review, Re*[200] Treacy J regarded a delay of five days in re-arranging the deportation of a German national, at the conclusion of his criminal sentence, as a failure to act with reasonable expedition.

(8) In *R (Belkasim) v Secretary of State for the Home Department*,[201] Haddon-Cave J held that a four month delay in responding to a fresh claim was not unreasonable 'given the Secretary of State's enormous workload'.

(9) In *R (Nourredine) v Secretary of State for the Home Department*,[202] Mitting J described a period of just over five months of detention as a 'relatively short period' and said that he was 'required' to consider it 'not with an overcritical eye but in a manner which accepts that the processing of difficult cases is not always impeccable'. The Secretary of State had detained the claimant, whose nationality was in dispute, for more than five months before she sought assistance from the 'country specialist investigation team'. In that period 'nothing much happened' but this was still held not to breach the fourth *Hardial Singh* principle.

(10) In *R (HE) v Secretary of State for the Home Department*,[203] the Deputy High Court Judge said that delay would have to be 'egregious' in order to be unreasonable and hence unlawful.

---

196 [2010] EWHC 3137 (Admin).
197 [2011] EWCA Civ 909 at [46].
198 [2011] EWHC 3358 (Admin) at [33].
199 [2012] EWHC 126 (Admin) at [170].
200 [2012] NIQB 6 at [22].
201 [2012] EWHC 3109 (Admin) at [187].
202 [2012] EWHC 1707 (Admin) at [97].
203 [2012] EWHC 3628 (Admin) at [56].

8.79 The most recent Court of Appeal authority on the fourth *Hardial Singh* principle is *R (Saleh) v Secretary of State for the Home Department*.[204] The claimant was detained pursuant to section 36(1)(a) of the UK Borders Act 2007—in other words, he was detained pending a decision by the Secretary of State as to whether one of the exceptions to automatic deportation applied. It took the Secretary of State 15 months to make that decision. During that period, there were three periods during which little or no administrative activity was taking place, measuring in turn three months, five months, and four a half months—i.e. a total of 12 months where the Secretary of State did nothing. At first instance, the Deputy High Court judge did not find a breach of the fourth *Hardial Singh* principle.[205] He said that, having regard to the Secretary of State's workload, it was it was 'not surprising' that it took eight months after the start of immigration detention to arrange an interview. His response to the fact that it took 12 months for the Secretary of State to reach a new decision was: 'more expedition would have been ideal, but the delay was not unlawful'.[206]

8.80 The Court of Appeal allowed Saleh's appeal and said that the first instance judge's analysis of the lawfulness of detention was 'totally inadequate'. The Court of Appeal acknowledged that the decision on whether to exempt Saleh from automatic deportation was serious and important and not to be rushed. They accepted that the dividing line between administrative failing and unreasonableness amounting to illegality was an exercise in judgment rather than mathematics. However, the Court found that at least two thirds of the twelve months of inactivity fell on the unreasonable side of the line. As a result, eight months of Saleh's detention was unlawful.

8.81 *Saleh* should now be seen as the leading authority in relation to the fourth *Hardial Singh* principle. In a deportation case, at least, the courts will not expect the Secretary of State to account for every day, or even every week, of detention.[207] The courts will not conduct a 'detailed time and motion study' of each day or week of detention.[208] However, the courts should no longer condone administrative delays that prolong detention substantially. The dividing line between administrative failing and unreasonableness will depend, of course, on the facts of the case.[209] However, this is a situation where guidance may be taken from other cases. Otherwise, the application of the fourth *Hardial Singh* principle will be arbitrary. Four months of unexplained inactivity crossed the line into unreasonableness in *Saleh*. Similar or greater periods of delay, in similar circumstances, are likely to be unreasonable.[210] If the person being detained was cooperative and posed little risk of absconding or offending, a great deal more expedition might be expected.

---

[204] [2013] EWCA Civ 1378.
[205] *Saleh v Secretary of State for the Home Department* [2013] EWHC 61 (Admin).
[206] [2013] EWHC 61 (Admin) at [45].
[207] *R (Saleh) v Secretary of State for the Home Department* [2013] EWCA Civ 1378 at [60].
[208] *R (Choy) v Secretary of State for the Home Department* [2011] EWHC 365 (Admin) at [24].
[209] See *Reuter (Hans), Application for Judicial Review, Re* [2012] NIQB 6 at [20].
[210] Although in *Ali Mahamed Abdi v Secretary of State for the Home Department* [2014] EWHC 929 (Admin), the Deputy High Court judge found, after considering *Saleh*, that it was reasonable

Of course, administrative inactivity will not always amount to administrative fail- **8.82** ing, let alone unreasonableness. Where the obstacle to removal is the delay of a third country in providing a travel document and there is reason to believe that the third country may provide a travel document in time, administrative inactiv- ity for several months might be reasonable and might have no causative effect on the length of detention because, in such a situation, frequent 'chivvying' might be counter-productive.[211] However, where the operative cause of detention is the Secretary of State's failure to make a decision, administrative inactivity is a failing, which will amount to unreasonableness when prolonged.

(2) Longer than it would have been

The second limb of the test in paragraph 12 of *Krasniqi* appears to be retrospec- **8.83** tive. Detention will have been unlawful if, viewed retrospectively, there was an unreasonable lack of expedition (i.e. more than mere administrative failing) which caused detention to be longer than it otherwise would have been.[212] However, the clarity of that principle is undermined by paragraph 14 of *Krasniqi* where Carnwath LJ appears to lay down a prospective test. He suggests that, in order to determine whether detention at any particular date in the past was unlawful, it is necessary to ask what the court would have done, on that date, if it had heard an application for release.[213] We consider that that this is wrong for the following reasons.

First, it is inconsistent with paragraph 12 of the same judgment. The inconsistency **8.84** is apparent if one considers the following example. X is detained at the start of a calendar year, pending deportation. X is a dangerous criminal who poses a high risk of absconding and offending. The only obstacle to X's deportation is a relatively simple administrative one which could be accomplished in a couple of weeks if the Secretary of State acted efficiently and with expedition—for example, the purchase of a plane ticket. For no good reason, the Secretary of State takes a whole year to buy X's ticket. Applying the retrospective test in paragraph 12 of *Krasniqi*, it seems clear that a large part of the detention was unlawful. Some delay in accomplish- ing a task that should take two weeks might count as mere 'administrative fail- ing'. However, at some point, certainly by the second half of the year, the delay must have crossed the line into unreasonableness. Moreover, that delay caused the

---

for the Secretary of State to take 10 months to come to the conclusion that the claimant could not be deported. During those 10 months there was a period of over three months where nothing happened other than the file being passed from one team to another (see at [104]–[105]). However, it was an unusually complex case –the claimant had been granted refugee status in error and the possibility of cancelling this status had to be investigated.

[211] *R (Giwa) v Secretary of State for the Home Department* [2013] EWHC 3189 (Admin) at [76].
[212] *R (Krasniqi) v Secretary of State for the Home Department* [2011] EWCA Civ 1549 at [12].
[213] *R (Krasniqi) v Secretary of State for the Home Department* [2011] EWCA Civ 1549 at [14].

detention to be longer than it otherwise would have been. As a result, one might say that a significant part of the detention was unlawful by reason of a breach of the fourth *Hardial Singh* principle. By contrast, if one were to apply the prospective test in paragraph 14 of *Krasniqi*, it would not lead to the same result. Assume X had applied for release after two or three months. His application would probably not have been heard until the second half of the year. What would have happened at a hearing in the second half of the year? In all probability, X would not have been released. Although there had been a lack of expedition, X was still a dangerous criminal who could, without doubt, be deported within a short period of time.[214] At best, the court might have made an order that put pressure on the Secretary of State—for example, an order that A be released if not deported within 21 days— and the Secretary of State would have been likely to comply with the order. Thus, the test at paragraph 14 of *Krasniqi* does not necessarily lead to the correct result.

8.85 Secondly, the test in paragraph 14 of *Krasniqi* has not been following by later Court of Appeal authority on the fourth *Hardial Singh* principle. In *R (Saleh) v Secretary of State for the Home Department*[215] the Court of Appeal held that past detention was unlawful because of a breach of the fourth *Hardial Singh* principle. In so finding, they referred to paragraph 12 of *Krasniqi* and not paragraph 14. They analysed past detention retrospectively, not prospectively. They did not ask whether the court would have ordered release at any particular point in the past.

8.86 Indeed, if the fourth *Hardial Singh* principle is to be effective, the lawfulness of past detention must be analysed retrospectively. The prospective test in paragraph 14 of *Krasniqi* conflates the third and fourth *Hardial Singh* principles. Taken at face value, it would allow egregious failures of expedition to be excused by the fact that there was, at all times, a reasonable prospect of removal within a reasonable period.

(3) Concurrent/sequential

8.87 Absent authority, one would have thought that there was a reasonably strong argument that, if the Secretary of State has different mechanisms to effect removal, she should generally pursue them concurrently rather than sequentially. The importance of the right to liberty and the obligation to act expeditiously where liberty is at stake would seem to suggest that time should not be wasted by pursuing each mechanism in turn. However, that is not the approach that the courts have taken. Several first instance judgments have found no breach of the first *Hardial Singh* principle where the Secretary of State has pursued different approaches to removal sequentially. So, for example, in *R (HE) v Secretary of State for the Home Department*,[216] Deputy High Court Judge Ockelton held that 'the Secretary of

---

214 See paragraph 8.10.
215 [2013] EWCA Civ 1378, discussed at paragraphs 8.79–8.81.
216 [2012] EWHC 3628 (Admin) at [29].

State is entitled to attempt strategies serially rather than simultaneously and still be regarded as acting with reasonable expedition'. Likewise in *R (Krawetskiy) v Secretary of State for the Home Department,*[217] MacDuff J found no breach of the fourth *Hardial Singh* principle where the Secretary of State attempted different methods to get round the claimant's non-cooperation one after another, rather than all together.

(4) Preparatory Steps

Absent authority, one might have thought that the Secretary of State was obliged **8.88** to minimize the period of immigration detention by taking all preparatory steps towards removal at the first possible opportunity and, if possible, in advance of immigration detention. However, the courts have not required this.

In *R (Q) v Secretary of State for the Home Department; and the Governor of Long* **8.89** *Lartin,*[218] the Divisional Court held that the Secretary of State was not obliged to apply for an emergency travel document from Q's home country while Q still had an appeal pending. In *R (Rashid Hussein) v Secretary of State for the Home Department,*[219] Nicol J held that the Secretary of State was not obliged to apply for a travel document before he has determined the claimant's asylum or human rights claim. In *R (Dimpl Singh) v Secretary of State for the Home Department*[220] the Deputy High Court judge held that the Secretary of State was not obliged to start the process of applying for an emergency travel document until immigration detention began because 'the circumstances might change'.

This particular issue arises frequently where detention is being maintained under **8.90** section 36(1)(a) of UKBA 2007. Section 36 was introduced to fill a gap in the pow-ers of detention pending deportation—prior to UKBA 2007, the Secretary of State could not detain a foreign national criminal at the conclusion of their criminal sentence unless she had made a decision to deport them. This created problems where there was no opportunity to make such a decision prior to the conclusion of the criminal sentence. For example, if a foreign national criminal was eligible for immediate release after sentencing, because he had already served his sentence on remand, the Secretary of State would have no power to detain him. Lord Bassam, the responsible Minister in the House of Lords, said that the purpose of section 36(1)(a) was to provide a power to detain in this kind of situation. He said that 'deportation action will, whenever possible, be commenced while the criminal sentence is being served' and that detention under section 36 would not be neces-sary 'in the majority of circumstances'.[221]

---

[217] [2013] EWHC 2325 (Admin).
[218] [2006] EWHC 2690 (Admin) at [20].
[219] [2009] EWHC 2492 (Admin) at [50].
[220] [2013] EWHC 380 (Admin) at [52].
[221] Hansard, HL Report 16 Oct 2007: Columns 661–662.

8.91 In practice, however, section 36(1)(a) of UKBA 2007 has frequently been used where there was no obvious reason why a decision on deportation could not have been made before the conclusion of the criminal sentence. The Court of Appeal in *Saleh* held that there was no 'blanket positive obligation' to start the decision making process while the foreign national criminal was still serving their sentence but that the court was entitled to question whether the Secretary of State should have started the decision making process earlier.[222]

G. Exceptions and Modifications

8.92 The *Hardial Singh* principles are based on a presumption that Parliament intended to impose limitations on the powers of immigration detention which it has provided.[223] In *Hardial Singh* itself, the power in question was under paragraphs 2(2) and 2(3) of Schedule 3 to IA 1971—i.e. discretionary detention pending deportation. Precisely the same principles apply to 'mandatory' detention pending deportation[224] and detention pending administrative removal.[225] The case-law which had suggested that there is an exception to *Hardial Singh*— i.e. that mandatory detention should not be subject to *Hardial Singh* limitations—is wrong.[226]

8.93 Although there is no exception to the *Hardial Singh* principles, there are situations in which they need to be modified. In their original formulation, the *Hardial Singh* principles are concerned with detention 'pending' expulsion from the United Kingdom. Different issues arise where the power of immigration detention is not pending expulsion but pending examination of immigration status[227] and/or a decision on immigration status, i.e.:

(1) a decision on whether to give, refuse, or cancel leave to enter;[228] or
(2) a decision on whether one of the exceptions to automatic deportation apply.[229]

---

[222] *R (Saleh) v Secretary of State for the Home Department* [2013] EWCA Civ 1378 at [50].

[223] *R (Francis) v Secretary of State for the Home Department* [2014] EWCA Civ 718 at [45].

[224] I.e. detention under paragraph 2(1) and the corresponding part of paragraph 2(3) of Schedule 3 to IA 1971. See *R (Francis) v Secretary of State for the Home Department* [2014] EWCA Civ 718.

[225] I.e. detention under paragraph 16(2) of Schedule 2 to IA 1971. See *R (FM) v Secretary of State for the Home Department* [2011] EWCA Civ 807 at [25].

[226] See paragraph 8.06.

[227] See paragraph 16(1), (1A)(a), and (1B) of Schedule 2 to IA 1971 and section 62(2)(a) of the Nationality, Immigration and Asylum Act 2002 ('NIAA 2002').

[228] See paragraph 16(1), (1A)(a) and (1B) of Schedule 2 to IA 1971 and section 62(1)(a) and 62(2)(b) of NIAA 2002.

[229] Section 36(1)(a) of UKBA 2007.

(1) Detention pending a decision on leave to enter

Where detention is under paragraph 16(1B) of Schedule 2 to IA 1971 (i.e. detention **8.94** for further examination) there is a time limit specified in statute—i.e. 12 hours. In other cases, detention pending examination is limited by common law principles which are 'analogous' to the *Hardial Singh* limitations—i.e. the power of detention has to be used reasonably.[230] The same 'fundamental principles' apply as in *Hardial Singh* and the court is to decide for itself whether the detention was lawful, rather than merely reviewing the decisions of the Secretary of State under *Wednesbury* principles.[231] Reasonableness is not to be equated with necessity. Detention for 10 days in Oakington IRC, in order to facilitate and expedite examination and decision making, is reasonable even if it is not necessary to prevent absconding.[232] However, some modifications to the *Hardial Singh* principles are necessary.

The first *Hardial Singh* principle requires detention to be for the statutory pur- **8.95** pose. It therefore needs to be modified to take account of the statutory purpose of the relevant provision. The Court of Appeal in *R (MS (Jamaica)) v Asylum and Immigration Tribunal and Secretary of State for the Home Department*[233] construed the statutory purpose of detention under paragraph 16(1) of Schedule 2 to IA 1971 as being 'to allocate [a] claim to the DFT[234] procedure'. In other words, the purpose of such detention is to speed up decision making. Detention pending examination and/or a decision on whether to give, refuse, or cancel leave to enter may only be used where the claim to be examined and decided upon is a relatively straightforward one which can be decided speedily in detention. Speedy decision making must be part of the purpose of detention if the first *Hardial Singh* principle is not to be breached. Public protection may also be a motive, so long as there is also the intention of speeding up decision making.[235]

The second *Hardial Singh* principle does not need to be modified. Detention may **8.96** still only be for a reasonable time.[236] However, that adds little to the other *Hardial Singh* principles.[237] The third *Hardial Singh* principle needs to be modified some- what. Where detention is under paragraph 16(1) of Schedule 2 to IA 1971, there must be a sufficient prospect of any examination being completed and any decision taken within a reasonable period of time. The fourth *Hardial Singh* principle does not need to be modified but it needs to be applied with the context in mind. The boundaries of reasonableness are drawn having regard to the relevant policies of

---

[230] *R (Saadi) v Home Secretary* [2002] UKHL 41; [2002] 1 WLR 3131 at [26].
[231] *Duggal v Secretary of State for the Home Department* [2011] EWHC 736 at [73].
[232] *R (Saadi) v Home Secretary* [2002] UKHL 41; [2002] 1 WLR 3131 at [26].
[233] [2011] EWCA Civ 938 at [46].
[234] Detained Fast Track. See Chapter 13.
[235] *R (MS (Jamaica)) v Asylum and Immigration Tribunal and Secretary of State for the Home Department* [2011] EWCA Civ 938 at [46].
[236] *R (Saadi) v Home Secretary* [2002] UKHL 41; [2002] 1 WLR 3131 at [26].
[237] See paragraphs 8.40–8.48.

the Secretary of State, for example the policy on how long the Detained Fast Track process should take.[238]

(2) Detention pending automatic deportation

8.97 The *Hardial Singh* principles also need modification when detention is pursuant to section 36(1)(a) of UKBA 2007. The first *Hardial Singh* principle, as modified, requires the Secretary of State to have the 'conditional intention' to deport, unless one of the exceptions applies. The intention of section 32(5) of UKBA 2007 is that the Secretary of State should deport 'foreign criminals'[239] wherever it is legally permissible.[240] As such, it is difficult to see when the first *Hardial Singh* principle could be breached by the detention of a 'foreign criminal'.[241]

8.98 The second *Hardial Singh* principle does not need to be modified.[242] Detention may still only be for a reasonable time. However, that adds little to the other *Hardial Singh* principles.[243] The third *Hardial Singh* principle needs to be modified somewhat. Where detention is under section 36(1)(a) of UKBA 2007, there must be a sufficient prospect of a decision being made and deportation being effected within a reasonable period of time.[244] The fourth *Hardial Singh* principle does not need to be modified but it needs to be applied with the context in mind.[245]

---

[238] *R (MS (Jamaica)) v Asylum and Immigration Tribunal and Secretary of State for the Home Department* [2011] EWCA Civ 938 at [50].

[239] Defined at section 32(1)–(3) of UKBA 2007.

[240] See *R (Rashid Hussein) v Secretary of State for the Home Department* [2009] EWHC 2492 (Admin) at [44(i)]; *R (Saleh) v Secretary of State for the Home Department* [2013] EWCA Civ 1378 at [16].

[241] See paragraphs 5.07–5.08 for a discussion of whether a British citizen can be liable to detention under this power in a case of mistaken identity.

[242] See *R (Rashid Hussein) v Secretary of State for the Home Department* [2009] EWHC 2492 (Admin) at [44(ii)]; *R (Saleh) v Secretary of State for the Home Department* [2013] EWCA Civ 1378 at [16].

[243] See paragraphs 8.40–8.48.

[244] See *R (Rashid Hussein) v Secretary of State for the Home Department* [2009] EWHC 2492 (Admin) at [44(iii)]; *Saleh v Secretary of State for the Home Department* [2013] EWCA Civ 1378 at [16].

[245] See *R (Rashid Hussein) v Secretary of State for the Home Department* [2009] EWHC 2492 (Admin) at [44(iv)]; *Saleh v Secretary of State for the Home Department* [2013] EWCA Civ 1378 at [16].

9

PUBLIC LAW ERRORS

A. Introduction

A public law error which bears on and is relevant to a decision to detain will, in **9.01** most cases, render immigration detention unlawful as a matter of public law, and give rise to the tort of false imprisonment in private law.[1]

(1) *Francis*

The sole exception to this general principle, as held by the Court of Appeal in *R* **9.02** *(Francis) v Secretary of State for the Home Department*,[2] is where a person is detained under a provision which requires (rather than permits) the Secretary of State to detain. In such a case there is no discretionary decision capable of being vitiated by a legal error; the decision to detain has been made by Parliament and the statute provides the authority for detention, unless and until the Secretary of State exercises the power to release.[3] It is arguable that the approach of the Court of Appeal in *Francis* is not compatible with Article 5[4] but, unless and until *Francis* is reversed

---

[1] *R (Lumba & Mighty) v Secretary of State for the Home Department* [2011] UKSC 12; [2012] 1 AC 245, *per* Lord Dyson at [68], with the agreement of the majority: see Lord Hope at [170]; Lady Hale at [196], [207]; Lord Collins at [219]–[221]; and Lord Kerr at [238]. Lord Hope's agreement is put beyond doubt by his judgment in *Kambadzi v Secretary of State for the Home Department* [2011] UKSC 23; [2011] 1 WLR 1299 at [41].

[2] [2014] EWCA Civ 718.

[3] *Per* Moore-Bick LJ at [20]–[22], [32] and Clarke LJ at [53]–[54].

[4] See Chapter 15, paragraphs 15.61–15.63.

or disapproved, it represents the law. In the remainder of this chapter, we have assumed *Francis* is correct.

9.03 *Francis* concerned detention under paragraph 2(1) of Schedule 3 to the Immigration Act 1971 ('IA 1971') (which provides that a person who is recommended for deportation by a criminal court 'shall' be detained unless the Secretary of State directs release) and detention under paragraph 2(3) following detention under paragraph 2(1).[5]

9.04 Section 36(2) of the UK Borders Act 2007 ('UKBA 2007') provides that the Secretary of State 'shall' exercise the (discretionary) power to detain under paragraph 2(3) of Schedule 3 to IA 1971, when a deportation order is made against a person in accordance with section 32(5) of UKBA 2007. It remains to be seen whether the reasoning in *Francis* will be applied in cases to which section 36(2) applies.

9.05 Although a material public law error will not undermine the legality of detention in a case to which *Francis* applies, such errors remain relevant to the question of release. If the Secretary of State acted unlawfully in her decision not to release such a detainee, the court might order the Secretary of State to reconsider release.[6] If release was the only lawful option open to the Secretary of State, the court might even order the Secretary of State to release the detainee. However, in neither case, would the detainee have a claim for damages in false imprisonment as a result of the public law error.[7]

9.06 The present chapter considers the circumstances in which public law errors will, or may, render detention unlawful. A finding that detention is unlawful as a result of a public law error will not in all cases lead to an award of compensatory (or 'substantial') damages for false imprisonment.[8]

B. Material Public Law Error

(1) Public law errors generally

9.07 It is beyond the scope of this work to attempt a detailed account of the various types of public law error that have been recognized by the courts.[9]

---

[5] N.B.: Detention under paragraph 2(3) following detention under paragraph 2(2) can be vitiated by a public law error.

[6] *Per* Moore-Bick LJ at [21].

[7] Although a claim for damages for detention in breach of the *Hardial Singh* principles would remain if it could be established on the facts.

[8] See Chapter 20, paragraphs 20.08 and 20.12–20.14, and *cf.* the discussion of Article 5 damages at paragraphs 20.57–20.68.

[9] See *Judicial Review Handbook*, Michael Fordham QC, Hart Publishing, 6th edition, 2012 Section C; *Judicial Review: Principles and Procedure*, Jonathan Auburn *et al*, Oxford University Press, 1st edition, 2013. For a helpful account of commonly occurring species of public law error see

The authorities to date show that most public law challenges to immigration **9.08** detention relate to policy. Allegations have included the application of unlawful policies;[10] detaining in contravention of a relevant policy absent good reasons to depart from it;[11] failing to take a relevant policy into account;[12] and failing to make sufficient inquiries in relation to the applicability of a policy.[13]

It is, however, clear from *Lumba* that any public law error is capable in principle **9.09** of vitiating the legality of detention. Other errors that might arise in the present context include, but are not limited to:

- making perverse or irrational decisions on matters material to the decision to detain;
- legal misdirection;
- breach of statutory duty;
- taking irrelevant matters into account;
- failing to take relevant matters (including but not limited to policies) into account;
- procedural irregularity or unfairness more generally; and
- arguably, a failure to give sufficient reasons for detention, although this remains controversial.

(2) Materiality

For a public law error to render detention unlawful it must be material to the **9.10** decision to detain and not to some other aspect of the detention and it must be capable of affecting the result. This is not the same as saying that the result would have been different had there been no breach.[14] The question may be said to be whether there is an 'adequate connection between compliance with the [public law] duty and the lawfulness of the detention'.[15] Insofar as the concept of an error of law amounting to an 'abuse of power' suggests a higher threshold, that is not the test.[16]

R (Iran & Ors) v Secretary of State for the Home Department [2005] EWCA Civ 982; [2005] Imm AR 535, *per* Brooke LJ at [9]–[10].

[10] *Lumba.*
[11] *R (LE (Jamaica)) v Secretary of State for the Home Department* [2012] EWCA Civ 597.
[12] *R (OM (Nigeria)) v Secretary of State for the Home Department* [2011] EWCA Civ 909.
[13] *R (Das) v Secretary of State for the Home Department* [2013] EWHC 682 (Admin) at [42]–[44], relying on the public law duty of inquiry as explained in *Secretary of State for Education and Science v Tameside Metropolitan Borough Council* [1977] AC 1014, *per* Lord Diplock at 1065B. For a recent summary of the law on the duty of inquiry, see *R (Plantagenet Alliance Ltd) v Secretary of State for Justice & Others* [2014] EWHC 1662 (QB) at [99]–[100].
[14] *Lumba, per* Lady Hale at [107], referring back to the question she posed at [196].
[15] *Kambadzi, per* Lord Kerr at [80].
[16] *Cf. Lumba, per* Lord Dyson at [69], Lord Hope at [170], Lord Walker at [193], Lord Kerr at [249]; and *Kambadzi, per* Lord Hope at [41].

9.11 There is a public law duty to give effect to published policy.[17] Whether a breach of that duty will render detention unlawful, and so a false imprisonment at common law, will depend upon whether the published policy is sufficiently closely related to the authority to detain to provide a further qualification of the discretion vested in the Secretary of State by the relevant statute.[18]

9.12 So far as the validity of a discretionary[19] decision to detain is concerned, there is no difference in principle between (i) detention which is unlawful because there was no statutory power to detain and (ii) detention which is unlawful because the decision to detain, although authorized by statute, was made in breach of a rule of public law. For example, a decision to detain which is unreasonable in the *Wednesbury*[20] sense 'is unlawful and a nullity'.[21]

9.13 Whether an error is 'material' to the decision to detain is a question distinct from whether the error caused detention to occur. In *Lumba*, the question for the court was whether detention was unlawful where a decision to detain was 'influenced'[22] by an unlawful, unpublished policy. The Court of Appeal had held that in such circumstances, if the decision to detain was inevitable in any event, 'the application of the policy [was] immaterial, and the decision [was] not liable to be set aside as unlawful'.[23] Lord Dyson characterized this as the application of a 'causation test'.[24]

9.14 Before the Supreme Court the Secretary of State's attempts to uphold the 'causation test' approach failed, being held to be contrary to principle both as a matter of the law of trespass to the person and as a matter of administrative law:[25]

> Neither body of law recognises any defence of causation so as to render lawful what is in fact an unlawful authority to detain, by reference to how the executive could and *would have* acted if it had acted lawfully, as opposed to how it *did in fact* act . . . the law of false imprisonment does not permit history to be rewritten in this way.

---

[17] See paragraph 9.26.

[18] *Kambadzi, per* Lord Hope at [51].

[19] The position is different where the statute requires detention unless the Secretary of State orders release: see paragraphs 9.02–9.06.

[20] *Associated Provincial Picture Houses Ltd v Wednesbury Corporation* [1948] 1 KB 223.

[21] *Lumba, per* Lord Dyson at [66]: 'A purported lawful authority to detain may be impugned either because the defendant acted in excess of jurisdiction (in the narrow sense of jurisdiction) or because such jurisdiction was wrongly exercised. *Anisminic Ltd v Foreign Compensation Commission* [1969] 2 AC 147 established that both species of error render an executive act *ultra vires*, unlawful and a nullity.'

[22] *Per* Lord Dyson at [56].

[23] *R (WL (Congo) & KM (Jamaica)) v Secretary of State for the Home Department* [2010] EWCA Civ 111; [2010] WLR 2168 at [89].

[24] At [59].

[25] *Per* Lord Dyson at [62].

As such, if an error is material in the sense described at paragraph 9.10 it is irrel- **9.15** evant, so far as the lawfulness of detention is concerned, whether detention could and would have been lawfully authorized in any event.[26]

Lumba did not, however, make the question of causation irrelevant. Rather, the **9.16** Court held that the relevance of causation lay in the realm of damages. Where detention was unlawful at public law, and so a false imprisonment, but it could and would have occurred in any event, the detainee will have suffered no loss and will recover no more than nominal damages for the false imprisonment.[27]

Lumba resolved questions of principle that had become increasingly irreconcilable **9.17** at Court of Appeal level. On its face, the rejection of a causation test was a victory for the claimants, who could not prove that a material public law error caused their detention. In practice, however, the victory was of little practical benefit to such claimants. Although, as Lord Hope observes in *Kambadzi*, an award of nominal damages affords recognition of the breach of a fundamental right,[28] it will be difficult for a litigant, whether privately or publicly funded, to pursue litigation where it is known from the outset that no more than declaratory relief and nominal damages can be achieved, save perhaps where a significant point of principle is in issue.[29]

C. The Need for Policy

Powers of detention under the Immigration Acts are far-reaching. In practice only **9.18** a small proportion of those liable to detention are detained at any given time. The *Hardial Singh* principles and Article 5 ECHR are not exhaustive of the applicable law. Were the position otherwise, there could be no room for the public law duty of adherence to published policy.[30]

The Secretary of State's policies guide decision makers in the exercise of their pow- **9.19** ers to detain. *Inter alia*, published policy establishes procedures to be followed upon detention and when reviewing detention, gives guidance as to when detention

---

[26] *Lumba, per* Lord Dyson at [71]. See at [62]–[88] for the full reasoning on this issue.

[27] *Per* Lord Dyson at [90]–[96]; see further Chapter 20, paragraphs 20.08 and 20.12–20.14. However, see Chapter 20, paragraphs 20.57–20.68 for a discussion of damages for breach of Article 5. A claimant in this position may, exceptionally, have a claim for exemplary damages; see Chapter 20, paragraph 20.45.

[28] At [56].

[29] *Cf. R (Hossein) v Secretary of State for the Home Department* [2011] EWHC 1924 (Admin), *per* Collins J at [5], addressing a ground which, in isolation went only to nominal damages: 'it would be wrong and a waste of public money for the court to permit that issue to be litigated because there would be no benefit in the end for the claimant'.

[30] *Lumba, per* Lord Dyson at [30].

powers should and should not be used, and identifies cases in which detention may only be justified in very exceptional circumstances.

9.20 The rule of law calls for a transparent statement by the executive of the circumstances in which the broad statutory powers of detention will be exercised.[31] Decisions are taken by a 'small army' of officials at different levels, and they need guidance to achieve consistency. People who may be subject to such decisions are entitled to know, at least in general terms, the content of the official policies. This is not a matter of being faithful to the purposes of statutory powers, 'but of seeing that they are exercised consistently and fairly'.[32]

D. The Duty to Apply Policy

9.21 A decision-maker must follow published policy (and not some different unpublished policy) unless there are good reasons for not doing so.[33] Policy must be consistently applied.[34] There is 'an independent duty of consistent application of policies, which is based on the principle of equal implementation of laws, non-discrimination and the lack of arbitrariness'.[35]

---

[31] *Lumba, per* Lord Dyson at [34].

[32] *Lumba, per* Lord Walker at [190]. See further *R (Refugee Legal Centre) v Secretary of State for the Home Department* [2004] EWCA Civ 1481; [2005] 1 WLR 2219, *per* Sedley LJ at [18]–[19]: 'Putting the relevant issues in writing—and we assume without question that what is put in writing will be made public—is not simply a bureaucratic reflex. It will concentrate official minds on the proper ingredients of fair procedure; it will enable applicants and their legal representatives to know what these ingredients are taken to be; and if anything is included in or omitted from them which renders the process legally unfair, the courts will be in a position to say so.' *B v Secretary of State for Work and Pensions* [2005] EWCA Civ 929; [2005] 1 WLR 3796, *per* Sedley LJ at [43]: 'It is axiomatic in modern government that a lawful policy is necessary if an executive discretion of the significance of the one now under consideration is to be exercised, as public law requires it to be exercised, consistently from case to case but adaptably to the facts of individual cases.'

[33] *Lumba, per* Lord Dyson at [26]. See also the discussion of this issue in the Court of Appeal's judgment, *R (WL (Congo) & KM (Jamaica)) v Secretary of State for the Home Department* [2010] EWCA Civ 111; [2010] 1 WLR 2168, *per* Stanley Burnton LJ at [58], in which it is suggested that obligations arise in relation to policy via the doctrine of legitimate expectation, and/or the *Wednesbury* duty to take relevant matters into account, and/or 'abuse of power': '. . . we may have arrived at the point where it is possible to extract from the cases a substantive legal rule that a public body must adhere to its published policy unless there is some good reason not to do so. The treatment of such concepts may vary in the cases and textbooks, but the differences are usually immaterial.'

[34] *Lumba, per* Lord Dyson at [26], citing *Administrative Law*, William Wade and Christopher Forsyth, Oxford University Press, 10th edition, 2009 at page 316.

[35] *Lumba, per* Lord Dyson at [26], citing *De Smith's Judicial Review*, Lord Woolf, Jeffrey Jowell and Andrew Le Sueur, Thomson, Sweet & Maxwell, 6th edition, 2007 at paragraph 12-039.

E. Unlawful Policies

It was established in *Lumba* that where a decision to detain was influenced by an **9.22** unlawful policy the detention was vitiated by material public law error and so unlawful. Lord Dyson endorsed three propositions as to the nature of a lawful policy:

(1) First, it must not be a blanket policy admitting of no possibility of exceptions.
(2) Second, if unpublished, it must not be inconsistent with any published policy.
(3) Third, it should be published if it will inform discretionary decisions in respect of which the potential object of those decisions has a right to make representations.[36]

Further points emerge from the authorities: **9.23**

(4) A policy which sets out 'normal practice' in relation to detention is unobjectionable.
(5) Policies the application of which will, or may, give rise to unlawfulness will, in certain circumstances, be unlawful.
(6) Where a public body is formulating policy it must have due regard to the obligations arising under section 149 of the Equality Act 2010 ('EA 2010') (the 'public sector equality duty').

(1) Blanket policies are unlawful

The prohibition on blanket policies reflects the principle that a policy should **9.24** not be so rigid as to fetter the discretion of the decision-maker.[37] A policy may lawfully be devised to deal generally with a regularly occurring species of case but it must always be possible to depart from the policy if the circumstances of an individual case warrant it.[38] It is 'a fundamental rule for the exercise of discretionary power that discretion must be brought to bear on every case: each one must be considered on its own merits and decided as the public interest requires at the time'.[39]

(2) Unpublished policies must not conflict with published policy

Where permitted at all, unpublished policies must not be inconsistent with **9.25** any published policy. This follows from the duty to apply published policy.

---

[36] At [20].
[37] *Lumba, per* Lord Dyson at [21].
[38] *Lumba, per* Lord Kerr at [245].
[39] *Administrative Law*, William Wade and Christopher Forsyth, Oxford University Press, 10th edition, 2009 at page 270, cited with approval by Lord Kerr at [245].

A decision-maker must follow published policy (and not some different unpublished policy) unless there are good reasons for not doing so.[40]

(3) Policy should be published

9.26 An individual has a basic public law right to have his or her case considered under whatever policy the executive sees fit to adopt provided that the adopted policy is a lawful exercise of the discretion conferred by the statute.[41] There is a correlative right to know what that currently existing policy is, so that the individual can make relevant representations in relation to it.[42] *R (Anufrijeva) v Secretary of State for the Home Department*[43] established that notice of a decision is required before it can have the character of a determination with legal effect because an individual must be in a position to challenge the decision in the courts if he or she wishes. The same is true of a detention policy.[44] Notice is required so that the individual knows the criteria that are being applied and is able to challenge an adverse decision.[45]

9.27 There is no obligation to publish policies in draft as they evolve, and there may be compelling reasons to withhold publication of certain policies, for example, where national security issues are in play; nor is there any requirement to publish matters 'irrelevant to the substance of decisions made pursuant to the policy'.[46] What must, however, be published is 'that which a person who is affected by the operation of the policy needs to know in order to make informed and meaningful representations to the decision-maker before a decision is made'.[47]

(4) A statement of 'normal practice' is unobjectionable

9.28 The question arose in *Lumba* whether the Secretary of State's published detention policy could lawfully stipulate that, in certain circumstances, detention would be the usual course. This was characterized in the proceedings as a 'presumption in favour of detention'.[48] The Supreme Court held that what was in issue was not in fact a 'presumption' at all. Lord Dyson distinguished between a 'legal presumption'—a rule regulating the burden of proof in legal proceedings—on the one hand and policy guidance on 'normal practice' on the other.[49]

9.29 Policy which regulated the conduct of the executive could not create a 'legal presumption'. However, it was unobjectionable for the Secretary of State to operate a

---

40 *Lumba, per* Lord Dyson at [26].
41 *Lumba, per* Lord Dyson at [35], citing *In re Findlay* [1985] AC 318, at p.338E.
42 *Lumba, per* Lord Dyson at [35].
43 [2003] UKHL 36; [2004] 1 AC 604, *per* Lord Steyn at [26].
44 *Lumba, per* Lord Dyson at [36].
45 *Lumba, per* Lord Dyson at [36].
46 *Lumba, per* Lord Dyson at [38].
47 *Lumba, per* Lord Dyson at [38].
48 See *per* Lord Dyson at [40]–[55].
49 *Per* Lord Dyson at [42]–[43].

policy which sets out the practice that she will normally follow in deciding whether or not to detain pending deportation or removal provided:

(1) the *Hardial Singh* principles are observed; and
(2) each case is considered individually.[50]

(5) Policies with unlawful consequences

The courts have recognized at least three, arguably four, circumstances in which a policy may be ruled unlawful by reference to the consequences of its application:[51] **9.30**

(1) First, a policy which, if followed, would lead to unlawful acts or decisions, or which permits or encourages such acts, will itself be unlawful.[52]
(2) Second, in an Article 3 case, a policy will be unlawful if it 'exposes a person to a significant risk' of the treatment prohibited by the Article.[53]
(3) Third, potential unfairness is susceptible to judicial intervention 'to obviate in advance a proven risk of injustice which goes beyond aberrant interviews or decisions and *inheres in the system itself*'.[54]

It is strongly arguable that a fourth, broader, test also applies. In *R (Medical Justice) v Secretary of State for the Home Department*,[55] at first instance, Silber J applied the test from *Refugee Legal Centre* (summarized at paragraph 9.30), but also referred to a broader test of 'unacceptable risk' of unfairness or curtailment of the right of access to justice.[56] In *R (Suppiah) v Secretary of State for the Home Department*[57] Wyn Williams J accepted that there was 'clear and binding authority for the proposition that a policy which is in principle capable of being implemented lawfully but which nonetheless gives rise to an unacceptable risk of unlawful decision-making is itself an unlawful policy'.[58] Foskett J in *MK v Secretary of State for the Home Department*[59] expressed the view that this proposition was 'supported by the **9.31**

---

[50] *Per* Lord Dyson at [53].

[51] See discussion in *R (Hassan Tabbakh) v Staffordshire & West Midlands Probation Trust & Ors* [2013] EWHC 2492; [2014] WLR 1022, *per* Cranston J at [42]–[52]. NB: At the time of writing *Tabbakh* is under appeal.

[52] *Gillick v West Norfolk and Wisbech Area Health Authority* [1985] UKHL 7; [1986] AC 112, *per* Lord Scarman at 177E, 181F; *per* Lord Bridge at 193G–194B. *Cf. R (Nadarajah & Amirhanathan) v Secretary of State for the Home Department* [2003] EWCA Civ 1768, *per* Lord Phillips of Worth Matravers at [60].

[53] *R (Munjaz) v (1) Ashworth Hospital Authority (now Mersey Care NHS Trust)* [2005] UKHL 58; [2006] 2 AC 148, *per* Lord Bingham at [29].

[54] *R (Refugee Legal Centre) v Secretary of State for the Home Department* [2004] EWCA Civ 1481; [2005] 1 WLR 2219, *per* Sedley LJ at [7] (emphasis added).

[55] [2010] EWHC 1925 (Admin).

[56] At [36].

[57] [2011] EWHC 2 (Admin).

[58] At [137].

[59] [2012] EWHC 1896 (Admin).

authorities to which he referred and indeed is consistent with the approach of the House of Lords in *Munjaz*.[60] However, in *Tabbakh*[61] Cranston J concluded that the approach was not in fact supported by authority, that the Court of Appeal in *Medical Justice* (which post-dated *Suppiah*) had not supported what Silber J had said at first instance,[62] and that the broader approach suggested in *Suppiah* 'should be avoided'.[63] At the time of writing *Tabbakh* is under appeal.

(6) The public sector equality duty

9.32   Section 149 of EA 2010 sets out a number of matters to which a public authority 'must, in the exercise of its functions, have due regard'. The duty applies to the formulation of policy, as well as to individual decisions taken by a public authority.[64]

F. The Role of the Court

9.33   It is settled that in a challenge brought under the *Hardial Singh* principles the court is not limited to reviewing the Secretary of State's decision to detain on *Wednesbury* grounds.[65] In a challenge brought on public law grounds, the position is more complex and some controversy remains.

(1) Allegations of material public law error

9.34   Although the point awaits final resolution, it has been said, *obiter*, that where it is alleged detention is unlawful as a result of a material public law error the court is limited to conducting a review of the decision on traditional public law grounds.[66] In contrast to the approach taken in *Hardial Singh* challenges, it does not adopt the role of primary decision maker.

9.35   The counter argument is founded upon two decisions of the Court of Appeal: *R (Anam) v Secretary of State for the Home Department*[67] (in particular the judgment

---

[60] At [156].

[61] See footnote 51.

[62] The significance of this is, in our view, questionable. Sullivan LJ held at [25]–[27] that, on a proper construction of Silber J's judgment, it was clear he had applied the test as formulated in *Refugee Legal Centre*. On the case as argued that was sufficient to dispose of the ground which was before him. He is silent as to the correctness or otherwise of the broader test.

[63] At [51].

[64] See, for example, *R (JL) v Islington LBC* [2009] EWHC 458 (Admin) at [114] and *R (HA (Nigeria)) v Secretary of State for the Home Department* [2012] EWHC 979 (Admin) at [192], addressing predecessor provisions in section 49A of the Disability Discrimination Act 1995 and section 71 of the Race Relations Act 1976. See further Chapter 11, paragraphs 11.65 and following.

[65] *R (A) v Secretary of State for the Home Department* [2007] EWCA Civ 804, *per* Toulson LJ at [60]–[62]; *per* Keene LJ at [71]–[75].

[66] *R (LE (Jamaica)) v Secretary of State for the Home Department* [2012] EWCA Civ 597 at [29].

[67] [2010] EWCA Civ 1140.

of Black LJ), which was decided before *Lumba*, and *AM v Secretary of State for the Home Department*,[68] which came after. Neither is wholly persuasive on the point.

In *Anam* Black LJ derives from the authorities on the approach to *Hardial Singh*[69] the proposition that 'the court must assume the role of primary decision maker' in relation to all aspects of the detention, giving 'appropriate weight in its deliberation to matters such as government policies, risk assessments, and the evidence as to likely time-scales for the deportation of the individual'.[70] There was no consensus on this issue.[71] Moreover, the suggested approach is very hard to reconcile with the later decision in *Lumba*, as it does not engage with the question of public law error, *per se*, at all.   **9.36**

In *AM*, it appears to have been common ground that it was for the court itself to decide whether detention was unlawful as a result of a breach of policy.[72] In support of that position, Rix LJ referred to *R (A)* and *Anam*. However, for the reasons given by Richards LJ in *LE (Jamaica)*,[73] it is strongly arguable those cases do not support that conclusion.   **9.37**

The contrary position—and, in our view, the position that is likely to be followed—is that taken by the Court of Appeal in *LE (Jamaica)*. In *LE* Richards LJ reasoned that, subject to the limits imposed by *Hardial Singh*, a decision whether to detain a person in any given case involves a true exercise of discretion. That discretion is vested in the Secretary of State, not in the court. As such, the role of the court is supervisory, not that of a primary decision-maker: 'the court is required to review the decision in accordance with the ordinary principles of public law, including *Wednesbury* principles, in order to determine whether the decision-maker has acted within the limits of the discretionary power conferred on him or her by the statute'.[74] The Court of Appeal's consideration of this issue in *LE (Jamaica)* was *obiter*.[75] However, it has been followed in a number of first instance decisions.[76]   **9.38**

---

[68] [2012] EWCA Civ 521.

[69] Specifically, *R (A)*.

[70] At [77].

[71] *Cf.* Longmore LJ at [85] and Maurice Kay LJ at [91]. *Anam* was the last case on these issues to be decided by the Court of Appeal before the Supreme Court gave its judgment in *Lumba*. By this point, as Maurice Kay LJ observes at [91], the various authorities on this issue were not 'entirely consistent in approach'.

[72] At [23], [26].

[73] At [29].

[74] At [28(iii)]. See further *R (OM (Nigeria) v Secretary of State for the Home Department* [2011] EWCA Civ 909, which is considered at Chapter 20, paragraphs 20.12 to 20.14.

[75] See at [29(ix)].

[76] See for example *R (EO & Ors) v Secretary of State for the Home Department* [2013] EWHC 1236 (Admin) at [15]–[16], in which it was common ground that *LE (Jamaica)* should be followed, but the claimants reserved their position in the event the case went further (it did not). See also *R (Agyeikum) v Secretary of State for the Home Department* [2013] EWHC 1828 (Admin) at [67].

(2) The meaning of a policy

9.39 The meaning of a policy is an objective matter. Where it is in issue, it falls to be determined by the court. On that issue, the court is not limited to reviewing the decision maker's interpretation of the policy on *Wednesbury* grounds.[77] Whether the policy was lawfully applied, however, is a different question and, as we explain at paragraphs 9.34–9.38, is likely to be approached by way of *Wednesbury* review.

(3) Nominal or substantial damages

9.40 Where detention is unlawful as a result of a public law error, substantial damages will be payable unless detention could and would have occurred in any event, in which case only nominal damages will be payable.[78] The approach taken by the courts to determining whether a claimant should recover substantial or nominal damages is considered in Chapter 20.[79]

G. Material Public Law Errors in Practice

9.41 Identifying whether a public law error is material to a decision to detain, and so renders detention unlawful, is not straightforward. In this section, we consider some of the circumstances in which the courts have held that the legality of detention was, or was not, vitiated by an error of law. Further examples are addressed in Chapters 11 and 12, dealing with aspects of Home Office detention policy.

(1) Unlawful policy

9.42 An official exercising discretion by applying a published policy is acting lawfully, but if the policy which is applied is unlawful, the exercise of discretion is unlawful.[80]

9.43 In *Lumba* the issue was the effect upon the legality of detention of unlawful, unpublished detention policies, in place from April 2006 until 9 September 2008.[81] Whilst the published policy provided for a presumption of release in all cases, the unpublished policies amounted to a 'near blanket ban' on release. The policies were unlawful because they were (a) blanket in nature, (b) inconsistent with published policy, and (c) unpublished.[82] They had been applied to the appellants.[83]

---

[77] *R (Raissi) v Secretary of State for the Home Department* [2008] EWCA Civ 72; [2008] QB 836 at [107]–[123]; *R (MD (Angola)) v Secretary of State for the Home Department* [2011] EWCA Civ 1238 at [12].

[78] *Lumba per* Lord Dyson at [71], [90]–[96], Lord Collins at [237], Lord Kerr at [252]–[256].

[79] Paragraphs 20.12–20.14.

[80] *Lumba, per* Lord Kerr at [247].

[81] See *per* Lord Dyson at [5]–[6], [11]–[18].

[82] See *per* Lord Dyson at [20], [39], and see discussion at paragraphs 9.22–9.32.

[83] At [19].

The majority of the Supreme Court held that this was a material public law error which rendered detention unlawful.[84]

In many subsequent cases challenging detention during the currency of the pol- **9.44** icy considered in *Lumba,* the Secretary of State has conceded that detention was unlawful. This is unsurprising, given that the Supreme Court accepted that there was 'clear evidence that [during the relevant period] caseworkers were directed to conceal the true reason for detention, namely the unpublished policy, and to give other reasons which appeared to conform with the published policy'.[85]

(2) Failure to review detention in line with policy

The issue in *Kambadzi* was whether a failure by the Secretary of State to review **9.45** detention at the intervals stated in her published policy[86] was an error of law which was material to the decision to detain. The Supreme Court held that it was. In *Lumba,*[87] and in *Kambadzi* itself[88] this was characterized as a public law error in relation to a *procedural,* rather than *substantive,* element of the published policy. Nevertheless, the breach vitiated the legality of detention, Lord Hope holding that the relationship of the review to the exercise of the authority was 'very close' and that, if the system worked as it should, 'authorisation for continued detention [was] to be found in the decision taken at each review'. Lady Hale endorsed the view of Munby J at first instance that detention reviews were 'fundamental to the propriety of the continuing detention' and 'a necessary prerequisite to the continuing legality of the detention'.[89] Lord Kerr added that 'where the review does take place but does not partake of the quality or character required to justify the continuance of detention, it becomes unlawful and gives rise to a right to claim false imprisonment'.[90] As such, in our view, a review which is itself marred by errors of law which are material to the decision to detain will not save the legality of detention.

---

[84] *Per* Lord Dyson at [89], Lord Hope at [170], Lord Walker at [194], Lady Hale at [218], Lord Collins at [219]–[221], and Lord Kerr at [238].

[85] *Per* Lord Dyson at [163], *per* Lord Collins at [220]. In R (*LK (Somalia)) v Secretary of State for the Home Department* [2012] EWHC 1229 (Admin) the Deputy Judge did not accept the unpublished policy had been applied to the claimant, noting that it 'appear[ed] clear' from the contemporaneous documentation that the correct criteria had been applied (at [49]–[50]). In our view this is a problematic conclusion, given the acceptance in *Lumba* that caseworkers were directed to conceal the true reasons for detention. Nevertheless, permission to appeal on this issue was refused. In *R (Mohammed) v Secretary of State for the Home Department* [2014] EWHC 972 (Admin), another case in which the point was not conceded, the Deputy Judge accepted the policy had been applied, noting that there was express reference to 'Operation Cullen' in a detention review (at [102]–[104]) (N.B. for the significance of 'Operation Cullen' see Lumba, per Lord Dyson, at [17] and [21]).

[86] See Chapter 10, paragraphs 10.43–10.46.

[87] *Per* Lord Dyson at [61].

[88] *Per* Lady Hale at [64], [69]–[72].

[89] *Per* Lord Hope at [52]; *per* Lady Hale at [73].

[90] At [86].

9.46 Although the failure to conduct reviews in line with the policy was a material public law error, the failure to provide written reasons for detention, month by month, in accordance with Rule 9(1) of the Detention Centre Rules 2001 was not. This was because, unlike the policy, the Rules were 'concerned with the regulation and management of detention centres, not with the way the discretion to detain is exercised'.[91]

(3) Mental and physical illness which cannot be managed in detention

9.47 A failure to have regard to, apply, or (arguably) to make appropriate inquiries in relation to the policy in Chapter 55, section 55.10, of the Secretary of State's Enforcement Instructions and Guidance ('EIG'), which provides that those suffering from serious medical conditions and serious mental illness which cannot be satisfactorily managed within detention should only be detained in very exceptional circumstances, will be a public law error material to the decision to detain.[92]

(4) Other findings of material public law error

9.48 In addition to the issues addressed at paragraphs 9.42–9.47, the courts have found detention to be unlawful as a result of material public law error in the following circumstances:

(1) Failure to conduct a medical examination in accordance with Rule 34 of the Detention Centre Rules 2001 within 24 hours of admission to detention: *R (EO & Ors) v Secretary of State for the Home Department*.[93]

(2) Error of approach in considering whether independent evidence of torture existed for the purpose of the unsuitability policy in EIG 55.10: *R (AM) v Secretary of State for the Home Department*.[94]

(3) Failure to consider section 149 of EA 2010 or the matters to which it required the Secretary of State have due regard: *R (D) v Secretary of State for the Home Department*.[95]

(4) Where, in a case involving the detention of a woman and her three children, there had been a failure to complete a family welfare form:[96] *R (N) v Secretary of State for the Home Department*.[97]

(5) Failure to obtain an Offender Assessment System ('OASYS') assessment of risk of reoffending from the National Offender Management Service,

---

[91] *Per* Lord Hope at [16].
[92] See further Chapter 11.
[93] [2013] EWHC 1236 (Admin); see further Chapter 11, paragraphs 11.42–11.48.
[94] [2012] EWCA Civ 521.
[95] [2012] EWHC 2501 (Admin) at [172]–[174]. See further Chapter 11, paragraphs 11.65–11.68.
[96] For the family welfare form see Chapter 12, paragraphs 12.17–12.20.
[97] [2012] EWHC 1031 (Admin).

in breach of EIG 55.3.2.6:[98] *R (Collin) v Secretary of State for the Home Department*.[99]

(6) Failure to consult the Office of the Children's Champion at the earliest possible opportunity in a case where detention continued the separation of a family, in breach of the relevant policy as in force at the time:[100] *R (Abdollahi) v Secretary of State for the Home Department*.[101]

(5) Immaterial errors

Examples of the court finding public law errors to have occurred but to be imma- **9.49**
terial to the decision to detain are, so far, uncommon. In *Lumba*,[102] Lord Dyson identified two legal errors which he said would not found a claim in false imprisonment: (i) 'a decision to detain made by an official of a different grade from that specified in a detention policy'; and (ii) 'a decision to detain a person under conditions different from those described in the policy'.[103] In *R (Mohammed) v Secretary of State for the Home Department*[104] a number of detention reviews stated, incorrectly, that the claimant had been convicted of indecent assault. The Deputy Judge said that she did not 'underestimate the significance of such an error', but that 'it is likely, given the claimant's history of failure to report and other offending that the error did not have a material effect', so did not go to the legality of detention. It may be that conclusion should have been directed to damages rather than liability. If the relevant officials, in authorizing detention month by month, took an irrelevant consideration into account then that was, in our view, a material error of law in the *Lumba* sense, notwithstanding it made no difference to the outcome.

H. Reasons

It is strongly arguable, but not yet settled, that a failure to give any, or any adequate, **9.50**
reasons for detention is a material public law error going to the legality of detention.

A failure to give reasons for detention under the Immigration Acts is a breach of **9.51**
Article 5(2) of ECHR.[105] It does not necessarily follow, however, that a failure to

---

[98] For the policy guidance on the requirement to obtain risk assessments see Chapter 10, paragraphs 10.26–10.36.
[99] Unreported, 7 June 2013, Westlaw. See also *AM v Secretary of State for the Home Department*, Central London County Court, 13 March 2012, Unreported, Westlaw, at [38(5)].
[100] For the current policy position on the OCC see Chapter 12, paragraphs 12.14–12.16.
[101] [2012] EWHC 878 (Admin) at [79].
[102] At [68].
[103] Applied in *R (Krasniqi) v Secretary of State for the Home Department* [2011] EWCA Civ 1549 at [16]. N.B.: Detention conditions may be relevant to a challenge under the *Hardial Singh* principles and may, in certain circumstances, engage Article 5(1) of ECHR.
[104] [2014] EWHC 972 (Admin).
[105] See paragraph 15.29.

give reasons for immigration detention is a public law wrong sufficiently connected
to the decision to detain that it renders detention unlawful at common law.

9.52 In *R (Saadi) v Secretary of State for the Home Department*,[106] a challenge to the legality of the Detained Fast Track ('DFT') at Oakington, Lord Slynn said that 'the
failure to give the right reason for detention and the giving of no or wrong reasons
did not in the end affect the legality of the detention'.[107] However, Lord Dyson
in *Lumba* observed that this passage was not part of the *ratio*, and Lord Hope in
Kambadzi noted that the first instance judgment in *Saadi* recorded that it had not
been argued that 'the muddle about reasons' rendered detention unlawful.[108]

9.53 *R (MS (Jamaica)) v Secretary of State for the Home Department*[109] was a challenge to
the claimant's detention in the DFT heard after *Lumba*. When the claimant was
detained on 6 June 2009 he was given reasons in a tick-box form which included
the assertions (a) that his release was not conducive to the public good and (b) that
his application could be decided quickly in the fast track.[110] Further reasons to
detain were given when his asylum claim was decided on 17 July 2009, in which
point (a) had been replaced by an assertion that he posed a risk of absconding,
but point (b) was maintained. The same day a letter was sent erroneously stating
that the claimant was held under the Detained Non-Suspensive Appeals ('DNSA')
(rather than DFT) procedure.[111] It was only when the case was underway before the
Court of Appeal that the Secretary of State disclosed an email sent the day before
the claimant's detention, stating that he should be detained and placed in the fast
track because (a) information had come to light fundamentally undermining the
credibility of his asylum claim, and (b) it had been discovered that he had been
convicted of rape in Jamaica.[112]

9.54 The judgment of Thomas LJ does not record any submission having been made that
detention was unlawful for want of sufficient reasons, and there is no consideration of the law on the duty to give reasons for detention. The three issues identified
by the court were (i) whether the detention power had been exercised for a lawful
purpose, (ii) *Hardial Singh*, and (iii) compliance with policies. In the course of his
reasoning on the first of those issues, having held that detention was for the permissible purpose of properly allocating the claimant's claim to the DFT, Thomas
LJ said:[113] 'Nor, in my view, does the fact that the UKBA [UK Border Agency] did
not give the real reasons impugn the validity of the exercise of the power: see *Saadi*

---

106 [2002] 1 WLR 3131.
107 At [48]. Mr Saadi pursued his challenge to the European Court of Human Rights. The Grand
Chamber held that there had been a breach of Article 5(2): (2008) 47 EHRR 17 at [81]–[85].
108 See *Lumba* at [84]; *Kambadzi* at [45].
109 [2011] EWCA Civ 938.
110 At [12].
111 See Chapter 13.
112 At [15].
113 At [47].

at paragraph 48.' He goes on to state,[114] in relation to the letter making mistaken reference to the DNSA process: 'The fact that an error was made in that letter makes no material difference to the analysis; it had been made clear in every other communication that he was detained under the DFT procedure. To the extent that a mistake in one letter may be thought material, it is clear the giving of a wrong reason does not affect the legality of the detention . . .'

The most recent consideration of the relevance of a failure to give reasons is to be found in *Mahajna (Raed Salah) v Secretary of State for the Home Department*.[115] Nicol J's judgment contains a detailed analysis of the authorities bearing on the issue, although it does not appear that *MS (Jamaica)* was before him, and it was accepted by the Secretary of State that 'the arrest and detention of the Claimant would only have been lawful if he was given reasons that were adequate in all the circumstances'.[116] The judge concluded that 'what is required in any particular situation is fact sensitive and dependent on all the relevant circumstances',[117] but Mr Mahajna was not given adequate reasons for his detention until two days had elapsed, and his detention was consequently unlawful for those days.[118] **9.55**

In our view there is force in the analysis in *Mahajna* notwithstanding what was said in *MS (Jamaica)*. It is strongly arguable that what is said about reasons in *MS* is *obiter*. The case was not advanced as a reasons challenge. Thomas LJ's discussion of reasons is in another context—i.e. whether detention was for the relevant statutory purpose. Moreover, on the facts of *MS*, there was arguably no material flaw in the reasons in any event. The document provided to MS reflected the central reasons for his detention. The Secretary of State's only failing was in not providing the detailed justification behind those reasons until a later stage. **9.56**

I. Legal Errors in Decisions to Deport or Remove

The final question we consider in this chapter is in what circumstances an error in an underlying decision to deport or remove might impact upon the legality of detention predicated upon that decision. Two propositions are clear: **9.57**

(1) First, where a person is detained pursuant to a decision to deport which was made in bad faith, or where there was in fact no intention to deport, detention will be unlawful;[119]

---

[114] At [49].
[115] [2011] EWHC 2481 (Admin).
[116] At [50].
[117] At [54].
[118] At [54]–[65].
[119] *Ullah (Mohammed) v Home Secretary* [1995] Imm AR 166.

(2) Second, where a person is detained in reliance on a decision to deport or remove which contains no error of law but is subsequently overturned on appeal because the Tribunal takes a different view of the facts, detention in the meantime will not be unlawful for that reason (although it may be unlawful for other reasons).[120]

9.58 Between those two extremes, however, lie a multitude of situations in relation to which the position is less clear cut.

9.59 *Ullah* concerned detention under paragraph 2(2) of Schedule 3 to IA 1971 following service of notice of decision to make a deportation order. The decision to deport had been taken without regard to all relevant factors, so was marred by public law error. Kennedy LJ held that 'all that is required by paragraph 2(2) of Schedule 3 in order to make detention legitimate is the giving of a notice of intention to make a deportation order'. Whilst that condition would not be met if no such intention had been formed, or if it had been formed in bad faith, in all other cirumstances, 'once notice is given . . . detention will be lawful even if the notice is later withdrawn or set aside'. Millett LJ dismissed the appeal for similar reasons, holding that paragraph 2(2) did not require 'that the decision should be the right decision, or without flaw, or otherwise impervious to successful challenge by way of judicial review'.

9.60 The judgment in *Ullah* was the subject of criticism in *R (ID) v Secretary of State for the Home Department*.[121] Brooke LJ held that the Court of Appeal was 'entitled to regard [itself] as not bound' by *Ullah* for five reasons, including that 'Kennedy LJ appears to have taken for granted that a pre-*Anisminic* approach to the decision of an officer of the executive was appropriate in the post-*Anisminic* world without explaining why'.[122]

9.61 In *Kullas v Secretary of State for the Home Department*[123] Nicol J accepted the Secretary of State's submission that, whilst a decision to detain can be rendered unlawful if the underlying refusal of leave to enter is 'tainted', the taint 'must take the form of either bad faith . . . or irrationality'.[124] This approach was applied in *Hatega v Secretary of State for the Home Department*.[125] The claimant, a failed asylum seeker, had been at liberty with outstanding representations pending before the Secretary of State. A decision was taken to refuse the representations

---

[120] *R (Draga) v Secretary of State for the Home Department* [2012] EWCA Civ 842, *per* Sullivan LJ at [60]. N.B.: In Chapter 14 we suggest that this general proposition may not hold good in cases involving the deportation or removal of EEA rights holders (see paragraphs 14.18–14.22).

[121] [2005] EWCA Civ 38; [2006] WLR 1003 at [110].

[122] At [119]. In considering the reach of *ID* it is important to note that another point of distinction identified by Brooke LJ was that *ID* was a case involving detention under Schedule 2 whereas *Ullah* involved detention under Schedule 3, 'which raises different considerations' (at [119]).

[123] [2009] EWHC 735 (Admin).

[124] At [5].

[125] [2009] EWHC 1980 (Admin).

without a right of appeal and to remove him from the United Kingdom, and he was detained on the ground that his removal was imminent. The decision on his representations was seriously flawed and unlawful. The Deputy Judge held that 'no reasonable Secretary of State could take the view that the submissions had been considered within the meaning of [the relevant rule], and accordingly no reasonable Secretary of State could regard removal as imminent'.[126] As such, the detention was unlawful.

The issue has most recently been considered by the Court of Appeal in *R (Draga)* **9.62** *v Secretary of State for the Home Department*.[127] In deciding to deport Mr Draga in August 2006 the Secretary of State had relied upon the terms of a statutory instrument which was subsequently, in June 2009, held to be *ultra vires*.[128] The decision to deport had therefore been in error of law, albeit this was not known either at the time it was taken or subsequently, when the Tribunal dismissed Mr Draga's deportation appeal. Mr Draga had been detained for most of the period August 2006 to September 2010, and the issue for the Court of Appeal was how, if at all, the unlawfulness which infected the deportation decision bore upon the legality of his detention.

Sullivan LJ said that, whilst it may appear obvious that an error of law in a decision **9.63** to deport was an error which bore upon and was relevant to the decision to detain (as without the prior decisions there could have been no decision to detain) that approach did not pay sufficient regard to the statutory scheme as a whole, having regard in particular to the existence of a statutory right of appeal against a decision to make a deportation order which encompassed (but was not limited to) points of law.[129]

Sullivan LJ discussed the circumstances in which a decision by the Tribunal over- **9.64** turning a deportation decision might, retrospectively, mean detention was unlawful. Uncontroversially, he said that where the Tribunal simply differed from the Secretary of State as to the correct view of the facts, that would not go to the legality of detention. However, he stopped short of accepting that whenever a deportation decision was set aside as being in error of law it would follow in every case that detention by reference to that decision was unlawful. He accepted that errors of the type identified in *Ullah* were 'examples' of breaches that would render detention unlawful (with the necessary implication that the categories in *Ullah* may not be exhaustive). Beyond that, he said, it was 'difficult to identify any principled basis for distinguishing between those public law errors which will render the decision

---

[126] At [36]–[39].
[127] [2012] EWCA Civ 842.
[128] In *R (EN (Serbia)) v Secretary of State for the Home Department & Another* [2009] EWCA Civ 630; [2010] QB 633.
[129] At [58]. N.B.: The Tribunal would have had no jurisdiction to rule upon the *vires* of a statutory instrument, the point of law which arose in *Draga*.

to detain unlawful and those which will not', given the post-*Anisminic* orthodoxy that 'there was a single category of errors of law, all of which rendered a decision *ultra vires*'.

9.65 Sullivan LJ further held that, where an appeal has been dismissed and appeal rights are exhausted, there was a strong case for treating the Tribunal's conclusions as determinative of the issues in the appeal. It would, he said, 'frustrate the operation of the statutory [appeal] scheme if the Secretary of State was not able to rely upon the Tribunal's decision, dismissing an appeal, once time for applying for permission to appeal . . . had expired . . .'.[130] Finality in litigation and legal certainty required this.[131] A subsequent clarification of the law was 'not a ground for re-opening the earlier decision by the Tribunal',[132] but would be a ground for an application to the Secretary of State to revoke a deportation order made in reliance upon the Tribunal's decision.[133]

9.66 The fact the Tribunal had upheld the decision to deport Mr Draga as lawful (even though it was not) meant that detention by reference to that decision was itself lawful. Detention only became unlawful after (i) the statutory instrument had been ruled unlawful; (ii) Mr Draga's representatives had made further representations on this basis; and (iii) the Secretary of State had responded to those representations in a way the Tribunal subsequently ruled was an unlawful device to maintain deportation.[134]

9.67 The judgment in *Draga* suggests that, at least where the underlying decision to deport or remove is one which attracts a right of appeal to the Tribunal,[135] an error of law in the decision to make a deportation order will not undermine the lawfulness of detention, pending deportation, unless either (a) the detainee brings a successful appeal under the statutory scheme, or (b) the unlawfulness is established by another route such as judicial review, this has been brought to the Secretary of State's attention, and she has had a reasonable period in which to reconsider the position. In other words, if the decision to deport has not been successfully appealed then, save in the circumstances just identified, the Secretary of State will be insulated from any challenge to detention based on the unlawfulness of that decision. This conclusion carves out a broad exception to the principle in *Lumba* that material errors of law vitiate the lawfulness of detention. It is unclear if the Supreme Court would uphold such an exception. It is also unclear what effect *Draga* will have when the Immigration Act

---

[130] At [61]–[62].

[131] At [61].

[132] At [62].

[133] At [64].

[134] See at [66]–[72].

[135] Given the centrality which Sullivan LJ attaches to the statutory scheme for appealing against a deportation decision, it is in our view arguable that the logic of *Draga* would not apply where (as was the case in *Hatega*) the underlying decision was not one which attracted a right of appeal.

2014 comes into force and the statutory appeal scheme changes. Section 15 of the Immigration Act 2014 will significantly reduce the scope of the statutory appeal scheme. As a result, there may be many kinds of error of law in the decision to deport which will no longer be within the jurisdiction of the Tribunal on appeal.

10

GENERAL DETENTION POLICY

A. Introduction

10.01 The rule of law requires a clear statement by the executive of the principles it will apply when using broad statutory detention powers.[1] The main policy document regulating the exercise of the powers of detention under the Immigration Acts is Chapter 55 of the Secretary of State's Enforcement Instructions and Guidance ('EIG').[2] EIG 55 states that to be lawful detention must, *inter alia*, 'accord with stated policy',[3] a statement which has been described as an 'important acknowledgement of the significance of the policy in public law'.[4]

10.02 This chapter considers the key principles which emerge from EIG 55. We look first at the principles which case owners are instructed to apply in all cases. We then look at the further guidance on the application of those principles in Immigration Enforcement Criminal Casework ('CC') cases involving the detention of foreign national offenders ('FNOs') facing deportation. The three chapters which follow address policy guidance on unsuitability for detention (Chapter 11), the detention of children and families (Chapter 12), and the Detained Fast Track (Chapter 13). The circumstances in which a failure to apply or have regard to published policy might render detention unlawful are considered separately in Chapter 9.

---

[1] See Chapter 9, paragraphs 9.18–9.20.

[2] At the time of writing, version 18.3, promulgated on 1 May 2014. In April 2008 EIG 55 replaced Chapter 38 of the Operational Enforcement Manual ('OEM') which dates back to December 2000. OEM 38 supplemented the more general policy statements in the White Papers of 1999 and 2002. NB: detention policy in port cases is set out in Chapter 31 of the Immigration Directorate Instructions ('IDIs').

[3] EIG 55.1.1; see also 55.1.4.

[4] *Kambadzi v Secretary of State for the Home Department* [2011] UKSC 23; [2011] 1 WLR 1299, *per* Lord Hope at [18].

B. General Detention Policy, All Cases

A number of core features of Home Office detention policy can be traced back **10.03** at least as far as the 1999 White Paper and the earliest iterations of OEM 38 including the presumption in favour of release, the circumstances in which detention is 'most usually appropriate', and the IS91R reasons document.[5]

(1) Presumption in favour of release

There is a presumption in favour of temporary admission or release and, **10.04** wherever possible, alternatives to detention are used.[6] EIG 55.3 adds that 'there must be strong grounds for believing that a person will not comply with conditions of temporary admission or temporary release for detention to be justified'.[7]

(2) Circumstances in which detention is 'most usually appropriate'

EIG 55.1.1 states that detention is most usually appropriate (a) 'to effect removal', **10.05** (b) 'initially to establish a person's identity or basis of claim', or (c) 'where there is reason to believe that the person will fail to comply with any conditions attached to the grant of temporary admission or release'.

(3) Shortest period necessary

EIG 55.1.3 states that detention must be used 'sparingly' and for 'the shortest **10.06** period necessary'.

(4) Factors influencing a decision to detain

EIG 55.3.1 states that 'all relevant factors' must be taken into account when con- **10.07** sidering the need for initial or continued detention. Eleven matters are identified for consideration:[8]

- 'What is the likelihood of the person being removed and, if so, after what timescale?'

---

[5] Significant aspects of current policy pre-date even these documents; see *R (Mohammed Liaket Ali) v Special Adjudicator and Secretary of State for the Home Department* , Unreported, 21 December 1999 at [8]–[11].

[6] EIG 55.1.1, EIG 55.3. Strictly speaking this is a statement of 'normal practice' rather than a 'presumption' in any legal sense; see *R (Lumba & Mighty) v Secretary of State for the Home Department* [2011] UKSC 12; [2012] 1 AC 245, *per* Lord Dyson at [42]–[44], and see further Chapter 9, paragraphs 9.28–9.29.

[7] This latter point is expressed as applying in all cases except fast track and CC cases.

[8] *Cf.* the factors identified as relevant to assessing *Hardial Singh* reasonableness; see Chapter 8, paragraph 8.55.

- 'Is there any evidence of previous absconding?'
- 'Is there any evidence of a previous failure to comply with conditions of temporary release or bail?'
- 'Has the subject taken part in a determined attempt to breach the immigration laws?'
- 'Is there a previous history of complying with the requirements of immigration control?'
- 'What are the person's ties with the UK?'
- 'What are the individual's expectations about the outcome of the case? Are there factors such as an outstanding appeal, an application for judicial review or representations which afford incentive to keep in touch?'[9]
- 'Is there a risk of offending or harm to the public (this requires consideration of the likelihood of harm and the seriousness of the harm if the person does offend)?'[10]
- 'Is the subject under 18?'[11]
- 'Does the subject have a history of torture?'[12]
- 'Does the subject have a history of physical or mental ill health?'[13]

(5) Form IS91R as an integral part of Home Office detention policy

10.08 Form IS91R is a pro forma document giving reasons for detention which must be served on every detained person at the time of initial detention in non-CC cases.[14] It identifies six possible 'reasons' for detention and 14 'factors' supporting those reasons. It has been described as 'an important part of the published policy,'[15] no doubt because it purports to identify an exhaustive list of reasons for detention, albeit the Court of Appeal in *Nadarajah* recognized that the 'factors' identified therein could not be exhaustive.[16]

10.09 The six 'reasons' identified in Form IS91R are as follows (case owners are instructed to 'tick **all** the reasons that apply to the particular case'):

(1) 'You are likely to abscond if given temporary admission or release.'

---

[9] See also EIG 55.1.3: 'A person who has an appeal pending or representations outstanding might have more incentive to comply with any restrictions imposed, if released, than one who is removable.'

[10] See further paragraphs 10.26–10.37.

[11] See further Chapter 12.

[12] See further Chapter 11, paragraphs 11.37–11.48.

[13] These factors may engage EIG 55.10, as to which see Chapter 11, paragraphs 11.20–11.36. They remain relevant even where EIG 55.10 is not engaged.

[14] EIG 55.6.3. In CC cases reasons for detention are set out in a letter (the ICD 1913 or ICD 1913AD). See further Chapter 9 paragraphs 9.50–9.56 for discussion of the duty to give reasons.

[15] *R (Nadarajah and Amirhanathan) v Secretary of State for the Home Department* [2003] EWCA Civ 1768, *per* Lord Phillips MR at [55].

[16] See *per* Lord Phillips MR at [57].

(2) 'There is insufficient reliable information to decide on whether to grant you temporary admission or release.'

(3) 'Your removal from the UK is imminent.'

(4) 'You need to be detained whilst alternative arrangements are made for your care.'[17]

(5) 'Your release is not considered conducive to the public good.'

(6) 'I am satisfied that your application may be decided quickly using the fast track asylum procedures.'

The 14 supporting 'factors' are:[18]   **10.10**

(1) 'You do not have enough close ties (for example, family or friends) to make it likely that you will stay in one place.'

(2) 'You have previously failed to comply with conditions of your stay, temporary admission or release.'

(3) 'You have previously absconded or escaped.'

(4) 'On initial consideration, it appears that your application may be one which can be decided quickly.'

(5) 'You have used or attempted to use deception in a way that leads us to consider that you may continue to deceive.'

(6) 'You have failed to give satisfactory or reliable answers to an immigration officer's enquiries.'

(7) 'You have not produced satisfactory evidence of your identity, nationality or lawful basis to be in the UK.'

(8) 'You have previously failed, or refused to leave the UK when required to do so.'

(9) 'You are a young person without the care of a parent or guardian.'

(10) 'Your health gives serious cause for concern on grounds of your own wellbeing and/or public health or safety.'[19]

(11) 'You are excluded from the UK at the personal direction of the Secretary of State.'

(12) 'You are detained for reasons of national security, the reasons are/will be set out in another letter.'

(13) 'Your previous unacceptable character, conduct or associations.'

---

[17] This reflects one of the exceptional circumstances in which EIG 55.9.3 states an unaccompanied child might be detained. However, arguments may arise as to whether detention for such reasons complies with the *Hardial Singh* principles; see further Chapter 8, paragraphs 8.26–8.29.

[18] In *Nadarajah* at [55] Lord Phillips MR analyses the connection between the six 'reasons' and the various 'factors' (which at the time were the same, save for the omission of factor (4)), and suggests that the final 'factor' is in fact a further reason.

[19] N.B.: The detention of a person 'cannot be justified by reference to that person's own wellbeing' *(R (Das) v Secretary of State for the Home Department & Ors* [2014] EWCA Civ 45, *per* Beatson LJ at [68]). Reliance on this factor may amount to a material public law error vitiating the legality of detention.

(14) 'I consider this reasonably necessary in order to take your fingerprints because you have failed to provide them voluntarily.'

10.11　Reliance on a 'reason' (or reasons) not borne out by the facts of the case is likely to be an error of law going to the legality of detention, as is detention in reliance upon a 'factor' which is not established. So, for example, detention on the ground that removal is imminent where this is not a conclusion reasonably open to the Secretary of State will be unlawful: *R (Hatega) v Secretary of State for the Home Department*.[20]

C. Criminal Casework Cases

10.12　Cases involving foreign national offenders ('FNOs') facing deportation are dealt with by Immigration Enforcement Criminal Casework ('CC').[21] They are subject to the general policy in EIG 55.1.1, including the presumption of release.[22] However, this is qualified by extensive guidance which states that detention may well be the appropriate course in any CC case and, in cases involving 'more serious offences', release is likely to be appropriate 'only in exceptional cases'.[23]

(1)　EIG 55.1.2; 55.1.3; 55.3.A

10.13　The starting point in CC cases 'remains that the person should be released unless the circumstances of the case require the use of detention'.[24] However, in any case in which the 'deportation criteria'[25] are satisfied, risk of re-offending and absconding should be weighed against the presumption of release, and:

> [d]ue to the clear imperative to protect the public from harm from a person whose criminal record is sufficiently serious as to satisfy the deportation criteria, and/ or because of the likely consequence of such a criminal record for the assessment of the risk that such a person will abscond, in many cases this is likely to result in the conclusion that the person should be detained, provided detention is, and continues to be, lawful. However, any such conclusion can be reached only if the

---

[20] [2009] EWHC 1980 (Admin) at [38]–[39].

[21] Previously, UK Border Agency Criminal Casework Directorate ('CCD').

[22] EIG 55.1.2.

[23] EIG 55.1.3.

[24] EIG 55.1.2.

[25] The deportation criteria are met where (i) the individual is liable to automatic deportation under the UK Borders Act 2007 ('UKBA 2007'); (ii) in the case of a non-EEA national: (a) there has been a court recommendation for deportation; (b) there has been a custodial sentence of any length for 'a serious drug offence'; or (c) the individual received a custodial sentence of 12 months or more, either as a single sentence or an aggregate of two or three sentences over a period of five years; or (iii) where, in the case of an EEA national, the individual received a sentence of at least 24 months (or 12 months where the offence involves sex, drugs, or violence) (EIG 55.1.2).

presumption of temporary admission or release is displaced after an assessment of the need to detain in the light of the risk of re-offending and/or the risk of absconding.[26]

The strong steer towards the use of detention powers in such cases is reiterated in **10.14** EIG 55.1.3 which states that where detention is indicated 'because of the higher likelihood of risk of absconding and harm to the public on release' it will 'normally' be appropriate to detain 'as long as there is still a realistic prospect of removal within a reasonable timescale'. EIG 55.1.3 envisages detention ending only (a) upon deportation; (b) upon the FNO's appeal against deportation succeeding; (c) upon a grant of bail by the Tribunal; or (d) where further detention would be unlawful.

In deciding whether continued detention might be unlawful, case owners are **10.15** instructed to attach 'substantial weight' to the risk of further offending or harm to the public.[27] Both the likelihood of re-offending and the level of harm if the person does re-offend must be considered'.[28]

A distinction is drawn in EIG 55.3.A between 'more' and 'less' serious offences. **10.16** More serious offences are those listed in the Annex to EIG 55 entitled *Crimes Where Release From Immigration Detention Or At The End Of Custody Would Be Unlikely*. Less serious offences are any offences not so listed.

Where a person has been convicted of a 'more serious' offence the guidance states **10.17** that the weight to be attached to further offending or harm to the public is 'particularly substantial' and in practice 'release is likely to be appropriate only in exceptional cases because of the seriousness of violent, sexual, drug-related and similar offences'.[29] Case owners are further instructed to balance against the increased risk the types of factors normally considered in non-FNO detention cases such as mental illness or the impact on any children affected by the individual's detention.[30]

In *BA v Secretary of State for the Home Department*[31] it was held that the policy con- **10.18** tained non sequiturs in its approach to risk of harm. It begins with an 'unobjectionable' requirement to assess risk of re-offending and harm and to give substantial weight where such risks are found. It then asserts that 'particularly substantial' weight should be given to risk in cases involving a listed offence. It concludes by stating that in such cases release will in practice be appropriate only in exceptional cases. The latter points, the judge said, do not follow from the initial premise: 'They

---

[26] EIG 55.1.2.
[27] EIG 55.1.3; see also EIG 55.3.2.
[28] This reflects the *Hardial Singh* authorities; see further Chapter 8, paragraph 8.69.
[29] EIG 55.1.3; and *cf.* EIG 55.3.A which re-states the position, stating that 'a conclusion that such a person should be released would only be reached where there are exceptional circumstances which clearly outweigh the risk of public harm and which mean detention is not appropriate'.
[30] EIG 55.3.A. See further Chapters 11 and 12.
[31] [2011] EWHC 2748 (Admin), at [169].

seem to be based on an assumption that everyone who has committed a listed offence ipso facto poses a risk of re-offending and of harm to the public. Common sense suggests that that is not so, and that the premise is correct in suggesting that the assessment of such risks must be done for each individual.' Although the judge did not say in terms that this aspect of the policy was unlawful, her reasoning calls this into question.[32]

10.19 As to 'less serious' offences, EIG 55.3.A states that risk of re-offending and absconding 'remain important' in assessing whether detention is reasonably necessary, but are given 'less emphasis' when balanced against other relevant factors.

(2) Further guidance on deciding to detain in CC cases (EIG 55.3.2)

(a) *PNC printout*

10.20 An up to date record of convictions must be obtained from the police national computer (PNC) to inform decisions to detain or maintain detention in CC cases.[33]

(b) *Family split*

10.21 Where the consequence of a decision to detain is that a family will be split (or a family split maintained upon the completion of a term of imprisonment), authority to separate the family must be obtained.[34]

(c) *The application in CC cases of the general factors influencing a decision to detain*

10.22 EIG 55.3.1 identifies 11 factors influencing a decision to detain, set out at paragraph 10.07. In the context of CC cases three of these—imminent removal, absconding risk, and risk of harm—are the subject of further guidance.

(d) *Imminent removal*

10.23 EIG 55.3.1 identifies likelihood of removal and timescale to removal (rather than imminence *per se*) as relevant factors. EIG 55.3.2.4 states, in the context of CC cases: 'As a guide, and for these purposes only, removal could be said to be imminent where a travel document exists, removal directions are set, there are no outstanding legal barriers and removal is likely to take place in the next four weeks.'[35]

10.24 Cases where removal is not imminent due to 'delays in the travel documentation process' may be considered for release on restrictions. However, where the FNO is frustrating removal by not cooperating with the documentation process, and

---

[32] See Chapter 9, paragraphs 9.22–9.32 for a discussion of the requirements of a lawful policy.
[33] EIG 55.3.2.1.
[34] EIG 55.3.2.3. See further Chapter 12, paragraphs 12.102–12.107.
[35] N.B.: In *R (FM) v Secretary of State for the Home Department* [2011] EWCA Civ 807 this definition of imminence was considered in the context of a non-CC case, suggesting that notwithstanding the clear words of the policy, it may be applied more broadly.

where that is a significant barrier to removal, 'these are factors weighing strongly against release'.[36]

(e) Risk of absconding

Case owners are instructed in EIG 55.3.2.5 that conviction for a more serious offence **10.25** 'may indicate a high risk of absconding'. The assessment should also take account of 'previous failures to comply with temporary release or bail', past failures to comply with immigration control or 'determined' attempts to breach the UK's immigration laws. Attempts to frustrate removal are relevant to absconding risk (but the exercise of appeal rights is not a relevant factor). Other relevant factors include conduct in prison or detention, family ties, and expectations about the outcome of the case.

(f) Risk of harm

(i) **General**   EIG 55.3.2.6 to 55.3.2.12 give detailed guidance to case owners on **10.26** the approach to be taken to risk of public harm.

(ii) **Requirement to obtain NOMS risk assessment**   Case owners are instructed **10.27** that risk of harm to the public 'will be assessed by the National Offender Management Service ('NOMS') unless there is no Offender Assessment System ('OASYS') or pre-sentence report available'. Where the sentence imposed was 12 months or more there should be in existence a licence and an OASYS report. NOMS will 'only be able to carry out a meaningful risk assessment in cases where a pre-sentence report exists (details of which can be obtained from the prison) or where the subject has a previous conviction resulting in a community order'.

Where NOMS can provide an assessment it can be obtained directly from the **10.28** offender manager in the Probation Service. This is done by completing a *Request for offender management information on a foreign national prisoner* on the form included at Annex A to Probation Circular 32/2007 (Form NOMS1).[37] The assessment 'should be received within three days'. Further reference to NOMS will also be 'essential' in cases where it is decided to end detention.

In every case where the subject would have been the subject of a licence (sentences **10.29** of 12 months or longer, sentences for shorter periods adding up to 12 months or longer, or offenders under 22 years or age) a risk assessment should be requested from the relevant offender manager and cases 'should not be taken forward without a reply from the offender manager being obtained'.[38] Given that, at least in principle,[39] the NOMS risk assessment will be an important factor to be taken into

---

[36]   EIG 55.3.2.4.
[37]   N.B.: The Probation Circular bears an expiry date of 30 September 2012, but at the time of writing has not been updated or replaced.
[38]   EIG 55.3.2.7.
[39]   *Cf.* the discussion of *BA* at paragraphs 10.18 and 10.36, and the judge's comments therein on the extent to which individualized risk assessments fall to be taken into account.

account when deciding whether or not to detain, in our view a failure, in breach of policy, to obtain such an assessment is likely to be held to be a material error of law vitiating the legality of detention.

10.30 (iii) **Case owner to assess risk where no NOMS assessment available** Where the offender manager advises that NOMS are unable to produce a risk assessment case owners are instructed that they 'will need to make a judgement on the risk of harm based on the information available to them'.[40] Relevant factors are said to include the nature of the original offence, any other offences committed, behaviour in prison and/or detention, and 'general record of compliance'. The guidance is silent on a number of relevant factors, including completion of offending behaviour courses, engagement with education and training more generally, and the deterrent effect of imprisonment.[41] In contrast to the approach of NOMS, risk assessments conducted by Home Office officials in this context do not apply any formal risk assessment methodology.

10.31 Where a person has been convicted of one of the 'more serious' offences identified in EIG 55.3.A case owners are instructed that, when considering whether to detain, 'the nature of the offence is such that the person presents a high risk'. Those with 'a long record of persistent offending are likely to be rated in the high or medium risk'. Those with 'a low level, one-off conviction and, with a good record of behaviour otherwise' are likely to be low risk.[42]

10.32 (iv) **Approach once risk has been assessed** If a NOMS report has been received it will, where possible, be based upon an OASYS assessment, and will include an indication of risk of harm on release, stated as low, medium, high or very high. It will also include an indication of risk of re-offending, expressed as low, medium, or high.[43]

10.33 Case owners are instructed that a marking of high or very high in either of these areas 'should be treated as an assessment of a high risk of harm to the public'. This is questionable. NOMS specifically assess risk of public harm. Where the risk is assessed as low or medium it would arguably be irrational to treat it as high by reference to the separate question of likelihood of reconviction. If that is right, a person who is assessed by NOMS as posing a high risk of re-offending but a low risk of harm, who is detained on the basis that he or she poses a high risk of harm may have grounds to challenge the legality of detention.[44]

---

[40] EIG 55.3.2.8.

[41] *Cf. R (MXL & Ors) v Secretary of State for the Home Department* [2010] EWHC 2397 (Admin) per Blake J at [70]: 'It cannot be assumed that a two year sentence on a woman who has never served a custodial sentence before and who is the mother of two young children from whom she has been separated throughout that sentence and have missed her would have no effect upon her.'

[42] EIG 55.3.2.8.

[43] EIG 55.3.2.9.

[44] The counter-argument may be that the Secretary of State is not obliged to adopt the definition of harm employed by NOMS.

Case owners are instructed to use the following table to 'translate the double assess- **10.34**
ment produced by NOMS into a single assessment' for the purposes of EIG 55:[45]

Seriousness of harm if offends on release	VH	VH	VH	H	H	H	M	M	M	L	L	L
Likelihood of re-offending	H	M	L	H	M	L	H	M	L	H	M	L
Overall assessment	H	H	H	H	H	H	H	M	M	H	L	L

VH = Very high, H = High, M = Medium, L = Low

Individuals assessed as low or medium risk 'should generally be considered for **10.35**
management by rigorous contact management',[46] albeit factors specific to the particular case might militate against this outcome. In cases involving 'more serious'
offences[47] 'a decision to release is likely to be the proper conclusion only when the
factors in favour of release are particularly compelling'. In practice, 'release is likely
to be appropriate only in exceptional cases because of the seriousness of violent,
sexual, drug-related and similar offences'.

This last instruction appears to override everything that goes before relating **10.36**
to individualized assessment, so far as convictions for any of the 'more serious'
offences are concerned. Even in a case in which NOMS assessed risk of harm *and*
risk of reconviction as low, the policy would indicate detention in the absence
of exceptional circumstances. This was noted by the judge in *BA*, who observed
that, whilst the policy 'appears to promise decisions based on an assessment of
individual risk,' it 'withdraws that promise in the case of FNPs who have committed "serious" offences'. Such an approach was 'inconsistent with other passages in
the policy which indicate that the assessment, and resulting balance, of relevant
factors, must be done in an individualised way'.[48] As we say at paragraph 10.18 in
relation to other comments made by the judge in *BA*, these conclusions call into
question the legality of this aspect of the policy.[49]

(v) Bail   Where an individual is refused bail by the first-tier Tribunal 'the opin- **10.37**
ions of the immigration judge will be relevant'.[50] If bail was refused due to the risk
of absconding or behavioural problems during detention, 'this would be an indication that the individual should not normally be released unless circumstances have
changed'. If bail was refused due to lack of sureties the case owner 'might want to
recommend release providing all the other criteria in [EIG 55.3.2] indicate release
is appropriate'.

---

[45] EIG 55.3.2.10.
[46] See further EIG 55.20.5 for instructions on release on contact management.
[47] See paragraph 10.16.
[48] [2011] EWHC 2748 (Admin), at [176].
[49] See Chapter 9, paragraphs 9.22–9.32 for a discussion of the requirements of a lawful policy.
[50] EIG 55.3.2.13.

D. Procedural Requirements

(1) Levels of authority for detention

10.38 Levels of authority for detention are addressed in EIG 55.5. EIG 55.5.3 addresses a number of special cases.

10.39 In *Lumba*, Lord Dyson said that 'a decision to detain made by an official of a different grade from that specified in a detention policy would not found a claim in false imprisonment'.[51] It is unclear how far this dictum will carry.[52] What might the position be where, because of the nature of the case, the policy required the decision to be taken at a very high level? For example, EIG 55.5.3 states that a decision to detain a child foreign national offender must have ministerial authorization. Were detention in such a case authorized not by the relevant minister but by a junior official, could it be said the procedural error was immaterial to the decision to detain? In our view, the answer is likely to be no. The requirement for high level authorization is a specific safeguard in a case in which detention powers must be exercised in only very exceptional circumstances. A failure to observe that safeguard is likely to render detention unlawful. It can be readily distinguished from the scenario Lord Dyson was considering in *Lumba*.

(2) Detention forms

(a) Written reasons for detention

10.40 Written reasons for detention should be given in all cases at the time of detention and thereafter at 28 day intervals.[53] In non-CC cases initial reasons for detention are given by way of a checklist in Form IS91R.[54] In CC cases a reasons letter[55] is sent in place of the IS91R.[56] Thereafter reasons are provided month by month on Form IS151A.[57]

---

[51] At [68]; followed, in the context of a detention review carried out by an official of the wrong grade, in *Kambadzi*; see *per* Lord Hope at [60].

[52] It is relevant that Lord Dyson was addressing a submission that, if the approach for which the appellants contended prevailed, 'a decision to detain made by an official one grade lower than that specified in the detention policy (but which is otherwise unimpeachable)' would be rendered equivalent to 'a decision to detain for which there is no statutory authority at all' (see at [67]).

[53] Rule 9(1) of the Detention Centre Rules 2001 states: 'Every detained person will be provided, by the Secretary of State, with written reasons for his detention at the time of his initial detention, and thereafter monthly.'

[54] EIG 55.6.

[55] ICD1913 or, in automatic deportation cases, ICD1913AD.

[56] EIG 55.6.

[57] These should be based on the outcome of the internal detention reviews: EIG 55.8.

(b) IS91 RA

Once a decision has been taken to detain, the risks in detention (as distinct from risk of harm) must be assessed and recorded on Form IS91 RA.[58] Risk assessment is an ongoing process. Should further relevant information become available it should be processed in line with the guidance in EIG 55.6.1. **10.41**

(c) IS91 Detention authority

Detention is authorized on Form IS91.[59] Form IS91 is issued only once for any continuous period of detention, irrespective of how many detaining agents there are during the course of a person's detention save (a) where there is an alteration in risk factors, and (b) in CC cases if the IS91 is re-issued when a deportation order has been signed. The pro forma reasons document Form IS91R is addressed at paragraphs 10.08–10.11. **10.42**

(3) Detention reviews

Once authorized, detention must be reviewed from time to time by the Secretary of State in accordance with the schedules applicable to different classes of case set out in EIG 55.8. Each review is, in effect, a reauthorization and, as such, a failure to review detention is a material public law error vitiating the legality of detention.[60] Likewise, where the review does take place but 'does not partake of the quality or character required to justify the continuance of detention', detention will be unlawful.[61] **10.43**

At each review, robust and formally documented consideration should be given to the removability of the detainee and to all other information relevant to the decision to detain.[62] Additional reviews may also be necessary on an ad hoc basis, for example, where there is a change in circumstances relevant to the reasons for detention.[63] **10.44**

Where detention involves or impacts on children under the age of 18, reviewing officers should have received training in children's issues and must demonstrably have regard to the need to safeguard and promote the welfare of children.[64] **10.45**

A review of detention by an official lower in rank than specified in the guidance will not amount to a material error of law impacting on the legality of detention.[65] **10.46**

---

[58] EIG 55.6.1. In CC cases, Form IS91 RA CCD.
[59] EIG 55.6.2.
[60] *Kambadzi, per* Lord Hope at [52].
[61] *Kambadzi, per* Lord Kerr at [86].
[62] EIG 55.8.
[63] EIG 55.8.
[64] EIG 55.8.
[65] See Chapter 9, paragraph 9.49, but *cf.* the discussion at paragraph 10.39.

11

UNSUITABILITY FOR DETENTION

A. Introduction and General Principles

(1) Introduction

11.01 Chapter 55, Section 55.10, of the Enforcement Instructions and Guidance (EIG) identifies eight categories of person 'normally considered suitable for detention in only very exceptional circumstances, whether in dedicated immigration accommodation or prisons'.[1] They are, in broad outline, and subject to certain caveats:

(1) unaccompanied children;

(2) the elderly;

(3) pregnant women;

(4) those suffering from serious medical conditions which cannot be satisfactorily managed within detention;

(5) those suffering from serious mental illness which cannot be satisfactorily managed within detention;

(6) those where there is independent evidence that they have been tortured;

(7) people with serious disabilities which cannot be satisfactorily managed within detention; and

(8) victims of trafficking.

---

[1] The same provisions are included in Chapter 31, Section 1, of the Immigration Directorate Instructions: *Detention and Detention Policy in Port Cases*, at Section 10B. Unless otherwise stated, references to EIG 55 in this chapter are to version 18.3, promulgated on 1 May 2014.

This chapter examines the application of this policy, and other related policy guidance, in relation to those falling within categories (2) to (8). Unaccompanied children are addressed separately in Chapter 12.[2]   **11.02**

All of the matters identified in EIG 55.10 are also relevant to the issue arising under the *Hardial Singh* principles of how long a period of detention is reasonable in a given case.[3] Detention of individuals who fall within the ambit of EIG 55.10 may also raise issues under Articles 3 and 8 of ECHR.[4]   **11.03**

(2) Release or relocation

EIG 55.10 has been consistently construed as giving guidance on the circumstances in which unsuitability for detention will necessitate release.[5] In most such cases, absent 'very exceptional circumstances', the policy will compel release. There will be rare circumstances, however, where the issue that engages the policy can be resolved by moving a person from an immigration removal centre ('IRC') or prison into a hospital.[6] In such a case, on the authority of *IM (Nigeria) v Secretary of State for the Home Department*,[7] the policy would not preclude continued detention in hospital under immigration powers.[8]   **11.04**

(3) Criminal Casework cases

EIG 55.10 applies to Criminal Casework ('CC') cases—that is, cases of ex-foreign national prisoners facing deportation, managed by Immigration Enforcement Criminal Casework. Earlier versions of EIG 55.10 drew no distinction between CC cases and other cases. On 9 September 2008 the policy was amended to state that, in CC cases, 'the risk of further offending or harm to the public must be carefully weighed against the reason why the individual may be unsuitable for detention'.[9] On 26 August 2010 the policy was amended again, to state that there may be cases 'where the risk of harm to the public is such that it outweighs factors that would otherwise normally indicate that a person was unsuitable for detention'.   **11.05**

---

[2] At paragraphs 12.21–12.53.

[3] *Cf.* Chapter 8, paragraph 8.55.

[4] See Chapter 15.

[5] For example, Cranston J's assertion in *Anam v Secretary of State for the Home Department* [2009] EWHC 2496 (Admin) at [55] that, where EIG 55.10 was engaged on mental health grounds, 'a strong presumption in favour of release will operate' has been adopted at Court of Appeal level; see, e.g., *R (OM (Nigeria)) v Secretary of State for the Home Department* [2011] EWCA Civ 909, *per* Richards LJ at [11]–[12].

[6] A hospital being a permissible place of detention; see Chapter 17, paragraph 17.4.

[7] [2013] EWCA Civ 1561.

[8] See further paragraphs 11.33–11.36.

[9] N.B.: on this date the Secretary of State amended EIG 55.10 to refer to a presumption in favour of detention in Criminal Casework cases, having secretly operated a blanket policy of detention in such cases since April 2006: see *R (Lumba & Mighty) v Secretary of State for the Home Department* [2011] UKSC 12; [2012] 1 AC 245 at [5], [6], [14], and [293]. The published policy presuming in favour of detention ended on 22 January 2009, but the change to the wording of EIG 55.10 remained.

These amendments make clear that in CC cases a high risk of harm to the public is relevant to deciding whether 'very exceptional circumstances' arise justifying the detention of a person who falls within the terms of EIG 55.10.[10]

(4) Very exceptional circumstances

11.06 Whether circumstances are sufficiently exceptional to justify detention in the face of the strong presumption of release created by EIG 55.10 requires consideration of a number of separate, interrelated factors. The issue has arisen most frequently in cases involving mentally ill detainees, but the approach which emerges from those cases applies to any case falling within the ambit of EIG 55.10.[11]

11.07 Cranston J's approach to this issue in *Anam* was upheld on appeal and subsequently adopted by the Court of Appeal in later cases.[12] *Anam* involved a claimant detained following a term of imprisonment who had been diagnosed with schizophrenia. He challenged his detention by reference to EIG 55.10 as it applied to those suffering from mental illness. Cranston J held that the 'very exceptional circumstances' proviso in EIG 55.10 did not 'stand in isolation'.[13]

11.08 *Anam* was a Criminal Casework case. As such, the qualifications in EIG 55.10 itself regarding such cases had to be taken into account, as did the guidance elsewhere in EIG 55. Although a person's mental illness meant 'a strong presumption in favour of release' would operate, other factors also had to be considered. 'Very exceptional circumstances' had to be 'construed in the context of the policy providing guidance for the detention of all those liable to removal, not just foreign national prisoners'. There was:

> a general spectrum which near one end has those with mental illness who should be detained only in 'very exceptional circumstances' along it—the average asylum seeker with a presumption of release—and near the other end has high risk terrorists who are detained on national security grounds. To be factored in, in individual cases, are matters such as the risk of further offending or public harm and the risk of absconding. When the person has been convicted of a serious offence substantial weight must be given to these factors. In effect paragraph 55.10 demands that, with mental illness, the balance of those factors has to be substantial indeed for detention to be justified.[14]

---

[10] See further the discussion of 'very exceptional circumstances' at paragraphs 11.06–11.10.

[11] See, e.g., *R (BE) v Secretary of State for the Home Department* [2011] EWHC 690 (Admin), *per* Stephen Morris QC, Deputy Judge, at [38], where the issue was disability. N.B.: In cases involving unaccompanied children, the circumstances in which detention may take place are so narrowly defined that there will be little room for the balancing exercise considered here.

[12] See, e.g. *R (Das) v Secretary of State for the Home Department* [2014] EWCA Civ 45, *per* Beatson LJ at [51]–[57].

[13] At [53].

[14] At [55].

In *R (S) v Secretary of State for the Home Department*,[15] the Deputy Judge stressed that the exceptionality provisions in EIG 55.10 had been set in the more general context of EIG 55.1 which creates a presumption of release in all cases. That remained the starting point even in Criminal Casework cases. In 'a genuine case of serious mental illness' the emphasis was not simply on the general presumption of liberty, but 'a specific presumption that detention will only take place in very exceptional circumstances'. EIG 55.10 did not preclude detention in all cases, but it 'undoubtedly creates a high hurdle to overcome if it is to be imposed'. A decision maker who approached such a case with only the general presumption of liberty in mind and did not properly apply the exceptional circumstances test may have asked 'the wrong question and approached the detention issue unreasonably'.[16]

11.09

As to what might constitute 'very exceptional circumstances', Beatson LJ in *Das* observed that 'mere liability to be removed and refusal to leave voluntarily cannot constitute the "very exceptional circumstances" required or the policy would be denuded of virtually all its operation' and that 'the detention of a person cannot be justified by reference to that person's own well-being . . . either in general or as an exceptional circumstance'. On the other hand, the balance might tip against a detainee 'where the case concerns a foreign national prisoner who poses a serious risk to the public, for example a person who poses a high risk of killing someone else, or where there are cogent grounds for believing that removal will take place in a very short time'.[17]

11.10

(5) Unsuitability and legality

The Secretary of State's policy on unsuitability bears directly upon a decision to detain or maintain detention. Where the facts of a case engage EIG 55.10 a failure to take the policy into account,[18] or a decision on the application of the policy which was *Wednesbury* unreasonable or marred by some other public law error[19] will render detention unlawful. It is also strongly arguable that where the Secretary of State is, or should be, aware of facts which show a 'a real (as opposed to a fanciful or insubstantial) possibility' that the policy is engaged, she is under a duty to make sufficient inquiries to satisfy herself as to whether the policy is in fact engaged, and a failure to conduct those enquiries will render detention unlawful.[20]

11.11

---

[15] [2011] EWHC 2120 (Admin).
[16] At [164].
[17] At [68].
[18] See, e.g., *OM (Nigeria)* at [21].
[19] See Chapter 9.
[20] This was the approach of Sales J in *Das* at first instance: [2013] EWHC 682 (Admin) at [42]–[45]. It was not challenged before the Court of Appeal, and is at least arguably endorsed by Beatson LJ at [66]. As to the duty of inquiry resting on the Secretary of State, see further Chapter 9, paragraph 9.08, footnote 13.

11.12 Although it now seems clear that the court is limited to reviewing the Secretary of State's application of policy on traditional public law grounds (and does not take on the role of primary decision maker),[21] at least one issue arising under EIG 55.10—the existence of 'independent evidence of torture'—has been held to be 'fairly hard edged', with the consequence that the question 'will often be less capable of two different answers'[22] than whether very exceptional circumstances exist. In our view, the same approach is likely to be taken to the existence of serious medical conditions, serious mental illness, and disability.

B. Unaccompanied Children

11.13 Unaccompanied children are addressed separately in Chapter 12 at paragraphs 12.21–12.53.

C. The Elderly

11.14 'The elderly' are normally considered suitable for detention in only very exceptional circumstances, 'especially where significant or constant supervision is required which cannot be satisfactorily managed within detention'. This head of unsuitability is not the subject of any further policy guidance and has not, to our knowledge, been considered by the courts.

D. Pregnant Women

11.15 For the purposes of enforcement action a pregnant woman is 'any woman who has been medically certified as being pregnant, or who claims to be pregnant unless a medical assessment has found no evidence of pregnancy'.[23]

11.16 EIG 55.10 states that pregnant women are unsuitable for detention in other than very exceptional circumstances 'unless there is the clear prospect of early removal and medical advice suggests no question of confinement prior to this'.[24] The detention of pregnant women is also addressed under *Special Cases* in EIG 55.9.1, which states:

> Pregnant women should not normally be detained. The exceptions to this general rule are where removal is imminent and medical advice does not suggest

---

[21] See Chapter 9, paragraphs 9.34–9.38.
[22] *R (EO & Ors) v Secretary of State for the Home Department* [2013] EWHC 1236 (Admin) *per* Burnett J at [16].
[23] EIG 45(a), paragraph 10.03.
[24] N.B.: 'confinement' in this context refers to childbirth, not detention.

confinement before the due removal date, or, for pregnant women of less than 24 weeks gestation, at Yarl's Wood as part of a fast-track asylum process.

The policy of not ordinarily detaining pregnant women implicitly recognizes that **11.17** detention places their welfare and the welfare of their unborn children at risk. That in turn will inform the construction of the elastic concept of 'early removal' or 'imminent removal' in such cases.[25] In our view, only very imminent removal will suffice to exclude a pregnant woman from the protection of the 'very exceptional circumstances' policy in EIG 55.10.[26]

If removal cannot take place as a matter of practicality or medical need, it can- **11.18** not rationally be characterized as imminent. As such, where a pregnant woman is unfit to fly, either because her pregnancy is too advanced[27] or because flight is counter-indicated by medical advice, it will not be open to the Secretary of State to detain on the grounds that removal is imminent.

The same holds true where removal cannot take place without a breach of the **11.19** Secretary of State's policy on the use of force against pregnant women. EIG 45(a) paragraph 13.02 states that force 'should only ever be used on a pregnant woman to prevent her from harming herself, any member of her family or any member of staff'. The use of force against a pregnant woman to effect removal is not permitted. Where a decision maker knows (or should know) that a pregnant woman cannot be removed without the use of force, removal cannot rationally be characterized as imminent (however defined).

---

[25] N.B.: It is unclear whether the (imprecise) term 'early removal' is intended to connote something other than the (imprecise) term 'imminent removal'. If the two concepts are not synonymous, the courts will inevitably read EIG 55.9.1 and EIG 55.10 together in the manner most protective of liberty.

[26] N.B.: The definition of 'imminent removal' in EIG 55.3.2.4 as meaning 'removal is likely to take place in the next four weeks' is expressly limited in its application to Criminal Casework cases, and in any event has been held to be simply illustrative of what the *Hardial Singh* principles are likely to require, the court recognizing that in some cases a greater degree of imminence will be necessary to justify detention: *R (FM) v Secretary of State for the Home Department* [2011] EWCA Civ 807 at [51]. In our view, the legality of the policy on the detention of pregnant women may be amenable to challenge on the basis that the lack of precision gives rise to a likelihood or risk of unlawful decision making; *cf.* the discussion of the requirements of a lawful policy in Chapter 9, at paragraphs 9.22–9.32.

[27] See further Detention Services Order 02/2013 *Pregnant women in detention* which details the Home Office position on fitness to fly during pregnancy and includes a table summarizing guidance from the International Air Transport Association (IATA). See also the Civil Aviation Authority guidance on pregnancy at <http://www.caa.co.uk/default.aspx?catid=923&pageid=13747> and the IATA Medical Manual at <http://www.iata.org/whatwedo/safety/health/Documents/medical-manual-2013.pdf>.

E. Serious Medical Conditions/Serious Mental Illness

(1) General

11.20 'Those suffering from serious medical conditions which cannot be satisfactorily managed within detention' and 'those suffering from serious mental illness which cannot be satisfactorily managed within detention'[28] are normally considered suitable for detention in only very exceptional circumstances.[29] We consider the two categories together. There is, however, one important point of distinction. In many (although not all) cases involving a 'serious medical condition' detention is unlikely to have any impact upon the course of that condition, whereas it is clear that detention—and *a fortiori* detention which, from the perspective of the detainee, is potentially indefinite in nature—can cause or significantly exacerbate mental ill health.[30]

(2) 'Suffering from'/seriousness/satisfactory management

11.21 The questions whether a person is (i) suffering from (ii) a serious medical condition or mental illness and, if so, (iii) whether that condition is satisfactorily managed are interrelated. 'Dissection' of the various elements is not appropriate; a 'purposive and pragmatic construction' is required.[31]

11.22 The Court of Appeal in *MD (Angola)*[32] approved as 'essentially correct' the reasoning of Cranston J in the court below that a person 'suffers from an illness if they are significantly affected by that illness' and that '[t]hose with a serious medical condition which is satisfactorily managed, albeit that its impact may vary, are not suffering from it'.[33]

11.23 The effects of the illness on the particular individual, the effect of detention on him or her, and on the way that person's illness would be managed if detained must be considered.[34] As to satisfactory management, relevant matters include the medication the person is taking and whether his or her demonstrated needs are such that they can or cannot be provided in detention.[35] Account should

---

[28] In 'exceptional' cases EIG 55.10 permits detention pending assessment or pending transfer under the Mental Health Act 1983 ('MHA 1983'). For transfer from detention to hospital under section 48 of MHA 1983, see Chapter 17, paragraphs 17.50–17.60. In Criminal Casework cases caseworkers are told to contact the specialist mentally disordered offender team.

[29] EIG 55.10.

[30] See *Mental health implications of detaining asylum seekers: systematic review*, Robjant *et al*, *The British Journal of Psychiatry* (2009) 194: 306–312, and the articles cited therein.

[31] *Das, per* Beatson LJ at [47]–[48].

[32] *R (MD (Angola) & Ors) v Secretary of State for the Home Department* [2011] EWCA Civ 1238.

[33] *Per* Maurice Kay LJ at [14].

[34] *Das, per* Beatson LJ at [57].

[35] *Das, per* Beatson LJ at [67].

be taken of the facilities available at the centre at which the individual is to be detained, and the expected period of detention before he or she is lawfully removed.[36]

(3) Evidential requirements

In *Anam*, in a section of his judgment subsequently approved by the Court of **11.24**
Appeal,[37] Cranston J said that 'mental health issues only fall to be considered under Chapter 55 where there is available objective medical evidence establishing that a detainee is, at the material time, suffering from mental health issues of sufficient seriousness as to warrant consideration of whether his circumstances are sufficiently exceptional to warrant his detention'. The same principle necessarily applies to 'serious medical conditions'. Such evidence could include a report under Rule 35 of the Detention Centre Rules 2001.[38] This general principle is subject to two caveats:

(1) First, it is strongly arguable that a duty of inquiry arises where the known facts disclose a 'a real (as opposed to a fanciful or insubstantial) possibility' that the policy is engaged;[39] and

(2) Second, it has been held[40] that generally it is no defence to an allegation of unlawful detention or breach of Convention rights for the Secretary of State to assert she was unaware of the mental (or, necessarily, physical) illness of a detainee 'if the condition was known to healthcare staff in a Detention Centre'. On the other hand, where the Secretary of State has 'conscientiously made reasonable inquiries as to the physical and mental health of the person who is being considered for detention, has obtained such reports of clinicians who had previously treated the person as have been made available, and considered the implications of the policy in §55.10 for the detention of that person, leaving aside cases in which there has been negligence by the clinicians at the detention centre, she should generally be entitled to rely on the responsible clinician'.[41]

---

[36] *Das, per* Beatson LJ at [67].

[37] [2009] EWHC 2496 (Admin) at [52].

[38] See further Chapter 17, paragraphs 17.18–17.28. Although most of the cases to date regarding Rule 35 have related to whether reports amount to 'independent evidence of torture' it is clear that reports made under Rule 35(1) and/or (2) could be sufficient to engage the provisions in EIG 55.10 regarding mental or physical health.

[39] See paragraph 11.11, footnote 20, and Chapter 9, paragraph 9.08, footnote 13.

[40] *R (EH) v Secretary of State for the Home Department* [2012] EWHC 2569 (Admin), *per* Lang J at [152].

[41] *Das, per* Beatson LJ at [70].

(4) Mental illness

11.25 The term 'mental illness' in EIG 55.10 applies to any person with a 'mental disorder' within the meaning of the MHA 1983 (which will include a personality disorder as well as a mental illness as strictly defined).[42]

11.26 Whether a person is suffering from serious mental illness which cannot be satisfactorily managed within detention is a different question to whether the condition meets the test for hospitalization under the MHA 1983. This was the conclusion of the Court of Appeal in *Das, inter alia* for the following reasons:[43]

- The purposes of and criteria for detention under MHA 1983 differ substantially from the purposes of and criteria for immigration detention and for the operation of EIG 55.10.
- Those whose condition is serious but untreatable cannot be detained in hospital under MHA 1983.
- The criteria in MHA 1983 seek to identify those who, because of their mental illness, *are* suitable for detention in a hospital in order to enable treatment to be given for the benefit of the patient, whereas the policy seeks to identify those who, because of their mental illness, are *not* suitable for detention in an immigration centre.
- To align the criteria in EIG 55.10 with those in MHA 1983 by regarding the policy as broadly only applicable where the criteria in the Act are met glosses over the important differences, and fails to reflect mental health practice. In particular, many people with serious mental illnesses are best treated in the community and some mental illnesses are exacerbated if the individual is placed in hospital.

(5) Change in wording of policy relating to the mentally ill

11.27 Until August 2010 EIG 55.10 referred to 'the mentally ill' alongside 'those *suffering from* serious medical conditions' (emphasis added). In *MD (Angola)* the difference in wording was said to be 'significant'.[44] On 26 August 2010 the policy was amended to refer instead to 'those suffering serious mental illness which cannot be satisfactorily managed within detention'.[45]

11.28 In *HA (Nigeria)*[46] Singh J held that the change in wording amounted to a change in policy and, as it had occurred without the Secretary of State taking the necessary

---

[42] *R (MC (Algeria)) v Secretary of State for the Home Department* [2010] EWCA Civ 347 at [41].
[43] At [61]–[63].
[44] At [16].
[45] Subsequently changed again to 'suffering from'.
[46] *R (HA (Nigeria)) v Secretary of State for the Home Department* [2012] EWHC 979 (Admin).

steps to comply with her public sector equality duties[47] (by carrying out an Equality Impact Assessment), the policy as amended was unlawful.

Two days after *HA* was decided, the Court of Appeal heard the appeal of *LE* **11.29** *(Jamaica).*[48] LE had been diagnosed with schizophrenia, but his condition was controlled by medication. He challenged his detention by reference to the pre-amendment form of EIG 55.10 (which referred simply to 'the mentally ill'). The issue which arose was whether there was an 'implicit requirement that a mental illness had to attain a minimum level of seriousness before [the policy] was engaged'.[49] The Court of Appeal held that there was.[50] Richards LJ accepted that the favoured approach involved 'reading in a substantial qualification which is not expressed in the original policy' but said that the qualification was implicit, 'and gives effect to the true meaning of the policy'.[51]

The conclusion in *LE (Jamaica)* would appear to support the position taken by **11.30** the Secretary of State in *HA (Nigeria)*. Following *LE* the Secretary of State withdrew her appeal to the Court of Appeal in *HA*. There has as yet been no ruling on whether the finding of unlawfulness in *HA* survives the judgment in *LE*.[52] In *Das* it was observed that, if there had in fact been no change in policy, authorities on the meaning of the pre-amendment policy were relevant to the construction of the policy subsequent to the amendment.[53]

(6) Serious medical conditions

Where a person is suffering from a serious medical condition which cannot be satis- **11.31** factorily managed in detention of any kind the position is straightforward: they must be released unless there are very exceptional circumstances justifying detention. However, where a person is suffering from a serious medical condition which cannot be satisfactorily managed within an IRC (or a prison, as the case may be) but which can be satisfactorily managed in hospital, the effect of EIG 55.10 may be to compel transfer to hospital rather than to compel release. This was the view of the Court of Appeal in *IM (Nigeria)*, which is considered at paragraphs 11.33–11.36 under 'Food and fluid refusal'.

Such cases will only arise very rarely and are likely to involve acute illness or seri- **11.32** ous injury. Where such circumstances arise, and treatment in hospital is viable, the

---

[47] Under section 71 of the Race Relations Act 1976 and section 49A of the Disability and Discrimination Act 2005.
[48] *R (LE (Jamaica)) v Secretary of State for the Home Department* [2012] EWCA Civ 597.
[49] At [32].
[50] At [41].
[51] At [41].
[52] See *R (S) v Secretary of State for the Home Department* [2014] EWHC 50 (Admin) *per* HHJ Thornton at [276].
[53] At [50].

detainee can be transferred to hospital[54] whilst remaining in detention under the Immigration Acts. However, if the continuation of detention during the period of hospitalization will impact upon the efficacy of treatment (for example, by imposing additional stress on a person with a heart condition) or the availability of treatment, the threshold of 'satisfactory management' may not be met.

(7) Food and fluid refusal

11.33   Difficult questions arise where a person in detention refuses food and/or fluids with the result that they come to suffer from a serious medical condition.[55] Where the detainee lacks capacity as a result of mental illness, or mental illness is contributing to the decisions to refuse food and/or fluids, EIG 55.10 will be engaged for that separate reason.[56] But what of the capacitous detainee engaged in a hunger strike which places his or her life at risk?

11.34   The issue came before the Court of Appeal in *IM (Nigeria)*. IM was gravely ill as a result of prolonged food and (intermittent) fluid refusal. Doctors at the IRC in which he was held considered he was unfit to be detained there because the medical needs arising from his food and fluid refusal could not be met.[57] However, his medical needs could be met in hospital and there was a power to transfer him to hospital without first releasing him.

11.35   The court accepted that IM fell within the ambit of EIG 55.10 as a person suffering from a serious medical condition which could not be satisfactorily managed within an IRC. In the court's view, however, it did not follow that absent exceptional circumstances IM had to be released. Rather, if his condition could be satisfactorily managed in hospital, the policy would ordinarily require his transfer to hospital, absent exceptional circumstances.[58] However, as he was withholding his consent to treatment the Secretary of State was entitled to conclude that was not required. The policy statements did not apply to IM 'because they simply did not envisage such a case'.[59]

---

[54]   See Chapter 17, paragraph 17.04.

[55]   The management of such cases is the subject of detailed guidance in Detention Services Order 03/2013: Food and Fluid Refusal in Immigration Removal Centres: Guidance.

[56]   As was the case in *R (BA) v Secretary of State for the Home Department* [2011] EWHC 2748 (Admin); see at [200], [227]. In one case pending at the time of writing, *Drammeh v Secretary of State for the Home Department* (CO/8758/2013), the judge who granted permission to apply for judicial review (Haddon-Cave J) observed that it was arguable that *IM (Nigeria)* is distinguishable 'on the grounds that the Claimant had a pre-existing mental illness which caused or materially contributed to his food/fluid refusal'. In contrast to *IM*, the Court was willing to order Mr Drammeh's release on bail pending resolution of his claim: [2013] EWHC 2980 (Admin).

[57]   [2013] EWCA Civ 1561, at [7(4)].

[58]   At [43].

[59]   At [43]. IM was refused permission to appeal by the Supreme Court. The panel which refused permission (Lady Hale, Lord Toulson, and Lord Hodge) noted that EIG 55 did not address the circumstances in which transfer to hospital otherwise than under section 48 of MHA 1983 should take place, and said that 'there may be a point of law of general public importance as to whether the

Although this meant the question of 'very exceptional circumstances' did not need **11.36**
to be addressed, Lloyd Jones LJ held that such circumstances did arise, not because
the condition was self-inflicted, but because of IM's continuing refusal to consent
to medical treatment unless released.[60]

F. Independent Evidence of Torture

(1) General

Individuals in respect of whom 'there is independent evidence that they have been **11.37**
tortured' should only be detained in very exceptional circumstances.[61] The ration-
ale of the policy is that those who have suffered torture in the past are disproportionately adversely affected by detention.[62]

'Torture' means any act by which severe pain or suffering, whether physical or **11.38**
mental, is intentionally inflicted on a person for such purposes as obtaining from
him or a third person information or a confession, punishing him for an act he or a
third person has committed, or intimidating or coercing him or a third person, or
for any reason based upon discrimination of any kind.[63]

A requirement of 'evidence' is not the same as a requirement of proof, conclusive or **11.39**
otherwise.[64] Whether the Secretary of State accepts an allegation of torture in light
of a given piece of evidence is irrelevant to the question whether it is independent
evidence of torture for the purposes of the policy.[65] However, an individual's credibility may inform the question whether very exceptional circumstances arise that
justify maintaining detention.[66] Doubts about credibility would be an insufficient
basis to conclude that such circumstances arise, but there may be cases in which
information available to the decision maker leads to the firm conclusion that the
torture claim is untrue or very unlikely to be true. It would be a 'perverse application of the policy' to require release of someone in respect of whom there was independent evidence of torture where it was clear the claim was untrue.[67]

Secretary of State's policy is required to be comprehensive', albeit the facts did not justify a grant of
permission.

[60] At [44].
[61] EIG 55.10.
[62] *EO & Ors* at [59].
[63] *EO & Ors* at [82]. Burnett J rejected an argument that the narrower definition of torture in
Article 1 of the United Nations Convention Against Torture, Inhuman and Degrading Treatment
or Punishment 1984 ('UNCAT') should apply in this context (at [75]–[82]).
[64] *AM (Angola) v Secretary of State for the Home Department* [2012] EWCA Civ 521, *per* Rix LJ
at [30].
[65] *AM (Angola)* at [31].
[66] *EO & Ors* at [69].
[67] *EO & Ors* at [69].

(2) Medical reports

11.40 Where a medical report is put forward as independent evidence of torture it will be relevant whether the report was prepared in accordance with the *Istanbul Protocol* of 1999.[68] The Protocol advises that where a physician is documenting scarring, '[f]or each lesion and for the overall pattern of lesions, the physician should indicate the degree of consistency between it and the attribution'.[69] Ultimately, however, it is the overall evaluation of all lesions and not the consistency of each lesion with a particular form of torture that is important in assessing the torture story.[70] Guidance is also given to the approach that should be taken when reporting psychological evidence of torture.[71]

11.41 An independent medical expert's belief in the truth of a person's claim to be a victim of torture following an expert examination and assessment, founded in part upon an account previously rejected by a judge, but not taking that account 'at face value', has been held to amount to independent evidence of torture.[72] Wherever an expert view is sought in a case in which a judge has previously made adverse credibility findings, this should be brought to the attention of the expert and the earlier conclusions should be fully taken into account by the expert.

(3) Reports under Rule 35 of the Detention Centre Rules 2001

11.42 Rule 34(1) of the Detention Centre Rules 2001 requires that every detained person shall be given a physical and mental examination by a registered medical practitioner within 24 hours of admission to an IRC. Rule 35(3) requires the medical practitioner to report on the case of any detained person who he is concerned may have been the victim of torture.[73]

11.43 The medical examination required under Rule 34 is an important part of the safeguards provided to assess whether a person should continue to be detained.[74]

---

[68] *The Manual on the Effective Investigation and Documentation of Torture and Other Cruel, Inhuman or Degrading Treatment or Punishment*, submitted to the United Nations High Commissioner for Human Rights on 9 August 1999, Revised 2004. See *AM (Angola)* at [14] and [30]; *cf. EH* at [163]–[165].

[69] Paragraph 187, which categorizes degrees of consistency in the following terms: '(a) Not consistent: the lesion could not have been caused by the trauma described; (b) Consistent with: the lesion could have been caused by the trauma described, but it is non-specific and there are many other possible causes; (c) Highly consistent: the lesion could have been caused by the trauma described, and there are few other possible causes; (d) Typical of: this is an appearance that is usually found with this type of trauma, but there are other possible causes; (e) Diagnostic of: this appearance could not have been caused in anyway other than that described.'

[70] Paragraph 188.

[71] Paragraphs 287–288.

[72] *AM (Angola)* at [30]. The expert in question was a nurse with 'a wealth of relevant experience' (at [17]).

[73] The requirements imposed by Rules 34 and 35 are considered in detail in Chapter 17 at paragraphs 17.18–17.28.

[74] *R (D & K) v Secretary of State for the Home Department and Others* [2006] EWHC 980 at [50].

Concerns as to torture identified by the medical practitioner following a Rule 34 examination are capable of constituting independent evidence of torture for the purposes of EIG 55.10.[75] This is recognized in published policy.[76] The weight to be attached to an expression of concern in such a report will depend upon the facts of the particular case.[77] The existence of, *inter alia*, the regime in Rules 34 and 35 displaces any notion that there is an overriding burden on a detainee always himself to come up with the relevant 'independent evidence'.[78]

The Asylum Process Guidance *Detention Rule 35 Process* gives the following **11.44** guidance to caseworkers on the approach to take when considering a Rule 35 report:

> A report which simply repeats an allegation of torture will not be independent evidence of torture.
>
> A report which raises a concern of torture with little reasoning or support or which mentions nothing more than common injuries or scarring for which there are other obvious causes is unlikely to constitute independent evidence of torture.
>
> A report which details clear physical or mental evidence of injuries which would normally only arise as a result of torture (e.g. numerous scars with the appearance of cigarette burns to legs; marks with the appearance of whipping scars), and which records a credible account of torture, is likely to constitute independent evidence of torture.[79] A failure to carry out or arrange a Rule 34 examination will render detention unlawful without more.[80]

Whether or not the failure caused the claimant to be detained will determine **11.45** whether substantial or only nominal damages are payable.[81]

In at least some circumstances there is a duty to make clear to a detainee the **11.46** significance of the Rule 34 examination: *R (RT) v Secretary of State for the Home Department*.[82] RT had declined an examination on admission to detention, despite previously having claimed to be a victim of torture. The Secretary of State argued that in those circumstances, no liability could flow from the failure to conduct an examination. Kenneth Parker J rejected this analysis as overly simplistic. The evidence suggested that when admitted to detention RT had not been asked

---

[75] *D & K*, at [50]. The approach in *D & K* was followed in *R (PB) v Secretary of State for the Home Department* [2008] EWHC 364 (Admin) (see at [19]–[27]).

[76] *Detention Rule 35 Process* Asylum Process Guidance, Section 3(i).

[77] *D & K* at [52].

[78] *D & K* at [53].

[79] N.B.: The examples given are very stark. In practice many cases fall between the second and third examples, and an exercise of judgement will be called for.

[80] This was the conclusion of Burnett J in *EO & Ors* at [51], departing from the pre-*Lumba* analysis in *D & K* and the cases which followed it, which endorsed a causation-based approach to liability.

[81] For causation and damages see Chapter 20, paragraphs 20.12–20.15.

[82] [2011] EWHC 1792 (Admin).

whether she was a victim of torture, as required. Had she been asked it was likely Rule 34(1) would have been applied to her. The correct procedure was to make explicit to her that it was in her best interests to have a medical examination so that if her allegations were true there might well be some independent medical evidence corroborating her allegations.[83]

11.47 Rule 35 is not prescriptive about what a report should contain,[84] but Detention Service Order 17/2012, *Application of Detention Centre Rule 35*, sets out detailed guidance for medical practitioners on the approach which should be taken.

11.48 In *EO & Ors* it was suggested, *obiter*, that there would be no failure by the Secretary of State to comply with her policy if a medical practitioner were to miss signs of torture even if, for the sake of argument, a claimant could show that the failure was negligent.[85]

G. Serious Disabilities

11.49 People with serious disabilities which cannot be satisfactorily managed within detention should only be detained in very exceptional circumstances.[86] There is a distinction to be drawn between the issue of whether a person is medically fit to be detained and the wider issue of the effect of his or her disability upon the experience of immigration detention. The former relates to an imminent threat to health, whilst the latter covers other aspects, such as increased distress, pressure, loss of privacy and dignity, and embarrassment.[87]

11.50 A decision maker who, in authorizing the detention of a disabled person, considers only medical fitness, is asking 'the wrong question',[88] and such a failing is likely to be a material error of law which goes to the legality of detention.[89]

11.51 The duties arising under equalities legislation are also relevant in this context. In a claim brought by reference to section 49A of the Disability Discrimination Act

---

[83] At [31]–[32].

[84] *EO & Ors* at [57].

[85] At [59]. This was said to be the case because there is 'no failure by the Secretary of State to comply with her policy' in such circumstances. In our view, there may be more to be said on this issue, particularly in light of the approach of the courts in other cases to the Secretary of State's liability for failings by those contracted to provide services in relation to detention (see the cases cited at Chapter 17, paragraph 17.61, footnotes 100 and 101). Moreover, if the *obiter dicta* in *EO & Ors* on this issue are correct, it leaves open the question whether the negligent doctor might him- or herself be fixed with liability. In his judgment in *Das* at [70] Beatson LJ leaves open the relevance of negligence by a medical practitioner working on behalf of the Secretary of State.

[86] EIG 55.10.

[87] *R (BE) v Secretary of State for the Home Department* [2011] EWHC 690 (Admin) at [160].

[88] *R (BE)* at [162].

[89] *R (BE)* pre-dates *Lumba*, so the analysis is not framed in the context of the the Supreme Court's analysis of material public law errors, but this conclusion is inevitable.

1995,[90] it was said that the effect of the duty to 'have due regard' to the matters identified therein was twofold:

> First, the Secretary of State was required to consider generally, and in advance, whether the detention estate as a whole had appropriate facilities and processes for disabled detainees generally. Secondly, in the case of individual disabled detainees . . . the Secretary of State was required to conduct an individual assessment before detention and before any transfer within the detention estate.[91]

That assessment involved asking whether an individual's disability '[can] be satisfactorily managed in the detention estate', which in turn involved 'consideration of the broader impact of being disabled upon a person's detention, as regards, facilities, transport and harassment by other detainees'.[92] The mere existence of the policy in EIG 55.10 was not of itself sufficient to constitute compliance with the section 49A duty,[93] although, in tandem with the existence of the *Hardial Singh* principles, it was held to be sufficient to meet a challenge brought by reference to section 21B of the Disability Discrimination Act 1995 which, at the material time,[94] provided that it was unlawful for a public authority to discriminate against a disabled person in carrying out its functions.[95]   **11.52**

H. Victims of Trafficking

(1) Policy in outline

Persons (i) identified as victims of trafficking,[96] and (ii) in respect of whom there are reasonable grounds for thinking they may be victims of trafficking and who are awaiting a final decision,[97] will not ordinarily be detained.   **11.53**

To place these categories in context, it is necessary to briefly consider the mechanisms which exist in the United Kingdom for identifying victims of trafficking, and the entitlements that flow to a person who is so identified.[98]   **11.54**

---

[90] Now repealed but replaced with similar provisions in section 149 of the Equality Act 2010 ('EA 2010').

[91] *R (BE)* at [42].

[92] *R (BE)* at [165]. This passage was subsequently relied upon in a challenge brought under section 149 of the EA 2010: see *R (D) v Secretary of State for the Home Department* [2012] EWHC 2501 (Admin) at [167].

[93] *R (BE) at* [165].

[94] See now section 29 of EA 2010.

[95] *R (BE)* at [166] to [168].

[96] EIG 55.10.

[97] EIG 9.9. NB: References to EIG Chapter 9 in this chapter are to version 5.3, promulgated on 27 November 2013.

[98] See further *Human Trafficking Handbook*, Parosha Chandran (ed.), Butterworths LexisNexis. 2011.

(2) Identification and protection of trafficking victims in the United Kingdom

11.55 The United Kingdom became a signatory to the Council of Europe Convention on Action against Trafficking in Human Beings ('CAT') in March 2007 and ratified it on 17 December 2008. CAT provides for a two-stage process for the determination of whether a person is a victim of trafficking:

(1) a decision is taken as to whether there are reasonable grounds to believe a person is a victim of trafficking; and

(2) if so, the 'competent authorities' shall move to determine whether the person is in fact a victim.

11.56 Where reasonable grounds are established the person shall not be removed from the territory of the state party until the identification process has been completed. In such a case the state party shall 'provide in its internal law a recovery and reflection period of at least 30 days'.[99]

11.57 The United Kingdom did not legislate to incorporate the provisions of CAT, but has established a National Referral Mechanism ('NRM') with a view to meeting its obligations thereunder. In briefest outline, the scheme which has been adopted takes the following form:

(1) A number of public bodies and non-governmental organizations (collectively known as 'first responders') are authorized to refer individuals into the NRM.

(2) When a first responder suspects a person is a potential victim of trafficking, they will, subject to the individual's consent, contact the UK Human Trafficking Centre ('UKHTC') within the National Crime Agency, who will log the referral.

(3) The 'competent authorities'[100] are located within the UKHTC and a number of bodies within the Home Office. The UKHTC deals with all cases involving UK or European Economic Area (EEA) nationals and acts as the first point of contact for referrals. If the UKHTC receives a case involving a non-EEA national who is subject to immigration control, they will refer the case to the Home Office competent authority unless the case involves a non-EEA national with no active immigration issues.

(4) The competent authority first takes a 'reasonable grounds' decision which acts as an initial filter before a more conclusive decision is taken. The reasonable grounds test considers if the statement 'I suspect but cannot prove that the person is a victim of trafficking' holds true. This decision will ordinarily be made within five working days.[101]

---

[99] Article 13(1). Article 13(3) states that: 'The Parties are not bound to observe this period if grounds of public order prevent it or if it is found that victim status is being claimed improperly.'

[100] See paragraph 11.55.

[101] But should be expedited where the person is detained; see paragraph 11.61.

(5) If reasonable grounds are made out, the individual must be granted a 45 day reflection and recovery period.[102] This temporary status provides the conditions for a full evaluation to conclusively decide if the person was a victim of trafficking at the date of the reasonable grounds decision.

(6) The expectation is that, following due investigation, a conclusive grounds decision will be made on day 45 of the recovery and reflection period. Where a positive conclusive grounds decision is made and the person is assisting with police enquiries, a period of discretionary leave to remain of 12 months may be granted, which may subsequently be extended. A person recognized as a victim of trafficking may have other claims for leave to remain (e.g. on protection grounds), but these are considered separately.

(7) Where a conclusive determination finds that the person is not a victim of trafficking, all entitlements flowing from the reasonable grounds decision end.

(3) Detention policy in trafficking cases

Victims of trafficking are not ordinarily detained. EIG Chapter 9, *Identifying* **11.58** *victims of trafficking*, section 9.1, states 'Officers should be aware that victims of trafficking are likely to be classified as vulnerable persons and detention will not normally be appropriate.' It then cross refers to EIG 55.

(4) Reasonable grounds cases

EIG 55.10 is silent as to the position of persons who are the subject of a positive 'rea- **11.59** sonable grounds' decision and who are in the 45 day reflection and recovery period awaiting a conclusive grounds decision. However, EIG 9.9 provides:

> Competent Authorities will aim to complete an assessment of whether there are 'reasonable grounds to believe' someone is a victim within 5 days of referral. A positive decision will trigger a 45 day 'recovery and reflection' period during which time individuals will not be detained (unless their detention can be justified on grounds of public order) and removal action will be suspended. Victims will have access to certain rights, including accommodation and advice.

Where a 'reasonable grounds' decision has been taken, EIG 9.9 requires deten- **11.60** tion to be justified 'on grounds of public order' but it does not require there to be 'very exceptional circumstances' before a person can be detained. EIG 9.9 has its source in Article 13(3) of CAT, which provides that parties are not bound to observe a 'recovery and reflection period' if 'grounds of public order prevent it or if it is found that victim status is being claimed improperly'. Whether, in practice, this imposes a different threshold to that found in EIG 55.10 remains to be seen.

---

[102] This is the United Kingdom's implementation of the obligation arising from Article 13(1) of CAT; see paragraph 11.56, fn 99.

11.61 Where a person is already detained when the first responder makes the referral to the competent authority, EIG 9.10 envisages that the reasonable grounds decision will be expedited: 'Where a case needs to be fast tracked, e.g. the person may be detained, the [competent authority] is expected to treat the case as a priority and reach the decision as soon as possible.' Where detention is prolonged by delays on the part of the Home Office competent authorities in taking a reasonable grounds decision it would be arguable that detention in the meantime was contrary to policy (due to the failure to expedite) and so unlawful.

(5) Conclusive grounds cases

11.62 EIG 55.10 states that those identified by the competent authorities as victims of trafficking are suitable for detention in only very exceptional circumstances. On its face this provision would appear to apply only to those who have been the subject of a positive conclusive grounds decision.

(6) Failings in the determination process

11.63 Although there has, to date, been no ruling on the point, it is clear that where a person who is the subject of a reasonable grounds decision or a conclusive grounds decision is detained (i) without due regard to the relevant policies in EIG 9.9 and/or EIG 55.10, or (ii) without a legally sustainable decision being taken that 'grounds of public order' or 'very exceptional circumstances' sufficient to justify detention arise, detention will be unlawful.

11.64 The position is perhaps less clear where there was a failure in the procedure for identifying victims of trafficking that delayed or prevented such a decision being taken. The issue has arisen to date in three cases. In two, the challenges failed on their facts without the underlying point of principle being resolved.[103] In the third, *R (Atamewan) v Secretary of State for the Home Department*,[104] the claimant had been detained and removed after it had been accepted that she was a victim of trafficking. The Secretary of State had taken the view that, because her experience of trafficking had ended some years previously, she was no longer 'a victim of trafficking in need of protection under the Convention'.[105] Her challenge to the NRM decision and to the legality of her removal succeeded, but at the time of writing the legality of her detention remains to be determined.

---

[103] *R (C) v Secretary of State for the Home Department* [2010] EWHC 1089 (Admin); *R (RT) v Secretary of State for the Home Department* [2011] EWHC 1792 (Admin).

[104] [2013] EWHC 2727 (Admin), a decision of a Divisional Court comprising Aikens LJ and Silber J.

[105] At [15].

I. Public Sector Equality Duty

Of the categories of person identified in EIG 55.10 as suitable for detention in only **11.65** very exceptional circumstances, a number are defined directly by reference to matters which are also 'protected characteristics' for the purposes of EA 2010, specifically age, disability,[106] and pregnancy. Moreover, the definition of disability in EA 2010 will encompass many (but not all) persons suffering from 'serious medical conditions' or 'serious mental illness'[107] within the meaning of EIG 55.10 (as well as, necessarily, people with 'serious disabilities which cannot be satisfactorily managed within detention').[108]

Section 149 of EA 2010 provides, *inter alia*: **11.66**

Public sector equality duty

(1) A public authority must, in the exercise of its functions, have due regard to the need to—

    (a) eliminate discrimination, harassment, victimisation and any other conduct that is prohibited by or under this Act;[109]

    (b) advance equality of opportunity between persons who share a relevant protected characteristic[110] and persons who do not share it;

    (c) foster good relations between persons who share a relevant protected characteristic and persons who do not share it.

(2) A person who is not a public authority but who exercises public functions must, in the exercise of those functions, have due regard to the matters mentioned in subsection (1).

---

[106] Section 6(1) of EA 2010 provides that 'A person (P) has a disability if—(a) P has a physical or mental impairment, and (b) the impairment has a substantial and long-term adverse effect on P's ability to carry out normal day-to-day activities.' Guidance under s.6(5) *(Guidance on matters to be taken into account in determining questions relating to the definition of disability, May 2011)* states: 'The term mental or physical impairment should be given its ordinary meaning' (A3).

[107] See *R(D)*, *per* Charles George QC at [172]–[174], finding a breach of section 149 in the case of a mentally ill detainee. The judge found detention to be unlawful by reference to the mental illness provisions in EIG 55.10 (at [163]), and identified the breach of section 149 'as a further reason why the detention was unlawful', albeit on his analysis that finding added nothing to the conclusions on policy.

[108] At A5 the *Guidance* states: 'A disability can arise from a wide range of impairments which can be: sensory impairments, such as those affecting sight or hearing; impairments with fluctuating or recurring effects such as rheumatoid arthritis, myalgic encephalitis (ME), chronic fatigue syndrome (CFS), fibromyalgia, depression and epilepsy; progressive, such as motor neurone disease, muscular dystrophy, and forms of dementia; auto-immune conditions such as systemic lupus erythematosus (SLE); organ specific, including respiratory conditions, such as asthma, and cardiovascular diseases, including thrombosis, stroke and heart disease; developmental, such as autistic spectrum disorders (ASD), dyslexia and dyspraxia; learning disabilities; mental health conditions with symptoms such as anxiety, low mood, panic attacks, phobias, or unshared perceptions; eating disorders; bipolar affective disorders; obsessive compulsive disorders; personality disorders; post traumatic stress disorder, and some self-harming behaviour; mental illnesses, such as depression and schizophrenia; produced by injury to the body, including to the brain.'

[109] N.B.: For the meaning of discrimination, harassment, and victimization see sections 13–19 (discrimination), section 26 (harassment), and section 27 (victimization).

[110] The protected characteristics are defined in section 4. Those relevant to section 149 are set out at section 149(7).

(3) Having due regard to the need to advance equality of opportunity between persons who share a relevant protected characteristic and persons who do not share it involves having due regard, in particular, to the need to—

(a) remove or minimise disadvantages suffered by persons who share a relevant protected characteristic that are connected to that characteristic;

(b) take steps to meet the needs of persons who share a relevant protected characteristic that are different from the needs of persons who do not share it;

(c) encourage persons who share a relevant protected characteristic to participate in public life or in any other activity in which participation by such persons is disproportionately low.

(4) The steps involved in meeting the needs of disabled persons that are different from the needs of persons who are not disabled include, in particular, steps to take account of disabled persons' disabilities.

(5) Having due regard to the need to foster good relations between persons who share a relevant protected characteristic and persons who do not share it involves having due regard, in particular, to the need to—

(a) tackle prejudice, and

(b) promote understanding.

. . .

(7) The relevant protected characteristics are—

age;

disability;

gender reassignment;

pregnancy and maternity;

race;

religion or belief;

sex;

sexual orientation.

. . .

11.67 The duty to have due regard must be fulfilled prior to the adoption or implementation of the decision, function, or policy in question. It requires the decision maker to embark upon a sufficient and proper decision making process so as to discharge the duty with an open mind. The issue is one of substance, not form: the decision need not refer to the statutory duties in terms, but the evidence adduced in any challenge must show that the substance of the duty was discharged.[111]

11.68 In the present context, the duty to have due regard to the matters identified in section 149 arises both in the context of decisions to detain in individual cases,[112] and in the context of carrying out functions and promulgating policy in relation to detention more generally.[113]

---

[111] *Per* Wyn Williams J, *R (Equality & Human Rights Commission) v Secretary of State for Justice and Secretary of State for the Home Department* [2010] EWHC 147 (Admin) at [45] summarizing the principles emerging from the leading cases. As to the meaning of 'due regard', see *per* Dyson LJ, *R (Baker & Ors) v Secretary of State for Communities & Local Government & Others* [2008] EWCA Civ 141 at [31]: 'What is due regard? In my view, it is the regard that is appropriate in all the circumstances.'

[112] See *R (D)* and *R (BE)* (in relation to a breach of the predecessor legislation).

[113] *R (HA (Nigeria)) v Secretary of State for the Home Department* [2012] EWHC 979 (Admin) at [192].

12

CHILDREN AND FAMILIES

A. Introduction

At the time of writing,[1] the powers of detention in the Immigration Acts apply to adult and child alike. However, the circumstances in which those powers might lawfully be exercised to detain a child, whether alone or as part of a family unit, are rare. Moreover, where the detention of an adult might impact upon the welfare of a child in the United Kingdom the best interests of that child must be taken into account as a primary consideration in any decision whether or not to detain. **12.01**

The detention of children is profoundly damaging to their wellbeing.[2] The coalition agreement of May 2010 included a commitment to 'end the detention of children for immigration purposes'.[3] There followed a review, the results of which were published in December 2010,[4] setting out proposals for improved decision making in family cases, and three routes to departure for families with children ('assisted', 'required', and 'ensured' return) to reduce to almost nil the detention of families with children for the purpose of removal. These measures (the Family Returns Process or 'FRP') were in force by 1 March 2011.[5] The policy that unaccompanied **12.02**

---

[1] See paragraph 12.04.

[2] See, for example, the discussion in *R (Suppiah) v Secretary of State for the Home Department* [2011] EWHC 2 (Admin) at [105]–[127].

[3] *Conservative Liberal Democrat coalition negotiations, Agreements reached*, 11 May 2010; repeated in *The Coalition: our programme for government*, 20 May 2010.

[4] *Review into ending the detention of children for immigration purposes*, December 2010.

[5] *Modernised Guidance, Criminal Casework, Detention of Families*, v.6.0, 14 November 2013 (*Detention of families*), p 3. The FRP is detailed in Enforcement Instructions and Guidance (EIG) Chapter 45, as amended from time to time. At the time of writing the Contents section of EIG 45 is dated January 2014 (EIG 45(index) v1.0), EIG 45(a) is dated 10 June 2014 (EIG 45(a) v2.0), EIG 45(b) is dated January 2014 (EIG 45b v1), and EIG 45(c) is also dated January 2014 (EIG 45(c) v1.0).

children could only be detained in very exceptional circumstances was already entrenched.

12.03 In this chapter, we begin by considering a number of general principles informing the use of detention powers in cases involving children.[6] We then examine in more detail the position of unaccompanied children and young people whose age is disputed,[7] the alternatives to detention created by the FRP and the limited circumstances in which families with children might still be detained,[8] and finally the law and policy governing the detention of adults which impacts upon the welfare of a child in the United Kingdom.[9]

12.04 At the time of writing there are amendments pending to Part 4 of the Borders, Citizenship and Immigration Act 2009 ('BCIA 2009'), Schedule 2 to the Immigration Act 1971 ('IA 1971'), and Part 8 of the Immigration and Asylum Act 1999 ('IAA 1999') by virtue of sections 3, 5, and 6 of the Immigration Act 2014 ('IA 2014') which will impact upon the law and guidance discussed in this chapter. Section 3 of IA 2014 will insert a new section 54A into BCIA 2009 which will place the Independent Family Returns Panel ('IFRP') on a statutory footing.[10] Section 5 of IA 2014 will amend paragraph 16 of Schedule 2 and add a new paragraph 18B, the combined effect of which will be (i) to limit the detention of unaccompanied children under paragraph 16(2) to a maximum period of 24 hours; and (ii) to restrict the place of such detention to short term holding facilities save where the child is being transferred to or from a short term holding facility or where paragraph 18(3) of Schedule 2 applies.[11] Further, by paragraph 18B(2) to (4), such detention will only be permissible where directions for the child's removal from the short-term holding facility within 24 hours are in force (or a decision is likely to be taken to give such directions) and the authorizing officer reasonably believes the child will be removed from the short term-holding facility within 24 hours. Section 6 of IA 2014 will amend section 147 of IAA 1999 to provide a statutory definition of 'pre-departure accommodation', a concept which already exists in published policy.[12] It will also put on a statutory footing the time limits currently set down in policy for the detention of families in pre-departure accommodation.[13]

---

[6] See paragraphs 12.05–12.20.
[7] See paragraphs 12.21–12.53.
[8] See paragraphs 12.54–12.87.
[9] See paragraphs 12.88–12.109.
[10] For the IFRP see further paragraphs 12.68 and 12.69.
[11] Paragraph 18(3) provides for a person to be taken, in custody, 'to and from any place where his attendance is required for the purpose of ascertaining his citizenship or nationality or of making arrangements for his admission to a country or territory other than the United Kingdom, or where he is required to be for any other purpose connected with the operation of this Act'.
[12] Presently in law the Secretary of State's pre-departure accommodation has the status of a short-term holding facility, as to which, see Chapter 17, paragraphs 17.47–17.48.
[13] See paragraphs 12.76–12.83.

B. General Principles

(1) UNCRC and ECHR

The United Nations Convention on the Rights of the Child 1989[14] ('UNCRC') contains a series of core principles relevant to the detention of children on immigration grounds. These are considered in Chapter 16.[15] Articles 3, 5, and 8 of the European Convention on Human Rights ('ECHR') are considered in Chapter 15.[16]   **12.05**

In cases involving children, ECHR rights must be read in harmony with the UNCRC.[17] The European Court of Human Rights ('ECtHR') has frequently held that the detention of unaccompanied children breached Article 5(1) of ECHR when it was read with Articles 3 and 37 of UNCRC.[18] The UNCRC also informs the common law: in *R (ID) v Home Office*, Brooke LJ said that a failure by an immigration officer to have regard to 'the fact that [a] prospective detainee is a child protected by Article 37(b) of the UN Convention on the Rights of the Child' would be an error of law vitiating the power to detain.[19]   **12.06**

(2) Section 55

Section 55 of the Borders, Citizenship and Immigration Act 2009 ('BCIA 2009') requires the Secretary of State to 'make arrangements for ensuring', *inter alia*, that any function she exercises in relation to immigration, asylum, or nationality, and any function conferred by or by virtue of the Immigration Acts on an immigration officer, is discharged having regard to the need to safeguard and promote the welfare of children who are in the United Kingdom.[20] A person exercising any such function must have regard to any guidance given by the Secretary of State under section 55.[21]   **12.07**

---

[14] The United Kingdom ratified the UNCRC on 16 December 1991, but entered a general reservation to the Convention concerning immigration matters. The reservation was lifted in 2008.

[15] Paragraphs 16.8, 16.27, and 16.29.

[16] Article 3 is addressed from paragraph 15.66, Article 5 from paragraph 15.7, and Article 8 from paragraph 15.84.

[17] *Neulinger v Switzerland* (2012) 54 EHRR 31 at [131]–[132]; *R (S & Ors) v Secretary of State for the Home Department* [2007] EWHC 1654 (Admin) at [38]–[41]; *R (Suppiah) v Secretary of State for the Home Department & Another* [2011] EWHC 2469 (Admin) at [168]; *R (MXL) v Secretary of State for the Home Department* [2010] EWHC 2397 (Admin) at [83]. See further paragraph 16.27.

[18] See discussion in *R (AAM (A Child)) v Secretary of State for the Home Department* [2012] EWHC 2567 (QB) at [137].

[19] *R (ID) v Home Office* [2005] EWCA Civ 38; [2006] WLR 1003 at [111].

[20] Section 55(1) and (2) of BCIA 2009. Section 71 of IA 2014, not in force at the time of writing, provides: 'For the avoidance of doubt, this Act does not limit any duty imposed on the Secretary of State or any other person by section 55 of the Borders, Citizenship and Immigration Act 2009 (duty regarding the welfare of children).'

[21] Section 55(3).

12.08 A correct understanding of section 55 includes the rights arising under Articles 3 and 8 of ECHR.[22] There should be a 'rigorous appraisal' of the matters which section 55 requires be considered.[23] A material breach of section 55 will render detention unlawful.[24] A decision to detain a child, or an adult in circumstances which materially impact upon the welfare of a child, that fails to have regard to the section 55 duty is likely to be a 'material breach'.[25] In *SM & FM v Secretary of State for the Home Department*, Beatson J held that a flawed consideration of the best interests of a child in a decision to deport rendered detention unlawful because it impacted on the question whether there was a reasonable prospect of removal within a reasonable time.[26]

(3) *Every Child Matters*

12.09 Guidance was issued under section 55(3) of BCIA 2009 entitled *Every Child Matters—Change for Children—Statutory guidance to the UK Border Agency on making arrangements to safeguard and promote the welfare of children* ('*Every Child Matters*'). Decision makers must take it into account and if they decide to depart from it must have 'clear reasons' for doing so.[27] The obligation extends to private or voluntary organizations commissioned to provide services on behalf of the Home Office.[28]

12.10 *Every Child Matters* is in two parts. Part 1 sets out arrangements for safeguarding and promoting the welfare of children as they apply generally to public bodies. Paragraph 1.04 defines 'Safeguarding and promoting the welfare of children' in line with statutory guidance issued under section 11 of the Children Act 2004 ('CA 2004'), as:

- protecting children from maltreatment;
- preventing impairment of children's health or development (where health means physical or mental health' and development means 'physical, intellectual, emotional, social or behavioural development');
- ensuring that children are growing up in circumstances consistent with the provision of safe and effective care; and

---

[22] *R (NXT & Ors) v Secretary of State for the Home Department* [2011] EWHC 969 (Admin) at [100].

[23] *R (Suppiah) v Secretary of State for the Home Department & Another* [2011] EWHC 2469 (Admin) at [201].

[24] *R (AA (Afghanistan)) v Secretary of State for the Home Department* [2013] UKSC 49; [2013] 1 WLR 2224, *Per* Lord Toulson, at [44].

[25] *Cf. R (Suppiah) v Secretary of State for the Home Department & Another* [2011] EWHC 2469 (Admin) at [166], [201].

[26] [2011] EWHC 338 (Admin), at [101].

[27] Introduction, paragraph 6.

[28] Introduction, paragraph 7.

- undertaking that role so as to enable those children to have optimum life chances and to enter adulthood successfully.

The duty in section 55 should be construed as encompassing each of these points.[29] **12.11** 'Promoting' a child's welfare is a different concept to 'safeguarding' his or her welfare.[30]

Part 2 of *Every Child Matters* sets out how the general arrangements identified in **12.12** Part 1 apply to what was the UK Border Agency.[31] The following principles, *inter alia*, are set out:[32]

(1) In accordance with the UNCRC the best interests of the child will be a primary consideration (although not necessarily the only consideration) when making decisions affecting children.
(2) Ethnic identity, language, religion, faith, gender, and disability are taken into account when working with a child and their family.
(3) Children should be consulted and the wishes and feelings of children taken into account wherever practicable when decisions affecting them are made, even though it will not always be possible to reach decisions with which the child will agree. In instances where parents and carers are present they will have primary responsibility for the children's concerns.

The secion 55 duty must be taken into account when new policies are developed. **12.13** Where appropriate, new operational and policy instructions should make reference to the duty and how it is to be taken into account.[33]

(4) Children's champion

The Home Office has a 'children's champion', who is responsible for: **12.14**

(1) promoting the section 55 duty;
(2) offering advice and support to staff on issues related to children; and
(3) identifying and escalating issues of concern.

Instructions to caseworkers in the policy document *Introduction to children and* **12.15** *family cases*[34] give guidance on a range of child welfare matters to be considered before a referral is made to the Office of the Children's Champion ('OCC'),[35] the

---

[29] *R (TS) v Secretary of State for the Home Department* [2010] EWHC 2614 (Admin), *per* Wyn Williams J at [29].
[30] *R (TS)* at [29].
[31] Now the Border Force, UK Visas and Immigration and, of most relevance for present purposes, Immigration Enforcement.
[32] Paragraph 2.7.
[33] Paragraph 2.13.
[34] *Modernised Guidance, Criminal Casework*, version 9.0, 24 January 2014.
[35] *Factors to consider before you request an OCC referral*, p 17.

circumstances in which a referral should be made,[36] and how to make a referral. Referrals should be made, *inter alia*, in cases that involve separating a family with a child, and the detention of a child. Where a referral to the OCC is made, its advice must be taken into account alongside all other relevant factors.[37]

12.16   In *R (Abdollahi) v Secretary of State for the Home Department*,[38] Beatson J held that a failure to consult the OCC before deciding to authorize the detention of the claimant, the father of three children, on his completing a term of imprisonment was an error of law which rendered detention unlawful (albeit on the facts, Mr Abdollahi failed to establish a claim to more than nominal damages).

(5) The family welfare form

12.17   The family welfare form ('FWF')[39] is an important record and safeguard in all cases involving families. It is the basis upon which key operational decisions including job-specific risk assessments are made in each family case. It is also used as part of the referral process to the Independent Family Returns Panel ('IRFP') in 'ensured return' cases.[40] Guidance on the completion of the FWF in Criminal Casework cases is set out in *Deportation of family members of foreign national offenders.*[41]

12.18   An FWF must be opened by Home Office staff on the first contact with a family then fully updated following each interaction.[42] It is important that an FWF is included on each family case file from the start of each family claim, and that the information in the FWF is detailed, fully accurate, and regularly updated with any changes to the family's circumstances.[43]

12.19   Any evidence of child welfare concerns, medical issues, or non-compliance recorded in the FWF will inform key operational decisions regarding the family, including planning their return. This information is also crucial for the IFRP to consider whether the case should proceed to the ensured return route.[44] The guidance on the FWF '*must* be followed'.[45]

12.20   In *R (Suppiah) v Secretary of State for the Home Department*[46] failure to complete an FWF was described as 'a significant breach of policy', and was held to be evidence

---

[36]   Page 21.
[37]   Page 22.
[38]   [2012] EWHC 878 (Admin) at [60].
[39]   Form ICD 3629, a template of which is annexed to EIG 45(b).
[40]   Asylum Process Instruction, *Processing Family Cases*, 1 March 2011, Section 3.2; EIG 45(b), Section 1.2. For the IFRP see paragraphs 12.68–12.69. For ensured return see paragraphs 12.64–12.66.
[41]   *Modernised Guidance, Criminal Casework* v9.0, January 2014, p 23.
[42]   EIG 45(b), Section 1.2.
[43]   *Processing Family Cases*, Section 3.2.
[44]   *Processing Family Cases*, Section 3.2.
[45]   *Processing Family Cases*, Section 3.2.
[46]   [2011] EWHC 2 (Admin).

that 'important parts of the policy and important material considerations were not considered either properly or at all',[47] contributing to a conclusion that detention of a family was unlawful. In *R (N) v Secretary of State for the Home Department*[48] a failure to prepare an FWF was held to be a material error of law bearing on the decision to detain, so rendering detention unlawful.[49]

C. Unaccompanied Children

(1) General policy

The Secretary of State's main policy guidance on the approach to the detention **12.21** of unaccompanied children and age disputed young people is in section 55.9.3 of EIG 55,[50] *Unaccompanied young persons.*

EIG 55.9.3 begins by asserting a strong presumption against the detention of **12.22** children:

> As a general principle, even where one of the statutory powers to detain is available in a particular case, unaccompanied children (that is, persons under the age of 18) must not be detained other than in very exceptional circumstances.[51]

Where 'very exceptional circumstances' arise, and unaccompanied children **12.23** are detained it should be 'for the shortest possible time, with appropriate care'. This may include detention overnight but a person detained as an unaccompanied child 'must not be held in an immigration removal centre in any circumstances'.

This guidance also applies in age dispute cases where the person concerned is being **12.24** treated as a child.[52]

(2) Very exceptional circumstances

Detention of unaccompanied children is permitted in 'very exceptional cir- **12.25** cumstances'. In contrast to the guidance on other categories of person who may only be detained in 'very exceptional circumstances', EIG 55.9.3 includes exhaustive definitions of the circumstances in which detention will be permitted.

---

[47] *Per* Wyn Williams J at [175].
[48] [2012] EWHC 1031 (Admin).
[49] Albeit on the facts only nominal damages were payable; see at [17]–[24].
[50] At the time of writing the current version is EIG 55, Version 18.3, 1 May 2014.
[51] Until the promulgation of EIG 55, version 18 on 27 August 2013, Home Office policy was that unaccompanied children 'must only ever be detained in *the most* exceptional circumstances...'
[52] See further paragraph 12.32.

(a) Alternative arrangements for care and safety (EIG 55.9.3A)

12.26   EIG 55.9.3A provides for the detention of unaccompanied children solely in 'unexpected situations where it is necessary . . . very briefly for their care and safety pending alternative arrangements being made'. Examples given include collection by parents, relatives, carers, friends, or local authority children's services ('LACS'). Efforts to secure alternative care arrangements in such cases should be made expeditiously.

(b)   Criminal casework cases (EIG 55.9.3B)

12.27   EIG 55.9.3B permits the detention of unaccompanied children in Criminal Casework cases 'where it can be shown that the [Foreign National Offender ('FNO')] poses a serious risk to the public and a decision to deport or remove has been taken'.[53] Detention is subject to ministerial authorization and the advice of the IRFP in respect of safeguarding matters.[54]

12.28   If Immigration Enforcement Criminal Casework considers a child FNO needs to be detained on completion of sentence a recommendation must be prepared after consultation with (i) immigration safeguarding coordinators and (ii) the OCC,[55] and a referral made to the IFRP before ministerial authority is sought.[56]

12.29   Unaccompanied FNOs under 18 who are facing deportation or removal may depart voluntarily under the early release scheme ('ERS') (if still serving a sentence) or otherwise. Should they not do so, Home Office policy envisages the three routes within the FRP,[57] 'voluntary', 'assisted', and 'required' return, being utilized.[58]

(c)   Returns (EIG 55.9.3C)

12.30   EIG 55.9.3C provides that unaccompanied children who are being removed may be detained in order to support their removal with appropriate escorts.[59] Such detention 'will occur only on the day of the planned removal to enable the child to be properly and safely escorted to their flight and/or to their destination'.

---

[53] See further *Review into ending the detention of children for immigration purposes,* December 2010, paragraph 5.15.

[54] For the IFRP see paragraphs 12.68–12.69.

[55] See paragraphs 12.14 to 12.16.

[56] *Detention of families,* p 11.

[57] See paragraphs 12.54–12.87.

[58] *Modernised Guidance, Criminal Casework, Managing foreign national offenders under 18 years old,* Draft, Version 0.7, 29 May 2013, p 48. NB: in non-Criminal Casework cases the removal of unaccompanied children is subject to procedures outside the FRP; see paragraph 12.54, fn 88.

[59] Further detail of the procedure adopted for the return of unaccompanied minors is set out in EIG 45(c), Section 3.2.

(3) Age dispute cases

The exercise of detention powers in disputed age cases is subject to the policy guidance in EIG 55.9.3.1. In both asylum and non-asylum cases this 'must be read in conjunction with' the Assessing Age Asylum Instruction ('*Assessing Age*').[60]   **12.31**

The starting point[61] when detention is under consideration in a disputed age case is that where an individual claims to be a child the Secretary of State will treat that person as a child (and so he or she will benefit from the very strong presumption against detention in EIG 55.9.3) unless: **12.32**

(1) there is 'credible and clear' documentary evidence that the person is over eighteen;

(2) a '*Merton* compliant' age assessment by a local authority 'is available' stating that they are 18 years of age or over;

(3) the person's appearance or demeanour suggests he or she is 'significantly' older than eighteen; or

(4) he or she has previously claimed to be an adult, and a number of other criteria are satisfied.[62]

The benefit of the protection afforded by EIG 55.9.3.1 does not extend to an individual who claims to be a child in detention if (a) he or she was previously sentenced by the criminal courts as an adult, and (b) there is no credible evidence to support their claim to be a child.   **12.33**

(a) Documentary evidence

EIG 55.9.3.1.A provides that, for detention purposes, the Secretary of State will treat an individual who is claiming to be a child as an adult where '[t]here is credible and clear documentary evidence that they are 18 or over'.   **12.34**

Assessing Age[63] gives guidance on the approach caseworkers should take when deciding whether to accept documentary evidence as proof of a person's claimed age. The guidance is directed to evidence advanced by an applicant to prove his or her age, but is of relevance insofar as it indicates the approach that will be taken to different categories of documentary evidence. If a particular type of document is considered insufficiently reliable to prove age when relied upon by an applicant, it is unlikely to amount to 'credible and clear' evidence to *disprove* age for the purposes of EIG 55.9.3.1.A. The problematic nature of apparently official documentation   **12.35**

---

[60] EIG 55.9.3.1. At the time of writing the current version of *Assessing Age* is version 6.0, dated 17 June 2011.

[61] See EIG 55.9.3.1.

[62] See paragraphs 12.49 to 12.50.

[63] Section 6, subsections 6.1 to 6.4.

from some countries is addressed in the Immigration Appeal Tribunal's decision in *Tanveer Ahmed v Secretary of State for the Home Department*.[64]

(b) Local authority age assessments

12.36 EIG 55.9.3.1.B provides that, for detention purposes, a young person who is claiming to be a child will be treated as an adult where a '*Merton* compliant' age assessment by a local authority 'is available' stating that he or she is 18 years of age or over.

12.37 **(i) A '*Merton* compliant' age assessment by a local authority** A local authority may be called upon to assess a person's age when considering whether he or she is entitled to assistance under Part III of the Children Act 1989 ('CA 1989'). This most commonly occurs with young asylum seekers who claim to be children but who lack proof of age and/or whose claimed age is disbelieved by the Home Office.

12.38 There is no proven method for the accurate assessment of age. The position of the Royal College of Paediatrics and Child Health is that 'age determination is extremely difficult to do with certainty . . . no single approach to this can be relied on . . . the margin of error can sometimes be as much as 5 years either side'.[65]

12.39 A '*Merton* compliant' age assessment is an assessment of age carried out by a local authority social services department in accordance with the guidance given by Stanley Burnton J in *R (B) v Merton LBC*, and refined in subsequent authority. The guidance was summarized in *R (FZ) v Croydon London Borough Council*[66] in the following terms:

> The assessment does not require anything approaching a trial and judicialisation of the process is to be avoided. The matter can be determined informally provided that there are minimum standards of inquiry and fairness. Except in clear cases, age cannot be determined solely from appearance. The decision-maker should explain to the young person the purpose of the interview. Questions should elicit background, family and educational circumstances and history, and ethnic and cultural matters may be relevant. The decision-maker may have to assess the applicant's credibility. Questions of the burden of proof do not apply. The local authority should make its own decision and not simply adopt a decision made, for instance, by the Home Office, if there has been a referral. It is not necessary to obtain a medical report, although paediatric expert evidence is sometimes provided in these cases, and there is some difference of view as to its persuasiveness in borderline cases. If the decision-maker forms a view that the young person may be lying, he should be given the opportunity to address the matters that may lead to that view. Adverse provisional conclusions should be put to him, so that he may have the opportunity to deal with them and rectify misunderstandings. The local authority is obliged to give reasons for its decision, although these need not be long or elaborate.

---

[64] [2002] UKIAT 439; [2002] Imm AR 318 at [31].
[65] Cited in *R (B) v Merton LBC* [2003] EWHC 1689 Admin at [22].
[66] [2011] EWCA Civ 59; [2011] PTSR 748 at [3].

In *FZ* the Court of Appeal confirmed two further preconditions for a *Merton* compliant assessment: **12.40**

(1) an applicant should be given a fair and proper opportunity, at a stage when a possible adverse decision is no more than provisional, to deal with important points adverse to his age case which may weigh against him; and[67]

(2) the young person being assessed should have the opportunity to have an appropriate adult present.[68]

(ii) '*. . . is available*' The requirement in EIG 55.9.3.1.B that a *Merton* compliant **12.41** assessment be 'available' raises the question of the steps the Secretary of State must take to satisfy herself of this. The prevailing approach is that of Coulson J in *R (J) v Secretary of State for the Home Department*,[69] adopted and approved by Lang J in *R(AAM (A Child)) v Secretary of State for the Home Department*:[70]

(1) There is 'an independent obligation' on the relevant official to consider the assessment and to reach his or her own conclusion as to whether it is *Merton* compliant.[71] The relevant Home Office official cannot assume that an age assessment conducted by a local authority is *Merton* compliant. He or she is expected to 'carry out an evaluation of the age assessment and satisfy [him- or herself] both that it is *Merton*-compliant and that its conclusion on age is reliable . . .'[72]

(2) The official's conclusion is subject to the supervisory jurisdiction of the court 'on traditional public law grounds'. Whether an assessment is *Merton* compliant is not an objective fact on which there can only be one correct answer. The official must make a judgment on whether the assessment is *Merton* compliant. This is a question upon which views may differ,[73] albeit that in some cases there will only be room for one view.[74]

---

[67] At [21].

[68] At [23] to [25].

[69] [2011] EWHC 3073 (Admin) at [31]–[32].

[70] [2012] EWHC 2567 (QB) at [110]–[111]. The judgment in *AAM* was considered by the Supreme Court in *R (AA (Afghanistan)) v Secretary of State for the Home Department* [2013] UKSC 49; [2013] 1 WLR 2224. One unrelated aspect of Lang J's reasoning was criticized, but Lord Toulson held that she had come to the right conclusion on the facts, and there was no criticism of her approach to the policy in EIG 55.9.3.1: see at [28]–[38], and [50]. A similar approach was adopted in *Durani v Secretary of State for Home Department & Anor* [2013] EWHC 284 (Admin) at [90] and in *HXT v Secretary of State for the Home Department* [2013] EWHC 1962 (QB) at [18].

[71] *R (J)* at [31].

[72] *AAM* at [107]–[108]. *Assessing Age*, at Section 5, includes guidance on what constitutes '*Merton* compliance' and the steps caseworkers should take to satisfy themselves of this. It envisages, at 5.3, that in some cases a local authority may be reluctant to provide a complete copy of the assessment and sets out the approach to follow where this occurs.

[73] *AAM* at [110].

[74] As was the case in *R (J)* itself; see at [18].

12.42   On this approach, a failure by an official to consider whether an age assessment was *Merton* compliant before deciding to detain, or a decision that an age assessment was *Merton* compliant which was not reasonably open to the decision maker, would be a material error of law which rendered detention unlawful.

12.43   The weight of current authority supports this approach and in our view it is clearly correct. However, there is at least one reported case in which the court takes a different approach. In *R (Hossein) v Secretary of State for the Home Department and Kent County Council*,[75] Collins J said that where detention was authorized on the basis that an age assessment was *Merton* compliant without the authorizing official having seen the assessment, there was not 'automatically' a breach of the guidance.[76]

12.44   **(iii) Challenges to local authority age assessments**   In *A v Croydon*[77] the Supreme Court ruled that, for the purposes of providing support under Part III of CA 1989, whether a young person is a child is not a matter of judgment within the discretion of the authority but a question of precedent or jurisdictional fact which, on an application for judicial review, the Court was required to determine for itself. Although this did not render the *Merton* principles redundant, the consequence of the decision in *A* was that most age assessment challenges brought against local authorities are now trials of fact on the issue of age rather than public law challenges to the authority's assessment.[78]

12.45   Where the Court does rule on age, the finding binds the local authority but does not bind the Home Office. However, in *R (AA (Afghanistan)) v Secretary of State for the Home Department*,[79] Lord Toulson observed that:

> [a]n asylum claimant who gives his age as under 18 is in practice likely also to be a claimant for local authority support under the Children Act. For both purposes there will be an age assessment by the social services department in any case of doubt. If the claimant is assessed as being over 18 and is also detained . . . any legal challenge is likely to be, as in this case, against both the local authority and the Secretary of State. In such a case the court would have jurisdiction under [*A v Croydon*] to determine the question of age as a primary fact finder under the Children Act. Its conclusion—if in the claimant's favour—would obviously affect the Secretary of State's future action under the Immigration Acts. It would give rise to a new situation and the Secretary of State could no longer properly rely on the accuracy of an age assessment which had been discredited by a judgment of a court.

---

[75] [2011] EWHC 1924 (Admin); a permission decision pre-dating *R(J)*.

[76] At [22]. *Cf. Safi v Secretary of State for the Home Department* [2013] EWHC 1619 (Admin) at [31]–[32] (under appeal at the time of writing).

[77] [2009] UKSC 8; [2009] 1 WLR 2557.

[78] In *R (Kadri & Ors) v Birmingham City Council* [2012] EWCA Civ 1432; [2013] 1 WLR 1755 at [28] the Master of the Rolls said that where an age assessment is challenged both on the facts and on orthodox public law grounds, 'it will be better for the court to decide all issues in one hearing, or transfer the case to the UT [Upper Tribunal] for that purpose'.

[79] [2013] UKSC 49; [2013] 1 WLR 2224 at [51].

(c) Appearance and demeanour

The Secretary of State will treat an individual who is claiming to be a child as an **12.46** adult where '[t]heir physical appearance/demeanour very strongly suggests that they are significantly over 18 year of age and no other credible evidence exists to the contrary'.

In such cases, 'the assessing officer's countersigning officer (who is at least a Chief **12.47** Immigration Officer (CIO) or Higher Executive Officer (HEO) must be consulted to act as a "second pair of eyes". They must make their own assessment of the individual's age.'

The threshold for a putative child to be treated as an adult in the absence of a **12.48** *Merton* compliant assessment or 'credible and clear' documentary evidence of age is very high. These provisions, bearing as they do on the individual's liberty, will be strictly and narrowly construed by the courts. A purported assessment which, for example, was not subject to the 'second pair of eyes' procedure (which is an evidential safeguard, not a mere administrative formality) would not be a lawful basis for detaining an age disputed young person. Reliance upon such a flawed assessment when detaining would in our view be likely to be held to be a material error of law rendering detention unlawful.

(d) Prior claim to be an adult

Since November 2012[80] EIG 55.9.3.1 has included a fourth scenario in which a **12.49** failed asylum seeker claiming to be a child will be treated as an adult. Seven separate criteria must be satisfied before this can be relied on. It must be the case that the individual:

(1) prior to detention, gave a date of birth that would make them an adult and/ or stated they were an adult;
(2) only claimed to be a child *after* a decision had been taken on their asylum claim;
(3) only claimed to be a child *after* they had been detained;
(4) has not provided credible and clear documentary evidence proving their claimed age;
(5) does not have a *Merton* compliant age assessment stating they are a child;
(6) does not have an unchallenged court finding indicating that they are a child; and
(7) his or her physical appearance/demeanour very strongly suggests that they are 18 years of age or over.[81]

---

[80] This provision appeared for the first time in EIG 55, Version 16, promulgated on 14 November 2012.

[81] This is a lower threshold than is applied under the 'appearance and demeanour' head, which requires that the appearance and demeanour of the person whose age is in issue suggests that they are '*significantly* over 18 years of age'.

12.50 The assessing officer's countersigning officer must be consulted to act as a 'second pair of eyes' in relation to the final point. Again, in our view, these provisions will be subject to a strict and narrow interpretation by the courts, and errors of law in a decision purportedly taken by reference to these provisions, which would include failing to follow the terms of the guidance without good reason, are likely to be held to be material to the decision to detain, so rendering detention unlawful.

(e) New evidence of age

12.51 In all cases, if the Home Office receives potentially material new evidence, the relevant official should 'promptly review any previous decision to treat an individual as an adult'. Any failure to do so is likely to be a material public law error rendering detention unlawful.

(f) Tribunal findings

12.52 Judicial findings on age may also arise in the context of immigration or asylum appeals. In such proceedings the Secretary of State is a party and, whilst not bound as a matter of law by specific factual findings, is unlikely to be able rationally to depart from them in the absence of further evidence calling them into question.[82] Difficult issues may arise where the decision of the High Court or Upper Tribunal on age in a judicial review of a local authority assessment is at odds with the findings of the Tribunal in an immigration appeal.[83]

(g) Habeas corpus and the role of the court as primary fact-finder

12.53 On the law as it stands, age is not a precedent or jurisdictional fact for the exercise of detention powers under the Immigration Acts.[84] In *AA* Lord Toulson suggested, *obiter*, that in the context of a challenge to detention, the Court may have the power to rule on a person's age as a matter of fact.[85] He was, he said, 'sympathetic to the view that the Court's habeas corpus jurisdiction in this type of situation should not be confined to determining whether the Secretary of State had acted lawfully in the detention of the claimant, but should extend to enable the court to make a

---

[82] See *Secretary of State for the Home Department v Danaie* [1997] EWCA Civ 2704; [1998] Imm AR 84.

[83] See *Safi v Secretary of State for the Home Department* [2013] EWHC 1619 (Admin) (under appeal at the time of writing), in which the Secretary of State maintained her reliance upon the Tribunal's finding in an immigration appeal that the claimant was an adult even after judicial review proceedings against a local authority had been compromised upon that authority accepting the claimant was a child.

[84] N.B.: When the amendments to Schedule 2 of IA 1971 which are to be made by section 5 of IA 2014 come into force age will be a statutorily defined limiting factor to detention in some circumstances; see paragraph 12.04. In those circumstances it may be arguable that age is a precedent fact to be determined by the Court as it is in the context of Part III of CA 1989 following *A v Croydon*; see paragraph 12.44.

[85] At [52]–[53].

fresh determination of the claimant's age, which would necessarily impact on the lawfulness of his continued detention'.[86]

D. The Family Returns Process

(1) General

The Family Returns Process ('FRP') is the name given to the various 'routes to departure'[87] intended to ensure that families with dependent children, who face removal or deportation from the United Kingdom, depart without being detained or, in exceptional cases, with only very limited use of detention powers.[88] It was instituted following the *Review into Ending the Detention of Children for Immigration Purposes* which reported in December 2010.[89] **12.54**

Families enter the FRP where there are no remaining legal barriers to removal, and any practical obstacles can be resolved in parallel with the returns process, or where the family has indicated a wish to leave the UK.[90] **12.55**

The full scheme of the FRP is detailed in EIG Chapter 45, Section (b), with further guidance specific to Criminal Casework cases set out in *Managing the return of families with children*.[91] There are three routes to departure: **12.56**

(1) Assisted return: encouraging and assisting the family to return voluntarily, whether through a formal voluntary return scheme or otherwise.
(2) Required return: return by way of 'self-check in removal directions' ('SCI RDs').
(3) Ensured return: where assisted and required return fail or are considered unsuitable there are five mechanisms for removal operated under the 'ensured return' rubric, all of which involve the use of detention to at least a limited degree at the point of removal.[92]

---

[86] Lords Neuberger, Clarke and Wilson agreed with Lord Toulson and gave no separate judgments. Lord Carnwath, at [56], expressed reservations.

[87] EIG 45(b), Section 2.2.3.

[88] In non-Criminal Casework cases the FRP is not used where unaccompanied minors face removal from the United Kingdom. Separate provision for such cases is made in EIG 45(c) ('Operational process outside of the FRP'), Section 3. For the position in Criminal Casework cases see paragraph 12.29. The detention of unaccompanied minors generally is considered at paragraphs 12.21–12.53.

[89] See paragraph 12.02. It has been fully in effect since 1 March 2011.

[90] See further EIG 45(b), paragraph 1.01.

[91] *Modernised Guidance, Criminal Casework*, Version 6.0, 11 November 2013.

[92] See paragraphs 12.64–12.83.

(2) The Family Returns Process and legality of detention

12.57 The FRP is intended to ensure that families with children are not detained for the purpose of removal save in exceptional circumstances. Where detention powers are used, their use is strictly curtailed in a number of ways, including the procedure by which detention is authorized, the duration of detention, the place of detention, and the level of authority required for detention.

12.58 Where a family that falls within the ambit of the FRP is detained, it is in our view likely that failures to comply with the policy guidance on the operation of the FRP will amount to material errors of law bearing on the decision to detain, and so render detention unlawful. There are, to date, no decided cases on this issue. However, we consider it likely that the following, *inter alia*, would be found to render detention unlawful:

(1) a failure without good reason to utilize the assisted and/or required returns route before instigating ensured return;

(2) failure to consult as required by the published policies with the IFRP;

(3) factual misdirection in a return plan which impacted upon the decision to authorize detention; and

(4) detaining for periods in excess of those set down in the policy guidance.

(3) The family welfare form

12.59 Where a case proceeds to the ensured return route within the FRP a 'return plan' must be presented to the IFRP[93] to seek authority for the chosen means of return. The return plan is included in section 6 of the FWF.[94]

(4) New mothers

12.60 New mothers who are to be removed with their children fall within the FRP.[95] There is no discretion in the policy to separate a nursing mother from her child; they must not be separated.[96] Guidance on 'Mother and Baby' cases in the context of Criminal Casework is given in *Detention of families*.

(5) Criminal Casework cases

12.61 Criminal Casework cases fall within the FRP, but such cases are subject to the further guidance in *Managing the return of families with children*.[97] If the FNO is living in the community the FRP will be the usual process.[98] Where the FNO is detained and a

---

[93] For the IFRP see paragraphs 12.68–12.69.

[94] EIG 45(b), Section 4.1. For the Family Welfare Form, see further at paragraphs 12.17–12.20.

[95] EIG 45(a), Section 10.4.

[96] EIG 45(b), Section 8.

[97] Page 2.

[98] *Managing the return of families with children*, p 10.

family declines voluntary return, required return may be the appropriate route for the non-detained family members whilst the FNO him- or herself is subject to ensured return.[99] In exceptional cases it may be appropriate to apply the ensured returns route to the entire family without first attempting the required return route.[100] In any case of ensured return Criminal Casework must seek the advice of the IFRP.[101]

(6) Assisted return

The first, and least intrusive, route of return under the FRP is 'assisted return'.[102] Assisted return is centred on a 'family returns conference' at which the family can consider their options for returning home. The options will be either to return voluntarily under assisted voluntary return ('AVR'),[103] where appropriate, or to return voluntarily without utilizing AVR.

12.62

(7) Required return

Where a family will not return voluntarily the 'required return' process is used. This involves 'self check-in removal directions' ('SCI RDs') being set.[104] SCI RDs are served at least two weeks prior to the scheduled return.[105] If a family which is subject to required return fails to depart in any of the circumstances identified in EIG 45(b), Section 3.2, the case will progress to the 'ensured return' route.

12.63

(8) Ensured return

(a) General

Ensured return, the most intrusive route of return within the FRP, encompasses five discrete mechanisms.[106] These are addressed at paragraphs 12.71–12.83.

12.64

Ensured return is used (a) where assisted and required return have failed; or (b) where assisted or required return are considered inappropriate, either (i) because the family has refused to cooperate with assisted or required return, or (ii) 'exceptionally' where a member of the family poses a high risk to themselves or others.[107]

12.65

Where, under the ensured return process, it is proposed to detain a child with his or her parents or guardians the caseworker must actively search for any information

12.66

---

[99] *Managing the return of families with children,* p 13.
[100] *Managing the return of families with children,* p 13.
[101] *Managing the return of families with children,* p 10. For ensured return see paragraphs 12.64–12.83.
[102] EIG 45(b), Section 2.
[103] See *Modernised Guidance, Assisted Voluntary Return* for details of the three AVR programmes currently in operation.
[104] EIG 45(b), Section 3.
[105] EIG 45(b), Section 3.
[106] EIG 45(b), Section 4.
[107] EIG 45(b), Section 4.

relevant to the requirement to have regard to the need to safeguard and promote the child's welfare.[108] Such a search is likely to involve a request for information from the relevant local authority children's services ('LACS') and primary care trust ('PCT').[109]

(b) The return plan

12.67 Where ensured return is chosen a decision must be taken as to which of the five options are suitable. The proposed mechanism of return will be presented as a 'return plan'[110] to the IFRP for consideration.[111] The return plan must, *inter alia*, explain the choice made; demonstrate how the duties arising under section 55 of BCIA 2009 are met, and stipulate how the welfare needs of each family member will be managed throughout the return.[112] It also includes further practical details about the management of the removal.

(c) The Independent Family Returns Panel

12.68 Ensured return is conducted with oversight by the IFRP.[113] The IFRP advises on the method of removal for individual families to help ensure compliance with section 55 of BCIA 2009. It also advises on safeguarding issues in cases involving the detention of unaccompanied child offenders on completion of sentence pending deportation or removal.[114]

12.69 No action may be taken to pursue ensured return until advice has been obtained from the IFRP. There is a presumption that the advice will be accepted. If it is considered unfeasible there must be further liaison and a new return plan submitted. In exceptional circumstances, the views of the panel may be overridden by the Immigration Minister. The panel will report publicly on any case in which its advice is not accepted.[115]

(d) Pre-departure accommodation

12.70 The last and most intrusive ensured return option involves a brief period of detention in what is termed 'pre-departure accommodation'.[116] Overnight detention in

---

[108] EIG 55.6.1, detailing completion of Risk Assessment Form IS91RA.

[109] EIG 55.6.1.

[110] In the FWF.

[111] EIG 45(b), Section 4.1.

[112] EIG 45(b), Section 4.2.

[113] At the time of writing the IFRP is a creation of policy. However, when section 3 of IA 2014 comes into force it will insert a new section 54A into BCIA 2009 which will place the IFRP on a statutory footing.

[114] See EIG 55.9.3B.

[115] EIG 45(b), Section 4.3.

[116] At the time of writing 'pre-departure accommodation' is a creation of policy, which in law is a short term holding facility (as to which, see Chapter 17, paragraphs 17.47–17.48). When pending amendments to the IAA 1999 come into force it will acquire a distinct legal identity; see further paragraph 12.4.

pre-departure accommodation is also possible as part of all three escorted check-in options.[117] The only pre-departure accommodation facility is Cedars in Crawley. Cedars is described as 'a secure facility which respects the privacy and independence of children and their families'.[118] It can accommodate up to nine families at a time in self-contained apartments.

(e) *The five ensured return mechanisms*

Within the ensured return route there are five separate mechanisms for removal.[119] **12.71**

(i) Escorted check-in without further notice If a family fails to comply with **12.72**
SCI RDs with no acceptable explanation they can be removed from the United Kingdom without further notice within ten working days of the failed removal.[120] The family will be arrested and transported to a designated place of detention from where they will be transferred to the escorting contractors. Arrest will be on the day of removal unless 'additional support' is required, in which case it may occur the previous day with the family held overnight in pre-departure accommodation.

(ii) Escorted check-in with further full notice This option involves serving **12.73**
removal directions on the family at least 72 hours in advance of the planned removal. The family will be arrested on the day of the proposed removal or, if 'additional support' is required, the day before, with detention overnight in pre-departure accommodation.[121]

(iii) Escorted check-in with limited notice This option allows the family to be **12.74**
informed that their departure will take place within a specified period, but not the exact date. This period cannot be less than 72 hours or more than 21 days from notification. The family will be arrested on the day of the proposed removal or, if 'additional support' is required, the day before, with detention overnight in pre-departure accommodation. This mechanism must not be used where immigration enforcement has been advised by a medical professional or children's/adult services that it will create a risk of suicide or self-harm.[122]

(iv) Return via open accommodation This option is only available to failed **12.75**
asylum seeking families who are supported under section 95 or section 4 of IAA 1999.[123] It cannot be used where a family member is subject to Multi Agency Public Protection Arrangements (MAPPA cases) or it is precluded on medical grounds.[124]

---

[117] See paragraphs 12.72–12.74.
[118] UK Visas and Immigration Guidance, *Cedars pre-departure accommodation information*, 28 February 2014.
[119] EIG 45(b), Section 4.6.
[120] EIG 45(b), Section 4.6.1.
[121] EIG 45(b), Section 4.6.2.
[122] EIG 45(b), Section 4.6.3.
[123] EIG 45(b), Section 4.7.
[124] EIG 45(b), Section 4.7.1.

It involves moving the family to full board residential accommodation, without cash support. It does not involve arrest or detention until the time of removal. Departure should be within 72 hours of arrival at the accommodation. If the departure fails the family can be returned to the accommodation, but must not remain there for more than 28 days from the date of arrival. Removal directions are to be served on the day of the move.[125] On the day of removal the family are arrested at the open accommodation and transferred to the escorting contractor for travel to the port of departure.[126]

12.76 **(v) Return via pre-departure accommodation** This is the most intrusive mechanism of ensured return, and involves a brief period of detention in Cedars, the 'pre-departure accommodation' operated by immigration enforcement.[127] It is a 'last resort'.[128]

12.77 Cedars is intended to accommodate families who have refused to cooperate with other return options, or for whom other return options are not suitable. It cannot be used to accommodate individuals who are serving a criminal sentence and are leaving under the early removals scheme ('ERS'), or who may present a risk to the public if they abscond and/or to staff/residents at Cedars. In such cases, caseworkers are advised to consider temporarily separating the family, detaining the individual who presents a risk in an immigration removal centre and accommodating the rest of the family in pre-departure accommodation.[129]

12.78 On 'rare occasions' a family may be detained together at Tinsley House IRC where they present risks which make the use of pre-departure accommodation inappropriate'.[130] The same time limits as for Cedars apply.[131] This can only take place following advice from the IFRP and requires ministerial authorization.[132]

12.79 Families can only be admitted to Cedars when removal directions have been set and all travel documentation is in place. The period of stay should be as limited as possible and will not normally exceed 72 hours, but can be extended to seven days with ministerial authorization. If a family reaches 72 hours in Cedars and ministerial authority is not in place the family must be released.[133]

12.80 If it is known in advance that the family needs to be accommodated for longer than 72 hours ministerial authority must be in place before the family enters Cedars.[134]

---

125 EIG 44(b), Section 4.7.3.
126 EIG 44(b), Section 4.7.5.
127 See paragraph 12.70.
128 EIG 45(b), Section 5.
129 EIG 45(b), Section 5.
130 EIG 45(b), Section 5; EIG 55.9.4.
131 EIG 55.9.4.
132 EIG 45(b), Section 5; EIG 55.9.4.
133 EIG 45(b), Section 5.1. When section 6 of IA 2014, which amends section 147 of IAA 1999, comes into force these time limits will have a statutory footing.
134 EIG 45(b), Section 5.2.

Where a first attempt at return fails or it is believed the scheduled return will fail, **12.81**
and a further set of removal directions can be secured without detention in Cedars
exceeding seven days in total, ministerial authority must be sought if detention
is to continue.[135] This is only permissible where it has been included as a contingency in the return plan. Advice received from the IFRP must be included in the
request for authorization, which must be obtained within 18 hours of a family's
failed return or within 72 hours of the family originally entering Cedars, whichever time period is the greatest. Detention operations duty director authority must
be obtained for a family to re-enter Cedars under these circumstances, pending
ministerial authority.

There is no provision to hold a family for longer than seven days in any **12.82**
circumstances.[136]

Pre-departure accommodation can be used again following a family's release from **12.83**
Cedars, provided that the failed return was not as a result of a procedural error
made by the Home Office or one of its contractors and it continues to be the most
suitable option for the family's return.[137]

(9) Separation of families in the FRP

During the FRP the aim is to ensure that the family remains together. However, **12.84**
temporary separation may be considered where there is potential for an ensured
return to fail as a result of disruptive behaviour by the family, and it is considered
in the best interests of the children to be temporarily separated from their parent(s)
in order to safely ensure the family's arrest and return.[138]

In such cases, consideration must be given to which parent is the most suitable **12.85**
to care for the children, taking into account all information about the family,
particularly any known safeguarding issues. All proposed separations must be for
as short a time as possible and the family must be informed why the separation is
necessary, as well as when, where, and under what circumstances they can expect
to be reunited.[139]

A child must not be separated from both adults for immigration purposes or from **12.86**
one in the case of a single-parent family if the consequence of that decision is that
the child is taken into care. Nursing mothers must not be separated from their
babies.[140]

---

[135] EIG 45(b), Section 5.2.
[136] EIG 45(b), Section 5.1.
[137] EIG 45(b), Section 5.3.
[138] EIG 45(b), Section 8.
[139] EIG 45(b), Section 8.
[140] EIG 45(b), Section 8.

(10) Cases outside the FRP

12.87 EIG 55.9.4 identifies two scenarios in which a family unit including a child might be detained which fall outside the ambit of the FRP:

(1) Where a mother and baby are being removed from a prison mother and baby unit during the early release scheme period, detention overnight in Tinsley House may be authorized, where transfer direct from the prison to the airport is not practical or desirable.[141]

(2) Second, in certain limited circumstances, where after reuniting a single parent deportee with their child at the airport for removal, either straight from prison custody or immigration detention, the removal does not proceed, a decision is taken to maintain the detention of the adult, and the child cannot be returned to the care of the person who had been looking after him or her in the parent's absence, the family unit at Tinsley House may be used to accommodate the parent and child until alternative, community-based arrangements for the care of the child are made.[142] The same time limits as for pre-departure accommodation apply, but, in most cases, 'the aim should be for the child's stay to be for no more than one night'.

E. Detention that Separates Families

(1) General principles

12.88 The obligations considered at paragraphs 12.05–12.08 arising under Article 3 of UNCRC, Article 8 of ECHR, and section 55 of BCIA 1999 are engaged where the detention of an adult has the potential to impact upon the welfare of a child. They will be engaged where the detention of a child's primary carer or carers is contemplated.[143] They will also be engaged where the person facing detention is a parent with whom a child has contact but does not reside and, depending upon the facts, in cases involving adult siblings or extended family members involved in a child's care.

12.89 The approach to be taken in such cases is subject to extensive and very detailed policy guidance. In this chapter we can do no more than highlight key aspects of that guidance.

---

[141] EIG 55.9.4(2).

[142] EIG 55.9.4(3).

[143] In *R (Abdollahi) v Secretary of State for the Home Department* [2013] EWCA Civ 366 Moses LJ at [44] referred to the 'important but obvious' proposition that 'separation of children from their parents due to incarceration will have a major impact on the well-being and psychological health of the child'.

Where detention is authorized in such cases without compliance with the processes **12.90** and safeguards set out in the relevant policies it is likely to be unlawful as a result of a material public law error.

EIG 55.1.1 states that, over and above the general presumption of liberty applicable **12.91** to all cases 'special consideration' must be given to cases where it is proposed to detain one or more family member(s) and the family includes children under the age of 18. Any information concerning the children that is available 'or can reasonably be obtained' must be considered.[144]

Home Office policy recognizes that if there is a 'subsisting relationship' between **12.92** a parent and a child the best interests of the child 'will almost always be in the liberty of the parent, unless there are child protection concerns around the parent',[145] and that separating children from either of their parents, unless a local authority has formally assessed the parents as unable to care for the children, 'can have a profound and long term impact on the child'.[146] It has been held that 'it is both common sense and the case-law of the Strasbourg court that the links between a mother and her children of a tender age should be presumed to exist unless there [is] evidence that they had been severed'.[147]

(2) Criminal Casework cases: further guidance

The detention of adults who are part of a family unit that includes a child will most **12.93** often be encountered in Criminal Casework cases where the adult is an FNO facing deportation. The approach to Criminal Casework cases generally is considered in Chapter 10. In cases involving children decision makers are instructed to take the following further matters, *inter alia*, into account:

(1) Where a 'serious offender' has dependent children in the United Kingdom careful consideration must be given not only to the needs such children may have for contact with the deportee 'but also to the risk that release might represent to the family and the public'.[148]

(2) Absent child protection concerns, where there is a subsisting relationship between parent and child, the best interests of the child will almost always be in the liberty of the parent. In such cases caseworkers are instructed to consider whether there are 'lawful grounds' whereby the best interests of the child can be 'justifiably overridden'.[149]

---

[144] EIG 55.1.4.2.
[145] *Detention of families*, p 12.
[146] *Introduction to children and family cases*, p 17.
[147] *R (MXL) v Secretary of State for the Home Department* [2010] EWHC 2397 (Admin), *per* Blake J at [40].
[148] EIG 55.1.3.
[149] *Detention of families*, p 12.

(3) If detention is likely to result in a long separation that will have a significant adverse impact on a child, the FNO must be considered for release unless the risk of absconding and/or harm to the public is assessed as 'high'.[150]

(4) Immigration enforcement is committed to not detaining both parents at the same time, or a single parent, if that decision will result in a child being taken into care save in the most exceptional circumstances.[151]

(5) A decision to detain may be taken where a child is already in care or is being cared for by a parent or other relative in the community. However, if the only reason for this is the parent's detention, there are no child welfare concerns, and the local authority intend to reunite the family after release, continued detention of the parent is only likely to be suitable in cases where the risk to the public and/or risk of absconding are assessed to be 'very high'.[152]

(6) Where the child is being cared for by another family member, consideration should be given to whether that person is prepared to continue caring for the child.[153]

(7) In cases of dangerous offenders whose detention is considered to be appropriate caseworkers must show the steps they plan to take to mitigate the potential damage to the best interests of the children.[154]

(3) Criminal Casework cases: decision making process

12.94 It is 'vital' that all relevant factors bearing on the best interests of the children are considered both at the point of detention and at each subsequent review.[155] Direct and indirect impact must be considered.[156]

12.95 The instructions in *Introduction to children and family cases* are directed both to decisions to deport and consequential decisions to detain. Under *Overall approach and key partners*[157] caseworkers are told to actively consider the needs of children if detention and/or deportation means separating their family unit.[158] Contact should 'immediately' be established with the relevant LACS and, if relevant, Children and Family Court Advisory and Support Service ('CAFCASS'), to

---

[150] *Detention of families*, p 12.

[151] *Modernised Guidance, Criminal Casework, Separating families for deportation and detention purposes*, v.8.0, 24 January 2014 (*Separating families*), pages 8 and 18.

[152] *Separating families*, p 8.

[153] *Separating families*, p 8.

[154] *Detention of families*, p 12.

[155] *Detention of families*, p 13.

[156] *Introduction to children and family cases*, p 15: Direct impact 'includes the practical and emotional effects the decision may have on the child'. Indirect impact 'includes the effects of the decision on other family members, caregivers or the family's circumstances, which have onward effects on the child'.

[157] Page 10.

[158] Page 10. Separating a family unit includes maintaining the separation of a family unit by detention following an FNO's release date (*Detention of families*, p 7).

gather information.[159] If a child is being split from his or her parent or usual carer or the report indicates a more complex need caseworkers should consider seeking advice from the OCC.

Detention of families augments this guidance. If enquiries with the relevant LACS **12.96** reveal the involvement of other agencies such as Youth Offending Teams ('YOTs') or Child and Adult Mental Health Services ('CAAMHS'), caseworkers should seek further information about the children's circumstances directly from these sources.[160] Where a child is in care caseworkers must establish from the LACS whether there are child protection or safeguarding issues in relation to the parent and whether it is intended to reunite the child and parent upon the parent's release.[161]

(4) Considering children's circumstances

Detailed guidance on considering the circumstances of children impacted by a **12.97** decision to detain is given in *Detention of families*.

Caseworkers are instructed first to consider whether an FNO has parental respon- **12.98** sibility for a child by reference to the criteria identified under *Determining parental responsibility*.[162] This criteria could be read as suggesting that a child's relationship with an adult will only be relevant to a child's best interests and/or constitute family life for Article 8 purposes if, as a matter of law, the adult has parental responsibility for that child. However, such an approach would be unduly restrictive.[163]

If parental responsibility is established caseworkers are instructed to consider **12.99** whether there is a 'subsisting family relationship' by reference to the matters identified under *Considering children's circumstances*.[164] These focus on past, current, and planned future care arrangements, who has custody of the child, any special needs, the impact of continued separation (taking into account advice from the relevant LACS and the OCC), and the nationality and immigration status of the children involved.

Once the family position is established, consideration must be given to the circum- **12.100** stances of the FNO, including timescale to removal, barriers to removal, the gravity of offences committed, sentencing comments, ongoing family proceedings, formal risk assessments, licence conditions, risk of absconding (with or without the children), and information from the relevant LACS.[165]

---

[159] Page 10.
[160] *Detention of families*, p 17.
[161] *Detention of families*, p 18.
[162] *Detention of families*, p 14.
[163] See, for example, *R (Senthuran) v Secretary of State for the Home Department* [2004] EWCA Civ 950; [2004] 4 All ER 365 at [15].
[164] *Detention of families*, p 19.
[165] *Detention of families*, p 21.

12.101   Having examined the relevant facts, caseworkers move to the instructions under *Making the decision*.[166] They are required to weigh risk of absconding and offending against the impact of continued detention on any children involved. Unless risk of absconding or offending is high, the parent should be 'considered for release' if the separation is likely to be long and continued separation may have a significant impact on the children.

(5) Separating the family

12.102   Where a decision is taken to detain, caseworkers must follow the procedures set out in *Separating families*. Authority to separate the family for deportation or detention purposes must be obtained from an assistant director ('AD'). It need only be obtained once, absent a significant change in circumstances.[167]

12.103   When making a proposal to separate a family unit, caseworkers must demonstrate that any safeguarding child welfare issues have been taken into account.[168] Caseworkers are instructed to take the following steps:[169]

(1) Contact should be made with the relevant LACS to establish if they have contact with the family, and to ask them for any relevant information regarding child protection issues.[170]

(2) Consideration must be given to seeking input from the OCC.[171]

(3) All information should then be considered to establish if child protection issues arise requiring the involvement of a UK child welfare agency[172] and whether the proposed action (detention, deportation) would impact on the child's welfare.

(4) Approval must be sought from a senior caseworker. If the senior caseworker agrees the separation, authority to separate the family must then be sought from the relevant assistant director. Thereafter, deportation proceeds in the usual way.

12.104   Authority to split a family must be obtained where it is proposed to detain and deport a parent whose child is already in care or already cared for by the other parent or another relative in the community. Before authority is sought in such cases, advice must be obtained from the OCC.[173]

---

[166] *Detention of families*, p 23.
[167] *Separating families*, p 16.
[168] *Separating families*, p 11.
[169] *Separating families*, p 13.
[170] *Separating families*, p 13.
[171] *Separating families*, p 13.
[172] *Separating families*, p 13.
[173] *Separating families*, p 21.

No authority is needed to separate a family for proposed deportation if they are to **12.105** be deported together unless it is proposed to separate the family by detention in advance of the departure.[174]

Detention must be reviewed in line with the timetable set out in EIG 55. However, **12.106** if any of the following matters come to light after an initial decision to detain detention must be reviewed immediately:[175]

- a child is in care and remains in care because of the detention;
- the FNO is a single parent and the child is living with family and/or foster carers because of the detention;
- concerns have been raised about child welfare;
- siblings will be split up by detention of a parent;
- both parents are FNOs and in custody and/or detention; or
- the child has special needs.

Where these circumstances arise, caseworkers are instructed to balance the welfare **12.107** of the child against the other risk factors in the case to decide if the risk of harm to the public or risk of absconding posed by the FNO outweighs the best interests of the child. Where any of the factors mentioned in paragraph 12.106 are identified, caseworkers are instructed that they 'must' prepare a release referral and get authorization from the strategic director.[176]

(6) Imminent release cases

In what are termed 'imminent release' cases (cases in which the Home Office **12.108** become aware of an FNO who is liable to deportation within the 48 hours prior to their proposed release from custody) the guidance permits detention for up to seven days without family separation being authorized.[177] During the seven days, the caseworker must gather the information necessary for the assistant director to make a fully informed decision. If authority is not obtained within seven days, it will be necessary to make arrangements to release.

In our view, it is arguable that this aspect of the guidance is unlawful.[178] It appears **12.109** to condone detention being authorized without the authorizing official being aware of all relevant facts. It instructs caseworkers to err in favour of detention pending receipt of information that might warrant release. Moreover, it does so in cases where (a) child welfare is likely to be engaged, and (b) where the FNO has served a 'short custodial sentence' so is likely to have committed a less serious offence.

---

[174] *Separating families*, p 17.
[175] *Separating families*, p 18.
[176] See also EIG 55.3.2.2.
[177] *Separating families*, p 17. *Detention of families*, p 8.
[178] See Chapter 9, at paragraphs 9.22 to 9.32 for a discussion of the law on the requirements of a lawful policy.

13

DETAINED FAST TRACK

A. Overview

13.01 The Detained Fast Track ('DFT') is the process whereby asylum seekers are detained for their applications for asylum and any subsequent appeal to be processed quickly under accelerated procedures. Cases within the DFT fall outside of general detention policy[1] and are not subject to the general presumption of liberty.[2] This chapter focusses on detention within the DFT. It does not address broader issues relating to the conduct of asylum claims or appeals.

B. History of the DFT

(1) Oakington

13.02 The original fast track scheme operated at Oakington Immigration Removal Centre ('IRC'). It was established on 16 March 2000. It sought to process initial claims within seven to ten days. However, it did not keep individuals detained if a decision could not be made within that timeframe or whilst their appeals were ongoing.

---

[1] *Detained Fast Track Processes* (formerly entitled *DFT & DNSA—Intake Selection (AIU Instruction)*) 11 June 2013, paragraph 2.01.
[2] EIG 55.3.

(2) Harmondsworth

On 18 March 2003 the Secretary of State announced a new fast track pilot scheme **13.03** to deal with certain asylum claims at Harmondsworth IRC.[3] Decisions were to be taken within three days. The Harmondsworth procedure included an accelerated appeals procedure. The whole process in the case of a refusal upheld by all relevant appellate bodies could be over within five weeks. It was limited to single male applicants from countries considered by the Secretary of State to be safe.

(3) Yarl's Wood

In May 2005 the DFT was expanded to include female applicants held at Yarl's **13.04** Wood IRC.

C. Challenges to the DFT

(1) *Saadi*

The lawfulness of the Oakington regime was challenged in the *Saadi* litigation, **13.05** and upheld as lawful in the House of Lords[4] and the Grand Chamber of the European Court of Human Rights ('ECtHR').[5]

Saadi was decided in the context of great pressure of numbers on the UK asylum **13.06** system. Giving judgment in the House of Lords, Lord Slynn[6] held that detention to process asylum claims quickly was 'not of itself necessarily and in all cases unlawful'.[7] The question, however, was whether detention 'for administrative convenience' fell within the permitted exception to the right to liberty in Article 5(1)(f) of the European Convention on Human Rights ('ECHR'), which allowed detention, *inter alia*, to 'prevent [an alien] effecting an unauthorised entry into the country', or whether there must be some other factor to justify the exercise of the power to detain such as a likelihood of absconding. Noting that the power to detain was to 'prevent' unauthorized entry, Lord Slynn held that 'until the State has "authorised" entry the entry is unauthorised. The State has power to detain without violating Article 5 until the application has been considered and the entry "authorised".'[8] Accepting that the arrangements at Oakington provided 'reasonable conditions'

---

[3] See *R (Refugee Legal Centre) v Secretary of State for the Home Department* [2004] EWCA Civ 1481, [2005] 1 WLR 2219, *per* Sedley LJ at [2], citing Collins J at first instance, at [1].
[4] *R (Saadi) v Secretary of State for the Home Department* [2002] UKHL 41; [2002] 1 WLR 3131.
[5] *Saadi v United Kingdom* (2008) 47 EHRR 17.
[6] With whom the whole court agreed.
[7] At [32].
[8] At [35].

and that the period involved was 'not in any sense excessive', he further held that detention under the Oakington procedure was 'proportionate and reasonable'.

13.07 *Saadi* progressed to the Grand Chamber of the ECtHR which found no violation of Article 5(1)(f). The national authorities had acted in good faith and the policy behind the creation of the regime was generally to benefit asylum seekers.⁹ Since the purpose of the deprivation of liberty was to enable the authorities quickly and efficiently to determine the applicant's claim to asylum, his detention was closely connected to the purpose of preventing unauthorized entry.¹⁰ The seven-day period of detention did not exceed that reasonably required for the purpose pursued.¹¹ In all the circumstances, it was not incompatible with Article 5(1)(f) to detain the applicant for seven days in suitable conditions to enable his claim to asylum to be processed speedily.¹²

(2) *Refugee Legal Centre*

13.08 In *R (Refugee Legal Centre) v Secretary of State for the Home Department*¹³ (*RLC*), the Court of Appeal considered whether the fast track system at Harmondsworth was inherently unfair. The evidence of the Secretary of State was that applicants whose claims transpired to be 'particularly complex' or to require expert evidence, or who had medical problems were removed from the system, and the appeal procedure rules in place at the time made analogous provision for removal from the appeal tier of the system in exceptional cases.¹⁴

13.09 The Court held that the existence of a right of appeal to the Immigration Appellate Authority (as was) was not in itself a sufficient answer to the claim of unfairness. An applicant was entitled not only to a fair appeal, but to a fair initial hearing and a fair-minded decision.¹⁵ Moreover, if the record of interview going before the adjudicator has been obtained in unacceptably stressful or distressing circumstances, so that it contained omissions and inconsistencies, the damage caused by an unfair system may not be curable.¹⁶

13.10 What was lacking from the Harmondsworth fast track, in the Court's judgment, was a clearly stated policy that recognized it would be unfair not to enlarge the standard timetable in a variety of instances.¹⁷ Nevertheless, the system did not carry an unacceptable risk of unfairness. There was a tension between flexibility, an 'essential part of the system', and the stated (albeit unwritten and imprecise)

---

⁹ At [77].
¹⁰ At [77].
¹¹ At [79].
¹² At [80].
¹³ [2004] EWCA Civ 1481; [2005] 1 WLR 2219.
¹⁴ See *per* Sedley LJ at [12].
¹⁵ *Per* Sedley LJ at [15].
¹⁶ *Per* Sedley LJ at [15].
¹⁷ At [18].

underlying policy of 'not compromising the system's integrity'.[18] However, provided the system was operated in a way that recognized the variety of circumstances in which fairness would require an enlargement of the standard timetable it was not inherently unfair. A 'written flexibility policy' to which officials and representatives could work would afford 'a necessary assurance' that the three-day timetable was in truth 'a guide and not a straitjacket'.[19]

(3) *Detention Action*

R (Detention Action) v Secretary of State for the Home Department[20] was a root and **13.11** branch challenge to the legality of DFT policy, practice, and procedure as operated in 2013. The claimants, a charity that campaigns on issues relevant to immigration detention, argued that the DFT in its current form operated in a way which was so unfair as to be unlawful, and that detention within the DFT breached the common law and Article 5(1)(f) of ECHR. Ouseley J accepted that the DFT as currently operated was sufficiently different from the regime in place at the time of *Saadi* and *Refugee Legal Centre* to mean those decisions 'may not give the current system an inevitable imprimatur of lawfulness'. The crucial question was 'whether the operation of the DFT now satisfies the requirements of the law'.[21]

Ouseley J held that neither the length of detention nor the criteria for inclusion **13.12** within the DFT, which had broadened significantly since the earlier cases, were in themselves unlawful,[22] and detention within the DFT was not rendered unlawful by its conditions.[23] Other aspects of DFT policy and practice were the subject of criticism, including the screening process,[24] the mechanism for identifying potential victims of torture and the operation of Rules 34 and 35 of the Detention Centre Rules,[25] the process for identifying victims of trafficking,[26] and the approach to applicants suffering from mental illness and learning difficulties.[27]

These 'remediable deficiencies' did not in themselves give rise to an unacceptable **13.13** risk of unfairness, in large part because the problems could be mitigated by the involvement of lawyers acting on behalf of applicants.[28] However, given those numerous shortcomings and the importance of legal representation in addressing

---

[18] At [22].
[19] At [23].
[20] [2014] EWHC 2245 (Admin).
[21] At [67].
[22] At [81]–[86] and [87]–[93].
[23] At [209].
[24] At [112].
[25] At [116]–[138].
[26] At [139]–[146].
[27] At [154]–[158].
[28] See at [195]: 'As I have gone through the various stages of the DFT process, I have commented on what appear to me to be remediable deficiencies which together fall short of showing that the detention is unlawful or that the process contains so high a risk of an unfair decision that it is inherently unlawful. At each stage, however, it has been the prospective use of lawyers, independent,

their consequences, the system was rendered unlawful by delays in providing access to legal representation. The DFT as operated carried 'an unacceptably high risk of unfairness, but one which . . . can be removed by the earlier instruction of lawyers'.[29] Remedial action was required.[30]

13.14 In a subsequent judgment addressing remedies, Ouseley J declined to make orders regarding the processing of future claims or regarding past claims that may have been affected by the illegality identified in the main judgment.[31] He made clear FTT judges were required to consider whether, in a given case, the process and the speed at which a claim had been processed affected its fairness.[32] As to past cases, it was for individual claimants facing removal to raise any issues they considered arose on their particular facts.[33] A suspension of the DFT was not necessary, although such a course may have operational advantages.[34] The court would not supervise the steps taken by the Secretary of State to remedy the problems identified.[35]

13.15 Unless the Secretary of State successfully appeals the decision in *Detention Action*, changes to the DFT regime to remedy the illegality identified are now inevitable. At the time of writing, the form these changes will take is not known. It also remains to be seen to what extent the conclusions in *Detention Action* might found either fresh asylum claims or actions for false imprisonment by individuals whose claims have been processed within the DFT.

D. The Current Position

(1) General

13.16 The DFT process currently operates in Harmondsworth, Colnbrook, and Campsfield IRCs (for men), and Yarl's Wood IRC (for women). It lasts until the exhaustion of appeal rights.

13.17 Also included in the DFT system are Detained Non-Suspensive Appeals ('DNSA') cases.[36] These are cases which are 'capable of being certified' as clearly unfounded pursuant to section 94 of the Nationality, Immigration and Asylum Act 2002,

---

giving advice, taking instructions having gained the client's confidence, which has seemed to me to be the crucial safeguard, the crucial ingredient for a fair hearing, whilst maintaining the speed of the process, but which can protect against failings elsewhere, and avoid an unacceptably high risk of an unfair process.'

[29] At [197]. See further at [195]–[200].
[30] At [198], [200].
[31] [2014] EWHC 2525 (Admin), at [4].
[32] At [6].
[33] At [8].
[34] At [9]–[12].
[35] At [14].
[36] These were included at Oakington IRC from November 2002 and Yarl's Wood IRC from the autumn of 2006; see Enforcement Instructions and Guidance Chapter 55, version 12, section 55.4.

with the consequence that a person whose claim is refused can only appeal after being removed from the United Kingdom.[37]

The current indicative timetable for an initial decision to be made within the fast track (DFT or DNSA) process is seven to 14 days.[38] However, DFT applicants will remain in the DFT pending the outcome of any appeal. Evidence before the Court in *Detention Action* showed that until November 2012, 44 days was the expected duration of the whole DFT process up to the exhaustion of appeal rights, if an appeal were pursued against a refusal, but then efficiency was improved and the expected duration was reduced to 28 days for that whole process.[39] **13.18**

Individuals who are subject to the DFT procedure can receive legal advice from one of the providers who have an exclusive contract with the Legal Aid Agency.[40] However, by the time cases reach the appeals stage many appellants are unrepresented. As discussed at paragraphs 13.11–13.15, the Administrative Court held in *Detention Action* that delays in providing access to legal advice, seen in the context of other significant flaws in the DFT system, were such as to render the DFT system as a whole unlawful. **13.19**

Where a decision is taken to refuse an asylum claim within the DFT, there is a right of appeal to the First-tier Tribunal (Immigration and Asylum Chamber) ('FTT'). The regime for fast track appeals is governed by the Asylum and Immigration Tribunal (Fast Track Procedure) Rules 2005[41] (the Fast Track Procedure Rules). Appeals are subject to the accelerated timescale set out in Part 2 of those Rules. There is provision in Rule 28 for the FTT to adjourn a case within the DFT, and within Rule 30 for the FTT to direct that a case ceases to be subject to the Fast Track Procedure Rules (with the necessary consequence that it is no longer in the DFT). **13.20**

A case remains within the DFT system whilst it proceeds through the appellate system. The Upper Tribunal ('UT') also sits as part of the DFT system. Individuals are also likely to remain in detention (albeit it is not entirely clear if they are still subject to the DFT) if their case is appealed to the Court of Appeal, at least initially. **13.21**

(2) Flexibility

The *Detained Fast Track Processes—Timetable Flexibility* policy states, at paragraph 2.01, in relation to the seven to 14 day period: **13.22**

> It is important that this timetable is maintained as far as is reasonably possible, and that the time an individual is detained is kept to a minimum. However,

---

[37] EIG 55.4.
[38] *Detained Fast Track Processes—Timetable Flexibility*, version 2, 11 January 2012, paragraph 2.01.
[39] [2014] EWHC 2245 (Admin) at [81].
[40] Subject to the normal means and merits tests.
[41] SI 2005/560.

the DFT and DNSA processes are built on an overriding principle of fairness, and as a consequence, *timetable flexibility or removal from the DFT and DNSA processes must be considered in all situations where fairness demands it* [emphasis in original].

(3) Selection criteria

13.23 An applicant may enter into or remain in DFT/DNSA processes only if there is a power in immigration law to detain,[42] and only if on consideration of the known facts relating to the applicant and their case obtained at asylum screening (and, where relevant, subsequently), it appears that a quick decision is possible, and none of the Detained Fast Track Suitability Exclusion Criteria apply.[43]

13.24 There are no requirements as to nationality or country of origin, and 'no other bases of detention policy need apply' (i.e. the applicant need not be someone who could be detained under EIG 55). There is no requirement that an application be 'late and opportunistic' but where it is known or suspected that it may be, particular consideration should be given to entering the applicant into DFT/DNSA.[44]

E. Suitability Exclusion Criteria

13.25 An applicant may enter into or remain in the DFT/DNSA process so long as a quick decision is possible and none of the DFT Suitability Exclusion Criteria apply. Those criteria, set out in *Detained Fast Track Processes* at paragraph 2.03, broadly reflect the general unsuitability provisions in EIG 55.10 and this section should be read alongside the detailed consideration of those factors in Chapter 11.

13.26 The following individuals are 'unlikely to be suitable for entry or continued management in the DFT or DNSA processes':

(1) 'Women who are 24 or more weeks pregnant';[45]

(2) 'Family cases';[46]

(3) children (whether applicants or dependants) and disputed age cases unless certain criteria are satisfied;[47]

---

[42] As to which, see Chapters 4 and 7.

[43] *Detained Fast Track Processes*, paragraph 2.01. See paragraphs 13.25–13.27 for the Suitability Exclusion Criteria.

[44] *Detained Fast Track Processes*, paragraph 2.01.

[45] *Cf.* the position in non-DFT cases, considered at Chapter 11, paragraphs 11.15–11.19.

[46] Further guidance as to the scope of this exclusion, which has no direct analogue in the general detention policy, is given at paragraph 2.3.1 of *Detained Fast Track Processes*.

[47] The prohibition on detaining children mirrors EIG 55.9.3 and 55.10; see Chapter 12, paragraphs 12.21–12.30. The approach to disputed age cases is broadly in line with EIG 55.9.3.1, although the guidance on when a local authority age assessment should be accepted is more explicit, requiring that a 'full and detailed local authority age assessment setting out the reasons for the

(4) 'Those with a disability which cannot be adequately managed within a detained environment';[48]

(5) 'Those with a physical or mental medical condition which cannot be adequately treated within a detained environment, or which for practical reasons, including infectiousness or contagiousness, cannot be properly managed within a detained environment';[49]

(6) 'Those who clearly lack the mental capacity or coherence to sufficiently understand the asylum process and/or cogently present their claim. This consideration will usually be based on medical information, but where medical information is unavailable, officers must apply their judgment as to an individual's apparent capacity';[50]

(7) those for whom there has been a reasonable grounds decision taken (and maintained) by a competent authority stating that the applicant is a potential victim of trafficking or where there has been a conclusive decision taken by a competent authority stating that the applicant is a victim of trafficking;[51]

(8) those in respect of whom there is independent evidence of torture.[52]

The Suitability Exclusion Criteria are supplemented by the *Medical Foundation Cases*[53] policy, giving guidance on the approach to take in cases in which the Medical Foundation for the Care of Victims of Torture (now known as Freedom From Torture) is involved. This provides that if the Medical Foundation has agreed to undertake a pre-assessment for a case in the DFT the asylum decision will be **13.27**

---

conclusion that the applicant is 18 years of age or over has been seen, and the local authority has stated that the assessment was conducted in compliance with the guidelines in the *Merton* case'. See further Chapter 12, paragraphs 12.31–12.53.

[48] For the position under EIG 55.10 see Chapter 11, paragraphs 11.49–11.52.

[49] For the position under EIG 55.10 see Chapter 11, paragraphs 11.20–11.36.

[50] The Suitability Exclusion Criteria include this further category, not found in EIG 55.10, but a necessary consequence of the underlying requirement that a case be capable of speedy resolution and can be dealt with fairly. The policy sets the bar very high. The requirement that the applicant 'clearly' lacks capacity or sufficient coherence to participate will permit borderline cases to remain in the DFT. In cases where concerns arise and there is no medical evidence officials are instructed to 'apply their judgement' rather than seek medical advice. In *R (S) v Secretary of State for the Home Department* [2014] EWHC 50 (Admin), the Court was highly critical of the decision of Home Office officials in the Harmondsworth DFT team to persist with an asylum interview in the face of circumstances which 'were such as to have put the interviewers on notice that S lacked capacity, was unfit to be interviewed, required the support of an appropriate adult and needed a legal representative to accompany him to any re-arranged interview once his health had improved' (see at [398]). This was one of a catalogue of failings which contributed to the judge's conclusion that S's detention was unlawful.

[51] This mirrors the position in EIG 9.1 and 55.10; see further Chapter 11, paragraphs 11.53–11.64. The requirement for a reasonable grounds decision to have been taken before the Suitability Exclusion Criteria are engaged means detention within the DFT will not be excluded where a trafficking claim has been made and a reasonable grounds decision is pending.

[52] For the position under EIG 55.10 see Chapter 11, paragraphs 11.37–11.48.

[53] 20 March 2007.

postponed and the individual will usually be removed from the DFT. This policy also applies to cases in which the Helen Bamber Foundation has accepted a referral.[54]

F. Removal from the DFT

13.28 Evidence suggests that a significant number of applicants admitted to the DFT are subsequently released.[55] There have been a number of cases challenging inclusion in the DFT.[56] DFT caseworkers are under a continuing duty to ensure that the suitability criteria remain satisfied.

13.29 An applicant who wishes to be removed from the the DFT has four options, depending on the stage the case has reached:

(1) make representations to the Secretary of State;
(2) apply for bail;
(3) make an application to the FTT under Rule 30; or
(4) potentially, judicial review.

(1) Representations

13.30 An applicant can make representations to the Secretary of State asserting that a case is unsuitable for the DFT either because it cannot be fairly determined within the indicative timescale or because the Suitability Exclusion Criteria are engaged. Representations can be made before an asylum decision is taken or subsequently, if an appeal is pending.

(2) An application for bail

13.31 A person detained in the DFT may seek bail in the same way as any other detainee.[57] Given that the Secretary of State should have satisfied herself that the case is suitable for the DFT, an application for CIO/Secretary of State bail is unlikely to succeed. As regards FTT bail nothing in the *Bail Guidance*[58] suggests a judge should

---

[54] Confirmed in a letter from the Home Office to Refugee and Migrant Justice dated 15 April 2009.

[55] In *Asylum: A Thematic Inspection of the Detained Fast Track System* July - September 2011, of 114 cases sampled it was found that 27% were removed from the DFT before a decision was taken (see Executive Summary at paragraph 2); see further *Detention Action* at [102]–[103].

[56] See, *inter alia*: *R (HBH) v Secretary of State for the Home Department* [2009] EWHC 928 (Admin) (disputed child held in the DFT at Oakington); *R (D & K) v Secretary of State for the Home Department* [2006] EWHC 980 and *R (HK) v Secretary of State for the Home Department* [2007] EWCA Civ 1357 (allegations of torture); *R (JB (Jamaica)) v Secretary of State of the Home Department* [2013] EWCA Civ 666; [2014] 1 WLR 836 (flaws in the screening process).

[57] See Chapter 18.

[58] See Chapter 18, paragraphs 18.55–18.109.

approach an application made by a detainee in the DFT differently to any other case. Nevertheless, the FTT will be mindful that a grant of bail will remove the case from the DFT, and is likely to attach great weight to its view of whether the case should remain in the DFT.

(3) Post-decision, if appeal pending, application to FTT under Rule 30

If an applicant's asylum claim has been refused and an appeal has been lodged with the FTT, he or she may apply under Rule 30 of the Fast Track Procedure Rules for the case to be removed from the Detained Fast Track. **13.32**

Rule 30(1) provides that where Part 2 (appeals before the FTT) or Part 3 (applications for permission to appeal to the UT) of the Rules applies to an appeal or application, the FTT must order that that Part shall cease to apply (with the consequence that the appeal or application is removed from the Detained Fast Track): **13.33**

(1) 'if all the parties consent';
(2) 'if it is satisfied by evidence filed or given by or on behalf of a party that there are exceptional circumstances which mean that the appeal or application cannot otherwise be justly determined';[59] or
(3) if it is satisfied that the appellant would be prejudiced by a procedural failing on the part of the Secretary of State if the appeal or application were determined in accordance with the Fast Track Procedure Rules.

If the Tribunal does not at the same time have before it an application for bail it has no jurisdiction to order release. However, once the Tribunal directs that a case be removed from the Detained Fast Track, release by the Secretary of State should follow (unless detention is maintained on some other ground). **13.34**

(4) Judicial review

An applicant can also apply to judicially review the Secretary of State's decision to include them in, and/or to refuse to remove them from, the DFT. However, judicial review is a remedy of last resort so the court will not grant relief where there is an alternative remedy. It has been suggested that applications for bail from the FTT and/or applications under Rule 30 of the Fast Track Procedure Rules[60] may be alternative remedies to judicial review.[61] **13.35**

---

[59] The test of 'exceptional circumstances' imposes no threshold additional to whether an appeal can be justly determined: *R (SH (Afghanistan)) v Secretary of State for the Home Department* [2011] EWCA Civ 1284, *per* Moses LJ at [3].

[60] As to which, see paragraphs 13.32–13.34.

[61] In *R (Irfan Ahmed) v Secretary of State for the Home Department* [2013] EWHC 1536 (Admin), HHJ Sycamore suggested that an application to the FTT to be removed from the DFT or an application for bail was an alternative remedy 'apart from the unlawful detention claim' (at [17]).

13.36 We do not think that there is an alternative remedy to judicial review if a decision on the applicant's asylum claim has not yet been made. At this stage an application under Rule 30 cannot be made.[62] The possibility of bail alone could not, in our view, constitute an alternative remedy. Although the FTT on an application for bail will have regard to all of the circumstances of the case, it can only determine whether release on bail is appropriate. It has no jurisdiction to decide on whether inclusion within the DFT is lawful or whether detention is lawful.

13.37 If a decision on the asylum claim has been made, it is arguable that an application under Rule 30 is an alternative to judicial review. However, this is not clear cut because the jurisdiction of the FTT is not co-extensive with that of the Administrative Court, and it could not engage with the legality of the underlying detention.

---

[62] On the authority of *RLC* (see *per* Sedley LJ at [15]) it could not be suggested that an asylum applicant should await refusal, lodge an appeal, and then make an application under Rule 30 as by that stage, irreparable damage may already have been done to his or her case.

14

EU LAW

A. Introduction

This chapter considers when and how EU law may limit the executive's powers of **14.01**
immigration detention.

The use of immigration detention does not always engage EU law. There must be **14.02**
something about the situation to bring the detention within the scope of EU law.

Judges and commentators have often struggled to determine the scope of EU law.[1] **14.03**
One kind of situation which clearly falls within the scope of EU law is where a person is exercising the fundamental freedoms guaranteed by the Treaty, in particular
those involving the freedom to move and reside within the territory of the Member
States.[2] Acts of Member States taken in the implementation of EU obligations,
including the exercise of a power of derogation recognized by EU law also fall
within the scope of EU law.[3]

In this context, it is probably easiest to consider the scope of EU law by reference to **14.04**
the different categories of person whose detention may fall within it. The immigration detention of the following is, or may be, within the scope of EU law:

(1) citizens of the EU member states, the EEA states, and/or Switzerland;

---

[1] *R (GI) v Secretary of State for the Home Department* [2012] EWCA Civ 867 at [38]–[43] where
Laws LJ suggested that the Court of Justice of the European Union ('CJEU') had strayed beyond its
competence in its judgment in *Rottmann v Bayern* [2010] ECR 1-1449.
[2] *Zanotti,* Case C-56/09 [2010] 3 CMLR 34.
[3] See *R (Sandiford) v SSFCA* [2013] EWCA Civ 581 and the discussion in the Opinion of the
Advocate General in *Zambrano* Case C-34/09 [2010] ECR nyr at 156–173.

(2) third country nationals who have, or had, certain kinds of family relationship to persons in the first category;

(3) persons with rights under the Agreement establishing an Association between the European Economic Community and Turkey ('the Ankara Agreement').

(4) persons who are being detained pending transfer to another Member State under Regulation 604/2013 ('Dublin III'); and

(5) asylum seekers.

14.05   Each of the sections in this chapter is concerned with one of these categories. In each case, we consider the situations in which each category may fall within the scope of EU law and the manner in which EU law will limit statutory powers of immigration detention.

B. Citizens of the EU, the EEA, and Switzerland

(1) Scope of EU law

14.06   EU citizens have a right to freedom of movement, conferred by the Treaties that establish the European Union and the measures which have implemented those Treaties, most recently Directive 2004/38/EC ('the Citizens Directive').[4] The Citizens Directive provides for all EU citizens to have a right to enter other Member States and reside there for three months.[5] EU citizens continue to have a right of residence after three months, under the Citizens Directive, if they fall within certain categories: i.e. workers, the self-employed, self-sufficient persons with comprehensive sickness insurance, and students with sickness insurance.[6] If immigration detention interferes with the rights of entry and/or residence guaranteed by the Citizens Directive, then plainly EU law will be engaged.[7]

14.07   The Citizens Directive is not exhaustive of the situations in which an EU citizen may have a right to be in a member state of which they are not a national. The case-law of the CJEU makes clear that EU citizens have a right to be in other member states for so long as they are receiving services (which includes being a tourist).[8] Any interference with this right to reside will clearly engage EU law.

---

4   The Immigration (European Economic Area) Regulations 2006 ('the EEA Regulations') were intended to implement this Directive—see paragraph 6.02.

5   Article 6 of the Citizens Directive.

6   Article 7 of the Citizens Directive.

7   For example, in *Salah Oulane v Minister voor Vreemdelingenzaken en Integratie*, Case C-215/03, there was no dispute that EU law was engaged by detention which interfered with a right of residence under Directive 73/148, one of the predecessors of the Citizens Directive. Likewise, in *Olazabal*, Case C-100/01, EU law was engaged by a decision to require a national of another Member State not to reside in certain parts of France.

8   *Cf. Luisi and Carbone v Ministero del Tesoro*, Case C-286/82 at [16].

Even if an EU citizen does not have a right to reside in another Member State **14.08** (e.g. because they have resided in another Member State for more than three months and are not self-sufficient and/or do not have comprehensive sickness insurance) their detention, for immigration purposes, will still engage EU law. The CJEU has stressed that the right of EU citizens to freedom of movement is the general rule and any condition imposed upon it (e.g. the condition of self-sufficiency after three months of residence imposed by Article 7(1)(b) of the Citizens Directive) is to be construed narrowly and in compliance with the limits imposed by EU law, such as proportionality.[9] The use of immigration detention against an EU national, on the basis that they no longer have a right to reside, is an interference with that general right and will need to comply with EU law.

It follows that the immigration detention of an EU citizen, from a country other **14.09** than the United Kingdom, will always be within the scope of EU law because of their constitutional right to freedom of movement.

The Agreement on the European Economic Area ('the EEA Agreement')[10] and **14.10** the bilateral agreement between Switzerland and the European Union on the Free Movement of Persons ('the Swiss Agreement') have provided for citizens of Norway, Iceland, Lichtenstein, and Switzerland to have a right to freedom of movement within the EEA and Switzerland. The differences between their freedom of movement and the freedom of movement of EU citizens are beyond the scope of this book. However, it is significant that the Immigration (European Economic Area) Regulations 2006, which the United Kingdom enacted to give effect to the Citizens Directive, make no distinction between citizens of the EU and citizens of Norway, Iceland, Lichtenstein, and Switzerland. In any event, given their right to freedom of movement, the detention of such citizens, under immigration powers, will also engage EU law.

(2) Effect of EU law

The detention of an EU national for immigration reasons must be authorized by **14.11** a derogating provision of EU law.[11] There are three provisions within the Citizens Directive which are of potential relevance.

First, Article 14 provides that EU citizens shall have a right of residence after three **14.12** months of residence 'as long as they do not become an unreasonable burden on the social assistance system of the host Member State'. Article 14 does not expressly provide for a right to expel or detain EU citizens who become such a burden but it is implicit, in Article 14.3 and recital 16 of the preamble, that such persons may

---

[9] *Brey*, Case C-140/12 at [69]–[70].
[10] Agreement between the European Community and its Member States, of the one part, and the Swiss Confederation, of the other, on the free movement of persons, Annex I.
[11] *Salah Oulane v Minister voor Vreemdelingenzaken en Integratie*, Case C-215/03 at [41].

become subject to expulsion measures (including, presumably, detention for the purposes of expulsion).[12]

14.13 Secondly, Article 27 of the Citizens Directive[13] provides, in so far as material:

1. Subject to the provisions of this Chapter, Member States may restrict the freedom of movement and residence of Union citizens and their family members, irrespective of nationality, on grounds of public policy, public security or public health. These grounds shall not be invoked to serve economic ends.

2. Measures taken on grounds of public policy or public security shall comply with the principle of proportionality and shall be based exclusively on the personal conduct of the individual concerned. Previous criminal convictions shall not in themselves constitute grounds for taking such measures. The personal conduct of the individual concerned must represent a genuine, present and sufficiently serious threat affecting one of the fundamental interests of society. Justifications that are isolated from the particulars of the case or that rely on considerations of general prevention shall not be accepted.

This provision authorizes restrictions on freedom of movement on grounds of public policy, public security, or public health. The CJEU has held in several cases that a failure to comply with 'legal formalities pertaining to aliens' access, movement and residence' does not constitute a threat to public policy or public security.[14] In other words, the fact that an EU national may not have a document which is required by domestic law, is not, in and of itself, sufficient justification for detention.[15]

14.14 Thirdly, Article 35 of the Citizens Directive[16] provides that:

Member States may adopt the necessary measures to refuse, terminate or withdraw any right conferred by this Directive in the case of abuse of rights or fraud, such as marriages of convenience. Any such measure shall be proportionate and subject to the procedural safeguards provided for in Articles 30 and 31.

14.15 The ECJ (as it then was) said this in *Royer*[17] about the power to detain:

As to the question whether a Member State may take measures for the temporary deprivation of liberty of an alien covered by the terms of the Treaty with a view

---

[12] Article 14 of the Citizens Directive is the source for the powers in Regulations 19(3)(a) and 24(2) of the EEA Regulations to detain and expel EEA nationals that no longer have a right of residence.

[13] Article 27 of the Citizens Directive is the source for the powers to exclude, expel and detain EEA nationals and their family members in Regulations 19(1), (1A), (1B), 19(3)(b) and 22, 23, and 24(1) and (3) of the EEA Regulations. Hence, it was Article 27 that the Court of Appeal focused on, in *R (Nouazli) v Secretary of State for the Home Department* [2013] EWCA Civ 1608, when considering detention under Regulation 24(1) of the EEA Regulations.

[14] For example, *Salah Oulane v Minister voor Vreemdelingenzaken en Integratie*, Case C-215/03 at [42].

[15] *Salah Oulane v Minister voor Vreemdelingenzaken en Integratie*, Case C-215/03 at [40].

[16] Article 35 of the Citizens Directive is, presumably, the source for the powers in Regulations 19(3)(c) and 24(2) of the EEA Regulations to detain and expel EEA nationals on the basis of 'abuse of rights'.

[17] Case 48/75 at [43].

to expelling him from the territory it must first be stated that no measure of this nature is permissible if a decision ordering expulsion from the territory would be contrary to the Treaty.

On the face of it, this suggests that someone with a right to reside under EU law **14.16** may only be detained, under immigration powers, when their expulsion would be compatible with EU law. Similarly, in *Olazabal*,[18] the CJEU held that an order restricting a Spanish national from living in certain parts of France was only permissible where there were reasons of public policy, public security, or public health which were serious enough to justify his expulsion from France.

The reasoning of the ECJ in *Royer, Olazabal*, and *Oulane* has potentially pro- **14.17** found effects on the Secretary of State's power, under domestic law, to detain EU nationals. In particular, it is arguable that those powers are limited in the following ways:

(1) detention may only be used where expulsion is justified—a mistaken but reasonable belief, by the Secretary of State, that an EU national can be expelled will not be sufficient to justify detention;
(2) detention of an EU national might not be justifiable on the basis of 'abuse of rights';
(3) detention must be proportionate; and
(4) detention must not offend against other general principles of EU law including the Charter of Fundamental Rights of the European Union ('CFR').

(a) Expulsion must be justified

First, it is arguable that EU law prevents the Secretary of State from justifying the **14.18** detention of an EU national on the basis of her opinions alone. The reasoning of the CJEU in *Royer* and *Olazabal* is that detention of an EU national will only be justified where their expulsion would also be justified. This is significant because there are several provisions of the EEA Regulations which provide for the detention of EEA nationals by reason of the Secretary of State's beliefs, suspicions or decisions alone, i.e.:

(1) a reasonable belief that the EEA national may be refused admission for certain reasons;[19]
(2) a decision that the EEA national should be refused admission;[20]
(3) a reasonable suspicion that the EEA national may be removed on grounds of public policy, public security, or public health;[21] or

---

[18] Case C-100/01 at [45].
[19] Regulation 22(1)(b) and (2) of the EEA Regulations.
[20] Regulation 23 of the EEA Regulations.
[21] Regulation 24(1) of the EEA Regulations.

(4) a decision that the person should be removed on one of the grounds in Regulation 19(3) of the EEA Regulations.[22]

14.19 On the face of the EEA Regulations, detention is still lawful even if a court later decides that the suspicion, belief, or decision of the Secretary of State was wrong— i.e. that there were insufficient grounds to justify a restriction on the EEA nationals' freedom of movement. It is questionable whether the detention of an EU national in such circumstances would be compatible with EU law. The case-law of the CJEU discussed at paragraphs 14.15-14.16 suggests that, if there are no grounds of public policy, public security, or public health to justify refusing an EU national admission, there will also be no grounds to justify detaining them. It matters not if the detaining authority reasonably suspected, believed, or decided that there were such grounds.

14.20 Taken to an extreme, this principle might result in the Secretary of State being liable for the wrongful detention of a person even when there was no fault on the part of the decision maker. This is not necessarily problematic, however, because the 'spirit and intent' of the Citizens Directive is that Member States should properly investigate whether the person in question has rights under EU law before taking any enforcement action against them.[23] There is no difficulty in holding the Secretary of State responsible for unlawful detention where she should have realized that the person she was to detain had a right to freedom of movement under EU law. But what of the situation where an EU national fails to mention their nationality? Is it unlawful to detain such a person pending removal? It might seem unjust to hold detention unlawful on the basis that the detainee had free movement rights which the detaining official did not know about, and could not reasonably have been expected to know about. However, it is arguable that that is the inevitable consequence of the reasoning of the CJEU in *Royer, Olazabal*, and *Oulane*.

14.21 The Court of Appeal in *R (Nouazli) v Secretary of State for the Home Department*[24] was not willing to accept a similar argument. The appellant was a family member of an EU national who had committed various criminal offences. He was detained under Regulation 24(1) of the EEA Regulations—i.e. on the basis that there were reasonable grounds for suspecting that he might be deported. He later won his appeal against deportation. Even so, his detention was held to be lawful. Eder J held, at first instance, that a decision to detain someone, pending a decision on whether to remove them on grounds of public policy or public security, could itself be justified on grounds of public policy or public security.[25] The Court of Appeal agreed.[26] It did not seem to matter that, ultimately, the grounds of public policy

---

[22] Regulation 24(2) and (3) of the EEA Regulations.
[23] *Bassey v Secretary of State for the Home Department* [2011] NICA 67 at [35].
[24] [2013] EWCA Civ 1608.
[25] [2013] EWHC 567 (Admin) at [38].
[26] [2013] EWCA Civ 1608 at [16].

and public security, relied on by the Secretary of State, were not strong enough to justify deportation.

It is difficult to reconcile the conclusion in *Nouazli* with the passage in *Royer* cited **14.22** at paragraph 14.15, which appears to suggest that someone with a right to freedom of movement may only be detained when they can be deported. Although *Royer* was cited in *Nouazli*, this point does not seem to have been taken. At the time of writing, the appellant in *Nouazli* has applied, to the Supreme Court, for leave to appeal. In the meantime, *Nouazli* is likely to be followed, at least until the issue reaches the Court of Appeal or the Supreme Court.

(b) Abuse of rights

The CJEU clarified in *Oulane*[27] that the detention of an EU national must be **14.23** justified on the basis of an express derogating provision. It is questionable whether Article 35 is sufficient to justify the detention of an EU national. It provides Member States with the power to adopt 'the necessary measures to refuse, terminate or withdraw any right conferred by this Directive in the case of abuse of rights or fraud, such as marriages of convenience'. We do not think that this allows Member States to strip EU nationals of a right to reside that they would otherwise have. We think that, unlike 'family members', EU nationals' right to freedom of movement is conferred by the Treaties that establish the EU, rather than by the Citizens Directive itself.

There is no case-law, so far as the authors are aware, on whether 'abuse of rights' **14.24** may be used as a reason to expel or detain an EU national. However, Article 35 is intended to implement the autonomous EU concept of 'abuse',[28] defined by the CJEU as follows:[29]

> Proof of such an abuse requires, first, a combination of objective circumstances in which, despite formal observance of the conditions laid down by the European Union rules, the purpose of those rules has not been achieved, and, secondly, a subjective element consisting in the intention to obtain an advantage from the European Union rules by artificially creating the conditions laid down for obtaining it. . .

The abuse principle, therefore, only has obvious application to artificially created **14.25** rights—e.g. third country nationals who are claiming a right of admission based on a sham marriage to an EEA national. It is difficult to see how it could be applied to an EU national, just because they intend to assist a third country national in an abuse of rights. The EU nationals' right to freedom of movement is not, after all, 'artificially created'. Furthermore, the abuse concept cannot be used to undermine

---

[27] *Salah Oulane v Minister voor Vreemdelingenzaken en Integratie*, Case C-215/03 at [41].
[28] *McCarthy v Secretary of State for the Home Department*, Case C-202/13, Opinion of Advocate General Szpunar of 20 May 2014 at [107]–[112].
[29] *O and B*, Case C-456/12 at [58].

the effectiveness of EU law.[30] It cannot be used to alter the scope of a provision of EU law or compromise the objectives pursued by it.[31] Detention of an EU citizen on the basis of 'abuse of rights' would undermine and compromise their right to freedom of movement. As the Advocate General said in *McCarthy*,[32] measures taken to fight against abuse should not deter EU citizens from making use of their right to free movement or unduly encroach on their legitimate rights.

(c) Proportionality

14.26 The detention of any EU national for immigration purposes must be proportionate.[33] The requirements of proportionality were described by the CJEU in *R (Omega Air Ltd) v Secretary of State for the Environment, Transport and the Regions*[34] as follows:

> measures adopted by Union institutions should not exceed the limits of what is appropriate and necessary in order to attain the objectives pursued by the legislation in question, and where there is a choice between several appropriate measures, recourse must be had to the least onerous and the disadvantages caused must not be disproportionate to the aims pursued.

14.27 The principle of proportionality, therefore, requires an alternative to detention to be used if it would be an appropriate means of attaining the objective pursued by detention. The principle of proportionality, under EU law, is more exacting than the principle of proportionality in ECHR law—the grounds of justification and test of necessity are narrower such that where there are less onerous means of achieving a legitimate aim, it would be disproportionate not to adopt them.[35] The use of immigration detention will only be proportionate where the objective necessity of detention has been established after an individualized assessment.[36]

14.28 Moore-Bick LJ suggested, obiter, in *Nouazli* that the proportionality principle provided protection 'similar to' the *Hardial Singh* principles.[37] In fact, proportionality provides significantly more protection than the *Hardial Singh* principles. The *Hardial Singh* principles do not prevent detention of someone who poses little or no risk of absconding, provided that there is a reasonable prospect of removal within

---

[30] *Hungary v Slovakia*, Case C-364/10 at [58].

[31] *Kefalas*, Case C-367/96 at [22].

[32] *McCarthy v Secretary of State for the Home Department*, Case C-202/13, Opinion of Advocate General Szpunar of 20 May 2014 at [127].

[33] Proportionality is expressly referred to in each of the provisions in the Citizens Directive which might justify detention—Articles 14, 27, and 35.

[34] Joined Cases C-27/00 and C-122/00 [2002] ECR I-2569 at [62]. See, also, Joined Cases C-286/94, C-340/95, C-401/95 and C-47/96 *Garage Molenheide BVBA v Belgian State* [1997] ECR I-7281 at [46]–[49].

[35] *R (Countryside Alliance) v (1) Attorney General; and (2) Secretary of State for the Environment, Food and Rural Affairs* [2006] EWCA Civ 817 at [158]–[172].

[36] *Arslan*, Case C-534/11 at [63].

[37] [2013] EWCA Civ 1608 at [16].

a reasonable period of time.[38] By contrast, if the person has a right to freedom of movement, EU law will make it unlawful to detain them—the detention of someone who poses little or no risk of absconding is unlikely ever to be proportionate under EU law.

(d) General principles and the Charter of Fundamental Rights

Because it engages EU law, the detention of an EU national will have to comply **14.29**
with the general principles of EU law and the CFR. There are two provisions of the CFR which may be of particular significance.

First, Article 6 of the CFR provides: 'Everyone has the right to liberty and security **14.30**
of the person.' There is no express exception for immigration control equivalent to Article 5(1)(f) of the ECHR but Article 52(1) of the CFR constitutes a general derogating provision which permits interferences with the rights in the CFR provided they are necessary and proportionate. It provides:

> Any limitation on the exercise of the rights and freedoms recognised by this Charter must be provided for by law and respect the essence of those rights and freedoms Subject to the principle of proportionality, limitations may be made only if they are necessary and genuinely meet objectives of general interest recognised by the Union or the need to protect the rights and freedoms of others.

Article 52(3) of the CFR requires EU fundamental rights with the same scope **14.31**
and meaning as counterpart rights in the ECHR to be interpreted by reference to ECtHR judgments. As a result, it is arguable that Article 6 of the CFR adds nothing to the protection afforded by Article 5(1)(f) of the ECHR. On the other hand, it is arguable that Article 6 of the CFR (read with Article 52 of the CFR) and Article 5(1)(f) of the ECHR do not have the same scope and meaning. Article 52 appears to impose a requirement that all detention be proportionate. This goes further than Article 5(1)(f) which does not impose any requirement of proportionality save that detention should not continue for an unreasonable period.[39] This issue is of no significance where the detainee has a right to freedom of movement—their detention will need to be proportionate regardless of how the CFR is interpreted. However, it may be of more significance where the detainee falls within the scope of EU law for another reason, e.g. because they are an asylum seeker.[40]

Secondly, Article 21 of the CFR provides: **14.32**

1. Any discrimination based on any ground such as sex, race, colour, ethnic or social origin, genetic features, language, religion or belief, political or any other

---

[38] See paragraph 8.71. Of course, the reasonable period of time in which removal must take place will be shorter if there is a low risk of absconding.

[39] *Saadi v United Kingdom*, Application No. 13229/03, 29 January 2008, at [73]; *Chahal v United Kingdom*, Application No. 22414/93, 15 November 1996, at [112]. See paragraph 15.16.

[40] See paragraphs 14.60–14.67.

opinion, membership of a national minority, property, birth, disability, age or sexual orientation shall be prohibited.

2. Within the scope of application of the Treaty establishing the European Community and of the Treaty on European Union, and without prejudice to the special provisions of those Treaties, any discrimination on grounds of nationality shall be prohibited.

14.33 This arguably goes further than Article 14 of the ECHR in that it affords a right, subject to limitations of EU law, not to be discriminated against by reason of nationality.

14.34 It was not in dispute in *Nouazli,* that persons exercising rights derived from EU law were in a less favourable position than aliens who were not within the scope of EU law in one respect—they could be detained, pending deportation, when no decision had been taken to deport them.[41] The power of detention under regulation 24(1) of the EEA Regulations exists where there are reasonable grounds for suspecting that someone may be deported. By contrast (save in automatic deportation cases under the UK Borders Act 2007) there is no power to detain a third country national, with no rights under the EEA Regulations, pending deportation unless there has been a recommendation for their deportation or a decision, by the Secretary of State, to make a deportation order.

14.35 The Court of Appeal in *Nouazli* held that this did not breach the EU principle of non-discrimination as that principle was concerned solely with discrimination between nationals of Member States.[42] The Court of Appeal thus suggested that EU law allows Member States to treat EU nationals less favourably than third country nationals, by reason of their nationality. This counter-intuitive conclusion was reached by reference to Article 18 of the Treaty on the Functioning of the European Union, rather than Article 21 of the CFR. The Court of Appeal also went on to find that there was no discrimination, in any event, because persons being removed under the EEA Regulations were not in an analogous situation to other deportees— they were subject to a different regime which had benefits as well as detriments.[43]

C. Family Members

(1) Scope of EU law

14.36 There are three kinds of relationship to an EU national which may give rise to rights under EU law:

(1) being a 'family member' as defined in Article 2(2) of the Citizens Directive;[44]

---

[41] [2013] EWCA Civ 1608 at [25].
[42] [2013] EWCA Civ 1608 at [28].
[43] [2013] EWCA Civ 1608 at [29].
[44] See paragraph 14.39.

(2) being an 'other family member' that meets the criteria in Article 3(2) of the Citizens Directive;[45]

(3) being someone on whom an EU citizen has a particular kind of dependency.[46]

Third country nationals with similar relationships to Swiss citizens have similar, **14.37** but not identical, rights under the Swiss Agreement.[47] The EEA Agreement does not yet expressly provide any rights to third country nationals with relationships to citizens of Norway, Iceland, or Lichtenstein. However, such rights may be the implicit consequence of EEA nationals' right to freedom of movement. In any event, the UK has chosen not to distinguish between third country nationals with relationships to EU citizens and third country nationals with relationships to citizens of Norway, Iceland, Lichtenstein, or Switzerland in the EEA Regulations.

(a) 'Family members'

The case-law of the CJEU has long recognized that the family members of EU **14.38** workers should have similar rights to the EU workers they are accompanying, otherwise it would be an obstacle to freedom of movement.[48]

The Citizens Directive codifies who are to be considered as family members **14.39** of an EU citizen and what their rights should be. Article 2(2) of the Citizens Directive defines who will always be treated as a 'family member' of an EU citizen,[49] e.g.:

(1) spouses;

(2) registered partners;

(3) direct descendants of the EU national or spouse or registered partner under the age of 21; and

(4) dependent direct relatives of the EU national or spouse or registered partner in the ascending line.

Such persons benefit from the rights under the Citizens Directive so long as they **14.40** are accompanying or joining an EU citizen who has moved to or resided in a Member State other than that of which they are a national.[50] They will receive the protections of EU law in the UK, even if they are the family member of a UK citizen, so long as the UK citizen has exercised their Treaty rights in another

---

[45] See paragraph 14.42.

[46] See paragraphs 14.44–14.45.

[47] See, for example, Article 3 of Annex I to the Swiss Agreement.

[48] *Gul v Regierungsprasident Dusseldorf* [1986] EWC 1573, Case 131/85 at [14].

[49] Regulation 7 of the EEA Regulations is intended to reflect this definition. However, if and in so far as regulation 7 is inconsistent with Article 2(2) of the Citizens Directive, the latter should be applied.

[50] Article 2(2) of the Citizens Directive.

Member State, e.g. by working in[51] or providing services to another Member State.[52]

14.41   The Citizens Directive also recognises that third country nationals who have fallen within the definition of 'family member' may continue to have a right of residence, when certain conditions are fulfilled, even if their relationship with an EU national has terminated, e.g. by reason of death or divorce.[53]

(b) 'Other family members'

14.42   Article 3(2) of the Citizens Directive also refers to 'other family members', who are defined as 'durable partners' and other family members that do not fall within the definition in Article 2(2) but who 'in the country from which they have come, are dependants or members of the household of the Union citizen having the primary right of residence, or where serious health grounds strictly require the personal care of the family member by the Union citizen'.

14.43   Unlike 'family members' within the definition of Article 2(2), the rights of these 'other family members' (or 'extended family members' as they are referred to in the EEA Regulations) are constituted only at the point at which the UK recognizes that they meet the necessary criteria. Article 3(2) is not sufficiently precise to enable 'other family members' to rely on it directly. A broad discretion is left to Member States to decide the relevant criteria.[54] They therefore only become assimilated to EU citizens in terms of their right to reside when they are recognised by the UK authorities as being 'extended family members'.[55]

(c) Dependency on the third country national

14.44   The Citizens Directive is not exhaustive of the situations in which a third country national may obtain a right of residence by reason of their relationship to an EU national. In *Chen*[56] a Chinese national had a child in Ireland. As a result, the child acquired Irish (and EU) citizenship. This conferred a right on the mother to reside, with her child, in the UK provided that they were self sufficient.[57]

14.45   This principle has been extended to situations where the EU citizen has not exercised their right to freedom of movement. *Zambrano*[58] concerned Belgian children, who had never left Belgium, and their father, who was a third country national. The

---

[51]   *Surinder Singh*, Case C-370/90, [1992] ECR I-4265.
[52]   *Carpenter*, Case C-60/00.
[53]   See, in particular, Article 17 of the Citizens Directive.
[54]   *Secretary of State for the Home Department v Rahman*, Case C-83/11.
[55]   Regulation 8 of the EEA Regulations defines when a third country national is an 'extended family member'.
[56]   Case C-200/02, [2004] ECR I-9925.
[57]   See also *Ibrahim*, Case C-310/08, [2010] ECR I-1065 and *Teixeira*, Case C-480/08, [2010] ECR I-1107.
[58]   Case C-34/09, [2011] ECR I-1177.

CJEU held that the EU citizenship of the children conferred a right of residence on the father. Otherwise, the children's genuine enjoyment of their EU citizenship rights would be nullified because they would be forced to leave the territory of the EU. In *Dereci*[59] the CJEU clarified that the principle would only apply in a 'static' citizenship case (i.e. a case where the person had not left their home state) where there was financial dependency.

(d) Conclusion

It follows from this discussion that the immigration detention of a third country **14.46** national will fall within the scope of EU law where:

(1) The third country national has one of the following connections to an EU citizen (other than a UK citizen who has not exercised Treaty rights abroad) who is present in the United Kingdom:
   (a) they are a 'family member' within the meaning of Article 2(2) of the Citizens Directive;[60]
   (b) they are an 'other family member' within the meaning of Article 3(2) of the Citizens Directive and that relationship has been recognized by the United Kingdom;[61]
(2) The EU citizen has a relationship of financial dependency with the third country national and as a result the EU citizen's rights would be nullified if the third country national were not given a right of residence.[62]
(3) The third country national once fell within category (1) and continues to have a right of residence by reason of the Citizens Directive.[63]

(2) Effect of EU law

If a third country national falls within one of the three categories identified at **14.47** paragraph 14.46, their detention will need to comply with general principles of EU law, in particular the principle of proportionality. This significantly reduces the situations in which detention may lawfully be used.[64]

Secondly, it is arguable that 'family members' of EU nationals may only be detained **14.48** in circumstances where EU nationals may be detained. After all, one of the intentions of the Citizens Directive was to ensure that the family members of EU citizens should have the same right to move and reside freely within Member States as EU citizens themselves.[65] The derogation in Article 27 of the Citizens Directive, from that

---

[59] Case C-256/11, [2011] ECR I-11315.
[60] See paragraph 14.39.
[61] See paragraph 14.42.
[62] See paragraphs 14.44–14.45.
[63] See paragraph 14.41.
[64] See paragraphs 14.26–14.28.
[65] See the fifth recital of the Citizens Directive.

right to freedom of movement, makes no distinction between EU citizens and their family members.[66]

14.49 This is not reflected in the EEA Regulations, which do not protect the rights of family members, in the same way that they protect the rights of EEA nationals. For example, regulation 22(1)(a) and (2) of the EEA Regulations provides for the detention of a third country national claiming a right of admission on the basis that they are a family member of an EEA national. On the face of the EEA Regulations, they are less protected from detention, in this situation, than EEA nationals—they are liable to detention even if there is no reason to believe they may be excluded under regulations 19(1), (1A), or (1B).[67] Instead, they are to be treated as if they were ordinary aliens.[68]

14.50 It is questionable whether this power of detention under regulation 22(1)(a) may be exercised compatibly with EU law. There is no express provision in the Citizens Directive to permit the detention of a family member with a right to enter and reside in the United Kingdom.

14.51 An example may clarify the effect of this limitation. Assume that X is a third country national, the 'family member' (as opposed to the extended family member) of Y, an EU national working in the United Kingdom. X arrives in the United Kingdom, claiming admission on the basis of their status as Y's 'family member'. There is no reason to think that X poses a risk to public policy, public security, or public health but the immigration officer is sceptical of whether X is really related to Y as claimed. The immigration officer has a power to detain X under regulation 22(1)(a) of the EEA Regulations. However, under Articles 5 and 6 of the Citizens Directive, X has a right to enter and reside in the United Kingdom. Exercising the power of detention would violate those rights. There is no derogating provision in the Citizens Directive which could justify X's detention.

14.52 This example is not academic. At present, the United Kingdom expects the family members of EU citizens to have EEA family permits or residence cards issued in the United Kingdom if they are to enter the United Kingdom.[69] This is reflected in the EEA Regulations which make no reference to residence cards issued in other Member States.[70] This is not consistent with Article 5(2) of the Citizens Directive which allows family members with residence cards issued

---

[66] See paragraph 14.13.
[67] Contrast regulation 22(1)(a) with 22(1)(b) of the EEA Regulations. See paragraph 6.36.
[68] See regulation 22(2) of the EEA Regulations. See also paragraphs 7.02–7.05 on the liability of ordinary aliens to detention on arrival.
[69] *McCarthy v Secretary of State for the Home Department*, Case C-202/13, Opinion of Advocate General Szpunar of 20 May 2014 at [26].
[70] Article 2 of the EEA Regulations.

by any Member State to enter a Member State without the need for an entry visa. It is possible that an immigration officer might refuse admission and/or detain the family member of an EU national, if the only evidence they had of their right of admission was a residence card issued in another Member State. In our view, this would be unlawful without good reason to suspect that the residence card was forged. Although regulations 22(1)(a)(i) and (2) and 23 of the EEA Regulations could be read as providing a power to detain in these circumstances, it would be unlawful to exercise that power because it would be incompatible with the family member's directly effective rights under Article 5(2) of the Citizens Directive. EU law requires the immigration officer to accept the residence card unless they can establish that it was procured by an abuse of rights.[71]

D. The Ankara Agreement

(1) Scope of EU law

The Member States of the European Community (as it then was) and Turkey **14.53** signed the Turkey EEC Association Agreement, which was later supplemented by the Brussels Protocol (collectively referred to as 'the Ankara Agreement'). The Ankara Agreement was intended as a first step towards Turkey obtaining the same right to freedom of movement as EU states. The purpose of the Ankara Agreement was purely economic—to promote the economic development of Turkey, rather than to allow Turkish nationals a right to freedom of movement comparable to EU citizens.[72] The Ankara Agreement provided for the creation of a Council of Association. This Council has adopted various decisions, the most important of which is Decision 1/80 because it provides for certain directly effective rights for Turkish nationals and their family members. These rights include:

(1) A right, under Article 41 of the Additional Protocol of 1970 (the 'standstill clause'), not to be subject to any new restrictions on the right to freedom to provide services with effect from the date of the Protocol.

(2) A right, under Article 6 of Decision 1/80, for Turkish workers who are 'duly registered as belonging to the labour force of a Member State' to continue in their employment and, after a period of time, to take any offer of employment they wish.

(3) A right under Article 7 of Decision 1/80 for family members of a Turkish worker, who was 'duly registered as belonging to the labour force', to take

---

[71] *McCarthy v Secretary of State for the Home Department*, Case C-202/13, Opinion of Advocate General Szpunar of 20 May 2014 passim and, in particular, at [137]; *Dias*, Case C-325/09.
[72] *Demirkan* Case C-221/11, at [50]–[53].

up job offers, after a period of time, if they have been 'authorised to join' the Turkish worker.

(4) A right under Article 7 of Decision 1/80 for children of Turkish workers, who have completed a course of vocational training in a host country, to take up employment when their parents have been employed for a certain period.

(2) Effect of EU law

14.54 The rights of Turkish nationals, and their family members, under Decision 1/80 are subject to limitations based on public policy, public security, or public health[73]—the same limitations imposed by Article 27 of the Citizens Directive on EU citizens' freedom of movement. The two derogations are to be construed in the same way.[74] As a result, the power to detain anyone with a right of residence in the United Kingdom by reason of the Ankara Agreement and Decision 1/80 is subject to limitations analogous to those which EU law imposes on the immigration detention of EU citizens with a right of residence.[75]

14.55 Detention which interferes with a right under the standstill clause is not subject to the same limitations. It does not need to be justified on the basis of public policy, public security, or public health. However, it will need to comply with general principles of EU law, such as proportionality, and to comply with rights under the CFR.[76]

E. Asylum Seekers

(1) Scope of EU law

14.56 There are two EU Directives, which the United Kingdom has opted into, which are, or may be, engaged by the immigration detention of asylum seekers. These Directives have subsequently been re-cast but the United Kingdom has not opted into the re-cast versions.

14.57 First, Article 7 of Directive 2003/9/EC ('the Reception Conditions Directive') provides:

1. Asylum seekers may move freely within the territory of the host Member State or within an area assigned to them by that Member State. The assigned area

---

[73] Article 14(1) of Decision 1/80.
[74] *Nazli v Stadt Nurnberg* [2000] ECR I-957, Case C-340/97 at [63]; *Cetinkaya v Land Baden-Wurttemberg*, Case C-467/02 at [47]; *Ergat v Stadt Ulm* [2000] ECR I-1487, Case C-329/97 at [56].
[75] See paragraphs 14.11–14.35.
[76] See paragraphs 14.26–14.35.

shall not affect the unalienable sphere of private life and shall allow sufficient scope for guaranteeing access to all benefits under this Directive.

2. Member States may decide on the residence of the asylum seeker for reasons of public interest, public order or, when necessary, for the swift processing and effective monitoring of his or her application.

3. When it proves necessary, for example for legal reasons or reasons of public order, Member States may confine an applicant to a particular place in accordance with their national law. . .

Secondly, Article 18 of Directive 2005/85/EC ('the Asylum Procedures Directive') provides: **14.58**

1. Member States shall not hold a person in detention for the sole reason that he/she is an applicant for asylum.

2. Where an applicant for asylum is held in detention, Member States shall ensure that there is a possibility of speedy judicial review.

It is reasonably clear that the immigration detention of asylum seekers falls within **14.59** the scope of EU law to some extent—i.e. at least in so far as such detention is covered by the Reception Conditions Directive and the Asylum Procedures Directive. What is not clear is the practical benefit of falling within the scope of EU law in this manner. This is discussed at paragraphs 14.60–14.67.

(2) Effect of EU law

Even if the provisions of the Reception Conditions Directive and the Asylum **14.60** Procedures Directive, cited earlier, are sufficiently clear to have direct effect, they are of questionable benefit. Asylum seekers are never detained in the UK for the sole reason that they are asylum seekers. The requirement that there be 'legal reasons' for detention is so vague as to have no obvious utility. It might be read as requiring Member States to give reasons for detention but, if so, it is not clear that that would add substantially to the obligation under Article 5(2) of the ECHR[77] and (arguably) the common law[78] to give such reasons.

This begs the questions of whether there are other, more useful principles of EU **14.61** law, such as the requirement of proportionality, on which asylum seekers may rely to challenge their immigration detention.

On the one hand, it is arguable that the detention of asylum seekers must be pro- **14.62** portionate. First, Article 7(3) of the Reception Conditions Detention appears to anticipate that asylum seekers' right to free movement within a Member State will only be interfered with where it 'proves necessary'. In the language of EU law, the requirement that a measure by a Member State be 'necessary' is effectively

---

[77] See paragraph 15.11(3).
[78] See paragraphs 9.50–9.56.

synonymous with a requirement that it be proportionate.[79] Secondly, it is arguable that Article 7 of the Reception Conditions Directive and Article 18 of the Asylum Procedures Directive bring the detention of asylum seekers within the scope of EU law, with the result that the CFR applies. It is arguable that the CFR requires detention to be proportionate.[80] Thirdly and in any event, proportionality is a general principle of EU law which applies whenever a member state acts within the scope of EU law.[81]

14.63 On the other hand, it is also arguable that the question of whether or not the detention of an asylum seeker is proportionate is outside the competence of EU law. The history of the drafting of the Asylum Procedures Directive reveals that Member States failed to agree on the grounds on which Member States may detain asylum seekers.[82] It is arguable that if the grounds for detaining an asylum seeker are outside the competence of EU law, so too must be the question of whether detention is proportionate to any grounds relied on.

14.64 The CJEU was required to consider some of these issues in *Arslan*.[83] The case concerned the detention of someone who made an asylum claim, while detained pending removal. The CJEU held that the Returns Directive did not apply while his asylum claim was being determined. As a result, the only provisions of EU law which applied to Mr Arslan were the Reception Conditions Directive and the Asylum Procedures Directive (the same provisions which have force in the UK). The CJEU recognised that the Member States had not yet agreed the grounds on which an asylum seeker might be detained. As a result, the CJEU said:[84]

> Therefore, for the time being it is for Member States to establish, in full compliance with their obligations arising from both international law and European Union law, the grounds on which an asylum seeker may be detained or kept in detention.

14.65 This ambiguous paragraph raises as many questions as it answers. At first sight, the CJEU appeared to acknowledge that it is for Member States to determine the basis on which they are to detain asylum seekers—the grounds of detention are not within the competence of the EU. However, the clarity of that principle is muddied by the caveat that Member States need to act 'in full compliance with their

---

[79] See e.g. Case 11/70 *Internationale Handelsgesellschaft* [1970] ECR 1125, 1146, *per* Advocate General de Lamothe.
[80] See paragraph 14.31.
[81] *R (Omega Air Ltd) v Secretary of State for the Environment, Transport and the Regions*, Joined Cases C-27/00 and C-122/00, [2002] ECR I-2569 at [62].
[82] Case C-534/11 at [55].
[83] Case C-534/11.
[84] Case C-534/11 at [56].

obligations arising from EU law'. This begs the question—what are the obligations arising from EU law?

To make matters even less clear, the CJEU in *Arslan* went on, later in the judgment, to examine the grounds of Mr Arslan's detention and found that it was 'objectively necessary' and compatible with Article 7(3) of the Reception Conditions Directive by reason of the risk of absconding.[85] This looks like an analysis of the proportionality of the grounds for detention. **14.66**

So, it appears from *Arlsan*, that the detention of asylum seekers does need to be proportionate in order to comply with the UK's obligations under EU law. However, it does not follow from *Arslan* that detention will only be proportionate where there is a risk of absconding. The Reception Conditions Directive and Asylum Procedures Directive allow for the detention of asylum seekers for any 'legal reason' provided that it is not the simple fact that the detainee is an asylum seeker. The swift processing of asylum claims is, in our view, a legal reason which can justify detention. Detention of asylum seekers under the detained fast track ('DFT') procedure will, therefore, be compatible with EU law so long as it is proportionate to the aim of processing asylum claims quickly. However, proportionality under EU law requires an analysis of whether detention is 'appropriate and necessary in order to attain the objectives . . . in question'.[86] Where there is an alternative to detention which would also attain the objective pursued, proportionality requires that less onerous alternative to be pursued.[87] **14.67**

F. Dublin III Transferees

(1) Scope of EU law

On 1 January 2014, Dublin III came into force. It is to apply to applications for international protection lodged from 1 June 2014.[88] Article 28 of Dublin III brings detention, for the purposes of transfer to another Member State, explicitly within the scope of EU law. It provides: **14.68**

1. Member States shall not hold a person in detention for the sole reason that he or she is subject to the procedure established by this Regulation.
2. When there is a significant risk of absconding, Member States may detain the person concerned in order to secure transfer procedures in accordance with

---

[85] Case C-534/11 at [57]–[59].
[86] *R (Omega Air Ltd) v Secretary of State for the Environment, Transport and the Regions,* Joined Cases C-27/00 and C-122/00, [2002] ECR I-2569 at [62].
[87] *R (Omega Air Ltd) v Secretary of State for the Environment, Transport and the Regions,* Joined Cases C-27/00 and C-122/00, [2002] ECR I-2569 at [62].
[88] Article 49 of Dublin III.

this Regulation, on the basis of an individual assessment and only in so far as detention is proportional and other less coercive alternative measures cannot be applied effectively.

3. Detention shall be for as short a period as possible and shall be for no longer than the time reasonably necessary to fulfil the required administrative procedures with due diligence until the transfer under this Regulation is carried out.

Where a person is detained pursuant to this Article, the period for submitting a take charge or take back request shall not exceed one month from the lodging of the application. The Member State carrying out the procedure in accordance with this Regulation shall ask for an urgent reply in such cases. Such reply shall be given within two weeks of receipt of the request. Failure to reply within the two-week period shall be tantamount to accepting the request and shall entail the obligation to take charge or take back the person, including the obligation to provide for proper arrangements for arrival.

Where a person is detained pursuant to this Article, the transfer of that person from the requesting Member State to the Member State responsible shall be carried out as soon as practically possible, and at the latest within six weeks of the implicit or explicit acceptance of the request by another Member State to take charge or to take back the person concerned or of the moment when the appeal or review no longer has a suspensive effect in accordance with Article 27(3).

When the requesting Member State fails to comply with the deadlines for submitting a take charge or take back request or where the transfer does not take place within the period of six weeks referred to in the third subparagraph, the person shall no longer be detained. Articles 21, 23, 24 and 29 shall continue to apply accordingly. . . .

(2) Effect of EU law

14.69 The domestic courts have held that Dublin II, the predecessor of Dublin III, was not intended to create any individual rights for asylum seekers.[89] Instead, it was concerned solely with the allocation of responsibility as between Member States. The intention of Dublin III, however, does seem to have been to confer rights to individual asylum seekers. Article 28, cited at paragraph 14.68, goes into detail on the situations in which Dublin transferees may be detained. There would be no purpose in that detail if Article 28 could not be enforced by detainees. Likewise, Article 4 ('Right to information') and Article 27 ('Remedies') of Dublin III appear to be intended to confer rights on the individual.

14.70 It follows that EU law imposes significant limitations on the power to detain someone pending their removal to a safe third country under Dublin III, in particular:

(1) the detainee must pose a significant risk of absconding;

---

[89] See *Habte v Secretary of State for the Home Department* [2013] EWHC 3295 (Admin) at [61] and the cases cited therein.

(2) the detention must be proportionate;

(3) the detention may only last 'for the shortest time possible'; and

(4) their detention is subject to express time limits (a maximum of three months in total, potentially less depending on when the request is made and replied to).

15

ECHR LAW

A. Introduction

15.01 When exercising her powers of immigration detention, the Secretary of State is under a duty to act compatibly with rights under the European Convention on Human Rights ('ECHR'). One Convention right—Article 5—is always engaged by immigration detention. Article 5 protects the right to liberty but allows for an exception, under Article 5(1)(f) for 'lawful' detention of a person:

(1) 'to prevent his effecting an unauthorised entry into the country'; or

(2) 'against whom action is being taken with a view to deportation or extradition'.

15.02 The detention, for immigration purposes, of vulnerable persons (e.g. children and the seriously ill) may engage Article 3 as it may amount to 'inhuman and degrading treatment'.

15.03 There is a reasonably strong argument that Article 8 is always engaged by immigration detention.[1]

15.04 There is considerable overlap between the limitations on detention imposed by the common law and the limitations imposed by these Convention rights. However, there are some limitations imposed by the Convention, which are not reflected in the common law. There is at least one reported judgment, for example, where immigration detention was held to breach Articles 3 and 8, even though it was consistent with the *Hardial Singh* principles and the Secretary of State's policies

---

[1] See, e.g., *R (Konan) v Secretary of State for the Home Department* [2004] EWHC 22 (Admin), *per* Collins J at [32] and the discussion at paragraph 15.87.

on who may be detained.[2] Moreover, it is arguable that Article 5 adds substantially, in several respects, to the protections of the common law.

Furthermore, even when the Convention does not limit the power of immigration detention any further than the common law, it may afford a better remedy. Substantial damages are only available at common law where the unlawfulness caused the claimant to spend longer in detention than they otherwise would have done. By contrast, substantial damages should be awarded for a breach of a Convention right that causes 'moral damage',[3] whether or not the breach caused detention to be longer than it otherwise would have been. A breach of Article 3 is likely to cause such moral damage and a distinct violation of Article 8 may also do so.[4] In addition, there is a strong argument, so far untested, that a breach of Article 5 should usually give rise to substantial damages, even if only nominal damages are available at common law. This is covered in paragraphs 20.61–20.68. **15.05**

The remainder of this chapter looks at the particular Convention rights, which are frequently in issue in immigration detention cases. We begin, in Part B, with Article 5 as it is the *lex specialis* of immigration detention. Part B examines the limitations imposed by Article 5 and then considers to what extent they may add to common law limitations. Part C focuses on Article 3 and begins with consideration of general principles before turning to some examples, from domestic and ECtHR case-law, of where immigration detention has breached Article 3. Part D is concerned with Article 8. **15.06**

B. Article 5

(1) Introduction

Article 5 protects the individual's liberty against arbitrary interference by the state.[5] Article 5(1) permits deprivation of a person's liberty 'in accordance with a procedure prescribed by law' on certain specified grounds, the most relevant of which is at Article 5(1)(f): **15.07**

> the lawful arrest or detention of a person to prevent his effecting an unauthorised entry into the country or of a person against whom action is being taken with a view to deportation or extradition.

Article 5(2) requires that everyone arrested should be informed 'promptly, in a language which he understands, of the reasons for his arrest and of any charge against **15.08**

---

[2] *R (D) v Secretary of State for the Home Department* [2012] EWHC 2501 (Admin).
[3] See paragraphs 20.49-20.50 for a discussion of what 'moral damage' is.
[4] See paragraphs 20.51–20.52 and 20.77–20.81.
[5] *Aksoy v Turkey* (18 December 1996), (1997) 23 EHRR 553, at [76].

him'. Article 5(3) has no relevance in the present context. Article 5(4) provides that everyone who has been arrested or detained should be 'entitled to take proceedings by which the lawfulness of his detention shall be decided speedily by a court and his release ordered if the detention is not lawful'. Article 5(5) requires that everyone who has been 'the victim of arrest or detention' in contravention of Article 5 shall have 'an enforceable right to compensation'.

15.09 This chapter is concerned with limitations on the power to detain. It focusses largely on Article 5(1) and 5(2) because they restrict the situations in which powers of immigration detention may lawfully be used. Articles 5(4) and 5(5) are more concerned with the remedies against detention which is, or may be, unlawful.[6]

15.10 This chapter focuses on two questions:

(1) What limitations does Article 5 impose on the power of immigration detention?
(2) In what ways, if any, do the limitations imposed by Article 5 go beyond those imposed by the common law?

(2) Article 5 limitations

15.11 Article 5(1)(f) and 5(2) impose three express limitations on the use of immigration detention:

(1) the detention must be lawful—i.e. 'in accordance with a procedure pre-scribed by law';[7]
(2) the detention must be on one of the specified grounds—either:
    (a) to prevent a person 'effecting an unauthorised entry into the country'; or
    (b) of a person 'against whom action is being taken with a view to deporta-tion or extradition'.[8]
(3) the detainee must be informed promptly, in a language which he under-stands, of the reasons for his detention.[9]

15.12 Each of these limitations is considered in turn below.

(a) Lawfulness

15.13 The first limitation requires that detention comply with the substantive and pro-cedural rules of national law.[10] As a result, any detention which is unlawful at common law will also violate Article 5.

---

[6] See further Chapter 20, paragraphs 20.55–20.76.
[7] Article 5(1) of the ECHR.
[8] Article 5(1)(f) of the ECHR.
[9] Article 5(2) of the ECHR.
[10] *Amuur v France* Application Number 19776/92 (25 June 1996), (1996) 22 EHRR 533 at [50].

However, the first limitation goes beyond that. It requires that the national law itself be 'certain'. As a result, the criteria for detention must be clearly defined and the application of the law must be sufficiently accessible and precise, in order to avoid all risk of arbitrariness.[11] **15.14**

(b) Permissible grounds

The second limitation limits permissible immigration detention to two situations: **15.15**

(1) Where the state is seeking to prevent 'unauthorised entry', which has been interpreted to include the detention of anyone seeking entry, when their entry has not yet been authorized,[12] but does not include the detention of illegal aliens who are trying to leave the Member State;[13] and

(2) When action is being taken with a view to the deportation[14] or extradition of the detainee.

Detention does not have to be 'reasonably considered necessary, for example to prevent the person concerned from committing an offence or fleeing'.[15] The principle of proportionality applies to detention under Article 5(1)(f) 'only to the extent that the detention should not continue for an unreasonable length of time'.[16] **15.16**

If immigration detention is on the basis of the second limb of Article 5(1)(f)—i.e. that action is being take with a view to deportation—there must be deportation proceedings in progress.[17] If those deportation proceedings are not pursued with due diligence, the detention will cease to be permissible under Article 5(1)(f).[18] On the face of it, this requirement for 'due diligence' is very similar to the fourth *Hardial Singh* principle—that the Secretary of State must act with reasonable expedition to effect removal.[19] However, in practice, there are significant differences in the way these similar tests have been applied.[20] **15.17**

The ECtHR has read the first and second limitations together and, from them, derived the following conditions which must be fulfilled if detention, which is alleged to be authorized by Article 5(1)(f), is not to be 'arbitrary' and hence in breach of Article 5(1):[21] **15.18**

---

[11] *Amuur v France* Application Number 19776/92 (25 June 1996), (1996) 22 EHRR 533 at [50].

[12] *Saadi v United Kingdom* Application Number 13229/03 (29 January 2008) at [65]

[13] *Rusu v Austria* Application Number 34082/02 (2 October 2008), 49 Eur HR Rep 28 (2009) at [57]–[60].

[14] 'Deportation' in Article 5(1)(f) includes administrative removal.

[15] *Saadi v United Kingdom* Application Number 13229/03 (29 January 2008) at [73]; *Chahal v United Kingdom* Application Number 22414/93 (15 November 1996) at [113].

[16] *Saadi v United Kingdom* Application Number 13229/03 (29 January 2008) at [73]; *Chahal v United Kingdom* Application Number 22414/93 (15 November 1996) at [112].

[17] *Chahal v United Kingdom* Application Number 22414/93 (15 November 1996) at [113].

[18] *Mikolenko v Estonia* Application Number 10664/05 (8 October 2009) at [59].

[19] See paragraphs 8.76–8.91.

[20] See paragraphs 15.54–15.58.

[21] *Saadi v United Kingdom* Application Number 13229/03 (29 January 2008) at [74].

(1) it must be carried out in good faith;

(2) it must be closely connected to the ground of detention relied on by the Government: i.e. either:
  (i) preventing unauthorized entry of the person to the country; or
  (ii) facilitation of deportation;[22]

(3) the length of the detention should not exceed that reasonably required for the purpose pursued; and

(4) the place and conditions of detention must be appropriate to the persons being detained. This requires account to be taken of whether the detainee is vulnerable, e.g. because they are a child;[23] or because they are asylum seekers who 'often fearing for their lives, have fled from their own country'.[24]

15.19 The first condition requires good faith. Member States are presumed to act in good faith.[25] However, that presumption can be rebutted where, for example, the evidence indicates that the real purpose of the authorities was different to their proclaimed purpose.[26] Detention will be unlawful if the real purpose differs from the 'outer one'.[27] Thus, the first condition is similar to the first *Hardial Singh* principle—immigration detention should only be used for its proper purpose, not for some ulterior motive.[28]

15.20 The second condition requires detention to be 'closely connected' to the purposes prescribed by Article 5(1)(f). This 'close connection' has been found to exist in the following circumstances:

(1) where detention was to enable the authorities quickly and efficiently to determine the applicant's claim to asylum;[29]

(2) where detention was with a view to removal to a safe third country;[30]

(3) where deportation had been prevented and detention was for a period of 20 days, authorized by a court, in order to check the detainee's identity before giving him leave to enter;[31] and

(4) where detention continued to be justified on the basis of the first detention order despite an error as to the facts giving rise to the new detention order.[32]

---

[22] *Aden Ahmed v Malta* Application Number 55352/12 (23 July 2013) at [141].

[23] *Popov v France* Application Numbers 39472/07 and 39474/07 (19 January 2012) at [118]–[119].

[24] *Saadi v United Kingdom* Application Number 13229/03 (29 January 2008) at [74].

[25] *Khodorkovskiy v Russia* Application Number 5829/04 (31 May 2011) at [255].

[26] *Bozano v France* Application Number 9990/82 (18 December 1986); (1987) 9 EHRR 297, at [60]; *Čonka v Belgium* Application Number 51564/99 (5 February 2002); (2002) 34 EHRR 54, at [42]; and *Khodorkovskiy v Russia* Application Number 5829/04 (31 May 2011) at [142].

[27] *Azimov v Russia* Application Number 67474/11 (18 April 2013) at [164].

[28] See paragraphs 8.26–8.39.

[29] *Saadi v United Kingdom* Application Number 13229/03 (29 January 2008) at [77].

[30] *Gebremedhin v France* Application Number 25389/05 (26 April 2007); (2010) 50 EHRR 29 at [74].

[31] *Gebremedhin v France* Application Number 25389/05 (26 April 2007); (2010) 50 EHRR 29 at [75].

[32] *Kanagaratnam v Belgium* Application Number 15297/09 (13 December 2011); (2012) 55 EHRR 26 at [90].

By contrast, in *Yoh-Ekale Mwanje v Belgium*[33] the ECtHR held there was an insuf-   **15.21**
ficient connection between detention and the goal of expulsion, where detention
lasted for over a year after a Rule 39 indication had prevented removal, the detainee
posed little risk of absconding, and the authorities had failed to consider a lesser
measure such as a temporary residence permit.

Thus, the second condition combines aspects of the first *Hardial Singh* prin-   **15.22**
ciple—that detention must be for the statutory purpose[34]—and aspects of the
second and third *Hardial Singh* principles—that detention must be reasonable
in light of all the circumstances including the risk of absconding.[35] *Mwanje*
is difficult to reconcile with the well-established principle that detention does
not need to be 'reasonably necessary to prevent the person . . . fleeing' to comply with Article 5(1)(f)[36] because it suggests that the court should consider
whether there is a sufficient link between the risk of absconding and the purpose
of detention.

The third condition—that detention should not be longer than that reasonably   **15.23**
required—is very similar, on its face, to the second *Hardial Singh* principle—that
detention should not exceed a reasonable period.[37] However, there are significant
differences in the manner in which that test has been applied by the ECtHR, as
opposed to the domestic courts.[38]

The last condition—that the place and conditions of detention must be appropri-   **15.24**
ate—has no exact parallel in the *Hardial Singh* principles. Detention has failed to
satisfy this principle where:

(1) a five-year old Congolese girl was detained for two months, alone among
    strangers, in an unadapted adult detention centre;[39]
(2) an asylum-seeking mother and three children were detained for four months
    in a closed transit centre for illegal aliens in conditions that were the same as
    those for adults and were not adapted to their vulnerable position;[40] and
(3) a family, with children, was detained in premises that were not adapted to the
    children's vulnerability.[41]

---

[33] *Yoh-Ekale Mwanje v Belgium* Application Number 10486/10 (20 December 2011); (2013) 56
EHRR 35 at [124]–[125].
[34] See paragraphs 8.26–8.39.
[35] See paragraphs 8.40–8.75.
[36] See paragraph 15.16.
[37] See paragraphs 8.40–8.48.
[38] See paragraphs 15.44–15.43.
[39] *Mayeka and Mitunga v Belgium* Application Number 13178/03 (12 October 2006); (2008) 46
EHRR 23 at [102]–[105].
[40] *Kanagaratnam v Belgium* Application Number 15297/09 (13 December 2011); (2012) 55
EHRR 26 at [86]–[88].
[41] *Popov v France* Application Numbers 39472/07 and 39474/07 (19 January 2012) at [119].

15.25   These conditions can combine together to create a violation of Article 5. In particular, the third condition—i.e. whether detention lasted too long—is affected by the last condition—i.e. whether the conditions are inappropriate. Thus, three months and six months detention have been held to be 'unreasonably lengthy' when coupled with 'inappropriate conditions'.[42]

15.26   The four conditions laid down in *Saadi v United Kingdom* are not exhaustive of what the principle of legal certainty may require, in the context of Article 5(1)(f). In several Bulgarian cases, the ECtHR has criticized the fact that someone may be detained pending expulsion from Bulgaria, without the expulsion order, or any other legal act, having to specify the state to which the detainee is to be expelled.[43] The ECtHR has found this to be incompatible with the legal certainty required by Article 5.[44]

15.27   The ECtHR has also held that legal certainty requires there to be a record of such matters as the date, time, and location of detention; the name of the detainee; the reasons for the detention; and the name of the person effecting it.[45]

15.28   Finally, in some recent cases, the ECtHR has held that the second limb of Article 5(1)(f)—i.e. detention of someone 'against whom action is being taken with a view to deportation or extradition' is only lawful where there is a 'realistic prospect' of removal. Otherwise, detention will not be 'with a view to deportation or extradition'.[46] This is similar to the third *Hardial Singh* principle, as it has been developed by the courts.[47]

(c) Giving reasons

15.29   Article 5(2) provides that: 'Everyone who is arrested shall be informed promptly in a language which he understands, of the reasons for his arrest and any charge against him.' This has been interpreted as follows:[48]

(1) any person arrested must be told in simple, non-technical language that they can understand, the essential legal and factual grounds for their arrest, so as to be able, if they see fit, to apply to a court to challenge its lawfulness;

---

[42] *Kanagaratnam v Belgium* Application Number 15297/09 (13 December 2011); (2012) 55 EHRR 26 at [94]–[95]; *Suso Musa v Malta* Application Number 42337/12 (23 July 2013) at [102].

[43] *Auad v Bulgaria* Application Number 46390/10 (11 October 2011) at [133]; *M and others v Bulgaria* Application Number 41416/08 (26 July 2011) at [76].

[44] *M and Ors v Bulgaria* Application Number 41416/08 (26 July 2011) at [76].

[45] *Shchebet v Russia* Application Number 16074/07 (12 June 2008).

[46] *A and Ors v United Kingdom* Application Number 3455/05 (19 February 2009) at [167]; *Amie v Bulgaria* Application Number 58149/08 (12 February 2013) at [77]–[79].

[47] See paragraph 8.49.

[48] See the judgment of the 4th section in *Saadi v United Kingdom* Application Number 13229/03 (11 July 2006) at [51], upheld by the Grand Chamber in *Saadi v United Kingdom* Application Number 13229/03 (29 January 2008) at [85].

(2) whilst this information must be conveyed *'promptly'*, it need not be relayed in its entirety by the arresting officer at the very moment of the arrest;

(3) whether the content and promptness of the information conveyed were sufficient is to be assessed in each case according to its special features;

(4) Article 5(2) does not demand that the detained person be informed of every charge which may later be brought, providing the information supplied is sufficient to justify the arrest. Where a person is arrested with a view to extradition, the information given may be even less complete.

(3) Article 5 and the common law

It has frequently been said that Article 5 adds nothing to the *Hardial Singh* principles.[49] It has been said the limitations imposed by Article 5 and the *Hardial Singh* principles are the same[50] and that, if anything, the common law may be more favourable.[51] **15.30**

In fact, there are strong arguments that, in certain situations, Article 5 does provide a greater protection than the *Hardial Singh* principles or the common law more generally, at least when the case-law of the ECtHR is applied. At the time of writing, there are relatively few reported judgments where immigration detention has been held to be incompatible with Article 5, even though it was otherwise compatible with the common law.[52] However, the case-law of the ECtHR is still relatively undeveloped, compared to domestic case-law, in regard to immigration detention. There are a number of cases pending before domestic courts and the ECtHR which could establish a difference in approach between Article 5 and the common law. **15.31**

In our opinion, there are at least six ways in which the ECtHR might find immigration detention to breach Article 5, even though it complies with the common law: **15.32**

(1) the location and conditions of detention were inappropriate;

(2) the detention was excessively long;

(3) removal was not pursued sufficiently vigorously;

(4) the ordinary common law limitations are precluded because there was a recommendation for deportation;

---

[49] See e.g. *R (Mohamed) v Secretary of State for the Home Department* [2003] EWHC 1530 (Admin) at [15]; *R (Anam) v Secretary of State for the Home Department (no. 2)* [2012] EWHC 1770 (Admin) at [63].

[50] *R (Lumba & Mighty) v Secretary of State for the Home Department* [2011] UKSC 12; [2012] 1 AC 245 at [30].

[51] *R (SK (Zimbabwe)) v Home Secretary* [2011] UKSC 23; [2011] 1 WLR at [58]–[59] and [94]-[95]; *R (MS (Jamaica)) v Asylum and Immigration Tribunal et al.* [2011] EWCA Civ 938 at [38].

[52] E.g. *R (C) v Secretary of State for the Home Department* [2009] EWHC 1989 (Admin), referred to at paragraph 15.35; *Saadi v United Kingdom* Application Number 13229/03 (29 January 2008) at [85] (but only in regard to Article 5(2)); *Chahal v United Kingdom* Application Number 22414/93, 15 November 1996 at [124]–[133] (but only in regard to Article 5(4)).

(5) insufficient reasons were given for detention; or

(6) the procedure did not comply with the requirement of lawfulness because there was no maximum period and no automatic judicial review of detention.

15.33 Moreover, even when Article 5 does not impose any greater limitation on the powers of immigration detention than the common law, it may afford a greater right to damages. This is discussed in more detail at paragraphs 20.55–20.76.

(a) Location and conditions

15.34 The requirement, in ECtHR case-law, that the place and conditions of detention be appropriate has no exact parallel in the common law. However, relevant factors, when assessing the legality of detention under the second and third *Hardial Singh* principles, are the conditions of detention and their effect on the detainee and his family.[53] Moreover, the common law requires the Secretary of State to follow her policies on who may be detained, unless there is good reason not to do so. This provides a significant amount of protection to certain categories of person who are not usually considered suitable for detention under the policies, e.g. children and pregnant women.[54] On the other hand, it is only the Secretary of State's policies on *who may be detained* that limit the power of detention. Under the common law, policies on *the conditions of detention* do not limit the power of detention. In other words, if the conditions of detention are inconsistent with the Secretary of State's policies that will not, in itself, render detention unlawful at common law.[55]

15.35 So far, there is only one authority where the conditions and location of detention have been held to breach Article 5, even though detention was consistent with *Hardial Singh* principles and not vitiated by any material public law error: *R (C) v Secretary of State for the Home Department*.[56] C was detained, under immigration powers, in prison. The crucial fact was that he was required, without his express agreement, to share a cell with a prisoner, in contravention of the applicable Prison Service Order.[57] HHJ Vosper QC, sitting as a Deputy High Court judge, held that this was a breach of C's Article 5 rights but dismissed all C's other challenges to detention.[58] In so finding HHJ Vosper QC said that detention was

---

[53] See paragraphs 8.55 and 8.66.

[54] See paragraphs 11.15–11.19 and 12.21–12.53.

[55] *R (Lumba & Mighty) v Secretary of State for the Home Department* [2011] UKSC 12; [2012] 1 AC 245 at [68]. NB: although detention in conditions which contravene published policy would not go to the legality of detention at common law, the breach of policy would be open to challenge on conventional public law grounds.

[56] [2009] EWHC 1989 (Admin) at [39].

[57] [2009] EWHC 1989 (Admin) at [49].

[58] [2009] EWHC 1989 (Admin) at [50]. C appealed unsuccessfully to the Court of Appeal against those findings: *R (MC (Algeria)) v Secretary of State for the Home Department* [2010] EWCA Civ 347.

lawful,[59] even though it violated Article 5.[60] Presumably, what HHJ Vosper QC meant was that C's detention did not amount to 'false imprisonment' at common law, even if it breached Article 5. Such a conclusion is consistent with later authority.[61]

By contrast, in *R (T) v Secretary of State for the home Department*,[62] the Administrative **15.36** Court dismissed a claim that immigration detention in a prison breached Article 5(1)(f) because there was an insufficient relationship between the ground and place of detention. However, this case turned on its own unusual facts: it had become public knowledge that the claimant was a registered police informer and he was being held in a prison because an immigration removal centre would not offer him sufficient security against attacks from fellow detainees.

In *R (Krasniqi) v Secretary of State for the Home Department*[63] the Court of Appeal **15.37** went further and said that there was nothing in the ECtHR case-law to support a submission that Article 5(1)(f) might be breached by the location of detention, in the absence of evidence that the conditions were 'unduly harsh'.

In fact, the test that conditions must be 'unduly harsh' in order to breach Article 5 **15.38** does not appear anywhere in the ECtHR case-law. There is at least one case where inappropriate conditions of detention have contributed to a finding that Article 5 was breached, even though there was no violation of Article 3.[64]

In a subsequent decision of the Administrative Court, *R (Gomes) v Secretary of State* **15.39** *for the Home Department*,[65] the Deputy High Court judge accepted that Article 5 might be violated by detaining an immigration detainee in a prison (although he made no reference to the decision in *Krasniqi*). On the facts of the case, he found no violation of Article 5 because the claimant would have posed a risk to children if she had been held in an immigration detention centre.[66]

In *R (Detention Action) v Secretary of State for the Home Department*[67] the court **15.40** did not accept that conditions of detention in the Detained Fast Track ('DFT') breached Article 5 ECHR. It was argued that conditions in the DFT as currently implemented were significantly less 'relaxed' than in the earlier Oakington DFT regime, and that the relaxed nature of that regime had been a factor in its being ruled lawful by the House of Lords and the ECtHR. Ouseley J was not persuaded

---

[59] [2009] EWHC 1989 (Admin) at [49]. There was no cross appeal against this finding.
[60] [2009] EWHC 1989 (Admin) at [50].
[61] *R (Lumba & Mighty) v Secretary of State for the Home Department* [2011] UKSC 12; [2012] 1 AC 245 at [68].
[62] *R (T) v Secretary of State for the Home Department* [2007] EWHC 3074 (Admin) at [42]–[44].
[63] *R (Krasniqi) v Secretary of State for the Home Department* [2011] EWCA Civ 1549 at [16]–[19].
[64] *Suso Musa v Malta* Application Number 42337/12 (23 July 2013) at [102].
[65] [2014] EWHC 1169 (Admin) at [113].
[66] [2014] EWHC 1169 (Admin) at [114]–[116].
[67] [2014] EWHC 2245 (Admin) at [201]–[209].

that 'the change in conditions contributed much to the argument about lawfulness of detention or its effect on the fairness of decision-making in the DFT'.

15.41 There are at least two pending cases, one before the domestic courts and one before the ECtHR, which might provide further guidance on when the location and conditions of detention will breach Article 5, even though there has been no 'false imprisonment' for the purposes of the common law.

15.42 The first is *VM v United Kingdom*,[68] which concerned a mentally ill woman who was detained, for several years, in an immigration removal centre despite medical evidence that her condition was exacerbated by detention. The Court of Appeal found that her detention for the first two years was unlawful, because it was pursuant to an unlawful policy, but awarded only nominal damages on the basis that she could and would have been detained in any event.[69] Further, the Court of Appeal found the last three months of her detention to be lawful.[70] The ECtHR has communicated the question of whether detention in these last three months was lawful in light of her mental health and the length of her detention. The ECtHR may find that detention in this period was 'arbitrary' by reason of the conditions and length of detention.

15.43 The second case is *R (Idira) v Secretary of State for the Home Department*.[71] The claimant is challenging, *inter alia*, the decision of the Secretary of State to detain him, under immigration powers, in the prison estate. He contends that the prison regime provides significantly less freedom than an immigration removal centre and other significant disadvantages, particularly in relation to accessing legal advice and communicating with the outside world. He further contends that the decision to detain him in prison was unlawful because it was not the product of an individualized assessment, but rather the result of a policy which requires that all foreign nationals detained on completion of a prison sentence remain in the prison estate until all of the prison beds available to the Home Office for that purpose have been filled.[72]

(b) Excessive length

15.44 The requirement which the ECtHR has read into Article 5(1)(f)—i.e. that 'the length of detention should not exceed that reasonably required for the purpose pursued'[73]—appears to mirror the second *Hardial Singh* principle.[74] In practice,

---

[68] Application Number 49734/12.
[69] *R (OM) v Secretary of State for the Home Department* [2011] EWCA Civ 909 at [38]–[39] and [57].
[70] *R (OM) v Secretary of State for the Home Department* [2011] EWCA Civ 909 at [47] and [57].
[71] CO/129/2014.
[72] For a discussion of the relevant policy provisions (EIG 55.10.1) see Chapter 17, paragraphs 17.29–17.33.
[73] *Saadi v United Kingdom* Application Number 13229/03 (29 January 2008) at [74].
[74] See paragraphs 8.40–8.48.

however, it is arguable that there is a significant difference in the way the domestic courts and the ECtHR have applied these similar tests. It is difficult to form any certain conclusions, however, because there are far fewer judgments of the ECtHR than the domestic courts on the length of immigration detention and the principles which the ECtHR applies are less clear.[75] However, an analysis of the conclusions in ECtHR and domestic case-law does suggest a difference in approach.

The domestic courts have at times been tolerant of long periods of immigration detention, stretching to several years, particularly in cases involving serious criminality and/or obstruction of the removal process. They have dismissed attempts by detainees to use the Returns Directive,[76] to which the UK was not a signatory, as a benchmark.[77] The Returns Directive sets a maximum period for immigration detention of six months,[78] with an additional 12 months if there is lack of cooperation by the third country national concerned or delays in obtaining the necessary travel documents.[79] There are examples of the domestic courts upholding periods of detention well in excess of 18 months—periods of 38 months,[80] 40 months,[81] and 53 months,[82] have been held to be compatible with *Hardial Singh* principles. **15.45**

It is arguable that the ECtHR has been much less tolerant of long periods of immigration detention. The ECtHR has accepted that the maximum time limits in the Returns Directive cannot be applied to Article 5.[83] Nonetheless, when immigration detention has exceeded 18 months, the ECtHR has relied on this fact as indicative of detention being excessive.[84] In *Mikolenko v Estonia*,[85] the ECtHR described detention for just under four years as 'extraordinarily long' and said that detention for three a half years could not be justified just by an 'expected change in legal circumstances'. **15.46**

In *Singh c. République Tchèque*,[86] the ECtHR considered that two and a half years of immigration detention, pending travel documents, was unreasonably long and noted that it was longer than the sentence of imprisonment for which the applicant was being deported. This can be contrasted with the approach of the **15.47**

---

[75] By contrast, the factors which are relevant to whether a period of detention is 'reasonable' at common law are well-established—see paragraph 8.55.

[76] Directive 2008/115/EC of the European Parliament and of the Council of 16 December 2008 on common standards and procedures in Member States for returning illegally-staying third-country nationals.

[77] *R (Azaroal) v Secretary of State for the Home Department* [2013] EWHC 1248 (Admin) at [41].

[78] Directive 2008/115/EC, Article 15(5).

[79] Directive 2008/115/EC, Article 15(6).

[80] *R (Noureddine) v Secretary of State for the Home Department* [2012] EWHC 1707 (Admin).

[81] *R (Davies) v Secretary of State for the Home Department* [2010] EWHC 2656 (Admin).

[82] *R (Giwa) v Secretary of State for the Home Department* [2013] EWHC 3189 (Admin).

[83] *Auad v Bulgaria* Application number 46390/10, 11 October 2011 at [128].

[84] *Raza v Bulgaria* Number 31465/08, 11 February 2010 at [74].

[85] Application Number 10664/05, 8 October 2009 at [64]–[66].

[86] Application Number 60538/00, 25 January 2005 at [61]–[68]. The ECtHR has not published an English translation of the judgment.

domestic courts, which have often upheld immigration detention for periods considerably longer than two and a half years in circumstances where the earlier term of imprisonment was substantially shorter—the claimants in *R (Noureddine) v Secretary of State for the Home Department*[87] and *R (Davies) v Secretary of State for the Home Department*,[88] for example, each received criminal sentences of 12 months but were subsequently detained for 38 and 40 months respectively under immigration powers.

15.48 In *Azimov v Russia*,[89] the ECtHR considered that two years and five months of immigration detention was unreasonably long. The first year was acceptable, in light of legal challenges that prevented removal, but the second was not, as removal was prevented throughout this time by a Rule 39 indication. The ECtHR noted, in so finding, that the period of 'preventative' immigration detention was significantly longer than the maximum period of 'punitive' imprisonment for the immigration offence of which the applicant was guilty. The ECtHR commented that this was 'unusual' and appears to have taken it into account in finding that detention was unreasonably long. This can be contrasted with the approach of the domestic courts. It is an offence, under section 35 of the Asylum and Immigration (Treatment of Claimants, etc.) Act 2004, to fail to cooperate in the process of obtaining a travel document necessary for removal when given notice to do so. The maximum sentence is two years' imprisonment, although punishments are usually less for a first offence.[90] Despite this, domestic courts have approved the use of immigration detention, for non-cooperative detainees, for periods considerably longer than two years.[91] In *R (BE) v Secretary of State for the Home Department*,[92] the Deputy High Court judge did not consider that the maximum sentence for an offence under section 35 was of 'any particular relevance to the reasonableness of the period of detention'.

15.49 On the other hand, there are some cases where the ECtHR has held that relatively long periods of immigration detention were not excessive. The most notable example is *Chahal v United Kingdom*,[93] where the ECtHR held that three years of immigration detention (prior to a Rule 39 indication)[94] was not excessive. However, in recent cases, the ECtHR has repeatedly distinguished this aspect of the judgment in *Chahal*, on the basis that the detention in *Chahal* was prolonged by complicated legal challenges to removal which were diligently pursued.[95]

---

[87] [2012] EWHC 1707 (Admin).

[88] [2010] EWHC 2656 (Admin).

[89] Application Number 67474/11, 18 April 2013 at [171]–[174].

[90] *R (BE) v Secretary of State for the Home Department* [2011] EWHC 690 (Admin) at [158].

[91] See paragraph 15.47.

[92] [2011] EWHC 690 (Admin) at [158].

[93] *Chahal v United Kingdom* Application Number 22414/93 (15 November 1996).

[94] I.e. a direction from the ECtHR that Mr Chahal should not be deported until his application to the ECtHR had been determined. The ECtHR in *Chahal* did not examine the two and a half years of detention after the Rule 39 indication—see paragraph 15.50.

[95] *Raza v Bulgaria* Application Number 31465/08 (11 February 2010) at [74]; *Massoud v Malta* Application Number 24340/08 (27 July 2010) at [66]; *M & Ors v Bulgaria* Application Number

The ECtHR has suggested that the conclusion in *Chahal* should have no application where the obstacle to removal was of a different kind—e.g. problems in obtaining the necessary travel documentation.[96]

Even where the obstacle to removal is legal proceedings, it is questionable whether **15.50** *Chahal* is a precedent that will be followed. The Convention is a living instrument and *Chahal* was decided in 1996, 12 years before the Returns Directive. Moreover, Mr Chahal was a suspected terrorist and the risks, if he were to be released, were high. The more recent case-law of the ECtHR shows a trend towards greater scrutiny of detention, even where the obstacle to removal is legal proceedings. In *Chahal* the ECtHR ignored the last two and half years of immigration detention on the basis that the only obstacle to deportation was a Rule 39 indication.[97] In the more recent cases, the ECtHR has examined detention where the only obstacle to deportation was a Rule 39 indication, saying that detention in such circumstances will be unlawful if it is 'unreasonably prolonged'.[98] The point at which such detention is 'unreasonably prolonged' is hard to define. In two cases where the detainee posed a threat to national security and there were regular reviews of detention, the ECtHR found it reasonable to use detention for 11 months after a Rule 39 indication.[99] In cases that do not involve national security, the maximum permissible period of detention, after a Rule 39 indication, appears to be shorter—the ECtHR has upheld detention for up to eight months[100] but found 11 months or more of such detention to be excessive (at least where no attempts were made to remove the detainee to a safe third country).[101]

More recently, the ECtHR agreed with the domestic courts that the detention of the **15.51** applicant in *Tabassum v United Kingdom*[102] for two and a half years did not breach

---

41416/08 (26 July 2011) at [68]; *Auad v Bulgaria* Application Number 46390/10 (11 October 2011) at [134]; *Amie v Bulgaria* Application Number 58149/08 (12 February 2013) at [78].

[96] *Raza v Bulgaria* Application Number 31465/08 (11 February 2010) at [74]; *Massoud v Malta* Application Number 24340/08 (27 July 2010) at [66]; *M & Ors v Bulgaria* Application Number 41416/08 (26 July 2011) at [68]; *Auad v Bulgaria* Application Number 46390/10, 11 October 2011 at [134]; *Amie v Bulgaria* Application Number 58149/08 (12 February 2013) at [78].

[97] *Chahal v United Kingdom* Application Number 22414/93 (15 November 1996) at [114].

[98] *Keshmiri v Turkey (No. 2)* Application Number 22426/10 (17 January 2012) at [34]; *SP v Belgium* (dec.) Application Number 12572/08 (14 June 2011); *Azimov v Russia* Application Number 67474/11 (18 April 2013) at [171]; *Kasymakhunov v Russia* Application Number 29604/12 (14 November 2013) at [171].

[99] *Al Hanchi v Bosnia and Herzegovina* Application Number 48205/09 (15 November 2011) at [49]–[51]; *Al Husin v Bosnia and Herzegovina* Application Number 3727/08 (7 February 2012) at [67]–[69].

[100] *Umirov v Russia* Application Number 17455/11 (18 September 2012) at [137]–[142]; *Bakoyev v Russia* Application Number 30225/11 (5 February 2013) at [164]–[168]; and *Kasymakhunov v Russia* Application Number 29604/12.

[101] *Azimov v Russia* Application Number 67474/11 (18 April 2013) at [171]–[174]; *Keshmiri v Turkey (No. 2)* Application Number 22426/10 (17 January 2012) at [34]–[35]; *M & Ors v Bulgaria* Application Number 41416/08 (26 July 2011) at [73]–[75].

[102] Application Number 2134/10, 24 January 2012.

Article 5.[103] The ECtHR relied on the fact that Mr Tabassum had contributed to the length of his own detention by insisting (falsely) that he was a British citizen and refusing to provide biographical details that were necessary if he was to obtain a travel document to Pakistan. The ECtHR distinguished *Mikolenko*[104] on the basis that it was 'entirely clear' that Mr Mikolenko would not cooperate and therefore could not be removed, whereas the attempts to remove Mr Tabassum were not 'bound to fail'. The reasoning of the ECtHR's judgment does not explain this distinction by reference to the facts of the case. It must be presumed that either Mr Tabassum or the Pakistani authorities gave reason to hope, at all times, that removal might be possible.

15.52 So far, the ECtHR has not yet found any period of immigration detention, condoned by British courts, to be excessively long. However, there have been hints that the ECtHR might do so. *Abdi v United Kingdom*[105] arose out of the domestic proceedings in *R (A) v Secretary of State for the Home Department*.[106] The Court of Appeal found that Mr Abdi's detention, pending deportation, for three years and three months was compatible with the *Hardial Singh* principles. Before the ECtHR, the United Kingdom conceded that detention had been unlawful, under domestic law, because it had not been subject to regular reviews as required by the Secretary of State's policy. The ECtHR declined to consider whether Mr Abdi's detention would have breached Article 5, even if the necessary reviews had taken place. However, the ECtHR awarded damages to Mr Abdi on the basis that it might have found a breach of Article 5 on the basis of the length of detention and the difficulties in effecting removal.[107] Thus, the ECtHR hinted that it might have taken a different approach to the domestic courts on how long immigration detention may be.

15.53 There is at least one pending case where the ECtHR will consider whether immigration detention, held to be compatible with *Hardial Singh* principles by the domestic courts, was excessively long[108] and there may be many more to come.

(c) Due diligence

15.54 The case-law of the ECtHR emphasises that deportation must be pursued with due diligence, if detention is to be justified under Article 5(1)(f) as being 'with a view to deportation'. Prima facie, this requirement for 'due diligence' is very similar to the fourth *Hardial Singh* principle—i.e. that the detaining officials must act with 'reasonable diligence and expedition' to effect removal.[109] However, there

---

103 *Tabassum v United Kingdom* Application Number 2134/10 (24 January 2012) at [19].
104 *Mikolenko v Estonia* Application Number 10664/05 (8 October 2009).
105 Application Number 27770/08 (9 April 2013).
106 [2007] EWCA Civ 804.
107 *Abdi v United Kingdom* Application Number 27770/08 (9 April 2013) at [92].
108 *VM v United Kingdom* Application Number 49734/12 which arose out of *R (OM) v Secretary of State for the Home Department* [2011] EWCA Civ 909.
109 See paragraphs 8.76–8.91.

is a reasonably strong argument that the approach of the domestic courts to this question is out of step with the approach of the ECtHR to 'due diligence' in at least two respects.

First, the domestic courts have generally been relatively tolerant of administrative **15.55** inactivity. The Court of Appeal in *R (Krasniqi) v Secretary of State for the Home Department*[110] drew a distinction between 'mere' administrative failing and unreasonableness amounting to illegality. Periods of up to six months of inactivity have been held to be 'mere administrative failing' not amounting to illegality.[111] Delay has been condoned on the basis of the Secretary of State's 'workload'[112] and it has been said that five months of inactivity was a 'relatively short period' which should not be looked at with an 'overcritical eye'.[113] Where applications for a travel document have been outstanding with a foreign embassy, the courts have accepted that there was no need to chase often as that might have been counter-productive.[114]

By contrast, the ECtHR's requirement of 'due diligence' has often been more **15.56** exacting, at least in its recent judgments.[115] In *Raza v Bulgaria*,[116] the ECtHR equated the need for due diligence, with a need for the Member State to pursue deportation 'vigorously' and this requirement of vigour has been adopted in subsequent cases.[117] The ECtHR has found an absence of due diligence in the following circumstances:

(1) where there was a three month period of inertia;[118]
(2) where the Member State maintained detention for periods of approximately 18 months pending an application for a travel document and all it did in the meantime was to chase the applicant's home country three or four times;[119] and

---

[110] *R (Krasniqi) v Secretary of State for the Home Department* [2011] EWCA Civ 1549 at [12].

[111] *R (OM) v Secretary of State for the Home Department* [2011] EWCA Civ 909 at [46]; *R (Noureddine) v Secretary of State for the Home Department* [2012] EWHC 1707 (Admin). See paragraph 8.78.

[112] *R (Belkasim) v Secretary of State for the Home Department* [2012] EWHC 3109 (Admin) at [187].

[113] *R (Noureddine) v Secretary of State for the Home Department* [2012] EWHC 1707 (Admin) at [97].

[114] *R (Giwa) v Secretary of State for the Home Department* [2013] EWHC 3189 (Admin) at [76].

[115] Daniel Wilsher argues convincingly that the ECtHR has 'raised the bar of due diligence' in light of the increasing numbers of de facto stateless persons held indefinitely—*Immigration Detention, Law, History and Politics*, Cambridge University Press, 2012, at p 145.

[116] *Raza v Bulgaria* Application Number 31465/08 (11 February 2010) at [73].

[117] *Massoud v Malta* Application Number 24340/08 (27 July 2010) at [66]; *Auad v Bulgaria* Application Number 46390/10 (11 October 2011) at [132]; *Amie v Bulgaria* Application Number 58149/08 (12 February 2013) at [77].

[118] *John c. Grèce* Application Number 199/05, 10 May 2007 at [35]. There is no English translation of the judgment.

[119] *Auad v Bulgaria* Application Number 46390/10 (11 October 2011) at [132]; *Amie v Bulgaria* Application Number 58149/08 (12 February 2013) at [77].

(3) where the Member State did nothing for two months other than interview the detainee.[120]

15.57 Secondly, in domestic case-law, a failure to act with reasonable expedition does not render detention unlawful unless it prolongs detention. In other words, the claimant must show not just unlawful delay but also that such delay was causative—i.e. there was a period when they would not have been detained if the Secretary of State had acted with all reasonable expedition.[121] By contrast, the ECtHR does not consider whether the absence of due diligence prolonged detention. In other words, the ECtHR does not apply a causation test. The applicant does not need to prove that there was a period when he would not have been detained if the Member State had acted with due diligence. If the Member State was not pursuing deportation 'vigorously' the ECtHR will find that detention was no longer permitted under Article 5(1)(f) because action was not being taken with a view to deportation.[122]

15.58 This difference in approach to 'due diligence' is most marked in non-cooperation cases. Domestic courts have condoned the detention of non-cooperative detainees for very long periods (often years) where little or nothing was being done to effect removal, on the basis that the Secretary of State was entitled to wait and see if the detainee changed their mind.[123] By contrast, in its recent case-law, the ECtHR has frequently found the detention of non-cooperative detainees in similar circumstances to be contrary to Article 5, on the basis that it must have been clear, relatively early on, that the detainee would not cooperate; and that not enough was done to find alternative means of removing the detainee.[124] The one exception is *Tabassum*, a case against the United Kingdom, where the ECtHR did not appear to analyse the domestic courts' conclusion that the Government had acted with due diligence.[125] It remains to be seen whether the approach in *Tabassum* will be followed—i.e. whether the ECtHR will follow domestic courts' findings that removal was pursued with 'reasonable expedition' without significant analysis of the facts—or whether a more intrusive approach will be taken. At the time of writing there are at least three cases pending before the ECtHR where the ECtHR

---

[120] *Suso Musa v Malta* Application Number 42337/12 (23 July 2013) at [104].

[121] *R (Krasniqi) v Secretary of State for the Home Department* [2011] EWCA Civ 1549 at [12].

[122] *Auad v Bulgaria* Application Number 46390/10 (11 October 2011) at [132]; *Amie v Bulgaria* Application Number 58149/08 (12 February 2013) at [77]; *Raza v Bulgaria* Application Number 31465/08 (11 February 2010) at [73]; *M & Ors v Bulgaria* Application Number 41416/08, 26 July 2011 at [66]–[75].

[123] E.g. *R (Davies) v Secretary of State for the Home Department* [2010] EWHC 2656 (Admin); *R (Giwa) v Secretary of State for the Home Department* [2013] EWHC 3189 (Admin) where detention was upheld for periods of 40 months and 53 months respectively.

[124] *Mikolenko v Estonia* Application Number 10664/05 (8 October 2009) at [64]; *Massoud v Malta* Application Number 24340/08 (27 July 2010) at [67].

[125] *Tabassum v United Kingdom* Application Number 2134/10 (24 January 2012) at [20].

may consider whether the 'due diligence' requirement has been properly applied by domestic courts.[126]

(d) No common law limitations

In *R (Francis) v Secretary of State for the Home Department*,[127] the Court of **15.59** Appeal held that Mr Francis's detention under paragraph 2(1) of Schedule 3 to the Immigration Act 1971 ('IA 1971') was not unlawful even though the Secretary of State had made errors of law in her consideration of whether to direct release—i.e. in the first period of detention the Secretary of State's decisions not to release Mr Francis were based on an unlawful policy; and in the second period of detention, the Secretary of State failed to conduct reviews of detention with the frequency required by her own policy. In the leading judgment, Moore-Bick LJ said that the mandatory wording of paragraph 2(1) of Schedule 3 to IA 1971 ('*shall* . . . be detained . . . unless the Secretary of State directs him to be released') meant that the decision to detain was made by Parliament. He held that paragraph 2(1) provided authority for the detention of someone who fell within its terms unless and until the Secretary of State exercised the power to release them.[128] Where someone was so detained, public law wrongs in the Secretary of State's consideration of release could not found an action for false imprisonment.[129] Christopher Clarke LJ agreed with Moore-Bick LJ and said that 'no claim will lie for damages for false imprisonment even if a decision not to direct his release is unlawful'.[130] Sedley LJ reached the same conclusions on the facts of the case but for different reasons. He rejected the test of 'material public law error', laid down by the Supreme Court in *Lumba*,[131] as 'too imprecise to do service in place of statutory construction'[132] and suggested that a causation test should be applied—i.e. if, absent public law error, someone detained under paragraph 2(1) of Schedule 3 would have been released, then their detention was unlawful.[133] However, Sedley LJ reached the same conclusion as the other judges because, on the facts of the case, Mr Francis would not have been released during the periods in question even if the public law errors had not been made.

The reasoning of the majority (Moore-Bick and Christopher Clarke LJJ) sug- **15.60** gests that detention, where there has been a recommendation by a court for

---

[126] *SMM v United Kingdom* Application Number 77450/12; *Mowleed Mohammed Hussein v United Kingdom* Application Number 19352/12; and *VM v United Kingdom* Application Number 49734/12.

[127] [2014] EWCA Civ 718 at [19]–[35].

[128] [2014] EWCA Civ 718 at [22].

[129] [2014] EWCA Civ 718 at [35].

[130] [2014] EWCA Civ 718 at [53].

[131] See *R (Lumba & Mighty) v Secretary of State for the Home Department* [2011] UKSC 12; [2012] 1 AC 245 at [68].

[132] [2014] EWCA Civ 718 at [59].

[133] [2014] EWCA Civ 718 at [61].

deportation,[134] will be always be lawful, so long as the *Hardial Singh* principles are complied with, even if it is inconsistent with the Secretary of State's own published policy. It is arguable that the same principles should apply to detention after the making of an automatic deportation order.[135] In such a case, section 36(2) of UKBA 2007 provides that the Secretary of State '*shall* exercise the power of detention under paragraph 2(3) of Schedule 3 to IA 1971 unless in the circumstances the Secretary of State thinks it inappropriate'. This is mandatory wording, similar to the wording of paragraph 2(1) of Schedule 3 to IA 1971 which was considered in *Francis*. On the other hand, Moore-Bick LJ emphasized that the word 'shall' can have different meanings in different contexts and statutory provisions need to be read fairly as a whole.[136]

15.61 The reasoning of the majority in *Francis* is difficult to reconcile with the requirement of 'lawfulness' inherent in Article 5. In order to be 'lawful' within the meaning of Article 5, the criteria for detention must be clearly defined and the application of the law must be sufficiently accessible and precise.[137] As the ECtHR put it in *Garayev v Azerbaijan*:[138]

> . . . where deprivation of liberty is concerned, it is particularly important that the general principle of legal certainty be satisfied. It is therefore essential that the conditions for deprivation of liberty under domestic law be clearly defined and that the law itself be foreseeable in its application, so that it meets the standard of 'lawfulness' set by the Convention, a standard which requires that all laws be sufficiently precise to allow the person—if need be, with appropriate advice—to foresee, to a degree that is reasonable in the circumstances, the consequences which a given action may entail, in order to avoid all risk of arbitrariness. . .

15.62 It is difficult to see how the conditions of detention can be sufficiently clearly defined, or detention sufficiently foreseeable, to meet the requirements of Article 5, if someone may lawfully be detained even though the Secretary of State's own policy indicates that they should have been released. The Court of Appeal did not examine this point in their judgment in *Francis*. Only Moore-Bick LJ referred to Article 5 and all he said about it was that the *Hardial Singh* principles 'provide the degree of protection against arbitrary detention in this context for which article 5 calls and it is therefore unnecessary to say any more about this aspect of the appellant's case'.

---

134 I.e. detention under paragraph 2(1) of Schedule 3 to IA 1971 and the corresponding parts of paragraph 2(3) of Schedule 3—see [2014] EWCA Civ 718 at [17] where Moore-Bick LJ said that detention under paragraph 2(3) should continue on the same basis as before.
135 I.e. a deportation order in respect of a foreign national prisoner under section 32(5) of the UK Border Act 2007 ('UKBA 2007').
136 [2014] EWCA Civ 718 at [17].
137 *Amuur v France* Application Number 19776/92 (25 June 1996); (1996) 22 EHRR 533 at [50].
138 Application Number 53688/08, 10 June 2010 at [96].

If *Francis* reaches the Supreme Court, or if a court considers whether to apply the   **15.63**
reasoning of the majority in *Francis* to detention after an automatic deportation
order,[139] it will be possible to revisit the effect of Article 5. Section 3 of the Human
Rights Act 1998 ('HRA') requires paragraph 2(1) of Schedule 3 to IA 1971 to be
read compatibly with detainee's rights under Article 5 of the ECHR. We consider
that the requirements of legal certainty, set out in paragraph 15.61, require paragraph 2(1) (and any provisions which have the same mandatory effect)[140] to be construed in the manner similar to that adopted by Sedley LJ—i.e. detention will be
lawful, unless and until the Secretary of State should have directed release (whether
because of a breach of the *Hardial Singh* principles or because of public law obligations, such as the duty to follow published policy unless there is good reason not
to). This is a 'possible' construction of paragraph 2(1)—it was, after all, adopted by
Sedley LJ. As a result, it should be adopted, even if it was not Parliament's intention
when paragraph 2(1) was originally drafted.[141] In the meantime, however, lower
courts are probably bound by *Francis*, at least when considering detention after a
recommendation for deportation by the court.[142]

(e) Insufficient reasons

There is, at present, doubt as to whether, at common law, a failure to give reasons   **15.64**
for detention is a material public law error which vitiates the lawfulness of detention.[143] By contrast, there is no doubt that a failure to provide the real reasons for
detention promptly will violate Article 5(2). A delay of three days is not compatible
with this obligation to give reasons promptly.[144]

(f) Insufficient safeguards

The ECtHR has held that in countries, like the United Kingdom, where there is   **15.65**
no maximum period for immigration detention, 'the necessity of procedural safeguards becomes decisive'.[145] In the United Kingdom, there is no automatic judicial oversight of immigration detention. The lawfulness of immigration detention
will only be considered if the detainee makes an application for judicial review or
habeas corpus. The ECtHR has said in *Shamsa v Poland*[146] that 'detention that
goes beyond several days which has not been ordered by a court or judge or other
person authorised to exercise judicial power cannot be considered lawful within
the meaning of Article 5(1)'. However, this point has not been taken up in any of

---

[139] See paragraph 9.04.
[140] See paragraphs 9.02–9.04.
[141] See *Mendoza v Ghaidan* [2004] UKHL 30; [2004] 2 AC 557 at [30]–[33].
[142] It is unclear whether the same approach will be applied to detention under section 36(2) of
UKBA 2007. See paragraphs 9.04 and 15.60.
[143] See paragraphs 9.50–9.56.
[144] *Saadi v United Kingdom* Application Number 13229/03 (29 January 2008) at [84]–[85].
[145] *Massoud v Malta* Application Number 24340/08 (27 July 2010) at [71].
[146] Application Numbers 45355/99 and 45357/99 (27 November 2003) at [59].

the later cases concerning the United Kingdom's use of immigration detention. Indeed, it is hard to reconcile with the cases where the United Kingdom's use of immigration detention for many months has been held to comply with Article 5(1) despite not being ordered by a court or judge or other person authorized to exercise judicial power.[147] It may be that the ECtHR will develop a more robust approach to the level of safeguards required. There are three communicated cases, pending before the ECtHR, where it will consider whether the lack of any time limits on immigration detention, taken alone or in conjunction with the lack of any automatic judicial oversight of detention, violates the requirement of lawfulness in Article 5.[148]

C. Article 3

(1) General principles

15.66 Article 3 provides that:

> 'No one shall be subjected to torture or inhuman and degrading treatment or punishment.'

15.67 This has been interpreted by the ECtHR as imposing negative and positive obligations on Member States:

(1) a negative obligation 'to refrain from inflicting serious harm on persons within their jurisdiction';[149] and

(2) a positive obligation 'to take measures designed to ensure that individuals within their jurisdiction are not subjected to torture or inhuman and degrading treatment or punishment, including such treatment administered by private individuals'.[150]

15.68 Where the complainant is a person with a mental illness in detention, the distinction between the negative and positive obligations is not always clear—it may be a combination of acts and omissions which leads to the overall conclusion that there has been a breach of Article 3.[151]

---

[147] *Chahal v United Kingdom* Application Number 22414/93 (15 November 1996); *Tabassum v United Kingdom* Application Number 2134/10 (24 January 2012).

[148] *SMM v United Kingdom* Application Number 77450/12; *Mowleed Mohammed Hussein v United Kingdom* Application Number 19352/12; and *VM v United Kingdom* Application Number 49734/12.

[149] *Pretty v United Kingdom* Application Number 2346/02 (29 April 2002); (2002) 35 EHRR 1 at [50].

[150] *Pretty v United Kingdom* Application Number 2346/02 (29 April 2002); (2002) 35 EHRR 1 at [52].

[151] *R (HA (Nigeria)) v Secretary of State for the Home Department* [2012] EWHC 979 (Admin) at [178].

There is a minimum threshold of severity of treatment which must be met if Article 3 is **15.69** to be breached. The ECtHR said the following about this threshold, in *Pretty v United Kingdom*:[152]

> As regards the types of 'treatment' which fall within the scope of Article 3 of the Convention, the Court's case law refers to 'ill-treatment' that attains a minimum level of severity and involves actual bodily injury or intense physical or mental suffering. Where treatment humiliates or debases an individual showing a lack of respect for, or diminishing, his or her human dignity or arouses feelings of fear, anguish or inferiority capable of breaking an individual's moral and physical resistance, it may be characterised as degrading and also fall within the prohibition of Article 3. The suffering which flows from naturally occurring illness, physical or mental, may be covered by Article 3, where it is, or risks being, exacerbated by treatment, whether flowing from conditions of detention, expulsion or other measures, for which the authorities can be held responsible.

Thus, if immigration detention exacerbates a detainee's mental or physical illness, **15.70** that may violate Article 3.[153] On the other hand, the mere fact that detention may exacerbate a mental or physical illness 'to a certain extent' does not necessarily mean that Article 3 will be breached.[154] Whether or not, in a given case, the Article 3 threshold has been breached 'will depend on all the circumstances of the case, such as the duration of the treatment, its physical and mental effects and, in some cases, the sex, age and state of health of the victim'.[155] In order for there to be a breach of Article 3, it is not necessary for the authorities to have any intention to inflict suffering.[156] However, the presence or absence of such intention is relevant to the question of whether Article 3 has been breached—if there is such an intention, it is more likely that Article 3 will be breached.[157]

In order to establish a breach of Article 3, it is not always necessary to prove that the **15.71** acts or omissions of the Member State caused the victim anguish and suffering.[158] For example, Article 3 may be breached by the unnecessary use of physical force on someone in detention, or by treatment of a mentally ill person that does not protect his dignity, even if they are unable to point to any specific ill-effects of such treatment.[159]

---

[152] Application Number 2346/02 (29 April 2002); (2002) 35 EHRR 1 at [52].
[153] *R (S) v Secretary of State for the Home Department* [2011] EWHC 2120 (Admin) at [192].
[154] *R (S) v Secretary of State for the Home Department* [2011] EWHC 2120 (Admin) at [198].
[155] *Kalashnikov v Russia* Application Number 470-95/99 (15 July 2002) at [95]; *R (S) v Secretary of State for the Home Department* [2011] EWHC 2120 (Admin) at [194].
[156] *Kalashnikov v Russia* Application Number 470-95/99 (15 July 2002) at [101]–[102]; *R (S) v Secretary of State for the Home Department* [2011] EWHC 2120 (Admin) at [199].
[157] *Kalashnikov v Russia* Application Number 470-95/99 (15 July 2002) at [101]–[102]; *R (S) v Secretary of State for the Home Department* [2011] EWHC 2120 (Admin) at [199].
[158] *Keenan v United Kingdom* Application Number 27229/95 (3 April 2001) at [113].
[159] *Keenan v United Kingdom* Application Number 27229/95 (3 April 2001) at [113].

15.72 Where someone with a serious mental illness is kept in immigration detention, the positive obligations under Article 3 will require adequate monitoring,[160] the obtaining of suitable medical advice,[161] and the employment of suitably trained, competent health care staff.[162] The Secretary of State cannot avoid these obligations by relying on the failures of external contractors, because it is the responsibility of the State to secure compliance with Article 3.[163] In the language of the common law, the Secretary of State has a non-delegable duty to protect detainees from harm.[164]

(2) Decided cases

15.73 There are various judgments of the ECtHR where Greece has been held to violate Article 3 on account of the deplorable conditions in which it keeps immigration detainees, including overcrowding, lack of hygiene (more than 100 people sharing two toilets), lack of beds or even mattresses, lack of access to fresh air or recreational activities, etc.[165] However, for present purposes, it is more helpful to focus on the other cases where either the ECtHR or the domestic courts have found immigration detention to violate Article 3. Those cases generally fall into one of two categories:

(1) the detention of children; and

(2) the detention of the ill.

(a) The detention of children

15.74 There are several ECtHR judgments where the detention of children has been found to violate Article 3.

15.75 The case-law of the ECtHR in this area began with the recognition that the detention of unaccompanied minors in unsuitable conditions is likely to violate Article 3. In *Mayeka and Mitunga v Belgium*,[166] the ECtHR held that the detention of an unaccompanied 5 year old for two months in a centre designed for adults, without anyone to look after her, violated Article 3.

15.76 The ECtHR has since developed this case-law to cover accompanied minors. In *Muskhadzhiyeva and Others v Belgium*,[167] the detention of four children, aged

---

[160] *R (S) v Secretary of State for the Home Department* [2011] EWHC 2120 (Admin) at [202].

[161] *R (S) v Secretary of State for the Home Department* [2011] EWHC 2120 (Admin) at [202].

[162] *Savage v South Essex Partnership NHS Foundation Trust* [2008] UKHL 74; [2009] 1 AC 681 at [50]; *R (S) v Secretary of State for the Home Department* [2011] EWHC 2120 (Admin) at [206].

[163] *Savage v South Essex Partnership NHS Foundation Trust* [2008] UKHL 74; [2009] 1 AC 681 at [50]; *R (S) v Secretary of State for the Home Department* [2011] EWHC 2120 (Admin) at [206].

[164] *Woodland v Essex County Council* [2013] UKSC 66 at [23(1)].

[165] E.g. *Tabesh v Greece* Application Number 8256/07 (26 November 2009) at [43]; *SD v Greece* Application Number 53541/07 (11 June 2009) at [51]; *Rahimi v Greece* Application Number 8687/08 (5 April 2011) at [85]–[86].

[166] Application Number 13178/03 (12 October 2006) at [50]–[59].

[167] Application Number 41442/07 (19 January 2010) at [59]–[63].

between 7 months and 7 years, was held to violate Article 3, even though they were accompanied in detention by their mother. The ECtHR placed emphasis on the fact that the detention facilities were unsuitable for children, and on medical evidence that the children were displaying serious physical and psychological symptoms of distress in detention. In *Popov v France*,[168] the ECtHR took this further and found that the detention of a family with children violated Article 3, even though there was no medical evidence of distress or suffering. The two children, aged 5 months and 3 years, were detained for 15 days. The ECtHR found a violation of Article 3 in light of their young age, the fact that the accommodation was ill-adapted to children, there were no activities to keep them occupied and there was a strong police presence. The Court was prepared to assume that this would have caused the children 'anxiety, psychological disturbance and degradation of the parental image' even in the absence of corroborative evidence.[169]

(b) The detention of the ill

There have been five domestic judgments where immigration detention has been held to violate Article 3. Each one involved the detention of someone with a serious mental illness.   **15.77**

The first was *R (S) v Secretary of State for the Home Department*.[170] The claimant   **15.78**
suffered from a mental illness which was aggravated by detention. The Secretary of State knew of the illness from the outset of detention and should have realized there was a risk of its deterioration.[171] The claimant hallucinated and self-harmed. After just under two months of detention, the Secretary of State was provided with medical evidence that the claimant's mental illness could not be addressed in detention. Despite this, the Secretary of State kept the claimant in detention for a further six weeks until his condition deteriorated so badly he was hospitalized and an order for his release was obtained from the court. David Elvin QC, sitting as a Deputy High Court judge, held that there had been a breach of the positive and negative obligations under Article 3:

(1) The Secretary of State's decision to detain the claimant and keep him in detention, while his condition deteriorated, notwithstanding the clearest of warnings from the medical experts was a breach of the negative obligation—the claimant had been subjected to inhuman and degrading treatment.[172]

---

[168] Application Numbers 39472/07 and 39474/07 (19 January 2012).
[169] Application Numbers 39472/07 and 39474/07 (19 January 2012) at [101]–[103].
[170] [2011] EWHC 2120 (Admin).
[171] *R (S) v Secretary of State for the Home Department* [2011] EWHC 2120 (Admin) at [209].
[172] *R (S) v Secretary of State for the Home Department* [2011] EWHC 2120 (Admin) at [211].

(2) The Secretary of State breached the positive obligation because she did not have in place measures to ensure that the claimant was not subjected to inhuman and degrading treatment and/or because the procedures that were in place where not utilized effectively or treated with the appropriate level of seriousness or urgency.[173]

15.79 The next case was *R (BA) v Secretary of State for the Home Department*.[174] The claimant had been recommended for deportation. The Secretary of State knew, at the outset of his immigration detention, that the claimant had a serious mental illness and a significant history of that illness being exacerbated by detention.[175] Nonetheless, Elisabeth Laing QC, sitting as a Deputy High Court Judge, did not consider that the first six months of immigration detention were in breach of Article 3. In her view, the claimant's immigration detention only began to breach Article 3 from the moment it was clear that detention was having a serious effect on his mental and physical health and the medical expert had reported that the claimant was 'unfit to be detained'.[176]

15.80 The third case was *R (HA (Nigeria)) v Secretary of State for the Home Department*.[177] The claimant in this case displayed 'odd' and 'bizarre' behaviour in immigration detention, such as sleeping on the floor, often naked, in the toilet area, drinking and washing from the toilet, and not washing or changing his clothes for over a year.[178] The medical advice was that the claimant should be transferred to a hospital to assess whether he suffered from a mental illness but the Secretary of State took five months to act on that advice. In the meantime, the use of force was frequently authorized against the claimant, he was not given appropriate medical treatment and he so alienated himself from the other detainees that he frequently had to be segregated. Singh J found a breach of Article 3 in all these circumstances.

15.81 The fourth case was *R (D) v Secretary of State for the Home Department*.[179] D was held in immigration detention even though he displayed disturbed behaviour and was 'floridly psychotic and thought disordered'.[180] Charles George QC, sitting as a Deputy High Court Judge, held that D's detention at Brook House and Harmondsworth IRC breached Article 3 because he was not provided with psychiatric treatment (i.e. no medication or access to a psychiatrist) and his mental state deteriorated as a result.[181] D's later detention at Colnbrook was held not to breach

---

[173] *R (S) v Secretary of State for the Home Department* [2011] EWHC 2120 (Admin) at [215].
[174] [2011] EWHC 2748 (Admin).
[175] [2011] EWHC 2748 (Admin) at [200].
[176] [2011] EWHC 2748 (Admin) at [237].
[177] [2012] EWHC 979 (Admin).
[178] [2012] EWHC 979 (Admin) at [179].
[179] [2012] EWHC 2501 (Admin).
[180] [2012] EWHC 2501 (Admin) at [7].
[181] [2012] EWHC 2501 (Admin) at [181]–[183].

Article 3 because he did receive some psychiatric treatment, albeit not as much as he should have done.[182]

Most recently, the claimant in *R (S) v Secretary of State for the Home Department*[183] **15.82** was suffering from 'florid and largely untreated psychosis' when he was taken into immigration detention pending administrative removal. He was kept in detention for 110 days and, in that time, he was never properly assessed save by an independent psychiatrist, whose reports were effectively ignored by those responsible for detention. HHJ Thornton QC, sitting as a Deputy High Court Judge, found that the failures to comply with the Secretary of State's policies were 'wilful or grossly negligent' and a breach of Article 3.[184] He noted that some of the systemic faults identified in *BA* had actually intensified—i.e. the 'uncaring attitude' of healthcare staff and the other defects identified in the report by HM Chief Inspector of Prisons in 2010.[185]

Aden Ahmed v Malta[186] suggests that the ECtHR may be applying a lower thresh- **15.83** old than the domestic courts in deciding when immigration detention violates Article 3. Ms Ahmed was an asylum seeker who had fled Eritrea. The ECtHR placed emphasis on the fact that she was 'in a vulnerable position' because she was an irregular immigrant, with a turbulent past and 'fragile health', including insomnia, recurrent pain, and episodes of depression.[187] Her health problems were, therefore, far less severe than those in the domestic cases referred to at paragraphs 15.78–15.82. Nonetheless, the ECtHR found that her detention for 14-and-a-half months violated Article 3 in light of the fact that her detention centre suffered from a lack of blankets, a lack of female staff, and a lack of access to fresh air.[188]

D. Article 8

Article 8 provides: **15.84**

1. Everyone has the right to respect for his private and family life, his home and his correspondence.
2. There shall be no interference by a public authority with the exercise of this right except such as is in accordance with the law and is necessary in a democratic society in the interests of national security, public safety or the economic well-being of the country, for the prevention of disorder or crime, for

---

[182] [2012] EWHC 2501 (Admin) at [184]–[186].
[183] [2014] EWHC 50 (Admin).
[184] [2014] EWHC 50 (Admin) at [417].
[185] [2014] EWHC 50 (Admin) at [269] and [417].
[186] Application Number 55352/12 (23 July 2013).
[187] *Aden Ahmed v Malta* Application Number 55352/12 (23 July 2013) at [97].
[188] *Aden Ahmed v Malta* Application Number 55352/12 (23 July 2013) at [91]–[99].

the protection of health or morals, or for the protection of the rights and freedoms of others.

15.85 Immigration detention has been held to give rise to distinct issues under Article 8 in the same kinds of situations as it gives rise to issues under Article 3, i.e.:

(1) where the private and/or family life of a child is affected by detention; and/or
(2) where the detainee suffers from a serious physical or mental illness which is adversely affected by detention.

15.86 In other situations, Article 8 has generally not been relied on, either in the domestic courts or before the ECtHR. There have been two cases in the ECtHR where an applicant argued that immigration detention violated Article 8 because it was arbitrary and disproportionate. However, in those cases, the ECtHR declined to consider the Article 8 complaint because it had already found a violation of Article 5(1) and Article 8 raised 'no separate issue'.[189] In *ID v The Home Office*,[190] the Court of Appeal struck out a claim that immigration detention breached Article 8 on the basis that the same issues would be considered under Article 5 and a 'free-standing' Article 8 claim would have no real prospect of success.

15.87 In fact, it is arguable that Article 8 claims do bring in a consideration which is not relevant to claims under Article 5(1)(f)—interference with the right to respect for private and family life needs to be 'necessary'; whereas, detention under Article 5(1)(f) does not need to be 'reasonably necessary to prevent a person committing an offence or fleeing'.[191] There is no obvious reason, in principle, why Article 8 should not be relied on in every claim against immigration detention. There is a strong argument that the use of immigration detention is always an interference with the right to respect for private life (even if the detainee does not have a family life). The ECtHR has recognized that the immigration detention of a child interferes with their right to respect for their private life because Article 8 is intended to ensure the development, without outside interference, of the personality of each individual in his relations with other human beings.[192] There is no obvious reason for taking a different approach when the detainee is an adult. In *R (Konan) v Secretary of State for the Home Department*,[193] one of the few judgments to discuss this issue, Collins J simply stated, without qualification, that detention was an interference with the right to private life.

---

[189] *M & Ors v Bulgaria* Application Number 41416/08 (26 July 2011) at [91]; *Amie v Bulgaria* Application Number 58149/08 (12 February 2013) at [89].
[190] [2005] EWCA Civ 38; [2006] 1 WLR 1003 at [127].
[191] *Saadi v United Kingdom* Application Number 13229/03 (29 January 2008) at [73]; *Chahal v United Kingdom* Application Number 22414/93 (15 November 1996) at [112].
[192] *Mayeka and Mitunga v Belgium* Application Number 13178/03 (12 October 2006) at [83].
[193] [2004] EWHC 22 (Admin), *per* Collins J at [32].

If that argument is correct—and immigration detention inevitably engages **15.88**
Article 8—the use of such detention will need to be proportionate. It is true that
the ECtHR has applied a kind of proportionality test when considering the lawfulness of detention under Article 5(1)(f) but it is, as one commentator put it,[194]
an 'attenuated' version of the usual proportionality test. It only requires that the
detention should not last too long, not that it be necessary in the first place.[195] If
detention were examined through the prism of Article 8, it might allow the courts
to balance the rights of the individual against the interests of society in a manner
they cannot do at present. For example, the detention, pending removal in the
near future, of someone who posed no risk of absconding might be said to breach
Article 8, even though it was compatible with *Hardial Singh* principles and Article
5.[196] On the other hand, Article 5 is the *lex specialis* in relation to detention. As
a result, it is arguable that the concept of proportionality should not be applied
differently under Article 8 to the way it is applied under Article 5, unless there is
some special feature of the detention raising issues which are more appropriately
considered under Article 8—e.g. detention interferes with family life or affects the
best interests of a child.

(1) Where children are affected by detention

Immigration detention which separates a child from their parent, or prolongs the **15.89**
separation of the child and parent, will interfere with the right to respect for the
parent and child's private and family life.[197] Even if the parent and child are
detained together, there is likely to be an interference with their rights under
Article 8(1), because the custodial living conditions interfere with the effective
exercise of family life.[198]

Where detention is for immigration purposes, there is likely to be a legitimate **15.90**
aim for such detention. As a result, the question of whether such detention

---

[194] Laura Dubinsky, *Foreign National Prisoners Law and Practice*, LAG, 2012 at 36.29.

[195] *Saadi v United Kingdom* Application Number 13229/03 (29 January 2008) at [73]; *Chahal v United Kingdom* Application Number 22414/93 (15 November 1996) at [112].

[196] It is questionable whether detention, in such circumstances, would be compatible with the Secretary of State's policies on detention, in particular the presumption against detention and the requirement that detention be used only as a 'last resort'—see paragraph 10.04. Even so, there would be advantages in a claimant relying on Article 8 as well as the Secretary of State's policy. Reliance on Article 8 would allow the courts to consider for themselves whether detention was proportionate—*R (A) v Chief Constable of Kent* [2013] EWCA Civ 1706 at [43]. By contrast, courts will only apply a *Wednesbury* test when considering a challenge to immigration detention based on the Secretary of State's policy—*R (LE (Jamaica)) v Secretary of State for the Home Department* [2012] EWCA Civ 597 at [29]; see paragraphs 9.34-9.38. The *Wednesbury* test allows for a far less intense review of the detention than an analysis of proportionality would do—*R (A) v Chief Constable of Kent* [2013] EWCA Civ 1706 at [36].

[197] *Mayeka and Mitunga v Belgium* Application Number 13178/03 (12 October 2006) at [75]–[82].

[198] *Popov v France* Application Numbers 39472/07 and 39474/07 (19 January 2012) at [134].

violates Article 8 turns on an assessment of proportionality. Where a child is affected by detention, the assessment of proportionality will involve consideration of the best interests of the child.[199] For that reason, Blake J said, in *MXL v Secretary of State for the Home Department*,[200] that where detention affects the welfare of children, the impact of detention is best considered under Article 8, rather than Article 5.[201]

15.91 The ECtHR has frequently found the detention of children for immigration purposes to be disproportionate and in breach of Article 8. In *Mayeka*,[202] the ECtHR found a violation of Article 8 in light of the fact that there was no risk of the applicant (an unaccompanied five year old) absconding. The ECtHR said detention was unnecessary and other measures should have been taken, such as placing the applicant in a specialized centre or with foster parents.[203]

15.92 In *Popov v France*,[204] the ECtHR found the detention of a family, including two children, violated Article 8 because there was no risk of absconding to justify detention. In so finding, the ECtHR expressly departed from *Muskhadzhiyeva and Others v Belgium*,[205] where it had held that the detention of a family did not violate Article 8 because they were not separated. The ECtHR justified this change in approach by reference to developments in its case-law and the fact that there is now a broad consensus in international law that the best interests of children must be 'paramount'.[206] The ECtHR held that Member States must take all necessary steps to limit, so far as possible, the detention of families accompanied by children.[207]

---

[199] *MXL v Secretary of State for the Home Department* [2010] EWHC 2397 (Admin) at [84]; *Popov v France* Application Numbers 39472/07 and 39474/07 (19 January 2012) at [140]. See paragraphs 12.05–12.08 and paragraph 16.08 for discussion of the best interests of the child in domestic and international law.

[200] [2010] EWHC 2397 (Admin) at [75].

[201] *MXL v Secretary of State for the Home Department* [2010] EWHC 2397 (Admin) at [82].

[202] *Mayeka and Mitunga v Belgium* Application Number 13178/03 (12 October 2006) at [75]–[87].

[203] *Mayeka and Mitunga v Belgium* Application Number 13178/03 (12 October 2006) at [83]–[85].

[204] Application Numbers 39472/07 and 39474/07 (19 January 2012) at [145].

[205] Application Number 41442/07 (19 January 2010).

[206] *Popov v France* Application Numbers 39472/07 and 39474/07 (19 January 2012) at [140] and [147]. N.B.: The concept of the best interests of a child being a 'paramount' consideration must be approached with caution. In *ZH (Tanzania) v Secretary of State for the Home Department* [2011] UKSC 4; [2011] 2 AC 166 Lady Hale referred at [21] to a similarly worded passage in *Neulinger v Switzerland* (2010) 28 BHRC 706, and at [22] to the various international instruments which had been considered, all of which 'refer to the best interests of the child, variously describing these as "paramount", or "primordial", or "a primary consideration"'. However, she cautions at [22] that 'To a United Kingdom lawyer . . . these do not mean the same thing.' In the domestic context, pursuant to section 55 of the Borders, Citizenship and Immigration Act 2009, the best interests of the child are a *primary* consideration but not a *paramount* consideration.

[207] *Popov v France* Application Numbers 39472/07 and 39474/07 (19 January 2012) at [147].

For some time, it has been the policy of the United Kingdom not to detain chil- **15.93**
dren in immigration facilities, save in exceptional circumstances.[208] As a result,
there are few recent domestic cases on when immigration detention will breach
Article 8 because of its effect on children. In *R (Suppiah) v Secretary of State for
the Home Department*,[209] Wyn Williams J found that the detention of children
with their mother was only in breach of Article 8 because it was unlawful under
domestic law. There was no distinct violation of Article 8 because the family
was held in appropriate accommodation and provided with appropriate medical
treatment.[210] In *R (Abdollahi) v Secretary of State for the Home Department*[211] the
Court of Appeal found that the immigration detention of the adult appellant
was proportionate, even though it had an adverse effect on his child (who was
not detained) because the appellant posed a high risk of absconding. The Court
of Appeal held that the appellant had brought detention upon himself by his
flouting of immigration law. These factors were sufficient to outweigh the best
interests of his child.[212]

(2) Mental and physical illness

There have been several domestic cases where a seriously ill detainee has argued **15.94**
that his immigration detention violated Articles 3 and/or 8 because of its
effect on his health. Article 8 has been used as a fall back in case the Article 3
claim fails.

In the majority of these cases, the courts have not given separate consideration **15.95**
to Article 8.[213] However, the case-law indicates that immigration detention may
breach Article 8 even where it does not breach Article 3—e.g. immigration detention which interferes disproportionately with the family and private life of someone
with a mental illness but which does not meet the high threshold of Article 3.[214]
And there are at least two cases where a period of immigration detention has been
held to violate Article 8, without violating Article 3.

First, in *R (S, C and D) v Secretary of State for the Home Department*,[215] a child **15.96**
in immigration detention developed rickets and anaemia, even though those

---

[208] See paragraph 12.02. When the Immigration Act 2014 comes into force, it it will impose
strict statutory limits on the places in which, and the time for which, unaccompanied children can
be detained under paragraph 16(2) of Schedule 2 IA 1971.
[209] [2011] EWHC 2 (Admin).
[210] [2011] EWHC 2 (Admin) at [190].
[211] [2013] EWCA Civ 366.
[212] *R (Abdollahi) v Secretary of State for the Home Department* [2013] EWCA Civ 366 at [56].
[213] *R (S) v Secretary of State for the Home Department* [2011] EWHC 2120 (Admin) at [222]; *R
(BA) v Secretary of State for the Home Department* [2011] EWHC 2748 (Admin) at [237]; *R (HA
(Nigeria)) v Secretary of State for the Home Department* [2012] EWHC 979 (Admin) at [182]; *R (S) v
Secretary of State for the Home Department* [2014] EWHC 50 (Admin) at [417].
[214] *R (S) v Secretary of State for the Home Department* [2011] EWHC 2120 (Admin) at [195].
[215] [2007] EWHC 1654 (Admin) at [82].

conditions were foreseeable and preventable. This was held to violate Article 8. Article 3 was not relied on.

15.97 Secondly, in *R (D) v Secretary of State for the Home Department*,[216] the claimant's detention at Colnbrook did not reach the high threshold of Article 3 because he received some treatment for his psychiatric illness.[217] However, this same period of detention did breach Article 8 because the treatment he received was insufficient.[218]

[216] [2012] EWHC 2501 (Admin).
[217] [2012] EWHC 2501 (Admin) at [185].
[218] [2012] EWHC 2501 (Admin) at [194]–[199].

16

OTHER INTERNATIONAL LAW

A. Introduction

This chapter is concerned with the way in which 'other international law', i.e. **16.01** international law other than the European Convention on Human Rights ('ECHR') and EU law, limits statutory powers of immigration detention. Section B provides an overview of the most important elements of 'other international law'. Section C identifies the ways in which 'other international law' might inform the approach of domestic courts in immigration detention cases.

B. Other International Law

This section provides an overview of the most important international law **16.02** relevant to immigration detention, other than the ECHR and EU law. It is divided into:

(1) international treaties and protocols, which are binding on states parties; and
(2) 'soft law' sources, which are not formally binding on states but which nevertheless contain important statements of international norms bearing on immigration matters.

(1) International treaties

The Convention relating to the Status of Refugees (1951) as amended and **16.03** added to by its Protocol (1967) ('the Refugee Convention') describes the basic

245

obligations of states regarding the treatment of refugees. The key provision, relevant to immigration detention, is Article 31 which provides:

Article 31
Refugees unlawfully in the country of refugee
1. The Contracting States shall not impose penalties, on account of their illegal entry or presence, on refugees who, coming directly from a territory where their life or freedom was threatened in the sense of article 1, enter or are present in their territory without authorization, provided they present themselves without delay to the authorities and show good cause for their illegal entry or presence.
2. The Contracting States shall not apply to the movements of such refugees restrictions other than those which are necessary and such restrictions shall only be applied until their status in the country is regularized or they obtain admission into another country. The Contracting States shall allow such refugees a reasonable period and all the necessary facilities to obtain admission into another country.

16.04 The prevailing view is that Article 31(1) of the Refugee Convention does not preclude the detention of asylum seekers for the purposes of examining their right of entry.[1] However, some commentators have suggested that Article 31(1) of the Refugee Convention may preclude some forms of detention as 'punitive'.[2]

16.05 Article 31(2) of the Refugee Convention requires restrictions on the freedom of movement of refugees to be 'necessary'. This appears to go further than Article 5(1)(f) of ECHR, which does not require detention to be 'reasonably considered necessary, for example to prevent the person concerned from committing an offence or fleeing'.[3]

16.06 Furthermore, Article 33 of the Refugee Convention prohibits 'refoulement'. This indirectly limits the powers of detention pending expulsion because it limits who may be expelled.

16.07 Article 9 of the International Covenant on Civil and Political Rights (1966) ('ICCPR') provides for the right to liberty and security of the person. Article 10 of ICCPR is also relevant to administrative detention situations, requiring that all persons deprived of their liberty be treated with dignity and humanity.

16.08 The UN Convention on the Rights of the Child (1989) ('UNCRC') contain a series of core principles relevant to the detention of children on immigration grounds:

---

[1] *Saadi v United Kingdom* Application Number 13229/03 (29 January 2008) at [65] and the 'soft' international law cited therein.
[2] Guy Goodwin-Gill, *Article 31 of the 1951 Convention Relating to the Status of Refugees: Non-penalization, Detention and Protection*, in Refugee Protection In International Law: UNHCR's Global Consultations On International Protection 185, 195–196 (Erika Feller, Volker Türk & Frances Nicholson eds., Cambridge University Press, 2003). See also Alice Edwards, *Back To Basics: The Right To Liberty And Security Of Person And 'Alternatives To Detention' Of Refugees, Asylum-Seekers, Stateless Persons And Other Migrants* UN High Commissioner for Refugees, April 2011.
[3] *Saadi v United Kingdom* Application Number 13229/03 (29 January 2008) at [73]; *Chahal v United Kingdom* Application Number 22414/93 (15 November 1996) at [113].

(1) in all actions taken concerning children states must make the best interests of the child a primary consideration;[4]

(2) children have the right not to be separated from their parents against their wishes and, where separation is unavoidable, both parents and child are entitled to essential information from the state on the whereabouts of the other unless such information would be detrimental to the child;[5]

(3) children should be guaranteed the right to express their views freely and their views given 'due weight';[6]

(4) a child temporarily or permanently deprived of his or her family environment must be provided with special protection and assistance from the state;[7]

(5) children may be detained only as a measure of last resort and for the shortest possible period of time;[8] and

(6) a child deprived of liberty must be separated from adults unless it is considered in the child's best interest not to do so and has the right to maintain contact with his or her family through correspondence and visits, save in exceptional circumstances.[9]

Article 16(1) of the International Convention on the Protection of the Rights of All Migrant Workers and Members of Their Families (1990) guarantees the right to liberty of migrant workers and members of their families. **16.09**

(2) UN declarations, principles, and guidelines

UN declarations, principles, and guidelines are not binding on states but contain authoritative statements of important international norms relevant to immigration detention. **16.10**

Article 3 of the Universal Declaration of Human Rights 1948 ('UDHR') affirms that 'everyone has the right to life, liberty, and security of person'. **16.11**

Rule 6(1) of the UN Standard Minimum Rules for the Treatment of Prisoners (1977) expressly provides that the standard minimum rules shall be applied impartially and without discrimination on grounds of race or nationality. **16.12**

The UN Body of Principles for the Protection of All Persons under Any Form of Detention or Imprisonment (1988) expands on the UN minimum standards, Principle 5(1) expressly providing that the Principles shall be applied without distinction on grounds of, *inter alia*, race, nationality, or ethnicity. **16.13**

---

[4] Article 3 of UNCRC.
[5] Article 9 of UNCRC.
[6] Article 12 of UNCRC.
[7] Article 20 of UNCRC.
[8] Article 37(b) of UNCRC.
[9] Article 37(c) of UNCRC.

16.14 The UN Rules for the Protection of Juveniles Deprived of their Liberty (1990) elaborate on norms contained in the UNCRC, in particular those regarding the deprivation of liberty of any person under the age of 18.

16.15 The UN Declaration on the Human Rights of Individuals Who Are Not Nationals of the Country in Which They Live provides, at Article 5, that all aliens shall enjoy the right to life and security of person, and that no alien shall be subjected to arbitrary arrest or detention, nor deprived of his or her liberty except on such grounds and in accordance with such procedures as are established by law.

16.16 In its case-law on Article 9 of the ICCPR, the United Nations Human Rights Committee ('the HRC') has held, *inter alia*, that the failure by the immigration authorities to consider factors particular to the individual, such as the likelihood of absconding or lack of cooperation with the immigration authorities, and to examine the availability of other, less intrusive means of achieving the same ends might render the detention of an asylum-seeker arbitrary.[10] In *A. v Australia*[11] the HRC observed that:

> the notion of 'arbitrariness' must not be equated with 'against the law' but be interpreted more broadly to include such elements as inappropriateness and injustice. Furthermore, remand in custody could be considered arbitrary if it is not necessary in all the circumstances of the case, for example to prevent flight or interference with evidence: the element of proportionality becomes relevant in this context.

16.17 In 2012, the UN High Commissioner for Refugees ('UNHCR') issued Guidelines on the Applicable Criteria and Standards relating to the Detention of Asylum-Seekers and Alternatives to Detention ('the Guidelines'), which reaffirm the consistent position of the UNHCR Executive Committee that the detention of asylum seekers should be an exceptional measure that can only be resorted to for a legitimate purpose. The exceptional grounds for detaining an asylum seeker, according to Guideline 4.1 are limited to the following:

(1) in connection with accelerated procedures for manifestly unfounded or clearly abusive claims;
(2) for initial identity and/or security verification;
(3) to protect public health; and
(4) to protect national security.

16.18 Additionally, Guideline 4.1.4 makes clear that detention is not justified on grounds of expulsion where asylum proceedings are ongoing or as a deterrent to seeking asylum. The Guidelines also outline procedural safeguards for detention, including the right to have the detention decision subjected to automatic review before

---

[10] see *A v Australia*, Communication no. 560/1993, CCPR/C/59/D/560/1993 and *C v Australia*, Communication no. 900/1999, CCPR/C/76/D/900/1999.
[11] Communication no. 560/1993, CCPR/C/59/D/560/1993.

an independent body, and the right to challenge the necessity of the detention and the right to legal representation.

In the face of the continued practice of detaining minors on immigration grounds, **16.19** the Committee on the Rights of the Child issued General Comment No. 7, emphasizing that detention should always be a measure of last resort and 'that all efforts, including acceleration of relevant processes, should be made to allow for the immediate release of unaccompanied or separated children from detention and their placement in other forms of appropriate accommodation'.[12]

C. Using International Law in Domestic Cases Bearing on Immigration Detention

The starting point is that international treaties and regimes are not part of domes- **16.20** tic law and that the UK's international obligations are not directly enforceable in domestic courts.[13]

Notwithstanding this principle, there are three ways in which international **16.21** instruments and norms may be relied on by courts adjudicating on immigration detention:

(1) construing domestic legislation and policies to be compatible with international law;

(2) construing obligations under the ECHR to be compatible with international law; and

(3) declaring whether the executive's acts and/or omissions are compatible with international law.

(1) Construction of domestic law

When construing ambiguous domestic legislation which was enacted to fulfil an **16.22** obligation under international law, the courts will prefer the interpretation which accords with international law.[14] This interpretative obligation does not go so far as the obligation to construe legislation compatibly with EU law or the ECHR. If the terms of legislation are clear and unambiguous they must be given effect to even if they are inconsistent with international law. It is only when the legislation

---

[12] CRC/GC/2005/6, paras. 61–63.

[13] See *Salomon v Customs and Excise Commissioners* [1967] 2 QB 116, at 143–144 referred to with approval by Lords Bingham and Carswell in *R (Al-Skeini) v Secretary of State for the Home Department* [2007] UKHL 26; [2008] 1 AC 153 at [12] and [147].

[14] See *Salomon v Customs and Excise Commissioners* [1967] 2 QB 116, at 143–144 referred to with approval by Lords Bingham and Carswell in *R (Al-Skeini) v Secretary of State for the Home Department* [2007] UKHL 26; [2008] 1 AC 153 at [12] and [147].

is reasonably capable of more than one meaning that international law becomes relevant.[15]

16.23 Even where the ambiguous domestic legislation was not enacted to fulfil an international obligation, the courts may apply a similar interpretative presumption— i.e. that Parliament intended the legislation to comply with the UK's obligations under international law. This principle was set out in the 3rd edition of *Bennion on Statutory Interpretation*[16] and endorsed by the Court of Appeal in *R (Diriye and Osorio) v Secretary of State for the Home Department*:[17]

> It is a principle of legal policy that the municipal law should conform to public international law. The court, when considering, in relation to the facts of the instant case, which of the opposing constructions of the enactment would give effect to the legislative intention, should presume that the legislator intended to observe this principle.

16.24 The Secretary of State's policies should also be construed in a manner that is compatible with international law, if that accords with a fair and objective reading of the policy. Mere differences in 'phraseology' and 'linguistic niceties' should not allow the policy to be construed incompatibly with international law.[18] This presumption is reinforced by the statement in paragraph 2.6 of the Secretary of State's guidance *Every Child Matters – Change for Children – Statutory guidance to the UK Border Agency on making arrangements to safeguard and promote the welfare of children*:

> The UK Border Agency acknowledges the status and importance of the following: the European Convention for the Protection of Human Rights and Fundamental Freedoms, the International Covenant on Civil and Political Rights, the International Covenant on Economic, Social and Cultural Rights, the EU Reception Conditions Directive, the Council of Europe Convention on Action Against Trafficking in Human Beings, and the UN Convention on the Rights of the Child. The UK Border Agency must fulfil the requirements of these instruments in relation to children whilst exercising its functions as expressed in UK domestic legislation and policies.

16.25 On its face, this statement only requires the Secretary of State to comply with the requirements of international law in relation to children. However, it is arguable that the acknowledgment of the status of international instruments in the first sentence of this statement is broader than that and that the Secretary of State's policies should be read so as to be compatible with those international instruments where possible.

---

[15] See *Salomon v Customs and Excise Commissioners* [1967] 2 QB 116, at 143–144.
[16] Butterworths, 1997
[17] [2001] EWCA Civ 2008; [2002] Imm AR 471 at [14]–[15], *per* Lord Phillips MR.
[18] *R (S) v Secretary of State for the Home Department* [2007] EWHC 1654 (Admin) at [44] and [48].

(2) Construction of ECHR law

The European Court of Human Rights ('ECtHR') has frequently said that the **16.26** ECHR 'cannot be interpreted in a vacuum but must be interpreted in harmony with the general principles of international law' and that account should be taken of 'any relevant rules of international law applicable in the relations between the parties, and in particular the rules concerning the international protection of human rights'.[19] Thus, the Convention rights which are engaged by immigration detention must be construed in the light of applicable international law.

So, for example, in *Popov v France*,[20] the ECtHR relied on the UNCRC to support **16.27** its findings that the detention of a family, including two children, violated Articles 3 and 8.[21] The finding that detention, which did not separate a family, interfered with the rights of the family under Article 8 was inconsistent with the conclusion of the ECtHR in an earlier case—*Muskhadzhiyeva and Others v Belgium*.[22] The ECtHR justified this difference in approach by reference to the fact that there was 'currently' a broad consensus, including in international law, that the best interests of children should be paramount.[23]

That does not, however, mean that the ECtHR will necessarily construe the right to **16.28** liberty, under Article 5, in the same way as other, similar provisions of international law have been construed by other organizations. In *Saadi v United Kingdom*,[24] the UNHCR submitted that Article 5 of the ECHR should be construed in the same way as it had construed Article 31(2) of the Refugee Convention and the HRC had construed Article 9 of the ICCPR—i.e. that immigration detention should be necessary, for example to prevent absconding, and not for reasons of administrative convenience.[25] The ECtHR expressly refused to adopt the same approach.[26]

Domestic courts, applying the ECHR, have also looked to international law to **16.29** inform their understanding of what the ECHR requires. The High Court has recognized that Article 5 of the ECHR should be read in the light of Articles 3 and 37(b) of the UNCRC.[27] The Supreme Court in *ZH (Tanzania) v Secretary of State*

---

[19] *Golder v United Kingdom*, 21 February 1975, Series A no. 18, at [29]; *Streletz, Kessler and Krenz v Germany* [GC] Application Numbers 34044/96, 35532/97 and 44801/98, ECHR 2001-II at [90]; *Al-Adsani v United Kingdom* [GC], Application Number 35763/97 at [55].

[20] Application Numbers 39472/07 and 39474/07 (19 January 2012) at [145].

[21] *Popov v France* Application Numbers 39472/07 and 39474/07 (19 January 2012) at [91], [139] and [141].

[22] Application Number 41442/07 (19 January 2010).

[23] *Popov v France* Application Numbers 39472/07 and 39474/07 (19 January 2012) at [140] and [147].

[24] *Saadi v United Kingdom* Application Number 13229/03, 29 January 2008.

[25] *Saadi v United Kingdom* Application Number 13229/03, 29 January 2008 at [54]–[57].

[26] *Saadi v United Kingdom* Application Number 13229/03, 29 January 2008 at [72]–[73].

[27] *R (S) v Secretary of State for the Home Department* [2007] EWHC 1654 (Admin) at [41]; *R (Suppiah) v Secretary of State for the Home Department* [2011] EWHC 2 (Admin) at [148].

for the Home Department[28] has construed Article 8 in light of the binding obligation, under international law, for states to have regard to the need to safeguard and
promote the welfare of children when taking decisions about asylum, deportation,
and removal. Baroness Hale drew on the requirements of Article 3 of the UNCRC,
the UNHCR's Guidelines on Determining the Best Interests of the Child, and
General Comment No 6 of the United Nations Committee on the Rights of the
Child (2005) when determining what was meant by 'bests interests of the child'
in this context.[29]

(3) Declarations

16.30   On some occasions domestic courts have made declarations as to whether domestic practice places the United Kingdom in breach of its international obligations.
Although such declarations do not, in themselves, bind the Secretary of State, they
may be used to support conclusions that domestic practice is incompatible with
obligations under international law and they may have political, if not legal, force.

16.31   For example in *R (European Roma Rights Centre) v Immigration Officer*[30] Lord Steyn
and Baroness Hale found that by operating a pre-clearance immigration system at
Prague Airport principally aimed at preventing Roma asylum seekers, the UK had
discriminated against Roma by treating them less favourably on racial grounds
than they treated other aliens and that, in doing so, the UK had breached its obligations under international law (i.e. Article 2 of the International Convention on
the Elimination of All Forms of Racial Discrimination, Article 26 of the ICCPR,
and the Refugee Convention) as well as domestic law (i.e. section 1(1)(a) of the Race
Relations Act 1976).

16.32   In *R (A) v Secretary of State for the Home Department,*[31] Lord Bingham relied upon
a range of international instruments, including the ICCPR and the Universal
Declaration of Human Rights, as a basis for rejecting the Attorney General's
submission that international law sanctions the differential treatment, including
detention, of aliens in times of war or public emergency.

---

[28] [2011] 2 AC 166.
[29] [2011] 2 AC 166 at [23]–[26].
[30] [2004] UKHL 55 See Lord Steyn at [44]–[46] and Baroness Hale at [98]–[103].
[31] [2005] 2 AC 68 at [57]–[63].

PART V

LOCATIONS AND CONDITIONS OF DETENTION

17

PLACES AND CONDITIONS OF DETENTION

A. Introduction

People subject to immigration detention in the United Kingdom are generally **17.01** detained in Immigration Removal Centres ('IRCs') or, increasingly, prisons, but may be detained in a number of other locations. Those places are selected by the Secretary of State, as determined by statute and policy. The requirement that individuals subject to detention be detained in specific designated places reflects, so far as asylum seekers are concerned, Guideline 8 of the UNHCR *Detention Guidelines*.[1]

The legislative authority for directing the places where a person may be detained **17.02** is derived from paragraph 18(1) of Schedule 2 to the Immigration Act 1971 ('IA 1971'), although it applies equally to detention under Schedule 3 and the other detention powers discussed in Chapter 4.[2] The places where a person may

---

[1] *Guidelines on the Applicable Criteria and Standards relating to the Detention of Asylum-Seekers and Alternatives to Detention*, UNHCR, 2012, paragraph 48(i); see also General Comment No. 20 (1992) of the UN Human Rights Committee at paragraph 11: 'To guarantee the effective protection of detained persons, provisions should be made for detainees to be held in places officially recognized as places of detention. . .'

[2] By virtue of paragraph 2(4) of Schedule 3 IA 1971. See also the preamble to the Immigration (Places of Detention) Direction 2014. The detention provisions in the Immigration and Asylum Act 1999 ('IA 1999'), the Nationality Immigration and Asylum Act 2002 ('NIAA 2002'), the UK Borders Act 2007 ('UKBA 2007') and the Immigration, Asylum and Nationality Act 2006 ('IAN 2006') apply paragraph

be detained are set out in the Immigration (Places of Detention) Direction 2014 ('the Direction'). The Direction distinguishes between those detained pending examination or removal (under paragraph 16(1), (1A), (1B) or (2) of Schedule 2 to IA 1971) and those detained pending deportation (under paragraphs 2(1), (2), or (3) of Schedule 3 to IA 1971 and section 36(1) of the UK Borders Act 2007 ('UKBA 2007')).

17.03 Pending amendments to Schedule 2 IA 1971, to be introduced by section 6 of the Immigration Act 2014 ('IA 2014'), will put on a statutory footing the concept of 'pre-departure accommodation', and the time limits for the use of such accommodation. At the time of writing, Home Office policy makes reference to pre-departure accommodation (a facility for the detention of families with children in very limited circumstances, as part of the Family Returns Process).[3] However, pre-departure accommodation is not referred to or defined in any statute or statutory instrument yet in force. The one facility that currently exists (Cedars) is, in law, a short-term holding facility.[4]

B. Permitted Places of Detention

17.04 Pursuant to paragraph 3 of the Direction, those detained under paragraph 16 of Schedule 2 IA 1971 may be held in any of the following locations:

(1) Any place, used by an immigration officer for the purposes of his functions, at the port at which that person is seeking to enter or has been refused leave to enter.[5]

(2) Any place specifically provided for the purpose of detention:
   (a) at any port;
   (b) at any place used by an immigration officer for the purposes of his functions;
   (c) in a control zone or a supplementary control zone.

(3) Any short-term holding facility, including:
   (a) any police station;
   (b) any premises at or near where appeals are heard.[6]

(4) Any hospital.[7]

---

18 of Schedule 2 IA 1971 to detention under those Acts (see section 10(7) IAA 1999, section 62(3) NIAA 2002, section 36(4) UKBA 2007 and section 47(3) IAN 2006 respectively).

[3] See further Chapter 12 paragraphs 12.54–12.87.

[4] As to which, see further paragraphs 17.47–17.48.

[5] Or in a control zone or a supplementary control zone (as defined in the Channel Tunnel orders) or a control area designated as such under paragraph 26 of Schdule 2 to IA 1971.

[6] Under the Nationality, Immigration and Asylum Act 2002 ('NIAA 2002'), Part IV of the Anti-Terrorism Crime and Security Act 2001 (now largely repealed), and the Special Immigration Appeals Commission Act 1997.

[7] 'Hospital' has the same meaning as in the Mental Health Act 1983 (MHA 1983): Immigration (Places of Detention) Direction 2014 at paragraph 2. See further *IM (Nigeria) v Secretary of State*

(5) Any young offender institution, prison or remand centre or, in the case of a person under the age of 18, any place of safety.

(6) Brook House Immigration Removal Centre, Gatwick Airport, West Sussex.

(7) Campsfield House Immigration Removal Centre, Kidlington, Oxford.

(8) Colnbrook Immigration Removal Centre, Colnbrook bypass, Harmondsworth, Middlesex.

(9) Dover Immigration Removal Centre, the Citadel, Western Heights, Dover, Kent.

(10) Dungavel House Immigration Removal Centre, Strathaven, Lanarkshire.

(11) Harmondsworth Immigration Removal Centre, Colnbrook bypass, Harmondsworth, Middlesex.

(12) Haslar Immigration Removal Centre, Gosport, Hampshire.

(13) Morton Hall Immigration Removal Centre, Swinderby, Lincolnshire.

(14) Tinsley House Immigration Removal Centre, Gatwick Airport, West Sussex.

(15) Yarl's Wood Immigration Removal Centre, Clapham, Bedfordshire.

(16) The Verne Immigration Removal Centre, Portland, Dorset.[8]

(17) Any vehicle which has been specially designed or adapted for use as a mobile detention facility and approved by the Secretary of State for such use.

17.05 Those detained subject to deportation proceedings may be detained in any of the above locations with the exceptions of (1) and (17).[9]

17.06 A person cannot be detained in the places referred to in (1), (2), (3), or (17) above if a period of five consecutive days has elapsed since they were detained there, unless the person is to be removed[10] within two days, in which case they may be held for two further days in those locations.[11] If a person is to be detained in a police cell for more than two days that decision must be approved by someone at the level of inspector or SEO.[12] The UNHCR *Detention Guidelines* stipulate that detention of asylum seekers in police cells is not appropriate.[13]

17.07 When it comes into force, section 5 of IA 2014 will amend paragraph 16 of Schedule 2 to IA 1971 and insert a new paragraph 18B, the combined effect

---

for the Home Department [2013] EWCA Civ 1561 at [19]-[23], *per* Lloyd Jones LJ, holding that the definition of 'hospital' in section 145 MHA 1983 was broad enough to include any hospital.

[8] Verne Immigration Removal Centre is currently HMP The Verne. At the time of writing plans to convert it into a removal centre have been postponed.

[9] Immigration (Places of Detention) Direction 2014 at paragraph 3(2).

[10] Under paragraphs 8–10 or 12–14 of Schedule 2 to IA 1971, or under section 10 of IAA 1999.

[11] Immigration (Places of Detention) Direction 2014 at paragraph 4.

[12] Enforcement Instructions and Guidance ('EIG'), Chapter 55, section 55.13.2. References in this chapter to EIG 55 are to version 18.3, current at the time of writing, unless otherwise stated.

[13] Guideline 8, paragraph 48(i).

of which will be to limit the period for which unaccompanied children can be detained under paragraph 16(2) to 24 hours, and to limit the location of such detention to short-term holding facilities, save in certain narrowly defined circumstances.[14]

C. Immigration Removal Centres

17.08 The regime under which IRCs[15] are regulated and managed comprises the Detention Centre Rules 2001, SI 2001/238[16] ('DCR 2001'), an array of Detention Service Orders (DSOs) giving detailed guidance on a broad range of issues,[17] and the Detention Services Operating Standards manual, designed to 'build on the Detention Centre Rules and to underpin the arrangements. . . for the management of removal centres'.[18]

17.09 The purpose of IRCs is stated as being:

> to provide for the secure but humane accommodation of detained persons in a relaxed regime with as much freedom of movement and association as possible, consistent with maintaining a safe and secure environment, and to encourage and assist detained persons to make the most productive use of their time, whilst respecting in particular their dignity and the right to individual expression.[19]

17.10 Further, '[d]ue recognition will be given at detention centres to the need for awareness of the particular anxieties to which detained persons may be subject and the sensitivity that this will require, especially when handling issues of cultural diversity'.[20]

The Detention Centre Rules 2001

17.11 The DCR 2001 comprise seven parts. Part I contains the interpretative provisions (Rule 2). Part VII provides for delegation of certain powers and duties. Parts II to VI are considered at paragraphs 17.12–17.17.

17.12 Part II, 'Detained Persons', addresses 'Admissions and Discharge' (Rules 4 to 11); 'Welfare and Privileges' (Rules 12 to 19); 'Religion' (Rules 20 to 25);

---

[14] See further paragraph 12.04.

[15] N.B.: The formal designation changed from 'detention centre' to 'removal centre' in February 2003 by way of an amendment to section 147 of IAA 1999 introduced by section 66 of NIAA 2002. The explanatory notes to NIAA 2002 stated: 'This reflects the part played by detention in the removal of failed asylum-seekers and others.'

[16] SI 2001/238, made under section 153 of IAA 1999. The change in terminology from 'detention centre' to 'removal centre' did not extend to the designation of the rules.

[17] <https://www.gov.uk/government/collections/detention-service-orders>.

[18] The manual is undated, and consists of a compendium of 'standards' issued between 2002 and 2005.

[19] DCR 2001, Rule 3(1).

[20] DCR 2001, Rule 3(2).

'Communications' (Rules 26 to 32); 'Health Care' (Rules 33 to 37); and 'Requests and Complaints' (Rule 38).

Rule 9(1) provides that 'Every detained person will be provided, by the Secretary **17.13** of State, with written reasons for his detention at the time of his initial detention, and thereafter monthly.' A breach of this rule—in contrast to a breach of the requirement in the Secretary of State's published policy to review detention month by month—has been held to be irrelevant to the legality of detention because the DCR 2001 'are concerned with the regulation and management of detention centres, not with the way the discretion to detain is exercised'.[21]

Part III addresses 'Maintenance Of Security and Safety', and includes provisions **17.14** for removal from association 'in the interests of security or safety'[22] and for the 'temporary confinement' of 'a refractory or violent detained person. . . in special accommodation',[23] as well as rules governing the use of force,[24] special control or restraint,[25] and compulsory drug and alcohol testing.[26]

Part IV of the DCR 2001 ('Officers of Detention Centres')[27] regulates the conduct **17.15** of IRC officers. Part V[28] regulates 'Persons Having Access To Detention Centres'.

Part VI of the DCR 2001 regulates 'Visiting Committees'. This relates to commit- **17.16** tees (also referred to as 'Independent Monitoring Boards') appointed under section 152 of IAA 1999. Rule 61 identifies the 'general duties' of the Committee, which include 'satisfy[ing] themselves as to the state of the detention centre premises, the administration of the detention centre and the treatment of the detained persons'. Rule 62 identifies a number of 'particular duties' attaching to members of the committee, specifically:

(1) A member shall visit any detained person who is subject for the time being to (a) removal from association under rule 40; (b) temporary confinement under rule 42; or (c) special control or restraint under rule 43 within 24 hours of his being made so subject, and thereafter as the Secretary of State may direct.[29]

(2) The committee and any member of the committee shall hear any complaint or request which a detained person wishes to make to them or him.[30]

---

[21] *R (Kambadzi) v Secretary of State for the Home Department* [2011] UKSC 23; [2011] 1 WLR 1299, *per* Lord Hope at [16].

[22] Rule 40(1).

[23] Rule 42(1): the detainee may only be so confined for so long as he or she remains refractory or violent, and the power cannot be used to punish.

[24] Rule 41.

[25] Rule 43.

[26] Rule 44.

[27] Rules 45–52.

[28] Rules 53–57.

[29] Rule 62(1).

[30] Rule 62(2).

(3) The committee shall arrange for the food of the detained persons to be inspected by a member of the committee at frequent intervals.[31]

(4) The committee shall inquire into any report made to them, whether or not by a member of the committee, that a detained person's health, mental or physical, is likely to be injuriously affected by any conditions of his detention.

17.17 Detailed guidance on practical and administrative issues relating to Visiting Committees/Independent Monitoring Boards, including the duties resting on IRC management to notify the chair or another designated member of certain eventualities is set out in Detention Service Order 02/2011, *Independent Monitoring Boards*.

D. Rules 33–35 of the Detention Centre Rules 2001

(1) General

17.18 As the DCR 2001 relate to the 'regulation and management of detention centres, not. . . the way the discretion to detain is exercised', breaches are generally not errors of law material to the decision to detain.[32] In this regard, however, rule 34 (which mandates medical examinations on entry to an IRC), and rule 35 (which requires the 'medical practitioner' to report to the Secretary of State should certain concerns arise) occupy a unique position.[33]

17.19 Underpinning this is the stipulation in policy[34] that certain people can only be detained in very exceptional circumstances including, *inter alia*, those suffering from a serious physical and/or mental illness which cannot be satisfactorily managed in detention, and 'those where there is independent evidence that they have been tortured'. This policy, in turn, necessitates mechanisms for identifying individuals who fall within its terms. It was said on behalf of the government in the House of Lords in 2002 that the policy in relation to torture victims was 'reinforced' by the terms of rule 35: 'There are systems in place to ensure that such information is passed to those responsible for deciding whether to maintain detention and to those responsible for considering the individual's asylum application.'[35]

---

[31] Rule 62(3).

[32] *Kambadzi, per* Lord Hope at [16].

[33] The current chapter considers the scheme which exists under rules 33, 34, and 35, and the guidance on its operation. The way in which this scheme impacts upon decisions by Home Office officials to release, and upon the legality of detention is considered further at paragraphs 11.42–11.48.

[34] EIG 55.10.

[35] HL Deb 15 July 2002, vol 637, col 1060; *R (D & K) v Secretary of State for the Home Department* [2006] EWHC 980 (Admin) at [34].

(2) The Rules

Rules 34 and 35 need to be read with rule 33, which imposes certain requirements regarding healthcare personnel in an IRC. The regime is summarized in the following paragraphs.   **17.20**

Every detention centre shall have a medical practitioner ('the medical practitioner'), who shall be vocationally trained as a general practitioner and a fully registered person within the meaning of the Medical Act 1983 who holds a licence to practise.[36]   **17.21**

The medical practitioner shall obtain, so far as reasonably practicable, any previous medical records located in the United Kingdom relating to each detained person in the detention centre.[37]   **17.22**

Every detained person shall be given a physical and mental examination by the medical practitioner[38] within 24 hours of his admission to the detention centre.[39] This requirement is subject to the detainee giving consent to the examination.[40]   **17.23**

Rule 35 (*Special illnesses and conditions (including torture claims)*) provides: **17.24**

(1) The medical practitioner shall report to the manager on the case of any detained person whose health is likely to be injuriously affected by continued detention or any conditions of detention.

(2) The medical practitioner shall report to the manager on the case of any detained person he suspects of having suicidal intentions, and the detained person shall be placed under special observation for so long as those suspicions remain, and a record of his treatment and condition shall be kept throughout that time in a manner to be determined by the Secretary of State.

(3) The medical practitioner shall report to the manager on the case of any detained person who he is concerned may have been the victim of torture.

(4) The manager shall send a copy of any report under paragraphs (1), (2) or (3) to the Secretary of State without delay.

(5) The medical practitioner shall pay special attention to any detained person whose mental condition appears to require it, and make any special arrangements (including counselling arrangements) which appear necessary for his supervision or care.

---

[36] Rule 33(1).

[37] Rule 33(8).

[38] Or another medical practitioner in accordance with rule 33(7), which permits a detainee to request that they are attended by a registered medical practitioner or dentist other than the medical practitioner if certain conditions are met, or rule 33(10) which permits a detainee to be examined only by a registered medical practitioner of the same sex, if they so wish.

[39] Rule 34(1).

[40] Rule 34(2). If a detained person does not consent to an examination under rule 34 (1), he or she shall be entitled to the examination at any subsequent time upon request: Rule 34(3). N.B.: In *R (RT) v Secretary of State for the Home Department* [2011] EWHC 1792 (Admin) Kenneth Parker J held at [32] that, where the claimant had claimed to be a victim of torture it was 'incumbent on those handling her at the detention centre' to make clear that refusal to consent to a medical examination may jeopardise her chances of corroborating her claim to have been tortured.

(3) The policy framework

17.25 If the system works as it should, the combined effect of rules 34 and 35 should be to bring to the attention of officials making decisions about detention individuals whose continued detention may breach the unsuitability policy in EIG 55.10. A policy framework has evolved with a view to securing this end in response to a number of decisions of the courts. The focus in this litigation has been primarily on the circumstances in which an examination under rule 34 might give rise to independent evidence of torture.[41]

17.26 EIG 55, Section 55.8A summarizes the terms and purpose of rule 35. It requires that, upon receipt of a report under rule 35 detention must be reviewed 'within two working days of receipt', and cross refers to Detention Service Order 17/2012 and the *Detention Centre Rule 35 Process*.

17.27 DSO 17/2012 gives guidance on the procedure to be followed by healthcare and Home Office staff for making and responding to rule 35 reports:

(1) Rule 35 reports should be prepared and submitted by medical practitioners only.[42]

(2) Specific administrative procedures must be followed.[43]

(3) Separate guidance is given in relation to reports generated by reference to Rule 35(1) ('. . . injuriously affected. . . '),[44] (2) (suicidality),[45] and (3) (possible victims of torture).[46]

(4) The steps required following a rule 35 report being made are set out.[47]

(5) Reports from third parties fall outside the terms of the DSO, but as a matter of best practice, where capable of engaging rule 35, they should be forwarded to the IRC medical practitioner and to the Home Office responsible officer for review.[48]

17.28 *Detention Rule 35 Process* gives further guidance to Home Office caseworkers on the approach to take, *inter alia*, when reviewing detention in light of a report.

---

[41] See Chapter 11, paragraphs 11.42–11.48.
[42] Paragraphs 9 and 10.
[43] Paragraphs 11–14.
[44] Paragraph 15.
[45] Paragraphs 16–19.
[46] Paragraphs 20–25. 'The medical practitioner should **always** state clearly the reasons why he/she has concerns arising from the medical examination—specifically the medical evidence which causes these concerns, including all physical and mental indicators' [emphasis in original] (Paragraph 20); 'Where there is medical evidence in support of an allegation, the medical practitioner must set out clearly all physical and mental indicators in support of his/her professional concerns. He/she should record any mental or physical health problems that are relevant to the torture allegation' (Paragraph 22). 'Medical practitioners are not required to apply the Istanbul Protocol or apply probability levels or assess relative likelihoods of different causes but if they have a view, they should express it' (Paragraph 25). For the Istanbul Protocol, see Chapter 11, paragraph 11.40.
[47] Paragraphs 28–37.
[48] Paragraphs 38–39.

It discusses when a report is likely to amount to independent evidence of torture.[49] This is considered further in Chapter 11.[50]

E. Policy on Detention in Prison

There is detailed provision in EIG Chapter 55 for the circumstances in which time-served Foreign National Offenders ('FNOs') will be detained in a prison (as permitted under the Direction) rather than an IRC.[51]

17.29

There is a Service Level Agreement ('SLA') between the Home Office and the National Offender Management Service ('NOMS') by the terms of which NOMS makes a specified number of beds available for immigration detention purposes.[52]

17.30

Prior to January 2012, Home Office policy was that immigration detainees should only be held in prison establishments 'when they present risk factors that indicate they pose a serious risk to the stability of immigration removal centres or to the safety of others being held there'.[53]

17.31

From 2 March 2010[54] this general approach had been subject to the caveat that there would be a cap on the total number of time-served FNOs in the IRC estate at any one time.[55] When this cap was reached, time-served FNOs would continue to be held in prison, even though there may have been free spaces within the IRC

17.32

---

[49] Section 3(i).

[50] See paragraph 11.44.

[51] EIG 55.10.1.

[52] The current SLA is not in the public domain, but in a letter sent to the Association of Visitors to Immigration Detainees and a number of other NGOs on 20 May 2013, the then Minister of State for Immigration, Mark Harper MP, confirmed that the number was 600. In the same letter it was said that, in autumn 2012, an agreement had been reached to temporarily halt transfers of time-served FNOs to the IRC estate until the number of such individuals in the prison estate reached 1,000.

[53] The last version of EIG 55.10 to articulate this position was version 12, in force 1 March 2011 to 24 January 2012. This policy of only detaining in prison in the face of specific risk factors can be traced back to the earliest version of EIG 55 (April 2008), and to Chapter 38 of the Operational Enforcement Manual before that. In the 1998 White Paper *Fairer Faster and Firmer—A Modern Approach to Immigration and Asylum* (Cm 4018, July 1998, at paragraph 12.12) the then government expressed its commitment to pursuing a strategy not to detain in prisons.

[54] When EIG 55.10, version 9, was promulgated.

[55] The level of the cap was not specified. When first introduced, this was said to be 'in the interests of maintaining security and control in the UKBA detention estate as a whole' (EIG 55.10.1, version 9, 2 March 2010). In January 2012, the following words were added: 'The cap may also be used as part of the day to day management of the UKBA detention estate in order to meet changing operational priorities for the use of IRC beds, which will have a consequence for the number of beds that will be available for allocation to time-served FNOs at any one time. As such, the level at which the cap is set is not static and will change as necessary to meet those priorities, as well as in the interests of security and control of the estate.' (EIG 55.10, version 13, 24 January 2012, and versions thereafter).

estate, and even though the individuals concerned may not themselves have met the risk-based criteria preventing their transfer to an IRC.

17.33 From 24 January 2012, the policy changed.[56] Reference to individualized risk assessment remained (albeit in amended form) but further provisions were added making clear that no time-served FNO would be transferred from the prison estate to the IRC estate until such time as all of the prison beds made available by UKBA to NOMS had been filled.[57] A waiting list would be operated, and when all of the prison beds became full, individuals who were suitable for transfer would be moved to the IRC estate, with transfers prioritized by reference to the length of time the individual had been held in the prison estate as an immigration detainee. The impact of this change in policy was increased by the fact that, from autumn of 2012, agreement was reached to increase the number of beds available to the Home Office in the prison estate.[58]

17.34 In the event that all of the places made available by NOMS are full and a person falls to be considered for transfer to an IRC, they may fall into one of the three broad groups in the following paragraph that are less (or much less) likely to be transferred.[59] These groups are not exhaustive, and even if a person does not fall into any of these categories the Home Office Detainee Escorting and Population Management Unit ('DEPMU') must consider whether there are other risks which make them unsuitable for transfer.[60]

17.35 There is a presumption that certain individuals will remain in prison and will only be transferred to IRCs in 'very exceptional circumstances'. These are:

(1) *National Security*: People considered a risk to national security, for example where there is specific, verifiable intelligence that the person is a member of a terrorist group or has been involved in the planning of terrorist activities.

(2) *Criminality*: People convicted of supply or importation of Class A drugs, or sexual offending involving a minor.

(3) *Specific Identification of Harm*: People who have been identified as posing a risk of serious harm to minors and those identified in custody as being subject

---

[56] EIG 55, version 13, 24 January 2012.

[57] N.B.: Prison Service Instruction 52/2011, which remains valid until 4 November 2015, continues to suggest that a fact-sensitive, risk-based approach is applied.

[58] See footnote 53. At the time of writing there is at least one case ongoing before the Administrative Court challenging the legality of the amendment made in January 2012 *R (Idira) v Secretary of State for the Home Department*, CO/129/2014).

[59] EIG 55.10.1.

[60] In *R (Mcfarlane) v Secretary of State for the Home Department* [2010] EWHC 3081 (Admin) it was held (at [12]) that the guidance as it then was could not 'be read as setting out exclusive categories of circumstances, which if they cannot be shown to exist in a given case, must mean that a person cannot be detained in prison'. See also *R (C) v Secretary of State for the Home Department* [2009] EWHC 1989 (Admin) at [43].

to formal harassment procedures under Prison Service Order 4400, preventing them from contacting their victim(s) whilst in custody.[61]

The second category of person will normally remain in or be transferred to prison   **17.36**
subject to some exceptions:

(1) *Criminality*: Detainees who are subject to notification requirements on the sex offenders register. Exceptions to this are persons who were sentenced to less than 12 months' imprisonment for a sexual offence (who may be considered for transfer on a case-by-case basis), and individuals subject to notification requirements on the sex offenders register who are assessed by the Home Office as suitable for transfer.
(2) *Security*: A person who has escaped from prison, police or immigration custody or escort, or planned or assisted others to do so.
(3) *Control*: A person who has engaged in, planned, or assisted others to engage in or plan serious disorder, arson, violence, or damage whilst in prison, police, or immigration custody.

The final category of person *may* be unsuitable for transfer to an IRC and must be   **17.37**
considered on a case-by-case basis. These are the following:

(1) *Behaviour during custody*: A person whose behaviour in prison or an IRC makes them unsuitable for transfer to an IRC. This includes someone who has had numerous proven adjudications against them in prison for violence or incitement to commit serious disorder which could undermine the stability of the IRC estate, or clear evidence of such behaviour within an IRC. Detainees who were originally convicted of a violent offence may be considered for transfer to an IRC depending on the nature of that offence and provided their behaviour in prison has not given rise to concerns.
(2) *Health Grounds*: Where in-patient medical care is being currently received in prison and a bed in the medical facility of an IRC is not available (transfer will only take place when an IRC healthcare bed becomes available, the person is fit to be moved, and their particular needs can be met at the IRC in question).

The policy also provides that individuals held in an IRC who are refusing food and/   **17.38**
or fluid may be transferred to prison medical facilities if this is considered necessary
to manage any resulting medical conditions.[62]

Those detained in the beds made available by NOMS who do not fall into the three   **17.39**
categories set out in paragraph 17.35 (or who are found to be suitable for transfer

---

[61] Prison Service Order 4400, Prisoner Communications Chapter 2: The Protection from Harassment Act 1997.
[62] This follows a change to EIG 55 in May 2013 and reflects the introduction of DSO 03/13 which addresses food and fluid refusal.

notwithstanding) will only be transferred to an IRC where the bed that they are occupying is required either by an individual who falls into the risk categories listed, or by an FNO who has more recently completed their sentence (where the maximum number of beds provided by NOMS has been reached).[63]

17.40 Where a decision is made not to transfer a time-served FNO to an IRC, the reasons for that decision (or for any delay) must be recorded. Where a request for transfer is made it must be considered promptly and written reasons provided for any refusal.[64]

17.41 DEPMU may decide that an individual currently held in an IRC or a short-term holding facility is unsuitable for detention there, and if so they will be referred to the Population Management Unit of NOMS,[65] who will consider their allocation to a prison. Written reasons must be provided for any decision to transfer a person from an IRC to a prison, and the decision must not be made on medical or care grounds.[66]

17.42 A person normally considered unsuitable for detention in an IRC may be detained there for a short period, for example, to facilitate either removal or an interview with a consular official.[67]

F. Conditions of Detention in Prison

17.43 Immigration detainees who are held in prison are subject to the Prison Rules 1999,[68] as supplemented by the relevant Prison Service Orders ('PSOs') and Prison Service Instructions ('PSIs'). The inapplicability of the DCR 2001 and the accompanying instructions and guidance, particularly in relation to Rules 34 and 35,[69] leaves a worrying lacuna. Unlike in IRCs, there is no automatic mechanism in prisons for identifying persons who should not be detained under immigration powers because they fall within one of the categories of person generally 'unsuitable for detention' according to EIG 55.10. So, for example, there is no mechanism equivalent to that provided by Rule 35(3) of DCR 2001 for bringing to the attention of Home Office officials concerns by medical staff that a detainee may be a victim of torture.[70]

---

[63] See paragraphs 17.30–17.34.
[64] EIG 55.10.1.
[65] Or in Scotland the Scottish Prison Service. There is provision for FNOs in Scotland to remain in prison in Scotland on completion of their sentence subject to the agreement of the Scottish Prison Service.
[66] Save, it would seem, in cases of food and/or fluid refusal; see paragraph 17.38.
[67] EIG 55.10.1.
[68] SI 1999/728.
[69] As to which see paragraphs 17.18–17.28.
[70] Discussed further in Chapter 11, paragraphs 11.42–11.48.

Prison Service Instruction 52/2011 *Immigration, Repatriation And Removal*   **17.44**
Services, addresses a number of issues relating to foreign nationals in the prison
estate, both as serving prisoners and as immigration detainees.[71] Where foreign
national prisoners have reached the end of their custodial sentence but continue to
be held in prison under immigration powers they should be treated as unconvicted
prisoners, with the same status and privileges.[72]

Rule 7(2) of the Prison Rules 1999 stipulates that unconvicted prisoners (a) shall   **17.45**
be kept out of contact with convicted prisoners as far as the governor considers it
can reasonably be done, unless and to the extent that they have consented to share
residential accommodation or participate in any activity with convicted prisoners;
and (b) shall under no circumstances be required to share a cell with a convicted
prisoner.[73]

As such, immigration detainees can only be detained otherwise than as uncon-   **17.46**
victed prisoners with their consent.[74] Where an immigration detainee opts to be
held with convicted prisoners, all reasonable efforts must be made to accommodate
the privileges to which unconvicted prisoners are entitled.[75]

G. Short-Term Holding Facilities

The IAA 1999[76] defines short-term holding facilities very broadly, as places where   **17.47**
a person may be detained for a period of seven days or 'such other period as may
be prescribed'.

Short-term holding facilities are found at airports and other points of entry to the   **17.48**
United Kingdom, but there are facilities at several other locations such as Lunar
House in Croydon.[77] Short-term holding facilities are largely run by private con-
tractors on behalf of the Border Force.[78] At the time of writing, there are no rules

---

[71] Prisoners held solely under immigration powers are addressed at paragraphs 2.60 to 2.74 of
the PSI.

[72] PSI 52/2011, paragraphs 2.65–2.66.

[73] See further Prison Service Order 4600, and in particular Annex B thereto, addressing the
Special Rights and Privileges of unconvicted prisoners.

[74] PSI 52/2011, paragraph 2.66. See further *R (C) v Secretary of State for the Home Department*
[2009] EWHC 1989 at [44]–[50].

[75] PSI 52/2011, paragraph 2.66.

[76] IAA 1999, section 147.

[77] For concerns about the use of short-term holding facilities see the reports by HM Chief
Inspector of Prisons following unannounced inspections: <http://www.justice.gov.uk/publica-
tions/inspectorate-reports/hmi-prisons/short-term>. Inspections have raised repeated concerns
about conditions and access to facilities and legal representation.

[78] The power to contract out these facilities arises from an extension to the powers under section 149 of IAA 1999 under the Immigration (Short-term holding facilities) Regulations 2002 (SI
2002/2538).

governing the operation of short term holding facilities. There have been two sets of draft Rules, first in 2005 and then again in 2009, neither of which were promulgated in final form.[79]

H. Places of Detention under the Fast Track

17.49 The places in which people may be detained while subject to the fast track procedure are set out in Schedule 2 to the Asylum and Immigration Tribunal (Fast-Track Procedure Rules) 2005 (SI 2005/560). They are:

(1) Campsfield House Immigration Removal Centre, Kidlington, Oxfordshire.
(2) Colnbrook House Immigration Removal Centre, Harmondsworth, Middlesex.
(3) Harmondsworth Immigration Removal Centre, Harmondsworth, Middlesex.
(4) Oakington Reception Centre, Longstanton, Cambridgeshire.
(5) Yarls Wood Immigration Removal Centre, Clapham, Bedfordshire.

I. Transfers under Section 48 of the Mental Health Act 1983

17.50 The Secretary of State for Justice[80] has a power to transfer a prisoner suffering from a serious mental illness to hospital in certain circumstances by virtue of section 47 of the Mental Health Act 1983 ('MHA 1983'). Section 48(2)(d) makes similar and overlapping provision for the transfer of persons detained under the Immigration Acts[81] in similar circumstances.

17.51 The conditions to be met before a person may be transferred to hospital under section 48 are as follows:

(1) the Secretary of State must be satisfied by reports of two registered medical practitioners that:

---

[79] *A review of short-term holding facility inspections 2005-2010* HM Inspectorate of Prisons, January 2011.
[80] N.B.: This power was previously vested in the Secretary of State for the Home Department.
[81] Specifically under IA 1971 or section 68 NIAA 2002. In *R (HA (Nigeria)) v Secretary of State for the Home Department* [2012] EWHC 979 (Admin) Singh J held (at [126]–[127]) that the power under section 48 does not extend to persons detained under section 36(1) of UKBA 2007, as a matter of plain statutory construction. Section 48 makes no reference to individuals detained under that power. He observed that 'there are other provisions available in the 1983 Act itself which would cater for the need for compulsory detention of a person in an emergency (section 4 or, in more limited circumstances, section 136), for the purpose of assessment (section 2) or for the purpose of treatment (section 3)'.

(a) the person is suffering from a mental disorder[82] of a nature and degree that makes it appropriate for that person to be detained in a hospital for medical treatment;

(b) the person is in urgent need of such treatment; and

(c) appropriate medical treatment is available; and

(2) the Secretary of State considers that having regard to:

(a) the public interest; and

(b) all relevant circumstances;

it is expedient to make the transfer.[83]

If a person cannot be treated then it follows that they cannot be detained for the purposes of such treatment.[84] There is moreover a requirement in section 48(1)(b) that the need for treatment be *'urgent'* which is absent from section 47. **17.52**

The transfer of a person under section 48 is made by a direction of the Secretary of State for Justice. The direction expires within 14 days unless the person in question has been received into the specified hospital, and has the same effect as a hospital order.[85] A transfer direction made under section 48 also ceases to have effect if a person ceases to be liable to immigration detention.[86] **17.53**

If a person either ceases to require treatment in hospital for mental disorder or cannot be treated in the hospital to which they have been transferred, the Secretary of State may remit them to any place where they might have been detained had they not been removed to hospital.[87] **17.54**

In *R (D) v Secretary of State for the Home Department*,[88] a section 47 case decided when responsibility for transfers still lay with the Home Office, Stanley Burnton J said, in the context of serving prisoners: **17.55**

> In my judgment, once the prison service have reasonable grounds to believe that a prisoner requires treatment in a mental hospital in which he may be detained, the Home Secretary is under a duty expeditiously to take reasonable steps to obtain appropriate medical advice, and if that advice confirms the need for transfer to a hospital, to take reasonable steps within a reasonable time to effect that transfer. In many cases, the medical advice as to the appropriateness of a transfer will serve

---

[82] A mental disorder is defined with some circularity in MHA 1983 as 'any disorder of the mind'. Learning disabilities and drug and alcohol addictions are expressly excluded for the purposes of section 48 (section 1(2A) and (2B) of MHA 1983).

[83] Sections 47–48 MHA 1983.

[84] See, e.g., *R (P) v Secretary of State for Justice* [2009] EWCA Civ 701 at [50].

[85] Section 47(2), (3) of MHA 1983, read with section 48.

[86] Section 53(1) MHA 1983. In *R(TF) v Secretary of State for Justice* [2008] EWCA Civ 1457 it was held that section 47 should not generally be employed at the end of a sentence or for the ancillary purpose of public protection. That latter principle must apply by analogy to section 48. See also *R (AA) v Secretary of State for the Home Department* [2010] EWHC 2265 (Admin) at [40].

[87] Section 53(2) of MHA 1983.

[88] [2004] EWHC 2857 (Admin); [2005] MHLR 17 at [33].

as the reports required by section 47. The steps that are reasonable will depend on the circumstances, including the apparent risk to the health of the prisoner if no transfer is effected.

17.56 This principle applies to those detained under the Immigration Acts.[89]

17.57 Section 86 of MHA 1983 makes express provision for the removal of 'alien patients' detained under, *inter alia*, section 48 of MHA 1983. It includes safeguards to protect patients.[90] However, in *X v Secretary of State for the Home Department*,[91] the Court of Appeal held that the power to remove under section 86 of MHA 1983 runs parallel with the powers of removal under IA 1971. If removal proceeds under IA 1971 the safeguards in section 86 of MHA 1983 are not engaged, albeit the mental illness 'will be a factor which [the Secretary of State] must take into account'. Where removal is carried out under section 86 of MHA 1983, the section 48 transfer direction ceases to have effect once responsibility is transferred to overseas clinicians either outpatient or at a hospital.[92]

17.58 There is policy guidance provided by the Department of Health in the form of its *Good Practice Procedure Guide*[93] which deals with section 48 transfers. The Guidance sets out appropriate timeframes and responsibility for various parts of the process. This provides that it is the Mental Health Casework Section ('MHCS') which makes a decision to transfer on behalf of the Secretary of State for Justice.

17.59 There is further guidance in PSI 50/2007 which must be read, in the case of children and young people, with PSI 62/2011.[94] Although PSI 50/2007 applies only directly to prisoners, it is treated by the Secretary of State as being equally applicable to immigration detainees and deals expressly with Immigration Act transfers under section 48.[95] PSI 50/2007 requires *inter alia* that Home Office caseworkers should be approached initially to see whether temporary admission is

---

[89] See *HA (Nigeria)* per Singh J at [169]–[171]; the principle extends to those detained under section 36 of UKBA 2007 even though there is no power to transfer such a person under section 48 of MHA 1983 (presumably on the basis identified earlier in the judgment that there are other mechanisms under MHA 1983 whereby persons detained under section 36 might be moved to a mental hospital); see footnote 81.

[90] The Secretary of State must be satisfied that adequate arrangements have been made both for removal and for care and treatment on return. The decision requires the approval of the 'appropriate tribunal' (section 86 of MHA 1983). For a discussion of the practical effects of this power see *R (MJ (Angola)) v Secretary of State for the Home Department* [2010] EWCA Civ 557.

[91] [2001] 1 WLR 740 at [28].

[92] Section 91 of MHA 1983.

[93] 1 April 2011.

[94] The Ministry of Justice website lists PSI 50/2007 as having been replaced by PSI 62/2011. However the latter document itself only purports to replace Appendix 1 of PSI 50/2007 and they are clearly designed to be read together.

[95] See *HA (Nigeria)* at [169].

appropriate, which may reflect the policy in EIG 55.10 not to detain those suffering from mental illnesses which cannot be satisfactorily managed in detention.[96] If a person who is detained in hospital under section 48 of MHA 1983 is to be released from immigration detention the treating psychiatrist must be notified in case it is necessary to consider detention under sections 2 and 3 of MHA 1983.[97]

Where a detainee is released, after having had treatment under section 48, he will **17.60** be entitled to 'aftercare' by virtue of section 117 of MHA 1983 until it is no longer required.[98]

J. Use of Contractors

There is express legislative provision for the contracting out of detention services.[99] **17.61** The Secretary of State will in some circumstances be liable for the acts or omissions of contractors in their conduct of those functions.[100] It has been held at first instance that the Secretary of State is on notice of matters known to those carrying out healthcare functions as her servants or agents.[101]

K. Challenges to Place and/or Conditions of Detention

The courts have been slow to intervene in the decision that a person should be **17.62** detained in a prison rather than an IRC, which has been held to be a 'matter of judgment'[102] and 'essentially an operational decision'.[103] However, the Home Office has changed its approach and now uses prisons much more frequently for immigration detention.[104] As a result, there is likely to be further litigation on the subject. Potential sources of controversy include concerns that there is no practical

---

[96] See paragraph 11.20 and following, but contrast the *Good Practice Procedure Guide* which states that: 'The aim is to return detainees to the IRC when inpatient treatment is no longer required' (at paragraph 4.42).

[97] PSI 50/2007, Section 5.

[98] This important provision is beyond the scope of this work.

[99] Section 149 of IAA 1999.

[100] *MT (Congo) v Secretary of State for the Home Department* [2008] EWHC 1788 (Admin) *per* Cranston J at [47]–[49]. See also: *R (S) v Secretary of State for the Home Department* [2014] EWHC 50 (Admin) at [274]; *R (HA (Nigeria)) v Secretary of State for the Home Department* [2012] EWHC 979 (Admin) at [182]; *R (EH) v Secretary of State for the Home Department* [2012] EWHC 2569 (Admin) at [156].

[101] *R (EH) v Secretary of State for the Home Department* [2012] EWHC 2569 (Admin) at [156].

[102] *R (C) v Secretary of State for the Home Department* [2009] EWHC 1989 (Admin) at [43].

[103] *R (Mcfarlane) v Secretary of State for the Home Department* [2010] EWHC 3081 (Admin) at [12].

[104] See further, paragraphs 17.29–17.34.

difference between imprisonment and immigration detention in prison, and the ability of detainees in prisons to access legal advice.[105]

17.63 The Committee for the Prevention of Torture has expressed concern at the detention of foreign national prisoners in prison conditions and recently recommended that they be transferred immediately on completion of their sentence to 'a facility which can provide conditions of detention and a regime in line with their new status of immigration detainees'.[106]

17.64 Article 5(1)(f) of ECHR expressly permits detention pending deportation, subject to the limits explored elsewhere in this work.[107] However, Article 5 of ECHR has been held to require that there should be some relationship between the ground of the permitted deprivation liberty and the place and conditions of detention.[108] Inappropriate conditions of detention can, certainly in extreme cases, give rise to a breach of Article 5(1)(f).[109] In any event, decisions as to where a person is detained must be made rationally[110] and in accordance with published policy. Where a decision is taken unlawfully, judicial review will be available. However, unless a breach of Article 5 is made out, the best available remedy will be an order compelling the Secretary of State to re-take the decision.

---

[105] See Bail for Immigration Detainees: *Detention under immigration powers in UK prisons: severe restrictions on access to justice,* 24 September 2013.

[106] Report to the Government of the United Kingdom on the visit to the United Kingdom carried out by the European Committee for the Prevention of Torture and Inhuman or Degrading Treatment or Punishment (CPT) from 17 to 28 September 2012. The visit was made to Scotland but the comments apply with equal force to England and Wales. The comments repeat earlier comments made following the visit to the United Kingdom in November 2008.

[107] See Chapter 15.

[108] *Aerts v Belgium* (2000) EHRR 29 at [46]; *Ashingdane v United Kingdom* (1985) 7 EHRR 528 at [44], and see further Chapter 15, paragraphs 15.24, 15.25, and 15.34–15.43.

[109] *Mayeka v Belgium* (2008) 46 EHRR 23 at [102]–[105]. Contrast the decision in *Ashingdane v United Kingdom* (1985) 7 EHRR 528 at [52]. See also the decision of the House of Lords in *R (Munjaz) v Ashworth Hospital Authority* [2005] UKHL 58.

[110] *R (Rangwani) v Secretary of State for the Home Department* [2011] EWHC 516 (Admin) at [52]. This case also held that no particular deference is due to the DEPMU risk assessment in the decision to transfer. See also *R (AE (Libya)) v Secretary of State for the Home Department* [2011] EWHC 154 (Admin).

PART VI

REMEDIES AGAINST DETENTION

18

STATUTORY POWERS TO RELEASE AND GRANT BAIL

A. Introduction

In this chapter we consider the powers which exist to release those who are liable **18.01** to detention and the statutory powers to grant bail. In Part B, we consider temporary admission or release under Schedule 2 to the Immigration Act 1971 ('IA 1971') and the release on restrictions under Schedule 3 of those facing deportation. In Part C, we consider the statutory sources of the power to grant bail. In Parts D, E, and F, we look in more detail at practice and procedure in relation to bail from:

(1) Immigration officers ('IOs') and the Secretary of State (Part D);
(2) The First-tier Tribunal ('FTT') (Part E); and
(3) The Special Immigration Appeals Commission ('SIAC') (Part F).

The power of the High Court and the Court of Appeal to grant bail is consid- **18.02** ered separately in Chapter 19.

(1) Pending amendments under IA 2014

Pending amendments to Schedule 2 to IA 1971, which will take effect when **18.03** section 7 of the Immigration Act 2014 ('IA 2014') comes into force, will create restrictions on repeat bail applications to the FTT and SIAC, and require the Secretary of State's consent to a grant of bail in certain circumstances.

18.04 Section 7(2) of IA 2014 will add a new paragraph 22(4) to Schedule 2, the effect of which will be to prohibit a grant of bail under paragraph 22[1] without the consent of the Secretary of State where removal directions are in force requiring the applicant to be removed from the United Kingdom within 14 days from the date on which the bail decision will be taken. Section 7(5) will amend paragraph 30(1)[2] to like effect, thereby imposing the same restriction on grants of bail pending appeal under paragraph 29.[3] Sections 7(3) and 7(6) of IA 2014 will amend Schedule 2 to require changes to the FTT procedure rules. The FTT will be required to refuse, without a hearing, any application for bail made within 28 days of an earlier refusal by the FTT unless the applicant demonstrates that there has been a material change in circumstances. Section 7(4) of IA 2014 will amend paragraph 29 of Schedule 2 ('Grant of bail pending appeal') to put beyond doubt that, where an appeal is pending, bail can only be sought under paragraph 29, and there is no simultaneous power to grant bail under paragraph 22.

18.05 Paragraph 10 of Schedule 9 IA 2014 will amend the provisions of the Special Immigration Appeals Commission Act 1997 ('SIACA 1997'). Section 5 will be amended such that a modification to the relevant procedure rules such that SIAC will be obliged refuse, without a hearing, any application for bail made within 28 days of an earlier refusal by SIAC unless the applicant demonstrates that there has been a material change in circumstances. Schedule 3 to SIACA 1997 will also be amended, changing the modifications it makes to IA 1971 Schedule 2. This is considered further at paragraph 18.40.

B. Temporary Admission, Temporary Release, Release on Restrictions

(1) Temporary admission or release

(a) General

18.06 A person liable to detention or detained under paragraph 16(1), (1A) or (2) (but not (1B)) of Schedule 2 to IA 1971 or section 62 of the Nationality, Immigration and Asylum Act 2002 ('NIAA 2002')[4] may be temporarily admitted to the United Kingdom without being detained or may be released from detention, but this shall not prejudice a later exercise of the power to detain.

18.07 The power to grant temporary admission ('TA') or temporary release ('TR') in a Schedule 2 case arises under paragraph 21 of that Schedule, which provides that

---

[1] For bail under paragraph 22 of Schedule 2 see paragraphs 18.20–18.25.
[2] For the current effect of paragraph 30(1), see paragraph18.31.
[3] For bail under paragraph 29 of Schedule 2 see paragraphs 18.26–18.34.
[4] For powers of detention see Chapter 4.

TA or TR may be granted under the written authority of an IO. Section 62(3) of NIAA 2002 provides, *inter alia*, that paragraph 21 of Schedule 2 shall apply to a person who is detained or liable to detention under section 62. For that purpose a reference in paragraph 21 to an IO shall be taken to include a reference to the Secretary of State.[5]

(b) Restrictions and conditions

A person granted TA or TR shall be subject to such restrictions as to residence, employment, or occupation,[6] and as to reporting to the police or an IO as may from time to time be notified to him in writing by an IO[7] or the Secretary of State.[8] **18.08**

Where a residence restriction is imposed on an adult he or she may be required to cooperate with electronic monitoring and a failure to so cooperate shall be treated for all purposes of the Immigration Acts as failure to observe the residence restriction.[9] Where a reporting restriction could be imposed on an adult he or she may instead be required to cooperate with electronic monitoring, and the requirement shall be treated for all purposes of the Immigration Acts as a reporting restriction.[10] **18.09**

In the case of a restriction imposed under paragraph 21 of Schedule 2 by virtue of NIAA 2002, section 62, a restriction imposed by an IO may be varied by the Secretary of State and a restriction imposed by the Secretary of State may be varied by an IO.[11] **18.10**

(c) Criminal offence

A person shall be guilty of an offence punishable on summary conviction with a fine[12] or with imprisonment for not more than six months, or with both if, without reasonable excuse, he or she fails to observe any restriction imposed, *inter alia*, upon a grant of TA or TR being made as to employment, occupation or reporting to the police, an IO or the Secretary of State.[13] **18.11**

Where an illegal entrant or person served notice of administrative removal is granted TA/TR, form IS96 must be served informing the subject of his or her release and the applicable restrictions.[14] **18.12**

---

[5] Section 62(3)(b).

[6] For details of the limited circumstances in which a person on TA or TR might be granted a right to work see Enforcement Instructions and Guidance ('EIG'), Chapter 23, Section 23.9 (at the time of writing, version 2, promulgated on 27 November 2013).

[7] Schedule 2, paragraph 21(2).

[8] Pursuant to section 62(3)(b) of NIAA 2002.

[9] Asylum and Immigration (Treatment of Claimants, etc.) Act 2004 ('AI(ToC)A 2004'), section 36(2).

[10] AI(ToC)A 2004, section 36(3).

[11] NIAA 2002, section 62(4).

[12] Of not more than level 5 on the standard scale.

[13] IA 1971, section 24(1)(e).

[14] EIG 56.6. The version current at the time of writing is version 2, dated 27 November 2013.

(2) Release on Restrictions

(a) General

18.13 A person who is liable to be detained under paragraph 2(1), (2) or (3) of Schedule 3 to IA 1971 or section 36(1) of the UK Borders Act 2007 ('UKBA 2007'), while he or she is not so detained, shall be subject to such restrictions as to residence, employment, or occupation, and as to reporting to the police or an IO as may from time to time be notified in writing by the Secretary of State.[15] They may also be subject to electronic monitoring in the same way as persons granted TA or TR.[16]

18.14 Where the release of a person recommended for deportation is directed by a court, that person shall be subject to such restrictions as to residence, employment, or occupation, and as to reporting to the police as the court may direct.[17] Where a person is so released without restrictions having been imposed the appropriate court shall have the power, on application, to impose restrictions.[18] Where restrictions have been imposed, the appropriate court may, on application, vary or lift the restrictions or give further directions as to residence and reporting.[19]

18.15 Guidance on the procedure for release and the conditions that are likely to be imposed when a person whose case is being managed by Immigration Enforcement Criminal Casework ('Criminal Casework') is released under Schedule 3 on restrictions is set out at EIG 55.20.5.[20] The default position is that release shall be subject to reporting twice weekly[21] and electronic monitoring may be imposed.

(b) Criminal offence

18.16 A person shall be guilty of an offence punishable on summary conviction with a fine[22] or with imprisonment for not more than six months, or with both if, without reasonable excuse, he or she fails to observe any restriction imposed under Schedule 3 as to employment, occupation or reporting to the police, an IO or the Secretary of State.[23]

---

15 IA 1971, Schedule 3, paragraph 2(5) read with paragraph 2(6); UKBA 2007, section 36(5).
16 AI(ToC)A 2004, section 36(2), (3); see paragraph 18.09.
17 IA 1971, Schedule 3, paragraph 4.
18 IA 1971, Schedule 3, paragraph 5(1), read with paragraph 5(2)(a).
19 IA 1971, Schedule 3, paragraph 5(1), read with paragraph 5(2)(b).
20 The version of EIG 55 current at the time of writing is version 18.3, 1 May 2014.
21 EIG 55.20.5.2.
22 Of not more than level 5 on the standard scale.
23 IA 1971, section 24(1)(e).

C. Statutory Bail Powers

(1) General

IOs not below the rank of chief immigration officer ('CIO'), the Secretary of **18.17** State, police officers not below the rank of inspector, the FTT, and the Special Immigration Appeals Commission ('SIAC') are all empowered by statute to grant bail in certain circumstances to persons detained under the Immigration Acts.

There is no right of appeal against a refusal of statutory bail. Judicial review is the **18.18** only route of challenge. Such challenges are rare.

(2) Bail from a CIO, the Secretary of State, the FTT, or a police officer

There is an important distinction to be drawn between (i) bail under paragraph 22 **18.19** of Schedule 2 to IA 1971, and (ii) bail pending appeal under paragraph 29 of that Schedule. At the time of writing, there is nothing on the face of paragraph 22 to suggest that it ceases to apply when an appeal is pending. If that is right, an applicant who falls within the scope of paragraph 22 and who has an appeal pending may have a choice as to the power under which he or she seeks bail. When section 7(4) of IA 2014 comes into force, it will amend paragraph 29 of Schedule 2 to make clear that where an appeal is pending, paragraph 22 does not apply.

(a) Bail under IA 1971, Schedule 2, paragraph 22

Paragraph 22 of Schedule 2 to IA 1971, as extended in its operation by a number **18.20** of other provisions,[24] empowers IOs not below the rank of CIO, the Secretary of State, and the FTT to grant bail. Bail may be granted under paragraph 22 to any person detained under the Immigration Acts save for (i) a person detained under paragraph 16(1) pending examination if less than seven days have elapsed since the person's arrival in the United Kingdom, (ii) a person detained under paragraph 16(1B) of Schedule 2, which provides for the detention for up to twelve hours of a person who has been required to submit to further examination under paragraph 3(1A), and (iii) a person to whom section 3(2) of SIACA 1997 applies.[25]

---

[24] Paragraph 34 of Schedule 2 extends the application of paragraph 22 to a person if directions for their removal from the United Kingdom are for the time being in force, and they are detained under Part I of Schedule 2. Section 62(3)(c) of NIAA 2002 extends the application of paragraph 22 to a person detained by the Secretary of State under section 62 of that Act. Paragraph 2(4A) of Schedule 3 to IA 1971 extends the application of paragraph 22 to persons detained under Schedule 3, paragraphs 2(1), (2) and (3). Section 36(4) of UKBA 2007 extends the application of paragraph 22 to detention in automatic deportation cases under section 36(1)(a) and (b).
[25] Section 3 and Schedule 3 of SIACA 1997 apply Schedule 2 of IA 1971 to such cases in modified form. The power to grant bail can only be exercised by the Special Immigration Appeals Commission; see further paragraphs 18.40–18.42.

18.21   Pending amendments to Schedule 2 to IA 1971 will require the Secretary of State's consent to a grant of bail under paragraph 22 in certain circumstances, and will require the FTT to dismiss an application for bail under paragraph 22 without a hearing where it is made within 28 days of an earlier refusal, absent a material change in circumstances. This is considered further at paragraphs 18.03–18.05.

18.22   Where an IO has sole or shared power to release a person on bail under Schedule 2 and an application for bail is made more than eight days after detention commenced, section 68(2) of NIAA 2002 provides that the power to release on bail is exercisable by the Secretary of State in place of the IO.

18.23   Bail may be granted upon the applicant entering into a recognizance (or, in Scotland, a bail bond) conditioned for his appearance before an IO at a time and place named in the recognizance or bail bond, or at such other time and place as may in the meantime be notified to him in writing by an IO.[26]

18.24   The conditions of a recognizance or bail bond may include conditions appearing to the IO or FTT to be likely to result in the appearance of the person bailed at the required time and place.[27] Any recognizance shall be with or without sureties as the IO or FTT may determine.[28] Paragraph 22(2) does not limit the conditions which can be imposed, and its scope is 'quite wide enough to enable conditions to be applied such as are applied routinely by the court in connection with the granting of bail'.[29]

18.25   Paragraph 22(1A) permits the time and place at which the applicant must answer bail (the 'primary condition'[30]) to be varied by an IO by giving notice in writing. There is no express power to vary any other condition which has been imposed under paragraph 22(2) (residence, reporting, etc; the 'secondary conditions'). EIG 57.11 suggests that the only way to 'vary' secondary conditions is to vary the primary condition and simultaneously impose new secondary conditions.[31] The FTT cannot vary bail granted under paragraph 22 (see paragraph 55 of the *Bail Guidance*). It appears the only remedy available to a person dissatisfied with a refusal or failure by an IO to vary bail under paragraph 22 is judicial review.

---

[26]   Paragraph 22(1A).
[27]   Paragraph 22(2).
[28]   Paragraph 22(2).
[29]   *R (Kelso) v Secretary of State for the Home Department* [1998] INLR 603, *per* Collins J.
[30]   N.B.: the terms 'primary condition' and 'secondary condition' are used in Presidential Guidance Note No 1 of 2012, *Bail Guidance for Judges Presiding over Immigration and Asylum Hearings* (the *Bail Guidance*).
[31]   The version of EIG 57 current at the time of writing is version 5, dated 27 November 2013.

(b) Bail where an appeal is pending (IA 1971, Schedule 2, paragraph 29)

18.26 Where a person has an appeal pending under NIAA 2002 Part 5 and is detained under Part 1 of Schedule 2, Schedule 3, section 62 of NIAA 2002, or section 36 of UKBA 2007, he or she may be released on bail under paragraph 29 of Schedule 2.[32]

18.27 Pending amendments to Schedule 2 to IA 1971 will require the Secretary of State's consent to a grant of bail under paragraph 29 in certain circumstances, and will require the FTT to dismiss an application for bail under paragraph 29 without a hearing where it is made within 28 days of an earlier refusal, absent a material change in circumstances. This is considered further at paragraphs 18.03–18.05.

18.28 The power to grant bail under paragraph 29 may be exercised by an IO not below the rank of CIO,[33] a police officer not below the rank of inspector,[34] or the FTT.[35] The power vested in an IO to release on bail transfers to the Secretary of State after a person has been detained for eight days.[36]

18.29 An appellant may be released upon his entering into a recognizance (or, in Scotland, bail bond) conditioned for his appearance before the FTT at a time and place named in the recognizance or bail bond.[37]

18.30 The person fixing bail can impose conditions appearing to be likely to result in the appearance of the person bailed at the required time and place.[38]

18.31 At the time of writing, paragraph 30(1) of Schedule 2 to IA 1971 provides that an appellant shall not be released under paragraph 29 without the consent of the Secretary of State if directions for the removal of the appellant from the United Kingdom are for the time being in force, or the power to give such directions is for the time being exercisable. When section 7(5) of IA 2014 comes into force, paragraph 30(1) will be amended such that the Secretary of State's consent will be required if removal directions are in place and removal is to take place within 14 days.[39]

18.32 Unlike bail under paragraph 22 of Schedule 2 to IA 1971, bail under paragraph 29 (bail pending appeal) is subject to paragraph 30(2) of Schedule 2, which provides that, on an application to the FTT for bail:

. . . the Tribunal shall not be obliged to release an appellant unless the appellant enters into a proper recognizance, with sufficient and satisfactory sureties if

---

[32] See Schedule 3, paragraph 3, section 62(3) NIAA 2002 and section 36(4) UKBA 2007.
[33] Paragraph 29(2).
[34] Paragraph 29(2). EIG 57.1.1 and 57.1.2 state that 'the police will normally refer such applications to the immigration office concerned'.
[35] Paragraph 29(3).
[36] Section 68(2) of NIAA 2002.
[37] Paragraph 29(2), (3).
[38] Paragraph 29(5).
[39] See paragraph 18.04.

required, or in Scotland sufficient and satisfactory bail is found if so required; and the Tribunal shall not be obliged to release an appellant if it appears to the Tribunal—

(a) that the appellant, having on any previous occasion been released on bail . . . has failed to comply with the conditions of any recognizance or bail bond entered into by him on that occasion;

(b) that the appellant is likely to commit an offence unless he is retained in detention;

(c) that the release of the appellant is likely to cause danger to public health;

(d) that the appellant is suffering from mental disorder and that his continued detention is necessary in his own interests or for the protection of any other person; or

(e) that the appellant is under the age of seventeen, that arrangements ought to be made for his care in the event of his release and that no satisfactory arrangements for that purpose have been made.

18.33 It has been argued that paragraph 30(2) can be read as imposing a presumption of bail in certain circumstances.[40]

18.34 There is no express provision in paragraphs 29 and 30 for varying bail.[41] The *Bail Guidance* states that when granting bail pending appeal the FTT should impose a condition that 'the terms of bail may be varied at any time during their currency by application or at the Tribunal's own motion',[42] and includes detailed guidance on the procedure for seeking variation of bail pending appeal.[43]

(c) Electronic monitoring

18.35 Bail may be granted to an adult subject to a requirement that he or she cooperate with electronic monitoring, and the requirement may (but need not) be imposed as a condition of a recognizance or bail bond.[44]

(d) Forfeiture

18.36 Schedule 2, paragraphs 23, 31, and 32 establish the framework for forfeiture proceedings before the FTT in relation to bail granted under paragraph 22 and paragraph 29 respectively.[45]

(e) Arrest

18.37 An IO or constable may arrest without warrant a person who has been released on bail if:

---

[40] See further paragraphs 18.77–18.79.
[41] *Cf.* paragraph 22(1A).
[42] *Bail Guidance*, paragraph 36(iii).
[43] *Bail Guidance*, paragraphs 55 to 59.
[44] Section 36(4) of AI(ToC)A 2004. Electronic monitoring is further defined at section 36(5). For the approach of the FTT to electronic monitoring, see paragraphs 18.97 and 18.98.
[45] See further at paragraphs 18.107–18.109.

(1) he or she has reasonable grounds for believing that that person is likely to break the condition of his or her recognizance or bail bond to appear at the time and place required or to break any other condition of it,[46] or has reasonable grounds to suspect that that person is breaking or has broken any such other condition; or

(2) he or she is notified in writing by any surety of the surety's belief that that person is likely to break the primary condition and of the surety's wish for that reason to be relieved of his or her obligations as a surety.[47]

If the person so arrested was not due to appear before an IO or the FTT within **18.38** 24 hours, he or she shall be brought before the FTT as soon as practicable or, in the event this is not practicable within 24 hours, brought instead before a justice of the peace ('JP') or, in Scotland, the sheriff. If the person was due to appear before an IO or the FTT within 24 hours he or she shall be brought before the IO or the FTT, as the case may be, within that period.[48]

The FTT, JP, or sheriff must determine whether the person has broken or is likely to **18.39** break any condition on which he was released. If not, the person must be released on his or her original recognizance or bail.[49] If so, they may either:

(1) direct that he or she be detained under the authority of the person who made the arrest; or

(2) release him or her, on the original recognizance or on a new recognizance, with or without sureties, or, in Scotland, on the original bail or on new bail.

(3) Bail Powers in SIAC Cases

Where a person is detained under IA 1971 or NIAA 2002 and: **18.40**

(1) the Secretary of State certifies that detention is necessary in the interests of national security;

(2) he or she is detained following a decision to refuse leave to enter the United Kingdom on the ground that his or her exclusion is in the interests of national security; or

(3) he or she is detained following a decision to make a deportation order against him on the ground that his deportation is in the interests of national security, he or she may seek bail from SIAC.[50]

---

[46] For the meaning of 'likely to break', see *Mohammed Othman v Secretary of State for the Home Department*, Unreported, SC/15/2005, 2 December 2008, *per* Mitting J (sitting as President of SIAC) at [6]–[12]. The test is one of 'serious risk or real possibility' (at [8]) or 'real risk or serious probability' (at [11]).

[47] Paragraph 24(1), 33(1).

[48] Schedule 2, paragraph 24(2), 33(2).

[49] Paragraphs 24(3) and 33(3).

[50] Special Immigration Appeals Commission Act 1997 ('SIACA 1997'), section 3. Schedule 3 to SIACA 1997 applies the provisions of Schedule 2, paragraphs 22 to 24 and 29 to 33 to such

18.41 SIAC's appellate jurisdiction extends to certain cases which do not have a national security element, such as those in which the Secretary of State has certified that the decision is or was taken wholly or partly 'in the interests of the relationship between the United Kingdom and another country',[51] or wholly or partly in reliance on information which in her opinion should not be made public 'in the interests of the relationship between the United Kingdom and another country', or 'otherwise in the public interest'.[52]

18.42 Where an appeal is proceeding before SIAC in such a case and the appellant is detained under the Immigration Acts, but the Secretary of State has not certified that detention is necessary in the interests of national security, the appellant does not, on the face of it, fall within the ambit of the SIAC bail jurisdiction and it appears that any application for bail would have to be made to a CIO, the Secretary of State, or the FTT in the usual way.[53]

D. Bail from a CIO or the Secretary of State

18.43 Decisions on bail taken by CIOs or Home Office officials are subject to the guidance in EIG 57.[54]

18.44 The starting point in all cases is a presumption of temporary release. Where this is not considered appropriate a grant of CIO/Secretary of State bail, 'upon application', may be an alternative to detention.[55] Use of bail enables the Home Office 'to retain greater control than temporary release'.[56]

18.45 A person who is eligible for bail must be notified of the right to apply for bail, and provided with 'bail information' and application forms.[57] A person need only be notified once.

18.46 The information to be included in an application for bail is set out at EIG 57.3. Where officials believe a detainee is a potential candidate for bail they should

---

cases in modified form. There is no concurrent power to grant bail vested in IOs, the FTT, or police officers. IA 2014, Schedule 9, paragraph 10(3), will amend Schedule 3 of SIACA 1997 so as to modify paragraph 29 of Schedule 2 to IA 1971, to include appeals brought under section 2 of SIACA 1997.

[51] NIAA 2002, section 97(1), (2)(b); SIACA 1997, section 2(1).
[52] Section 97(3)(b) and (c) of NIAA 2002; SIACA 1997, section 2(1).
[53] To our knowledge, this issue remains untested.
[54] EIG 57 also contains instructions for Home Office officials on the steps to be taken when a detainee seeks bail from the FTT.
[55] EIG 57, *Introduction*.
[56] EIG 57.7.
[57] See EIG 57.3. The forms are Form IS98 and IS98A for CIO or Secretary of State bail and form B1 for Tribunal bail.

consider inviting an application, if appropriate stipulating the level of sureties which would be acceptable.[58]

(1) Consideration of a bail application

EIG 57.5 identifies a number of factors to be considered when deciding whether or not to oppose bail. They are: **18.47**

(1) 'the likelihood of the applicant failing to appear when required';
(2) 'the period of time likely to elapse before any conclusive decision is made or outstanding appeal is disposed of';
(3) 'the diligence, speed and effectiveness of the steps taken . . . to effect removal';
(4) 'any special reason for keeping the person detained . . .';
(5) 'the reliability and standing of sureties'; and
(6) 'in deportation cases, the views of the relevant senior case-worker in the relevant casework section'.

(2) Risk of absconding

EIG 57.5.1 identifies a number of indicators of absconding risk: escape attempts, failures to comply with release conditions, terrorist connections or other public interest concerns, disruption of removal, failing to cooperate with the documentation process, and failing to attempt to regularize immigration status until apprehended. **18.48**

Where a person is unlikely to abscond and there are no other grounds for detention the usual course will be a grant of temporary release rather than bail. Bail may, however, be granted where, despite an adverse background or history, 'sufficient and satisfactory sureties are produced'.[59] **18.49**

(3) Level of bail

EIG 57.6.1 states that, whilst each case should be assessed on its merits, a recognizance of between £2,000 and £5,000 per surety is suggested. In our view these figures are arbitrary; they will be beyond the reach of some sureties and of no concern to others. An appropriate level of recognizance (i.e. a level which is both realistic and represents a sufficient incentive) can only be identified by considering a surety's circumstances in the round. **18.50**

---

[58] EIG 57.7.
[59] EIG 57.5.

(4) Sureties

18.51 EIG 57.6.2 gives guidance on acceptable sureties: a surety should be able to exert control over the bail applicant to ensure compliance with bail conditions. To be acceptable a surety should:

(1) have sufficient assets to pay the recognizance if bail is forfeited;

(2) be over 18 and settled in the United Kingdom;

(3) be a householder 'or at least well-established in the place where he lives';

(4) be free of any criminal record, although the relevance of any given conviction will be a matter for the CIO/Secretary of State;

(5) not have come to adverse notice in other immigration matters, particularly past bail cases or applications for temporary admission; and

(6) 'Have a personal connection with the applicant, or be acting on behalf of a reputable organisation which has an interest in his welfare.'

(5) Conditions

18.52 Conditions which might be imposed to ensure a person answers bail include:[60]

(1) reporting to an immigration reporting centre or an immigration office/police station, 'normally on a monthly basis';[61]

(2) a requirement to live at a nominated address; and

(3) where appropriate, surrender of the applicant's passport.

(6) Refusal of bail

18.53 CIO or Secretary of State bail can be refused orally or in writing, and at the same time the applicant should be advised that he or she can seek bail from the FTT.[62] Absent a change in circumstances following a refusal, bail is likely to be refused again. However, passage of time with little progress towards removal may be a sufficient change in circumstances to warrant a grant of bail.[63]

(7) Re-detention following a grant of bail

18.54 Where a decision is taken to re-detain a person following a grant of bail ('normally because that person has become removable') the procedure at EIG 57.12 should be followed. Bail will be varied to require the individual to report to an IO on a given date, and on reporting, he or she will be re-detained.

---

[60] EIG 57.7.

[61] *Cf.* the *Bail Guidance* at paragraph 38(v) which suggests that the usual frequency of reporting when bail is granted will be weekly, and EIG 55.3.2.14 which states that, in a Criminal Casework case, where a decision is taken not to oppose a grant of bail by the FTT, a condition to report twice weekly should be sought.

[62] EIG 57.7.2.

[63] EIG 57.7.3.

E. FTT Bail

(1) Procedure

(a) Rules and guidance

Applications to the FTT for bail are governed by Part 4 of the Asylum and **18.55** Immigration Tribunal (Procedure) Rules[64] ('the FTT Procedure Rules'). The Senior President's Practice Directions, *Immigration and Asylum Chambers of the First-tier Tribunal and the Upper Tribunal* of 10 February 2010 ('the IAC Practice Directions') contain some limited directions on procedure. Presidential Guidance Note No 1 of 2012, *Bail Guidance for Judges Presiding over Immigration and Asylum Hearings* ('the *Bail Guidance*'),[65] gives detailed guidance on law, practice, and procedure.

(b) Cases pending before the Upper Tribunal

The Upper Tribunal (UT) has no free-standing jurisdiction to grant bail under **18.56** IA 1971, and bail applications should normally be made to the FTT. A judge of the UT may exercise bail jurisdiction by reason of being also a First-tier judge.[66] However, where an application for bail is made whilst an appeal is pending before the UT it should normally only be made to a UT judge where the appeal 'is being heard by the Upper Tribunal, or where a hearing before the Upper Tribunal is imminent'. In cases of doubt applicants should consult the bails section of the FTT.[67]

(c) Making the application

An application for bail is made by filing with the FTT an application notice in a **18.57** form approved for the purpose by the Senior President of Tribunals,[68] currently Form B1. The application must contain the information specified in Rule 38(2), including the grounds on which the application is made and, where a previous application has been refused, full details of any change in circumstances since the earlier refusal.[69] It must be signed by the applicant or his or her representative or, in the case of an applicant who is a child or is for any other reason incapable of acting, by a person acting on his or her behalf.[70]

---

[64] SI 2005/230.
[65] This supersedes the *Bail Guidance Notes for adjudicators from the Chief Adjudicator* ('the 2003 *Bail Guidance Notes*'), 3rd edition, May 2003.
[66] Section 4(1)(c) of the Tribunals, Courts and Enforcement Act 2007.
[67] IAC Practice Directions, paragraph 13.04.
[68] FTT Procedure Rules, Rule 38(1).
[69] Rule 38(2)(h).
[70] Rule 38(3).

(d) Listing the hearing

18.58 Where an application for bail is filed the FTT must, as soon as reasonably practicable, serve a copy of the application on the Secretary of State and fix a hearing.[71] An application for bail must if practicable be listed for hearing within three working days of receipt by the FTT of the notice of application,[72] but where an application is received after 3.30 pm then for the purposes of the three-day listing target, it will be treated as if it were received on the next business day.[73]

(e) The bail summary

18.59 If the Secretary of State wishes to contest an application for bail she 'must' file with the FTT and serve on the applicant a 'written statement' of her reasons for doing so not later than 2.00 pm on the business day before the hearing or, if she was served with notice of hearing less than 24 hours before that time, as soon as reasonably practicable.[74] The statement takes the form of a *pro forma* 'bail summary' which will include an account of 'facts pertaining to the person's detention' (in the form of a chronology) and reasons for resisting a grant of bail.[75] It will also include details of the conditions the Secretary of State will seek in the event bail is granted.

18.60 Where the Secretary of State fails to file and serve a bail summary the *Bail Guidance* states that a judge 'may be able to infer the reasons for detention from other available information' and that the absence of the bail summary 'is not of itself a reason to grant or refuse bail or to invite withdrawal of the application'.[76] However, it goes on to state that such a failure 'will be taken seriously' and will mean 'the application may be regarded as unopposed'. In such circumstances, the FTT must exercise its discretion on the facts known to it. Before making a final decision, the *Bail Guidance* requires that the judge 'have regard to all the circumstances, particularly any public interest factors which may be relevant to the individual application'.[77]

18.61 It is good practice for advisers to take an applicant's instructions on the contents of the bail summary as early as possible and, where time permits, to put the Home Office on notice of any points of dispute. It is for the Home Office to provide the evidence on which it relies to say that it is reasonable for detention to continue. Failure to provide relevant evidence of any disputed matter that is reasonably available should result in the judge giving less weight to the arguments opposing bail.[78]

---

[71] Rule 39(1)(a) and (b).
[72] IAC Practice Directions, paragraph 13.01.
[73] IAC Practice Directions, paragraph 13.02.
[74] Rule 39(2)(a) and (b).
[75] EIG 57.7.1.
[76] *Bail Guidance*, paragraph 6.
[77] *Bail Guidance*, paragraph 10.
[78] *Bail Guidance*, paragraph 28.

EIG 57.7.1 recognizes the need for the Home Office to provide evidence in support of allegations in the bail summary relating to an applicant's behaviour whilst in detention (such as lack of cooperation with travel documentation or disrupting removal attempts), stating that 'wherever possible, evidence should be submitted along with the bail summary to support these claims'. It continues: 'this evidence should only be sent for the attention of the Presenting Officer,[79] to be used in the hearing if any of the assertions are challenged: it should not be forwarded on to the representatives or the applicant'.[80] **18.62**

(f) Video link

Most bail hearings are conducted by video link.[81] Video link bail hearings are addressed in Annex 6 to the *Bail Guidance*. Standard directions[82] require representatives to attend 30 minutes before the commencement of the hearing, and permit a private consultation 'of no more than 10 minutes'. Documentary evidence relied upon by both parties, as well as the bail summary, must be filed and served no later than 2.00 pm on the day before the hearing. **18.63**

Where it is considered that 'exceptional circumstances' exist preventing an applicant from using the video link medium an *ex parte* application should be made to the Resident Judge at the relevant hearing centre providing reasons.[83] **18.64**

(g) Conduct of the hearing

At the time of writing, the *Bail Guidance* states that, where bail has been refused within the past 28 days and the application contains no new evidence or grounds for bail, the FTT will restrict the length of the hearing, the evidence that will be heard, and the opportunity for an applicant to consult with his or her representative.[84] When section 7 IA 2014 comes into force, the Tribunal will be required to dismiss without a hearing any application for bail made within 28 days of an earlier refusal unless the person demonstrates to the Tribunal that there has been a material change in circumstances. **18.65**

---

[79] The Home Office advocate who will present the bail hearing.

[80] This policy is inconsistent with the model directions for video link bail hearings in Annex 6, Appendix A, of the *Bail Guidance* which require both parties to serve on the FTT and on each other copies of all documents relied on no later than 2.00 pm on the day before the hearing. There can be no good reason for adopting a general position that relevant evidence is withheld until the bail hearing takes place, *a fortiori* when most hearings take place by video link. This aspect of the policy is arguably unlawful. If an applicant is prejudiced by late production of evidence the failure to serve the material in advance may, in our view, properly be taken into account by the FTT in considering the weight it should be given.

[81] *Bail Guidance*, paragraph 67.

[82] *Bail Guidance*, Annex 6, Appendix A.

[83] *Bail Guidance*, Annex 6, Section 7.

[84] *Bail Guidance*, paragraph 67.

18.66 The judge must keep a clear record of proceedings. It is good practice for the judge to minute the reasons for granting bail, albeit written reasons for granting bail are not ordinarily given. Where bail is refused the reasons for refusal should be set out in writing and with sufficient detail that the applicant knows why they have not been granted bail.[85]

18.67 Judges have a broad discretion as to the conduct of the hearing.[86] Some judges take a view on the merits of the application 'in principle', only going on to consider the evidence of potential sureties where a *prima facie* case for bail is made out.[87] In our view this approach risks unfairness where the evidence of a surety is capable of informing the judge's view of suitability for bail. A holistic approach, where all evidence is considered before a decision is taken on any issue is preferable. Absent specific reasons for excluding a surety from part or all of a hearing, he or she should be permitted to be present in the hearing room throughout the hearing.

18.68 A practice has developed of some judges giving a provisional indication at the outset of a hearing if they are minded to refuse bail. This allows an application to be withdrawn, avoiding the consequences that a formal refusal might have for a subsequent application (a consideration that will acquire greater significance when the amendments to Schedule 2 to IA 1971 pending by virtue of section 7 of IA 2014 come into force). However, taking that course also risks a potentially successful application being abandoned before it is fully ventilated.

(h) Adjourning bail hearings

18.69 Rule 47 of the FTT Procedure Rules provides that '[s]ubject to any provision of these Rules, the Tribunal may adjourn any hearing'. Neither the Procedure Rules nor the statutory scheme nor the IAC Practice Directions prevent a judge from adjourning a bail hearing. The 2003 *Bail Guidance Notes* discouraged the adjournment of bail hearings on grounds of practicality.[88] The current *Bail Guidance* is silent on the point. The power to adjourn bail hearings is seldom used. Nevertheless, there may be circumstances in which good grounds for adjourning a bail application arise. For example, the *Bail Guidance* suggests that in certain circumstances it will be appropriate for the FTT to give directions for the production of evidence on risk of harm.[89] It is difficult to see how this could be done in practice if the hearing was not adjourned to allow time for the evidence to be produced.

---

[85] *Bail Guidance*, paragraph 68.
[86] *Bail Guidance*, paragraph 67.
[87] Such an approach was suggested in the 2003 *Bail Guidance Notes* (see fn 65) which suggested (at paragraph 2.7.4) that judges deal with an application in three stages: 'First, is this a case where bail is right in principle, subject to suitable conditions if necessary? Second, are sureties necessary? Third, are the sureties and recognizances offered satisfactory?'
[88] Paragraph 2.7.5.
[89] *Bail Guidance*, paragraph 13.

(i) Bail in principle

The *Bail Guidance* contains an important innovation to assist in dealing with cases **18.70** in which it is accepted bail should be granted but a practical or logistical obstacle (generally relating to accommodation) remains. Where there is sufficient information to decide bail should be granted in principle but 'information is missing to complete the conditions to be imposed' it is undesirable that bail should be refused or that hearing time is spent on repeat applications on the same point. To address this difficulty the *Bail Guidance* provides for a grant of 'bail in principle', with the applicant remaining in detention until such time as the missing information is provided to the judge's satisfaction.[90]

Where bail is granted in principle the reasons for doing so and the missing infor- **18.71** mation should be noted by the judge in the bail file and notified in writing to the parties.[91] The *Bail Guidance* suggests a window of 48 hours in which to provide the missing material. If it is produced to the judge's satisfaction 'the order for release can be completed without any further hearing'.[92] If it is not, bail will be treated as having been refused and it will be for the applicant to make a fresh application. The subsequent provision of the missing information will be treated as a change in circumstances.[93] It is unclear whether a judge might allow a window of more than 48 hours. In our view, there is no reason in principle why this should not happen, so long as the period is finite and relatively brief. If a longer period is required there may be a case for adjourning the hearing rather than granting bail in principle.[94] Circumstances where the procedure may be of utility include:

(1) Where, in a Criminal Casework case, licence conditions require residence at an address approved by the applicant's offender manager, this has yet to be done, but is anticipated by a specific date;
(2) Where an address is available but material information such as proof of the landlord's consent to the applicant residing there is missing;
(3) Where a 'section 4' address is to be granted but has been delayed.

(j) Bail hearings in Scotland and cross border issues

Annex 7 to the *Bail Guidance* adapts certain aspects of that guidance to hearings **18.72** before the FTT in Scotland, and also addresses potential cross-border issues that might arise, such as forfeiture against a surety resident in Scotland where bail was

---

[90] *Bail Guidance,* paragraph 46.
[91] *Bail Guidance,* paragraph 47.
[92] *Bail Guidance,* paragraph 48. Where bail in principle is contemplated and cross border issues arise, see Annex 7, paragraphs 6 and 7.
[93] *Bail Guidance,* paragraph 50. Assuming it remains in place, this guidance will take on particular importance when Schedule 2 to IA 1971 is in due course amended by section 7 of IA 2014 to require that bail applications be dismissed without a hearing if made within 28 days of an earlier refusal in the absence of 'a material change in circumstances'. See paragraph 18.04.
[94] See *Adjourning bail hearings* at paragraph 18.69.

granted in England, and how to approach applications for bail by people detained in Scotland where the sureties reside in England.

(2) Decisions

(a) General

18.73 The *Bail Guidance* explains 'when and how' a judge of the FTT should consider granting bail.[95] It does not purport to be exhaustive and it does not purport to be a source of law.[96] Nevertheless, it should be taken into account, and a judge '*may need to give reasons if it cannot be applied in a particular situation*'.[97] A failure to take it into account and/or a decision to depart from it without good reason may be open to challenge by way of judicial review.[98]

(b) Legality of detention as a factor in an application for bail

18.74 A grant of bail presupposes the existence of a power to detain[99] and a decision on bail is not a determination of the legality of detention, whether at common law or for Article 5(4) purposes.[100] In practice, however, the distinction is less hard edged than might at first be assumed.

18.75 Risk of absconding and offending are central to any decision whether to grant bail and are 'paramount' considerations when deciding whether detention is lawful by reference to the second and third *Hardial Singh* principles. As such, reasons given by an FTT judge for refusing bail might inform a judge's consideration of the legality of detention.[101] Equally, 'concerns about the lawfulness of detention' can be taken into account in deciding whether bail should be granted, albeit the FTT lacks jurisdiction to rule on the issue.[102] In *R (Othman) v Special Immigration Appeals Commission and Others*[103] the Divisional Court said that '[a]ny tribunal charged with considering bail is bound sometimes to have to ask, en route to its decision, whether the detention is still lawful or not . . .'[104]

---

[95] *Bail Guidance*, paragraph 3.
[96] *Bail Guidance*, paragraph 2.
[97] *Bail Guidance*, paragraph 3.
[98] As to challenging bail decisions by way of judicial review, see paragraph 18.18.
[99] *R (Konan) v Secretary of State for the Home Department* [2004] EWHC 22 (Admin), *per* Collins J at [30].
[100] *R (Lumba & Mighty) v Secretary of State for the Home Department* [2011] UKSC 12; [2012] 1 AC 245, *per* Lord Dyson at [118].
[101] *MA & TT v Secretary of State for the Home Department* [2010] EWHC 2350 (Admin), *per* Ian Dove QC at [15]. In deciding how much weight to accord bail decisions 'it is . . . necessary to have regard to the extent and quality of the information which was available to the Immigration Judges who considered those applications. It is necessary to examine the evidence before [the Administrative Court] to see whether or not there is a broader range of material . . . than that which was available to the Immigration Judges when forming their decisions.'
[102] *Konan, per* Collins J at [30].
[103] [2012] EWHC 2349 (Admin).
[104] *Per* Hughes LJ at [18].

The *Bail Guidance* states that judges should normally assume detention is lawful **18.76**
but that 'it will be a good reason to grant bail if for one reason or another continued detention might well be successfully challenged elsewhere'.[105] The guidance which then follows stresses the importance of a number of factors going to
the legality of detention: adherence to policy;[106] adequacy of reasons;[107] length
and likely future length of detention;[108] adherence to the statutory purpose of
detention;[109] and compliance with Article 8 of ECHR and section 55 of the
Borders, Citizenship and Immigration Act 2009 ('BCIA 2009').[110]

(c) Presumptions, burden and standard of proof, evidence

The *Bail Guidance* characterizes the 'primary function' of a bail judge as one **18.77**
of 'risk assessment': weighing the evidence to decide whether continued detention is 'proportionate' in the circumstances.[111] It states that there is no statutory
presumption of bail,[112] although it notes that Home Office policy provides for a
presumption of liberty in all cases, and that a 'policy in favour of release would be
a persuasive reason to grant bail'.[113]

The *Bail Guidance* states that 'bail should not be refused unless there is good **18.78**
reason to do so, and it is for the respondent to show what those reasons are'.[114]
Attempts to apply strict burdens of proof 'may be misleading'.[115] The standard
of proof is described as 'whether there are substantial grounds for believing that
detention should be maintained'. Where there are substantial grounds for both
granting and refusing bail, regard must be had to whether bail conditions may
assist to make release appropriate.[116]

As to matters of evidence: **18.79**

(1) Either party may need to provide relevant evidence to support their
case.[117]

---

[105] *Bail Guidance*, paragraph 5.
[106] *Bail Guidance*, paragraph 7.
[107] *Bail Guidance*, paragraph 8.
[108] *Bail Guidance*, paragraph 17.
[109] *Bail Guidance*, paragraphs 18–20.
[110] *Bail Guidance*, paragraph 21.
[111] *Bail Guidance*, paragraph 27.
[112] *Cf.* Section 4 of the Bail Act 1976 which provides that, in the criminal context, bail 'shall be
granted' except as provided for in Schedule 1 to that Act. There is an argument that so far as applications to the FTT for bail pending appeal are concerned, there is a presumption of bail arising from
paragraph 30(2) of Schedule 2 to IA 1971, which provides that the Tribunal 'shall not be obliged' to
grant bail where certain circumstances arise. The 2003 *Bail Guidance Notes* referred to 'a common
law presumption in favour of bail, subject to the restrictions on the granting of bail' in paragraph 30.
[113] *Bail Guidance*, paragraph 27, fn 15.
[114] *Bail Guidance*, paragraph 27.
[115] *Bail Guidance*, paragraph 28.
[116] *Bail Guidance*, paragraph 31.
[117] *Bail Guidance*, paragraph 28.

(2) It is for the immigration authorities to provide the evidence on which they rely to say that it is reasonable for detention to continue.[118]

(3) It is necessary for the applicant to provide the evidence to challenge this case and show that it is reasonable to grant bail.[119]

(4) Failure by one side or the other to provide relevant evidence that is reasonably available should result in the judge giving less weight to that party's arguments.[120]

(5) Both parties have a 'duty to bring to the judge's attention any relevant evidence in their possession'.[121] The respondent may have evidence of past compliance which is obviously relevant to the assessment the FTT must conduct.[122] Equally, bail summaries may omit matters adverse to an applicant. A failure by an applicant's representative to correct the position risks misleading the FTT by omission.

(d) Decision making guidance

18.80   The *Bail Guidance* states that in reaching a decision on bail a judge should consider the reasons for detention; the length of detention and its likely future duration; alternatives to detention; the effect of detention upon the detainee and his or her family; and the likelihood of the person complying with conditions of bail.[123] Of these reasons, duration and compliance are the subject of detailed discussion.

18.81   **(i) Reasons**   The Secretary of State's reasons for detention should be stated in the bail summary.[124] The judge should consider whether they are 'proportionate to the need to continue to detain' and may also consider whether they are consistent with published Home Office policy.[125] Reasons which are unsupported by evidence or fail to take account of the applicant's circumstances are likely to attract less weight than reasons which are clear and supported by evidence.[126]

18.82   Risk of harm is not in itself a sufficient basis to detain but where a person is detained pending investigation or expulsion and has a history of criminality the judge will have to assess the risk the person poses of reoffending and the consequences of such offending. High risk will weigh against release.[127]

18.83   The immigration authorities must substantiate any allegation that a person poses a risk of harm to the public or a risk of reoffending.'[128] In cases involving foreign

---

[118] *Bail Guidance*, paragraph 28.
[119] *Bail Guidance*, paragraph 28.
[120] *Bail Guidance*, paragraph 28.
[121] *Bail Guidance*, paragraph 29.
[122] *Bail Guidance*, paragraph 29.
[123] *Bail Guidance*, paragraph 4.
[124] *Bail Guidance*, paragraph 6.
[125] *Bail Guidance*, paragraph 7.
[126] *Bail Guidance*, paragraphs 8–9.
[127] *Bail Guidance*, paragraph 11.
[128] *Bail Guidance*, paragraph 12.

national offenders an 'Annex A/NOMS 1' report should be made available by the Home Office.[129]

The *Bail Guidance* contemplates the FTT requiring the immigration authorities **18.84** to provide details of a person's criminal record, recent risk assessments, and/or licence conditions. Where such information is not provided the *Bail Guidance* suggests giving directions under Rules 45(1) and 50(1) of the FTT Procedure Rules.[130] Unless directions can be issued and complied with on the day of hearing, this will necessitate an adjournment.[131]

Licence conditions should be taken into account, and any bail conditions should **18.85** be consistent with those conditions. A requirement to report regularly to a probation officer may negate the need for stringent bail conditions.[132]

(ii) Length of detention The approach in the *Bail Guidance* to length of deten- **18.86** tion draws heavily on the *Hardial Singh* jurisprudence.[133] Whilst the bail judge cannot rule on lawfulness, length of detention 'will be informative about why the person remains detained and whether they should continue to be'.[134] The guidance on length of detention refers to Annex 2 of the *Bail Guidance*, which sets out key passages from two authorities that discuss the application of the *Hardial Singh* principles.

The Secretary of State will have to show that the reasons for detention remain con- **18.87** nected to the pending investigation or removal,[135] mirroring the first *Hardial Singh* principle. Where she cannot do so, bail should be granted 'as continued detention may well be unlawful'.[136] Where there is some continued connection but detention has become prolonged the weight to be attached to the contention that detention is necessary in the interests of immigration control 'should diminish'.[137]

The *Bail Guidance* arguably goes beyond the *Hardial Singh* case-law, specifying **18.88** periods of detention that will call for particular justification. Whilst noting that the senior courts have been reluctant to identify a period of time after which detention will be deemed excessive, and stressing that each case must be considered on its own facts, it states: 'it is generally accepted that detention for three months would

---

[129] See Annex 3 to the *Bail Guidance*, and Probation Circular 32/2007. The NOMS1 will be completed by the applicant's offender manager and will include information about assessed levels of risk of serious harm, Multi-agency Public Protection ('MAPPA') arrangements, likelihood of reconviction, licence conditions, any concerns about the proposed bail address, and past compliance with national standards, licence requirements and bail.

[130] *Bail Guidance*, paragraph 13.

[131] See paragraph 18.69 for further consideration of adjournments.

[132] *Bail Guidance*, paragraph 15.

[133] *Bail Guidance*, paragraphs 16–21. See further Chapter 8.

[134] *Bail Guidance*, paragraph 17.

[135] *Bail Guidance*, paragraph 18.

[136] *Bail Guidance*, paragraph 18.

[137] *Bail Guidance*, paragraph 18.

be considered a substantial period of time and six months a long period. Imperative considerations of public safety may be necessary to justify detention in excess of six months.'[138]

18.89   Whether a detainee has obstructed removal should be taken into account as should any periods spent pursuing appeals or other legal challenges that prevented removal moving forward.[139] However, the FTT 'must continue to consider what alternatives there are to detention that will not interfere unreasonably with the functions of the immigration authorities, in order to reach a proportionate decision regarding bail'.[140]

18.90   Judges are further advised that in family cases detention would have to be compatible both with Article 8 of ECHR and the best interests of the child principle recognized by the UN Convention on the Rights of the Child ('UNCRC') and section 55 of BCIA 2009.[141]

18.91   **(iii) Likelihood of compliance**   Judges should grant bail 'where a less intrusive alternative to immigration detention is sufficient to protect the relevant public interest'.[142] Regard should be had to an applicant's personal circumstances, 'including their incentives for keeping in contact with the immigration authorities', as well as any conditions that might ensure 'reasonable control'.[143]

18.92   A good record of past compliance is likely to attract significant weight when considering whether a person is likely to comply with conditions.[144] However, even in cases where there is a good record of compliance, a person's incentive to comply with bail may be low if removal is imminent. If a person is likely to comply with a grant of bail, bail should normally be granted and stringent conditions may be unnecessary.[145]

(3) Conditions

18.93   The first, or 'primary', condition of bail is to appear before an IO or the FTT, as the case may be, at a specified time and place:

(1)   Where there is no appeal pending, the judge should grant bail on the condition that the applicant surrenders to an IO at a time and place specified in

---

[138] *Bail Guidance*, paragraph 19.
[139] *Bail Guidance*, paragraph 20.
[140] *Bail Guidance*, paragraph 20.
[141] *Bail Guidance*, paragraph 21. For Article 8 of ECHR see further Chapter 15, paragraphs 15.84–15.97; for the UNCRC see further Chapter 12, paragraphs 12.05 and 12.06 and Chapter 16, paragraphs 16.08 and 16.27–16.29; for section 55 of BCIA 2009 see further Chapter 12, paragraphs 12.07–12.08.
[142] *Bail Guidance*, paragraph 22.
[143] *Bail Guidance*, paragraph 23.
[144] *Bail Guidance*, paragraph 24.
[145] *Bail Guidance*, paragraph 26.

the bail grant (or a subsequent variation).[146] The period will often be seven days,[147] after which a further grant of bail should be made by a CIO absent a change in circumstances justifying re-detention;[148]

(2) Where an appeal is pending and bail is granted under paragraph 29 of Schedule 2 to IA 1971 the *Bail Guidance* requires that the primary condition be formulated as follows:

(a) to attend the next and every subsequent hearing of the appeal at such places and times as shall be notified or as otherwise varied in writing by the Tribunal;

(b) following final determination of the appeal, unless bail is revoked by the Tribunal or by operation of law, to appear before an IO at such time and place as directed by the Tribunal; and

(c) the terms of bail may be varied at any time during their currency by application or at the Tribunal's own motion.[149]

Secondary conditions may be imposed to 'enable the Tribunal to promote the achievement of the primary condition'.[150] The most common secondary conditions are as to place of residence, contact with the immigration authorities, and electronic monitoring. **18.94**

(a) Residence

The *Bail Guidance* states that the proposed place of residence must be set out clearly in the application for bail 'so that the immigration authorities can consider its suitability and make representations if they believe it is not suitable'.[151] However, the 'bail in principle' mechanism means that in certain limited circumstances a decision on bail may be taken subject to final details of accommodation being provided to the FTT after the hearing.[152] A late change in the proposed address is likely to result in the refusal of bail.[153] There may be circumstances in which an applicant does not have a release address but is entitled to accommodation under section 4(1)(c) of the Immigration and Asylum Act 1999. Protocols exist between the FTT and the Home Office regarding the provision of addresses in such circumstances, to which the FTT must have regard.[154] **18.95**

---

[146] *Bail Guidance*, paragraph 33.
[147] *Bail Guidance*, paragraph 34.
[148] *Bail Guidance*, paragraph 35.
[149] *Bail Guidance*, paragraph 36.
[150] *Bail Guidance*, paragraph 37. The power arises from paragraphs 22(2) and 29(5) of Schedule 2 of IA 1971.
[151] *Bail Guidance*, paragraph 38(i).
[152] See paragraphs 18.70 and 18.71.
[153] *Bail Guidance*, paragraph 38(ii).
[154] See *Bail Guidance*, paragraph 38(iii) and Annex 4.

(b) Reporting

18.96 A person granted bail is likely to be made subject to a condition requiring them to maintain contact with the immigration authorities.[155] The most common is a requirement to report weekly to an immigration reporting centre. However, it is for the judge to determine the appropriate frequency.[156] A failure to maintain contact in breach of a condition of release may be taken by the immigration authorities to disclose reasonable grounds for believing that the person should be re-detained.[157]

(c) Electronic monitoring

18.97 The FTT has the power to direct that an adult be made subject to a requirement of electronic monitoring or 'tagging' as a condition of bail.[158] This condition should not be imposed as a matter of course. It is most likely to be imposed where bail is granted to an applicant who has previously committed an offence, and where the respondent has requested it as an additional safeguard for public protection.[159] Whether such safeguards are necessary is a matter for the judge, and the respondent must substantiate such a request.[160]

18.98 Form B1 requires a bail applicant to indicate whether, in the event electronic monitoring is considered to be an appropriate condition, he or she consents to remaining in detention for a period not exceeding two working days so this can be arranged. Annex 5 to the *Bail Guidance* states that this form of consent was agreed between the President of the FTT (IAC), Ministry of Justice lawyers, and the Home Office 'to ensure lawful detention until the tag has been fitted'. Where bail is granted with a condition of electronic monitoring, the grant of bail is expressed as being subject to 'the applicant cooperating with the arrangement for electronic monitoring' and the Home Office 'arranging electronic monitoring within two working days of this grant of bail'.[161] The grant of bail will also state that if electronic monitoring is not set up within the stipulated two-day period the applicant will be released on specified conditions without electronic monitoring.[162]

(d) Sureties

18.99 A judge can require an applicant to produce sureties. This is not mandatory. The FTT must have 'due regard' to the fact that people recently arrived in the country may have nobody who can stand surety for them.[163] The purpose of a surety is to

---

155 *Bail Guidance*, paragraphs 37, 38(v).
156 *Bail Guidance*, paragraph 38(v).
157 *Bail Guidance*, paragraph 38(v).
158 Section 36(4) of AI(ToC)A 2004.
159 *Bail Guidance*, paragraph 38(vi). See further Annex 5 to the *Bail Guidance* and the model bail conditions at Annex 8.
160 *Bail Guidance*, paragraph 38(vi).
161 *Bail Guidance*, Annex 8.
162 *Bail Guidance*, Annex 8.
163 *Bail Guidance*, paragraph 39.

reduce the risk of a breach of bail conditions. If there are no reasonable grounds for thinking an individual might abscond a surety may well be unnecessary.[164]

The surety's principal obligation is to ensure that the applicant answers bail.[165] The surety need not reside with the applicant, and the level of supervision is a matter for them.[166] Nevertheless, where the evidence establishes that a surety is able to influence and monitor the actions of the person seeking bail that may increase the judge's confidence that bail conditions will be met.[167] **18.100**

Confidence in a surety 'may be increased by the amount of the recognisance offered'.[168] The *Bail Guidance* is silent as to what sum will be appropriate in a given case. The approach in the 2003 *Bail Guidance Notes* was, in our view, instructive. They stated that the sum 'must be fixed with regard to the surety's means . . . There is no tariff figure and the sums involved are always a matter for the individual adjudicator.'[169] The following factors were identified as material: **18.101**

(1) '[the sum] must be realistic in the sense that it must be well within the resources of the surety, and not so high as to be prohibitive';
(2) 'it must be assessed in relation to the means of the surety alone';
(3) 'it must be sufficient to satisfy [the adjudicator] that it will ensure that the applicant and the surety will meet their obligations'; and
(4) 'it must be realisable in the event of forfeiture'.[170]

A surety with no immigration status, regular address, means of subsistence, or knowledge of the applicant may well be unsuitable to act as such, as will a surety with unspent convictions.[171] Details of sureties offered should be supplied in advance to the respondent who may well make background checks.[172] **18.102**

A judge will need to verify the identity and residence of a proposed surety and their ability to stand in the sum offered.[173] The surety should bring evidence of their ability to pay the recognizance. What constitutes sufficient proof 'may depend on the size of the recognisance and other circumstances of the case. There is no inflexible rule'.[174] Bank statements 'for three months before the hearing date', or details of a building society or other savings account of similar duration may be sufficient.[175] **18.103**

---

[164] *Bail Guidance*, paragraph 39.
[165] *Bail Guidance*, paragraph 40.
[166] *Bail Guidance*, paragraph 40.
[167] *Bail Guidance*, paragraph 41.
[168] *Bail Guidance*, paragraph 41.
[169] 2003 *Bail Guidance Notes*, paragraph 2.3.3.
[170] 2003 *Bail Guidance Notes*, paragraph 2.3.3.
[171] *Bail Guidance*, paragraph 42.
[172] *Bail Guidance*, paragraph 42.
[173] *Bail Guidance*, paragraph 43.
[174] *Bail Guidance*, paragraph 43.
[175] *Bail Guidance*, paragraph 43.

Where a person offers wage slips as evidence of means 'some inquiry may be needed as to outgoings'.[176]

(4) When does bail end?

18.104 Bail ends when:

(1) the person granted bail ceases to be liable to detention under the Immigration Acts (having been granted leave to enter or remain, or having left the United Kingdom);

(2) the person is re-detained; or

(3) the period of bail granted comes to an end.[177]

18.105 Where a person is re-detained and there has been no change in circumstances, it is 'likely a First-tier Tribunal Judge will grant bail on the same conditions as before'.[178]

18.106 If bail was granted by an IO, and the person surrenders as required, a further period of bail should be granted unless there has been a change in circumstances or unless a decision is taken to grant temporary admission or release.[179]

(5) Forfeiture

18.107 Where a person fails to answer bail at the time and place required a judge of the FTT can find the recognizance of the person on bail and of any surety is forfeit.[180] The judge has the power to decide if the person entering into a recognizance is bound in full or in part.[181]

18.108 Failure to comply with secondary conditions of bail (residence, reporting, compliance with electronic tagging, etc) is not a basis for the commencement of forfeiture proceedings (although it may amount to a change in circumstances sufficient to justify re-detention).[182]

18.109 When assessing whether or not there should be forfeiture of any recognizance and the amount to be forfeited, a judge will take account of the following matters in particular with regard to the sureties:

(1) the level of their responsibility for the applicant's failure and the steps taken by them to ensure compliance;

(2) any steps taken by them to report any concerns to the immigration authorities;

---

[176] *Bail Guidance,* paragraph 43.
[177] *Bail Guidance,* paragraph 60.
[178] *Bail Guidance,* paragraph 61.
[179] *Bail Guidance,* paragraphs 35 and 63.
[180] *Bail Guidance,* paragraph 64. See paragraphs 23, 31, and 32 of Schedule 2 to IA 1971.
[181] *Bail Guidance,* paragraph 64.
[182] *Bail Guidance,* paragraphs 65 and 38(v).

(3) whether the applicant failed to comply with any secondary conditions and any steps taken by the sureties to ensure compliance; and

(4) any other explanations offered by the sureties.[183]

F. SIAC Bail

(1) SIAC Procedure Rules

Where a person is detained under the Immigration Acts in a national security case[184] an application for bail must be made to the Special Immigration Appeals Commission (SIAC) under Part 6 of the Special Immigration Appeals Commission (Procedure) Rules 2003 (the 'SIAC Procedure Rules'). **18.110**

When exercising its functions SIAC 'shall secure that information is not disclosed contrary to the interests of national security, the international relations of the United Kingdom, the detection and prevention of crime, or in any other circumstances where disclosure is likely to harm the public interest'.[185] Part 7 of the SIAC Procedure Rules provides for the mechanisms by which the purposes of SIAC are achieved including, *inter alia*, the use of 'special advocates' (rules 34–36) and the deployment by the Secretary of State of 'closed material'[186] (rules 37–38A). **18.111**

The SIAC bail procedure is found in Part 6 of the SIAC Procedure Rules. Rule 29 stipulates the information that must be provided on an application for bail to the Commission. Where an application for bail is filed the Commission must, as soon as reasonably practicable, serve a copy of the application on the Secretary of State and fix a hearing (unless a hearing has already been fixed under rule 9A(3)(a)).[187] **18.112**

If the Secretary of State wishes to contest the application, she must file with the Commission a written statement of her reasons for doing so not later than 2.00 pm the day before the hearing; or where she received notice of the hearing less than 24 hours before that time, as soon as reasonably practicable.[188] If the Secretary of State objects to such a statement being disclosed to the applicant or his representative, rules 37 (Closed material) and 38 (Consideration of Secretary of State's objection) shall apply.[189] Rule 37(2) provides that the Secretary of State may not rely upon **18.113**

---

[183] *Bail Guidance,* paragraph 66.
[184] See paragraphs 18.40–18.42.
[185] SIAC Procedure Rules, rule 4.
[186] Closed material is defined in rule 37(1) as 'material which the Secretary of State would otherwise be required to disclose to the appellant or his representative under rule 10, 10A, or 10B, but which the Secretary of State objects to disclosing to the appellant or his representative'.
[187] Rule 30(1).
[188] Rule 30(2).
[189] Rule 30(3).

closed material unless a special advocate has been appointed to represent the interests of the appellant.

18.114   The Commission must serve written notice of its decision and, if and to the extent that it is possible to do so without disclosing information contrary to the public interest, the reasons for its decision on the applicant, the Secretary of State, and the person having custody of the applicant.[190] Where bail is granted, the notice must include the conditions of bail and the amounts in which the applicant and any sureties are to be bound.[191] Rules 30(6) and (7) set out further requirements in relation to the recognizance of the applicant and/or any surety.

18.115   Rule 31 makes the necessary modifications for applications in Scotland.

(2) Bail decision-making in SIAC

18.116   There is no statutory test for granting or withholding bail. Prior to 2009, SIAC consistently held that two factors were of great importance: (i) risk of absconding; and (ii) risk to national security, including the risk posed if an applicant were to abscond,[192] and these remain of fundamental importance. In that period, SIAC assumed that the SIAC Procedure Rules were 'undiluted by any obligation to ensure that an individual appellant had disclosed to him any minimum standard of information about the grounds upon which the Secretary of State opposed the grant of bail or sought its revocation'.[193]

18.117   In *R (Cart and Others) v Upper Tribunal and Others*[194] the Divisional Court held that this assumption was wrong. It held that decisions by SIAC to revoke and refuse bail on the basis of closed material violated the claimants' rights under Article 5(4) of ECHR because the claimants were not given the gist of that closed material.[195]

18.118   Following *Cart* Mitting J gave guidance on the approach that SIAC would adopt to bail applications henceforth in *U & Others v Secretary of State for the Home Department*.[196] He said an applicant 'must be told sufficient about the grounds

---

[190] Rule 30(4).

[191] Rule 30(5).

[192] See, e.g. *Mohammed Othman v Secretary of State for the Home Department*, Unreported, SC/15/2005, 2 December 2008, *per* Mitting J at [4].

[193] *U & Ors v Secretary of State for the Home Department* [2009] UKSIAC 80/2009, *per* Mitting J at [2].

[194] [2009] EWHC 3052 (Admin); [2010] 2 WLR 1012.

[195] *Per* Laws LJ at [101]–[113]. The Court of Appeal subsequently ruled that the same does not hold in relation to the Secretary of State's case in support of the imposition of particular bail conditions, so long as the bail conditions are not so onerous as to amount to a deprivation of liberty within the meaning of Article 5. Article 5(4) would not assist in such a case, Article 6 of ECHR was not engaged, and Article 8 of ECHR, whilst engaged, did not compel the procedural safeguards for which the appellant contended: *R (BB (Algeria)) v Secretary of State for the Home Department* [2012] EWCA Civ 1499; [2013] 1 WLR 1568 *per* Dyson LJ at [32] and [52].

[196] [2009] UKSIAC 80/2009.

upon which the grant of bail is opposed and/or its revocation is sought, to permit him to give effective instructions to the Special Advocates about them',[197] although:

(1) the Secretary of State could rely on closed material to support a ground, provided that sufficient information was given to permit effective instructions to be given about the ground; and

(2) the Secretary of State may elect not to rely upon a ground which she is, for one or more of the reasons set out in Rule 4(1) of the SIAC Procedure Rules, unwilling to disclose, in which case SIAC would consider only those grounds which have been sufficiently disclosed to an appellant.[198]

The inability to rely on closed material is characterized in *U & Others* as the loss of **18.119** a 'vital tool' that had permitted balanced judgments to be made about the risk to national security and the risk of absconding posed by an individual appellant, and had informed the management of one or both risks in the event that the Secretary of State contended a breach of bail conditions was likely.[199] The loss of this tool necessitated reconsideration of the grounds on which SIAC might grant or refuse bail. Henceforth, a 'precautionary approach' was to be followed:[200]

> In the case of a new appellant, it is unlikely that the national security case will be fully deployed at the start, at least in the open material. We do not start with a presumption that he must be detained but, save in exceptional cases, we are unlikely to be able to determine, at least on the open material, whether or not the two risks could be managed if an appellant were to be admitted to bail. A precautionary approach will be adopted. Removal of the vital tool of reliance on closed material will make it unlikely that SIAC will grant bail. The means of ensuring that detention is not arbitrary or even unduly prolonged will be to insist upon a tighter timetable for the taking of steps preparatory to an appeal than has hitherto been customary. The aim will be to ensure that all cases involving appellants who are detained will be heard within about six months of the filing of a notice of appeal. If only the national security case can be determined within that time, we will determine it and adjourn the issue of safety on return to be determined separately.

Mitting J went on to state that, in the case of an applicant whose appeal had been **18.120** finally determined, and against whom a deportation order had been made, a precautionary approach to any application for bail by him would be adopted, 'subject to two provisos which arise from the fact that SIAC is likely to have far more information about him than it would have about a new appellant'.[201] The provisos were:

(1) that it would not be necessary to 'revisit the grounds for finding that he posed a risk to national security, whether those grounds were open or closed or both'; and

---

[197] At [2].
[198] At [2].
[199] At [3].
[200] At [7]. The lawfulness of the 'precautionary approach' was challenged in *R(U) v Special Immigration Appeals Commission* [2010] EWHC 813 (Admin) but the Divisional Court concluded that it had not impacted upon the decision under challenge, so declined to rule on the issue (see *per* Laws LJ at [25]–[26]).
[201] At [9].

(2) SIAC would take into account what is known about the appellant's history and circumstances, including compliance with bail conditions, in determining whether or not he can be readmitted to bail.

18.121 The lawfulness of SIAC's approach to bail applications in this scenario (i.e. after SIAC had determined the appeal) came before the Divisional Court in *R (BB) v Secretary of State for the Home Department*.[202] Richards LJ held that it was impermissible for SIAC to rely upon conclusions it had reached in closed proceedings in reaching decisions on bail without giving the applicant the opportunity of challenging those findings by reference to material that had been withheld and not conveyed in gist in the main proceedings.[203]

18.122 In *M1 v Secretary of State for the Home Department*,[204] which followed soon after *BB*, Mitting J observed that 'SIAC's bail jurisdiction is in a state of flux',[205] and that it must be approached 'without much in the way of guiding principles'.[206] Nevertheless, at least in relation to a pre-hearing case, the following points of principle appeared to be clearly established:[207]

> First, it is wrong, in principle, to form or to express a firm view about the material, which will be relied upon by either side at the final hearing. To do so would either demonstrate, or give the impression of demonstrating a mind made up. That is plainly wrong in a case . . . in which [the same judge will] hear the application for bail and will preside over the final hearing.
>
> Secondly, if the Secretary of State relies on specific grounds to resist bail, she must provide sufficient information to permit the appellant and his open representatives to give effective instructions to the special advocates about those grounds.[208]
>
> Thirdly, as is the case in all appeals involving immigration decisions and children, where children are involved their best interests must be treated as a primary consideration.
>
> Fourthly, when, as here and in many other cases, the interests of a family are involved, respect must be shown to the rights of the family under Article 8.
>
> Fifthly, if the decision is to detain and, possibly, even to impose bail conditions which deprive of liberty for the purposes of Article 5, the decision must be lawful

---

[202] [2011] EWHC 336 (Admin); [2012] QB 146.
[203] *Per* Richards LJ at [35]–[37].
[204] [2011] UKSIAC 101/10.
[205] At [1].
[206] At [5].
[207] At [6].
[208] As required by Article 5(4). In *D2 v Secretary of State for the Home Department*, Unreported, SC/116/12, 8 May 2012, the applicant's advisors indicated he was willing to waive his right to disclosure of subsequent grounds for revocation of bail were bail to be revoked. Mitting J held that this course was in principle open and, had it tipped the balance in favour of bail, he would have accepted the undertaking (see at [4]–[7]).

on *Hardial Singh* principles, which are, in effect, identical to those expressed by the Strasbourg Court in *Chahal*.

Sixthly, and I express this view tentatively because I invited no submission on it, and have heard no argument upon it, there is no presumption either for or against the grant of bail.

Absent any further guidance from SIAC or the higher courts, these propositions are for the time being the last word on SIAC's approach to bail. **18.123**

SIAC's jurisdiction to rule on the legality of detention

Whilst there has yet to be a definitive ruling from the higher courts on the point, it seems clear that, unlike the FTT, the bail jurisdiction of SIAC extends to determining the legality of detention. This approach was adopted, for example, in the *Othman* litigation in which Mitting J declared that SIAC had jurisdiction to review the lawfulness of the claimant's detention.[209] This was then challenged before the Divisional Court in *R (Othman) v Special Immigration Appeals Commission*. The claimant argued SIAC had exceeded its jurisdiction by purporting to determine the legality of detention.[210] The Secretary of State argued:[211] **18.124**

(1) That since SIAC was created by Parliament 'to provide a court such as the ECHR requires to be available to determine (*inter alia*) the lawfulness of any deprivation of liberty', it followed that the power to determine the *Hardial Singh* question was implicit in the statutory power to grant or refuse bail;[212] and

(2) 'SIAC alone has the evidence, and the evidence-handling procedures, which provide the essential means of deciding this question'.

Mitting J had agreed that approach, 'whilst accepting the concurrent jurisdiction of the High Court'.[213] **18.125**

Ultimately, the Divisional Court declined to make a definitive ruling on the jurisdictional issue, holding that the *Hardial Singh* principles were in any event relevant to the exercise of the discretion to grant bail and, on any view, SIAC was entitled to address them.[214] However, Hughes LJ expressed the Court's agreement with the approach of Mitting J below. He went on to observe that even if SIAC can exercise **18.126**

---

[209] See *R (Othman) v Special Immigration Appeals Commission, Secretary of State for the Home Department and Governor of HMP Long Lartin* [2012] EWHC 2349 (Admin), *per* Hughes LJ at [11].

[210] At [17].

[211] At [17].

[212] At [17].

[213] At [17]. At [19] Hughes LJ approves this aspect of Mitting J's approach: 'Mitting J dealt with this bail application, as is frequently the practice, sitting alone, but he brought to it vast experience of cases such as this generally and of this one in particular. *Qua* high court judge, he might himself perfectly properly have considered an application for judicial review of the decision to detain; indeed in January/February of this year, at the invitation of the claimant, he did exactly that concurrently with entertaining, *qua* SIAC, a bail application.'

[214] At [18].

jurisdiction to rule on the legality of detention, 'the overarching jurisdiction of the High Court to intervene if necessary to review the decision of the Secretary of State and to determine whether detention is or is not lawful is not ousted by the ability of SIAC to decide or address the question. What matters is when this court ought to do so and when it ought to decline to exercise its undoubted power'.[215] Given the unique position occupied by SIAC, the High Court ought not to interfere with its judgment on *Hardial Singh* issues 'unless some hard-edged or florid error of law or approach is demonstrated to have occurred'.[216]

---

[215] More recently, in *B v Secretary of State for the Home Department* (SC/09/2005, 13 February 2014), SIAC applied the *Hardial Singh* principles when considering whether there was an underlying power to detain an appellant who had been released on very stringent bail conditions. It found there was 'no reasonable prospect of removing the Appellant to Algeria and thus the ordinary legal basis for justified detention of B under the Immigration Acts has fallen away' (at [51]). However, as the bail conditions did not amount to a deprivation of liberty, there was no requirement that the conditions for a lawful detention be met (at [65]).

[216] At [19].

19

LITIGATING UNLAWFUL DETENTION

A. Introduction

This chapter focuses on the routes available to those detained under the Immigration Acts to challenge the legality of their detention through the courts with a view to securing release, and/or damages, and/or declaratory relief. It also examines a number of procedural issues of particular importance in claims challenging detention. **19.01**

It is beyond the scope of a work such as this to consider all the procedural elements of a judicial review claim or civil claim in detail. In the light of a series of cases decided in the wake of the Jackson reforms[1] it is clear that the courts will henceforth show little tolerance for procedural error and delay. It has been held that the 'spirit of the Jackson reforms' applies to public law cases as much as to private law claims.[2] As a result, claimants and defendants (and their advisors) face potentially severe consequences if they fail to comply with the relevant procedure rules and practice directions. **19.02**

---

[1] See in particular *Mitchell v News Group Newspapers* [2013] EWCA Civ 1537; [2014] 1 WLR 795.

[2] *R (Singh & Ors) v Secretary of State for the Home Department* [2013] EWHC 2873 (Admin), *per* Hickinbottom J at [27]. The approach in *Mitchell* was applied to the resolution of a costs issue in a judicial review claim in *R (Royal Free London NHS Foundation Trust) v Secretary of State for the Home Department and Brent Borough Council* [2013] EWHC 4101 (Admin), *per* Coulson J at [23]–[26].

B. Routes of Challenge in Outline

19.03 Where a claimant is detained and seeks an order for release, the route of challenge is either a claim for judicial review under Part 54 of the Civil Procedure Rules ('CPR'); or exceptionally (and if the only remedy sought is release) an application for habeas corpus using the procedure in Schedule 1 to the CPR.[3] Where a claimant is at liberty and seeks damages for past false imprisonment the options are a claim for judicial review, if it can be brought in time, or a claim for damages in the county court or Queen's Bench Division of the High Court ('QBD') brought under CPR Part 7 (an 'ordinary civil claim').

C. Anonymity and Private Hearings

19.04 A claimant challenging detention before the courts may have good reason to apply for the case to be heard in private or to seek an anonymity order. Experience suggests that press interest can be significant, particularly in cases involving ex-offenders.

19.05 The general rule is that a hearing should be in public.[4] Parties and witnesses are not normally afforded anonymity.[5] However, it has long been recognized that the courts have the power to permit the identity of a party or a witness to be withheld from public disclosure where that is necessary in the interests of justice.[6]

19.06 CPR 39.2(3) allows for hearings to be in private *inter alia* where this is necessary to protect the interests of any child or protected party[7] and where the court considers this to be necessary in the interests of justice.[8] CPR 39.2(4) permits the court to order that the identity of any party or witness must not be disclosed if it considers non-disclosure necessary in order to protect the interests of that party or witness.

19.07 Where there is a power in the court to order that a name or other matter be withheld from the public, section 11 of the Contempt of Court Act 1981 empowers the court to 'give such directions prohibiting the publication of that name or matter

---

[3] Which preserves Order 54 of the Rules of the Supreme Court of 1965.

[4] CPR 39.2(1).

[5] For the principle of open justice and the exceptions to that principle, see *A v British Broadcasting Corporation (Secretary of State for the Home Department intervening)* [2014] UKSC 25; [2014] 2 WLR 1243, *per* Lord Reed at [23]–[41]; *R (M) v Parole Board and Another* [2013] EWHC 1360 (Admin) *per* Pitchford LJ at [22]; *Practice Guidance (Interim Non-Disclosure Orders)* [2012] 1 WLR 1003 at [13].

[6] *A v BBC* at [38]. In *Guardian News and Media Ltd and Ors, In re* [2010] 2 AC 697, Lord Rodger considers at [26] to [32] the scope of the power to give anonymity orders to give effect to rights under Article 8 of ECHR.

[7] CPR 39.2(3)(d).

[8] CPR 39.2(3)(g).

in connection with the proceedings as appear to the court to be necessary for the purpose for which it was so withheld'.

A number of principles emerge from the cases regarding the making of anonymity orders: **19.08**

(1) The general rule is that parties to proceedings are named and that an anonymity order has to be justified.[9]

(2) In an extreme case identification of a party or witness may put that person's life at risk. In such cases, anonymity will be sought to help secure the individual's rights under Articles 2 and 3 of ECHR.[10] Those are the rights that are most likely to be relevant if the person is seeking asylum.[11]

(3) Notwithstanding the position taken in *Practice Note (Court of Appeal: Asylum and Immigration Cases)*[12] asylum seekers are not entitled to anonymity as a matter of course.[13]

(4) Where, in a case involving an asylum seeker, anonymity is under consideration by reference to Articles 2 and 3 of ECHR, 'the position that the asylum seeker himself adopts will always be an important factor. He is likely to be in the best position to assess the risks and to say whether or not he needs anonymity for his protection.'[14]

(5) Where the basis for a claim for anonymity is not Articles 2 and 3 but Article 8 of ECHR, the party's Article 8 rights must be balanced against the Article 10 rights of the press to publish reports of legal proceedings.[15]

In *Secretary of State for the Home Department v AP (No. 2)*,[16] in the absence of submissions as to why Article 10 of ECHR might weigh against maintaining anonymity, the Supreme Court upheld an anonymity order on Article 3 and Article 8 grounds in relation to a foreign national previously subject to a control order and **19.09**

---

[9] R (*Kambadzi*) v Secretary of State for the Home Department [2011] UKSC 23; [2011] 1 WLR 1299, *per* Lord Brown at [122]. See further *R (M) v Parole Board and Another* [2013] EWHC 1360 (Admin) *per* Pitchford LJ at [68], confirming that an application for anonymity in judicial review proceedings should be sought at the permission stage or, if made later, by way of a formal application, and in either case should be supported by evidence. He declined (at [69]) to give broader guidance in the absence of consultation, but observed that 'attention is required to the issue as to what, if any, notice should be given to media organisations of an application either at the permission stage or in advance of the substantive hearing for judicial review for the purpose of enabling any interested person or organisation to make representations if so advised'. At the time of writing, a working group had been established under the chairmanship of Cranston J to consider this issue further.

[10] *In re Guardian News and Media Ltd* at [26]; *A v BBC* at [39]–[41], [45], and [49].

[11] *Kambadzi, per* Lord Hope at [6].

[12] [2006] 1 WLR 2461. This states that all appeals 'raising asylum and immigration issues' will be anonymized unless a judge gives a specific direction to contrary effect.

[13] *Kambadzi, per* Lord Hope at [6], referring to the position before the Supreme Court.

[14] *Kambadzi, per* Lord Hope at [7]; see also *per* Lord Kerr at [78].

[15] *In re Guardian News and Media Ltd and others per* Lord Rodger at [43]; see discussion at [33]–[43].

[16] [2010] UKSC 26; [2010] 1 WLR 1652.

at the time of judgment the subject of deportation proceedings, where there was a real risk of racist and extremist abuse and physical violence, and publication of his identity might have further exacerbated his social isolation.[17]

19.10 In *A v BBC* the Supreme Court upheld an anonymity order made in favour of a convicted sex offender who had been deported to an unspecified country on the grounds that, if his identity became known, he would be exposed to a real risk of vigilante attacks in his home country in breach of his protected rights under Articles 2 and 3 of ECHR.[18]

D. Time Limits and Limitation

(1) Judicial review time limit

19.11 A claim for judicial review must be brought (a) promptly; and (b) in any event not later than three months after the grounds to make the claim first arose.[19] The Court has a discretion to extend time, but the time limit may not be extended by agreement between the parties.[20]

19.12 The practice in judicial review proceedings is to treat a period of immigration detention as a continuing act. Where a person is in detention or brings a claim challenging detention within three months of release, there will be no barrier on grounds of delay to challenging the legality of the most recent detention dating back more than three months from the date the claim is brought.[21] However, where it is sought to challenge more than one period of detention and the earlier period or periods ended more than three months prior to the date of issue, a challenge in relation to those earlier periods will have to be brought by way of an ordinary civil claim in the county court or QBD.[22] In practice, unless the claimant is still detained, all such challenges should be brought in the same civil claim.

(2) Limitation periods in tort claims

19.13 A comprehensive treatment of the law of limitation is beyond the scope of this work, and what follows is intended only to provide a short account of some key principles.

---

[17] *Per* Lord Rodger at [15]–[18].

[18] At [72]–[76].

[19] CPR 54.5(1)(a) and (b).

[20] CPR 54.5(2).

[21] We are unaware of any authority on this point but the practice has been followed without dissent in countless cases including both *R (Lumba & Mighty) v Secretary of State for the Home Department* [2011] UKSC 12; [2012] 1 AC 245 and *Kambadzi* in the Supreme Court.

[22] N.B.: See R (*MC (Algeria)) v Secretary of State for the Home Department* [2010] EWCA Civ 347 at [34] for consideration of when there is an 'effective break' in the continuity of detention for the purpose of a challenge brought by reference to the *Hardial Singh* principles; see further Chapter 8, paragraph 8.61.

The limitation period for a claim for damages for false imprisonment is six years from the date on which the cause of action accrued.[23] A claim should be brought, at the latest,[24] within six years of the date on which it is alleged detention became unlawful. The authors are not aware of any authority directly on point, but the cases on limitation periods for 'continuing torts' suggest that a new cause of action will accrue on each day that the imprisonment continues.[25] If that is right, then a claim for damages for false imprisonment in relation to a period of detention which began more than six years before the claim was brought but ended less than six years before that date would be time barred in relation to the earlier period but not the later period. Where a claim includes damages for personal injury the limitation period is three years from the date on which the cause of action accrued; or from the date of knowledge (if later) of the person injured.[26] In the context of private law claims founded upon public law wrongs it has been said that delay in commencing proceedings is a factor which can be taken into account in deciding whether the proceedings are abusive, even if the limitation period has not been exceeded.[27]

A claim alleging a breach of a Convention right brought under section 7(1)(a) of **19.14** the Human Rights Act 1998 must be brought before the end of (a) the period of one year beginning with the date on which the act complained of took place; or (b) such longer period as the court or tribunal considers equitable having regard to all the circumstances (subject to any rule imposing a stricter time limit in relation to the procedure in question).[28] In *Home Office v Mohammed & Others*[29] Sedley LJ said that '[i]n measuring time from "the date on which the act complained of took place", both the language and the purpose of s.7(5) are apt to include the last day of a continuing act'.[30]

The facts of a detention challenge may disclose a cause of action beyond false **19.15** imprisonment. These are beyond the scope of this work.[31]

---

[23] Limitation Act 1980, section 2. The limitation period can be postponed in cases of fraud or concealment; see section 32. Special rules apply where the claimant is under a disability: see section 28.

[24] See the discussion of the relevance of delay later in this paragraph.

[25] See *Iqbal v Legal Services Commission* [2005] EWCA Civ 623; *Cartledge and Others v E. Jopling & Sons Ltd* [1962] 1 QB 189 *per* Pearson LJ at pp. 206-207; and *cf. Hardy v Ryle* (1829) 9 B & C 603 *per* Bayley J at p 608.

[26] Limitation Act 1980, section 11(4); *A v Hoare* [2008] UKHL 6, [2008] 1 AC 844. N.B.: the court has a discretion to extend the time limit in personal injury cases; see section 33.

[27] *Clark v University of Lincolnshire and Humberside* [2000] EWCA Civ 129; [2000] EWCA Civ 129, *per* Lord Woolf at [35].

[28] Section 7(5).

[29] [2011] EWCA Civ 351; [2011] 1 WLR 2862.

[30] At [5]. N.B.: This was held in the context of a claim for damages for breach of Article 8. The extent to which that reasoning might apply in the context of Article 5 has not been tested. Whilst it is in our view strongly arguable that a claim brought within one year of the last day of a period of detention would be in time, this is not settled.

[31] The facts giving rise to a claim in false imprisonment may also disclose, for example, a viable claim for damages for assault, misfeasance in public office, or negligence.

E. Pre-Action Protocol

(1) Judicial review

19.16 Save in the most urgent cases and in post-release cases in which the end of the three month longstop time limit is imminent, the judicial review pre-action protocol should be followed where proceedings challenging the legality of past or continuing detention are contemplated. The protocol requires the parties to consider alternative dispute resolution.[32] Where the proposed challenge is to continuing detention, this is unlikely to be a realistic course, but in post-release claims there may be scope for ADR.

19.17 The standard format letter annexed to the pre-action protocol requires a proposed reply date to be specified. The protocol suggests 14 days as a reasonable period but this is not mandatory and a shorter timescale may be appropriate in a detention claim. In the most urgent cases it may be appropriate to allow no more than a few hours.

(2) Civil claim

19.18 The personal injury pre-action protocol is intended to apply to 'all claims which include a claim for personal injury' and it applies to the entirety of the claim, not only the PI element (paragraph 2.01). The focus of the PI protocol is primarily on relatively low value, routine claims (paragraph 2.02), but 'the "cards on the table" approach advocated by the protocol is equally appropriate to higher value claims' and the 'spirit, if not the letter of the protocol, should still be followed for multi-track type claims' (paragraph 2.03). ADR should be considered (paragraphs 2.16 to 2.19). Where a claim is brought for damages for false imprisonment and there is no PI claim the claim is not covered by a specific protocol. It will, however, be subject to the guidance in the Practice Direction – Pre-action Conduct (see in particular paragraphs 6 to 9 and Annex A). Again, the Practice Direction requires the parties to consider ADR (paragraphs 6.01, 8.01 to 8.04).

F. The Correct Defendant

19.19 Judicial review proceedings challenging the legality of detention are brought against the Secretary of State for the Home Department. An ordinary civil claim for damages in the county court or the QBD is brought against the Home Office.[33]

---

[32] Paragraph 3.01.
[33] List of Authorised Government Departments published by the Minister for the Civil Service in pursuance of Section 17 of the Crown Proceedings Act 1947.

G. Challenging Removal and Detention: Abuse of Process

In *BA & Others v Secretary of State for the Home Department*[34] the Court of Appeal   **19.20**
held that it may be an abuse of process to pursue a civil claim for damages for false
imprisonment arising out of a period of immigration detention where the legality of that detention was, or could have been, addressed in earlier judicial review
proceedings brought to challenge removal directions ('RDs') and permission was
refused. The High Court has since held that the principles emerging from *BA* are
not limited to cases in which permission was refused.[35]

The High Court has recently held in *R (Ashraf) v Secretary of State for the Home*   **19.21**
Department[36] that it may be an abuse of process to challenge detention in judicial review proceedings which challenge RDs where the detention challenge lacks
'obvious distinct merit'.[37]

The decisions in *BA* and in *Ashraf* appear to pull in different directions and—   **19.22**
particularly given the pressured circumstances in which challenges to RDs are
often commenced—taken together, may confront practitioners with real difficulties. On the one hand, a failure to pursue a meritorious detention challenge at the
same time as a challenge to RDs without good reason could, following *BA*, result in
a subsequent detention claim being struck out as an abuse (with the representative
facing potential liability in negligence). On the other hand, pursuit of a detention
challenge alongside a challenge to RDs could, on one reading of *Ashraf*, result in
serious sanctions being visited upon representatives if the detention aspect of the
claim is found to lack 'obvious distinct merit'.

(1) *BA & Ors*

The Court of Appeal in *BA* emphasized that there is a need for finality in litiga-   **19.23**
tion, and generally a party should not be vexed twice.[38] As a result, if a challenge
to detention should have been raised in earlier proceedings (e.g. a judicial review
of RDs), it might well be an abuse of process to make that challenge in subsequent
proceedings (e.g. a civil action for damages). Whether or not it does is to be decided
by reference to the principles identified in *Johnson v Gore Wood*.[39] There should

---

[34] [2012] EWCA Civ 944, *per* Sir John Thomas at [27].
[35] *HHF v Secretary of State for the Home Department* [2012] EWHC 4261 (QB), *per* Cranston J at
[4]. *HHF* was a case in which an earlier claim had been discontinued before a ruling on permission.
BA was held to apply, but on the facts the judge considered that there was no prospect of the later
claim being ruled abusive (at [5]).
[36] [2013] EWHC 4028 (Admin), *per* Cranston J at [2].
[37] *R (Ashraf) v Secretary of State for the Home Department* [2013] EWHC 4028 (Admin), *per*
Cranston J at [2].
[38] *BA & Ors* at [26].
[39] [2000] UKHL 65; [2002] 2 AC 1.

be 'a broad, merits-based judgment which takes account of the public and private interests involved and also takes account of all the facts of the case, focusing attention on the crucial question whether, in all the circumstances, a party is misusing or abusing the process of the court by seeking to raise before it the issue which could have been raised before'.[40]

19.24 In *BA*, Sir John Thomas[41] identifies a number of general factors which are likely to inform a decision as to whether a false imprisonment claim brought subsequent to a judicial review of RDs is an abuse of process.

19.25 It will, in general, be an abuse of process to bring an unlawful detention claim if there were earlier proceedings in which that claim could have been brought and it was not. There will, however, be an exception to that rule if the claimant can show good reason for not having brought the unlawful detention claim earlier. This might include there having been insufficient time to obtain the necessary evidence before issuing the judicial review claim.[42] It might also include the fact the public funding regime made it impractical to pursue the two issues together.[43] On the particular facts of *BA* it was also relevant, *inter alia*, that the focus of the judicial review had been removal and not detention,[44] that the claimants had not behaved in any way which was culpable,[45] and that the Secretary of State had been notified that the civil claim was contemplated before permission had been refused in the judicial review proceedings.[46] In isolation, however, these last three factors are unlikely to be determinative in any future case.

(2) *Ashraf*: bringing an unmeritorious detention challenge in a removal judicial review

19.26 Following the transfer to the Upper Tribunal ('UT') of most immigration and asylum judicial review work on 1 November 2013, challenges to RDs will ordinarily be brought in the UT. Judicial review proceedings challenging detention remain in the Administrative Court.[47] A claim challenging both detention and RDs must therefore also be brought in the Administrative Court.

19.27 In *Ashraf* the claimant challenged RDs and the legality of detention, so his claim was issued in the Administrative Court. Cranston J considered that the detention challenge lacked merit. He perceived a concern that if challenges to detention were

---

[40] *BA* at [26] citing Lord Bingham in *Johnson* at p 31D.
[41] At [27].
[42] At [27(e)].
[43] This weighed heavily with the Court of Appeal in its conclusion that BA's claim was not an abuse of process; at [29]–[30].
[44] At [32].
[45] At [33].
[46] At [34].
[47] Paragraph 3 of the Direction of the Lord Chief Justice of 21 August 2013.

routinely included with challenges to RDs the transfer of immigration judicial review claims to the UT would have little practical effect.[48] He said it should not be possible to 'circumvent' the rules about issuing in the UT 'by the inclusion of an unmeritorious unlawful detention claim',[49] adding that lodging a challenge to removal in the Administrative Court including a ground going to the lawfulness of detention when there was no 'obvious distinct merit' could well constitute an abuse of process by the lawyers engaged in the case.[50] Where such an abuse was found it could be addressed 'within the framework' of *R (Hamid) v Secretary of State for the Home Department*[51] and the cases following it.[52] Costs penalties, he said, were another possibility.

In our view *Ashraf* should be approached with caution. The suggestion that sanctions may follow where a challenge to detention is included alongside a challenge to removal and lacks 'obvious distinct merit' was *obiter*. The judge found that despite Mr Ashraf 'never [having] had any basis for alleging unlawful detention' his claim did not lack 'obvious distinct merit'.[53] This suggests, at the very least, that the merits of the detention challenge must be far below the permission threshold before an allegation of abuse might gain traction. **19.28**

Nothing that is said in *Ashraf* can detract from two fundamental and long standing propositions: **19.29**

(1) the test for permission in judicial review is one of arguability, and this is not a high threshold;[54] and
(2) a judicial review claim is not an abuse of process simply because it is subsequently ruled to be unarguable.

Ashraf must be read in a manner that is consistent both with these statements of general principle, and also with the importance that the common law and the European Convention on Human Rights attach to the right of access to the court to challenge the legality of detention. If a detention challenge, brought in isolation, would not be an abuse of process it cannot be the case that it becomes abusive simply because it is raised at the same time as a removal challenge. **19.30**

---

[48] At [34].
[49] At [34].
[50] At [35].
[51] [2012] EWHC 3070 (Admin); [2013] CPR 6.
[52] The *Hamid* line of cases deal with the sanctions to be imposed following serious procedural shortcomings by lawyers making urgent injunction applications.
[53] At [30] and [36], albeit he suggests that he applied leniency because the evidence which was relied on in challenging detention arrived with the claimant's advisers late in the day.
[54] *Inland Revenue Commissioners v Federation of Self-Employed and Small Businesses* [1982] AC 617 *per* Lord Diplock at 644A: 'If, on a quick perusal of the material then available, the court thinks that it discloses what might on further consideration turn out to be an arguable case in favour of granting to the applicant the relief claimed, it ought, in the exercise of a judicial discretion, to give him leave to apply for that relief.'

19.31 In our view, whilst there may be cases in which the inclusion of a challenge to detention in a judicial review claim challenging RDs amounts to an abuse of process, this will only be where the detention challenge is obviously unmeritorious and is being used as a tactical device to bring a claim in the Administrative Court that should be brought in the UT. Moreover, the reference to 'distinct' merit must not be read as suggesting merit distinct from the removal challenge. Much of the reasoning in *BA*[55] is premised upon the fact that the merits of a detention challenge will often be bound up with the merits of a removal challenge.

19.32 Those acting for claimants in such circumstances can mitigate any risks arising from *Ashraf* by ensuring that any challenge to detention is pleaded in sufficient detail, making reference to the relevant legal principles.

H. Appropriate Venue for Post-Release Challenges

19.33 *ID v The Home Office*[56] established that there is no objection to a claim for false imprisonment, based upon an allegation of unlawful immigration detention, being pursued as an ordinary civil action in the county court. The Secretary of State's argument that issuing the claim in the county court was an abuse of process circumventing the safeguards in the judicial review process was rejected. Brooke LJ noted that 'it is always possible for a circuit judge to direct the transfer of part of a private law action to the High Court for trial by a judge with Administrative Court experience if this is thought desirable on case management grounds',[57] and that there were 'a number of sound reasons why cases of this kind, if they are viable at all, should be entrusted to a judge with Administrative Court experience at any rate until matters settle down and clear principles emerge from the caselaw'.[58] However, these were case management issues and did not impact upon whether it was wrong in principle to issue a claim in the county court (or by extension, the QBD).

19.34 If a claim is brought outside the three month longstop deadline for judicial review without a good reason to extend time, then the claimant will have little choice but to proceed by way of an ordinary civil claim.

19.35 In *BA & Others* Sir John Thomas said that whether immigration detention is lawful raises issues 'which the Administrative Court is best placed to determine'.[59] This could be read as meaning the Administrative Court is the appropriate venue in all such cases. However, it does not have to be read in this way—cases can be heard in the county court or the QBD by a judge with Administrative Court experience

---

[55] Which does not appear to have been cited in *Ashraf*.
[56] [2005] EWCA Civ 38; [2006] 1 WLR 1003.
[57] *Per* Brooke LJ at [103].
[58] At [109].
[59] At [27(a)].

if necessary. Moreover, since *ID* was decided in January 2005, much of the legal controversy relating to immigration detention has indeed 'settled down', and 'clear principles' have emerged. The majority of challenges involve allegations of a breach of *Hardial Singh* principles (ii) and (iii) or a breach of the policy guidance on suitability in EIG 55.10 which raise no novel points of law.

If the claimant has been released, the most appropriate venue to bring a claim is **19.36** likely to be the county court,[60] unless the claim is of high value and complex, in which case the claim should be issued in the QBD.[61]

Where a claimant is released in the course of a judicial review claim, leaving only **19.37** a claim for declaratory relief and damages, the approach should be no different. The case should be transferred out of the Administrative Court to the county court or the QBD unless there are good reasons for it to remain in the Administrative Court. If the court does not intervene of its own motion, the parties should apply for such a transfer. This will avoid the problem discussed in *Swaran*—i.e. the Administrative Court being burdened with false imprisonment claims that are more suitable for another court.[62]

I. Candour and Disclosure in Judicial Review Proceedings

(1) Defendant's duty

There is no duty of general disclosure in judicial review proceedings.[63] However **19.38** there is a 'very high duty' on public authority respondents, not least central government, to assist the court with full and accurate explanations of all the facts relevant to the issue the court must decide.[64] Judicial review is a process 'which falls to be conducted with all the cards face upwards on the table and the vast majority of the cards will start in the authority's hands'.[65]

A respondent authority 'owes a duty to the court to cooperate and to make can- **19.39** did disclosure, by way of affidavit, of the relevant facts and (so far as they are not apparent from contemporaneous documents which have been disclosed) the reasoning behind the decision challenged in the judicial review proceedings'.[66]

---

[60] In this regard see *Swaran v Secretary of State for the Home Department* [2014] EWHC 1062 (Admin), *per* Dingemans J at [32]–[33].

[61] For detailed guidance on where to start proceedings see Practice Direction 7A to CPR Part 7 at paragraphs 2.01 to 2.10.

[62] See fn. 60.

[63] CPR PD54A, paragraph 12.01: 'Disclosure is not required unless the court orders otherwise.'

[64] *R (Quark Fishing Ltd) v Secretary of State for Foreign and Commonwealth Affairs* [2002] EWCA Civ 1409 *per* Laws LJ at [50].

[65] *R (Huddlestone) v Lancashire County Council* [1986] 2 All ER 941 *per* Sir John Donaldson MR at p 945.

[66] *Bacongo v Department of the Environment* [2004] UKPC 6; [2004] Env LR 761 at [86].

That is to say, the duty is 'information-based and not restricted to documents'.[67] It extends to documents or information which will assist the claimant's case and/or give rise to additional (and otherwise unknown) grounds of challenge.[68]

19.40 Affidavits should be in clear unambiguous language, which must not deliberately or unintentionally obscure areas of central relevance. There can be no place in affidavits in judicial review applications for 'spin'. Public bodies and central government agencies in particular are involved in the provision of fair and just public administration and must present their cases dispassionately and in the public interest.[69]

19.41 The duty clearly arises at least from the point at which permission to apply for judicial review is granted.[70] The *Treasury Solicitors Guidance* suggests that the duty arises as soon as a department is aware that someone is likely to test a decision or action affecting them, and to every stage of the proceedings including letters of response under the pre-action protocol.[71] It continues to apply throughout the proceedings.[72]

19.42 If the court is not given a true and comprehensive account, but has had to tease the truth out of late discovery, it may be appropriate to draw inferences against a defendant upon points which remain obscure.[73] Where liberty is in issue the court should not be left to try and make findings as best it can on inadequate evidence.[74]

(2) Disclosure applications and requests for further information

19.43 Historically, disclosure was seldom ordered in judicial review proceedings, in part because they often turned on issues of law in which the facts were uncontroversial. The growth in human rights challenges has changed the position to some degree, with such cases at times requiring enquiry into the factual position. In detention claims, the facts may well be controversial and will always require detailed scrutiny. If there is reason to think that the Secretary of State has failed to comply with her duty of candour, it may be appropriate to make an application for specific disclosure

---

[67] *Guidance on discharging the duty of candour and disclosure in judicial review proceedings*, Treasury Solicitor's Department ('*Treasury Solicitor's Guidance*'), January 2010, J.R. 2010, 15(3), at 1.2.

[68] *Treasury Solicitor's Guidance* at 1.2, citing *R v Barnsley Metropolitan Borough Council ex p. Hook* [1976] 1 WLR 1052, *per* Lord Denning at 1058C–E.

[69] *Downes, Re Application for Judicial Review* [2006] NIQB 77, HCNI, *per* Girvan J.

[70] *R (Huddlestone) v Lancashire County Council* [1986] 2 All ER 941 *per* Sir John Donaldson MR at p 945.

[71] *Treasury Solicitor's Guidance* at 1.2.

[72] *Treasury Solicitor's Guidance* at 1.2.

[73] *Quark Fishing, per* Laws LJ at [50].

[74] *R (I & Ors) v Secretary of State for the Home Department* [2010] EWCA Civ 727 *per* Munby LJ at [54].

under CPR Part 31 or seek further information using the mechanism in CPR Part 18 and the practice direction thereto.

(3) Claimant's candour duty

Whilst the focus of much of the jurisprudence on the duty of candour has been **19.44** on public authority defendants, a similar duty rests upon claimants. In the present context in particular, it will not always be the case that the defendant 'holds all the cards'. The following passage from the *Judicial Review Handbook*[75] has been approved by the Court:[76]

> Judicial review claimants have always been under an important duty to make full and frank disclosure to the court of all material facts and any procedural hurdles (eg, ouster, alternative remedy, delay) . . . Claimant candour remains a necessary virtue, both at the outset and in alerting the court as to any key development as the case proceeds.

J. Bail and Interim Relief in the Administrative Court

(1) General

Where a judicial review claim is pending before the Administrative Court chal- **19.45** lenging the legality of continuing detention, the claimant can seek an order for his or her release pending the final hearing. There are, broadly, two bases in law for the court to grant release:

(1) First, in its inherent jurisdiction the High Court has a power to grant bail whilst there are proceedings pending before it.

(2) Second, pursuant to CPR Part 25, the High Court has the power to grant an interim injunction against the Secretary of State compelling the claimant's release from detention on temporary admission/release/restrictions as the case may be or, in our view, on statutory bail.

Applications for release pending the outcome of a judicial review claim are often **19.46** made very early in proceedings. The application can in principle be made without notice and on paper, but it is most unlikely that a judge would grant bail or order release without hearing from the Secretary of State. The most appropriate course, save in the most urgent cases, is to seek an urgent interim relief hearing at which, if appropriate, permission may also be considered.[77] If the claimant applies for an

---

[75] Michael Fordham QC, Hart Publishing, 4th edition, paragraph 10.03; see now 6th edition, paragraph 10.03 to like effect.

[76] *R (Khan) v Secretary of State for the Home Department* [2008] EWHC 1367 (Admin), *per* Sedley LJ, sitting in the Administrative Court.

[77] Although, in a complex case in which an application for release is heard very swiftly there may be good reasons for deferring consideration of permission. For example, it may be clear that continued detention is injurious to the claimant's health, such that an order for immediate release

order to be made, without notice to the Secretary of State, they must ensure that the court is apprised of all relevant facts within their knowledge, including facts adverse to the application.[78]

(2) High Court/Court of Appeal bail

19.47 It is settled at Court of Appeal level that the High Court has an inherent jurisdiction to grant bail in proceedings which are ongoing before it.[79] The power is to be regarded as ancillary to ongoing proceedings; the Court has no power to grant bail *in vacuo*.[80] The power exists pre-permission, following a grant of permission, and following a paper refusal of permission whilst a renewed application for permission is outstanding.[81]

19.48 When permission to apply for judicial review is refused at an oral hearing, the Administrative Court has no power to grant permission to appeal.[82] It is *functus officio*. There are no proceedings before it, to which an application for bail could be ancillary, so it has no power to grant bail.[83]

19.49 An application for permission to appeal the refusal of permission to apply for judicial review can be made directly to the Court of Appeal.[84] Where such an application is made, the Court of Appeal will itself be seized of the matter, and will have a power to grant bail.[85]

19.50 It has been said that in light of the statutory powers available to the Secretary of State and what is now the First-tier Tribunal to grant bail, it will only be in exceptional cases where the High Court's power should be exercised, and then only where permission has been granted.[86] However, this observation was made in the

---

is appropriate, but also the case that the defendant has not had time to consider her position or formulate any defence.

[78] See *R (Hamid) v Secretary of State for the Home Deparment* [2012] EWHC 3070 (Admin); [2013] CPR 6 and, *inter alia*, *R (Awuku & Ors) v Secretary of State for the Home Department* [2012] EWHC 3298 (Admin); *R (Butt & Ors) v Secretary of State for the Home Department* [2014] EWHC 264 (Admin).

[79] *R (Swati) v Secretary of State for the Home Department* [1986] 1 WLR 477, *per* Sir John Donaldson MR at 485H.

[80] *R (Turkoglu) v Secretary of State for the Home Department* [1988] 1 QB 398, *per* Sir John Donaldson MR at 400F.

[81] See *Turkoglu, per* Sir John Donaldson MR at 401D.

[82] CPR 52.15(1).

[83] *Turkoglu*, 401E–F.

[84] CPR 52.15(1).

[85] See Senior Courts Act 1981, section 15(3)(b), and *R (Sezek) v Secretary of State for the Home Department* [2001] EWCA Civ 795; [2002] 1 WLR 348, *per* Peter Gibson LJ at [16]. This conclusion seems to have been reached with reluctance, the Court owning to 'some doubts as to whether there is room for an inherent jurisdiction to grant bail in relation to a civil appeal in judicial review proceedings when Parliament has given the Secretary of State the power to detain and the substance of the complaint is the exercise of that power'. In *In re Corey* [2013] UKSC 76; [2013] 3 WLR 1612, in which submissions touched upon the decisions of the Court of Appeal in *Turkoglu* and *Sezek*, Lord Kerr (at [30]) stopped short of endorsing either decision.

[86] *Swati* at 485H–486A.

context of bail being sought in proceedings in which the legality of detention was not in issue. Where detention is the subject matter of the claim, the position is, in our view, different. The High Court will be seized of the question of the legality of detention and in many cases it will be appropriate for the same court to consider the merits of a claim for release pending the final hearing.

A refusal (or grant) of bail by the High Court can be appealed to the Court of Appeal.[87] **19.51**

The discretion to grant bail is a broad one. The judge must 'decide for himself on the material put before him whether it is an appropriate case for bail'.[88] In practice, the factors which are likely to weigh with the court will be the factors considered in Chapter 18, albeit the Administrative Court will be better placed to take a preliminary view on the substantive merits of the challenge to the legality of detention. **19.52**

On its face, the test for bail differs from the test for release by way of interim relief, which will be approached by reference to the *American Cyanamid* principles.[89] In practice, however, given the overlap between the factors relevant to bail and the factors going to the merits of the underlying claim, it will be a very rare case in which the two tests would not result in the same outcome. **19.53**

In granting bail, the High Court can require sureties and impose such conditions as it thinks fit. **19.54**

(3) Release by way of interim relief

The Administrative Court has jurisdiction to grant an interim injunction.[90] An injunction may be prohibitory or mandatory. On an application for an interim injunction the Court can order the release of a person detained under the Immigration Acts by making a mandatory injunction compelling the Secretary of State to release the person on temporary admission, temporary release, or restrictions under Schedule 3 or, in our view, compelling the Secretary of State to release the person on bail under Schedule 2, paragraph 22 or 29 of the Immigration Act 1971.[91] **19.55**

The test for a grant of an interim injunction is whether it is just and convenient. In judicial review proceedings, the principles governing the grant of interim relief are **19.56**

---

[87] Senior Courts Act 1981, section 16(1). See *R (Turkoglu) v Secretary of State for the Home Department* [1988] 1 QB 398, referring to s.16(1) of what was then the Supreme Court Act 1981 in similar terms.

[88] *R (Kelso) v Secretary of State for the Home Department* (unreported), 12 March 1998, *per* Collins J.

[89] *American Cyanamid Company v Ethicon Limited* [1975] AC 396.

[90] The jurisdiction arises under sections 31(2) and 37(1) of the Senior Courts Act 1981 and is regulated by CPR Part 25 and the Practice Direction thereto.

[91] As to which, see Chapter 18, paragraphs 18.17–18.42.

those contained in *American Cyanamid Company v Ethicon Limited*,[92] modified as appropriate to public law cases:[93]

(1) there must be a real prospect of succeeding at trial;[94] and

(2) the balance of convenience must lie in favour of granting the interim injunction sought.[95]

19.57 In addition the Court has to take account the importance of the public interest when considering the grant of interim relief against a public authority.[96]

19.58 The court has a wide discretion to take the course which seems most likely to produce a just result or put 'less ambitiously', to minimize the risk of an unjust result.[97]

19.59 In the present context, it is also relevant that the grant of interim relief in the form of release has the potential to pre-determine the outcome of the proceedings.[98] In practice, therefore the approach to whether an interim injunction should be granted compelling release is often very close to that taken on an application for bail: judging whether or not there is a meritorious case and whether the balance of convenience favours release will often involve asking the same questions that a judge considering bail would ask: is there a risk of absconding and offending; if so, can it be managed?

(4) Practical differences between High Court bail and a mandatory injunction

19.60 Where the High Court releases a person on bail in its inherent jurisdiction, it can impose a wide range of conditions. As such, in a case in which release is only likely to be viable if strictly managed, or if sureties are relied upon, this may be the most appropriate course.

---

[92] [1975] AC 396.

[93] *R (Medical Justice) v Secretary of State for the Home Department* [2010] EWHC 1425, *per* Cranston J at [6]–[8].

[94] *Medical Justice* at [6], citing *Smith v Inner London Education Authority* [1978] 1 All ER 411, *per* Brown LJ at 419B–C: 'The first question is whether the plaintiffs have satisfied the first requirement laid down by the House of Lords in *American Cyanamid Co v Ethicon Ltd*: is their action not frivolous or vexatious? Is there a serious question to be tried? Is there a real prospect that they will succeed in their claim for a permanent injunction at the trial? The first two questions were clearly intended to state the same test, because they are joined by the phrase "in other words", and the third cannot, I think, have been meant to state any different one.'

[95] *American Cyanamid* per Lord Diplock at 408B; *Medical Justice per* Cranston J at [12].

[96] *Medical Justice* at [7]. See further *Sierbein v Westminster City Council* [1987] 86 LGR 431, *per* Dillon LJ at p 440: 'the ordinary financial considerations in a Cyanamid case, though no doubt to some extent relevant, must be qualified by a recognition of the public interest'.

[97] *Bacongo, per* Lord Walker at [39].

[98] See, e.g., *R (Muhammad & Ors) v Secretary of State for the Home Department* [2013] EWHC 3157 (Admin), *per* Stewart J at [20].

It is arguable that release on bail by the High Court is not release 'on bail from **19.61** detention *under any provision of the Immigration Acts*' within the meaning of section 4(1)(c) of the Immigration and Asylum Act 1999. If that is right, a person so released will be ineligible for a grant of accommodation under that provision. In cases in which section 4(1)(c) accommodation is required, there-fore, a mandatory order compelling the Secretary of State to release on bail may be more appropriate, because: (i) the range of possible conditions is the same as a court can impose when granting bail (so broader than when the Secretary of State is granting temporary admission, etc)[99] and (ii) it would unquestionably be release on bail from detention *under [a] provision of the Immigration Acts*' within the meaning of section 4(1)(c), with the consequence that the claimant could take up section 4 accommodation upon release (assuming eligibility and a grant of such accommodation).

K. Habeas Corpus

(1) General

The ancient writ of *habeas corpus ad subjiciendum*, an order requiring a detainer **19.62** to bring the detainee before the court to justify the lawfulness of detention, is of great historic significance.[100] The existence of the procedure for seeking a writ of habeas corpus in Order 54 of the Rules of Supreme Court (RSC) was preserved when the RSC were replaced by the CPR in 1998. However, the procedure is now seldom used, and the question arises whether it has any continuing utility in the present context, given the broad powers and procedural flexibility vested in the Administrative Court.

(2) Procedure for seeking a writ of habeas corpus

Applications for habeas corpus are governed by RSC 54, preserved in Schedule 1 **19.63** to the CPR. An application is made to court for the writ. If issued by the court the writ requires the detainer to produce the detainee at court at the appointed time and date, and to make a 'return' by affidavit, justifying the detention. The court then considers and decides the lawfulness of detention. The writ does not secure the detainee's release; it secures access to the court: a hearing on the lawfulness of detention.

---

[99] See *Kelso, per* Collins J.
[100] See, for example, *The Law of Habeas Corpus*, Judith Farbey and R. J. Sharpe, 3rd edition, 2011, OUP; *Habeas Corpus From England to Empire*, Paul Halliday, Harvard University Press, 2010.

(3) Powers of the court on an application for habeas corpus

19.64   The powers of the court on an application for a writ of habeas corpus are limited. It can order release immediately upon the application being made,[101] or it can order release at the hearing of the writ if the detainer fails to establish lawful authority for detention. It has no power to award damages, to grant declaratory relief, or to compel the detainer to do anything other than release the detainee.

(4) Nature of the illegality to which the remedy is directed

19.65   It has been held that writ of habeas corpus will issue where someone 'is detained without any authority or the purported authority is beyond the powers of the person authorising the detention and so is unlawful' whereas judicial review is available 'where the decision or action sought to be impugned is within the powers of the person taking it' but, due to a public law error it should never have been taken'.[102]

19.66   The cases do not, however, reflect that apparently hard-edged distinction. *R (Hardial Singh) v Governor of Durham Prison Governor,*[103] itself was brought as an application for habeas corpus and Woolf LJ would have ordered release but for the possibility of an imminent change in circumstances. Yet, as Lord Brown observed in *R (Khadir) v Secretary of State for the Home Department,*[104] *Hardial Singh* was a case 'about the exercise of the power to detain (when properly it can be exercised and when it cannot)', not about its 'existence'. In *In re Mahmod (Wasfi Suleman),*[105] which came some years after *Cheblak,* a breach of the *Hardial Singh* principles was held to warrant release on an application for habeas corpus. In *R (AA) v Secretary of State for the Home Department,*[106] Lord Toulson suggested *obiter,* but with the agreement of the majority of the Supreme Court, that the court's habeas corpus jurisdiction might extend to permitting it to enquire into a claimant's age, as this would 'impact on the operation thereafter of the Secretary of State's [detention] policies introduced for the purpose of implementing section 55 [of the Borders, Citizenship and Immigration Act 2009]'.[107]

19.67   Put another way, the distinction drawn in *Cheblak* suggests that habeas corpus will lie only where the legality of detention is vitiated by 'jurisdictional errors' as understood prior to the decision of the House of Lords in *Anisminic Ltd v Foreign Compensation Commission.*[108] However, *Lumba* makes clear that that distinction

---

[101]   Rule 4.
[102]   *R (Cheblak) v Secretary of State For the Home Department* [1991] 1 WLR. 890, *per* Lord Donaldson MR at 894D.
[103]   [1984] 1 WLR 704.
[104]   [2005] UKHL 39; [2006] AC 207 at [33].
[105]   [1994] EWHC 3 (Admin); [1995] Imm AR 311.
[106]   [2013] UKSC 49; [2013] 1 WLR 2224.
[107]   At [52]–[53].
[108]   [1969] 2 AC 147.

has no relevance when considering the legality of detention,[109] and the cases do not suggest that such a strict division has been observed in practice.

In our view habeas corpus will in principle lie not only in 'no authority' cases, in **19.68** the narrow pre-*Anisminic* sense, but also in cases in which the legality of detention is vitiated by a breach of the *Hardial Singh* principles or a material public law error.

(5) Current status of the writ in challenges to immigration detention

Although a number of the older authorities cited in this work were habeas corpus **19.69** applications,[110] during the great proliferation of litigation in this area over the past decade very few cases have been brought by way of habeas corpus.

This reflects a broader move away from habeas corpus to judicial review as the **19.70** appropriate mechanism for challenging the legality of administrative detention. In *B v Barking and Havering & Brentwood Community Health Case NHS Trust*,[111] in which the claimant had sought both judicial review and habeas corpus, Woolf J noted the 'veneration which is paid to habeas corpus because of its historic role in protecting the liberty of the subject', but observed that this was 'probably no longer justified in view of the ability of judicial review to provide a remedy equally expeditiously whenever the liberty of the subject is threatened'.[112] He went on to consider a number of apparent advantages in the habeas corpus procedure but suggested that these were matters of form rather than substance,[113] and noted the limited remedies available in a habeas corpus application, before stating: 'I would discourage applications for habeas corpus unless it is clear that no other relief will be required.'[114]

In our view, although habeas corpus remains open as a means of challenging **19.71** ongoing immigration detention, judicial review will be the appropriate course in most cases.

---

[109] See Chapter 9, paragraph 9.12.

[110] *Hardial Singh* and *Mahmod*, being two examples. In *R (I) v Secretary of State for the Home Department* [2003] INLR 196; [2002] EWCA Civ 888, there were linked proceedings for habeas corpus and judicial review. The Court of Appeal made no comment on this.

[111] [1998] EWCA Civ 1347, [1999] 1 FLR 106.

[112] At 114G–H.

[113] At 115A–D.

[114] At 116F. See also *R (Hunt) v Leeds Crown Court* [1999] 1 WLR 841, a challenge by way of judicial review and habeas corpus to a judge's decision to extend the custody time limit, in which Lord Bingham CJ said: 'The concurrent application for Habeas Corpus was wholly unnecessary and served only to increase costs unnecessarily. It should not have been made.'

20

DAMAGES

A. Introduction

20.01 Where a person is detained unlawfully, whether in breach of the *Hardial Singh* principles, as a result of a material public law error, or for simple want of authority, the detaining authority is liable in the tort of false imprisonment and for breach of a Convention right.[1] As a result, the person so detained is entitled to damages under the common law for any resultant loss of liberty, damage to reputation, pecuniary loss or physical injury flowing from the imprisonment and/or under section 8 of the Human Rights Act 1998 ('HRA').

20.02 *Lumba* established that liability in the tort of false imprisonment is not subject to a causation test.[2] However, on normal compensatory principles,[3] if detention would have occurred in any event there will have been no loss, and the claimant will be entitled to only nominal damages at common law.[4] The majority of the justices in *Lumba* rejected the possibility of an award of 'vindicatory' damages—a 'conventional sum to mark the invasion of important rights'[5]—in the absence of any right to compensatory damages.[6]

---

[1] I.e. breach of Article 5 of the European Convention on Human Rights ('ECHR'); breaches of Article 3 and 8 of the ECHR may also arise. See Chapter 15.

[2] *R (Lumba & Mighty) v Secretary of State for the Home Department* [2011] UKSC 12; [2012] 1 AC 245. See further Chapter 9, paragraphs 9.07–9.17.

[3] *R (Kambadzi) v Secretary of State for the Home Department* [2011] UKSC 23; [2011] 1 WLR 1299, *per* Lord Hope at [56].

[4] *Lumba, per* Lord Dyson at [90]–[96].

[5] See *per* Lady Hale at [216].

[6] Lord Hope, Lord Walker, and Lady Hale favoured such an award; see at [176]–[180], [195], and [213]–[217]. The other six justices did not: see *per* Lord Dyson at [101], Lord Collins at [222]–[237],

If a claim to 'substantial' (or 'compensatory') damages (rather than nominal dam- **20.03** ages) is made out, a claimant will be entitled to general damages for loss of liberty (as well as any damage to reputation and/or physical or psychiatric injury). In *Thompson v Commissioner of Police for the Metropolis* and *Hsu v Commissioner of Police for the Metropolis*[7] the Court of Appeal used the term 'basic damages' to refer to damages for loss of liberty.[8] A person who establishes an entitlement to substantial damages for loss of liberty may be able to make good a claim for pecuniary loss ('special damages').

Aggravated damages will be payable where there are 'aggravating features about **20.04** the defendant's conduct which would justify [such an award]'.[9] Although compensatory in nature, they 'will in fact contain a penal element as far as the defendant is concerned'.[10] Exceptionally, exemplary damages may be awarded to punish a defendant's conduct, rather than compensate the claimant.

Where a breach of ECHR rights is made out, the court can make an award of dam- **20.05** ages where it considers this 'necessary to afford just satisfaction to the person in whose favour it is made'.[11]

In this chapter we consider the approach to deciding whether substantial or only **20.06** nominal damages are recoverable (Section B). We then address compensatory damages (Section C) and exemplary damages (Section D). We conclude by examining damages for breach of Convention rights (Section E). Appendix I contains summaries of a number of quantum decisions.

Where we refer to levels of damages we state the award made at the time, and **20.07** what that figure would be when adjusted for inflation by reference to the May 2014 Retail Price Index. When considering past awards with a view to quantifying basic or general damages, it will be necessary in most cases to adjust any award pre-dating 1 April 2013 upwards by a further 10 per cent to take account of the guidance in *Simmons v Castle*.[12]

B. Substantial or Nominal Damages

False imprisonment is a tort actionable *per se*: a claimant need show no loss to **20.08** establish liability.[13] However, where no loss flows the victim will be entitled to

---

Lord Kerr at [254]–[256], Lord Phillips at [335], and Lord Brown, with whom Lord Rodger agreed, at [361].

[7] [1997] EWCA Civ 3083; [1998] QB 498.

[8] This appears to be a narrower concept than 'general damages'; *cf.* the discussion in *McGregor on Damages*, Harvey McGregor, Sweet & Maxwell, 18th edition, 2009 at 37–012.

[9] *Thompson, per* Lord Woolf at p 514H.

[10] *Thompson, per* Lord Woolf at p.516G.

[11] Under section 8 HRA.

[12] [2013] 1 WLR 1239; see paragraphs 20.26–20.27.

[13] See Chapter 9, paragraphs 9.10–9.17.

no more than nominal damages.[14] We consider how that causation test applies in three kinds of cases where detention under the Immigration Acts is unlawful at common law:

(1) where detention is unlawful because of a breach of the *Hardial Singh* principles;
(2) where detention is unlawful because the decision to detain was vitiated by a material public law error; and
(3) where there was no power, under the Immigration Acts, to detain.

(1) Detention in breach of the *Hardial Singh* principles

(a) Principles (ii), (iii), and (iv)

20.09 Where detention is unlawful as a result of a breach of the second or third *Hardial Singh* principles it follows that, but for the unlawful conduct, the detention would not have taken place. Where a court has concluded that detention was of unreasonable duration (or prospective duration), there is no room for an argument that, on a different approach, the same period of detention might have been reasonable, such that the claimant suffered no loss.[15]

20.10 A lack of expedition by the Secretary of State will only result in detention being ruled in breach of *Hardial Singh* principle (iv), and so unlawful, if a claimant can 'show a specific period during which, but for the failure, he would no longer have been detained'.[16] As such, as with principles (ii) and (iii), it will follow in such a case that the breach led to a loss of liberty. There can be no question of only nominal damages being payable.

(b) Principle (i)

20.11 There are few cases in which a breach of the first *Hardial Singh* principle has been found in isolation. In such a case, the overwhelming likelihood is that, but for the established illegality, the individual would not have been detained so substantial damages will be payable. However, it is possible to envisage a case in which a person is detained for a purpose other than the permitted statutory purpose yet detention

---

[14] An award which recognizes the commission of the wrong but has no compensatory effect; in *Lumba* the award was £1: [2012] 1 AC 245 at p 360D–E.

[15] N.B.: In *Sino v Secretary of State for the Home Department* [2011] EWHC 2249 (Admin) at [236] the judge left open the question 'whether, but for his detention, [the claimant] would not have been at liberty in any event, but rather in prison', and the relevance of this to damages. In our view, if such an extreme proposition could be made good on the facts it might be relevant to quantum but would not extinguish an entitlement to substantial damages. Cf. *HXA v The Home Office* [2010] EWHC 1177 (QB) *per* King J at [212]: '. . . the fact the Claimant may or may not have gone straight into police custody pursuant to domestic criminal process had he been released earlier' was irrelevant to 'the question of liability' but 'might be relevant to damages'.

[16] *R (Krasniqi) v Secretary of State for the Home Department* [2011] EWCA Civ 1549, *per* Carnwath LJ at [12].

would and lawfully could have been authorized. For example, if detention was authorized solely for the impermissible purpose of compelling an uncooperative detainee to depart,[17] it might nevertheless be possible for the Secretary of State to establish that it could and would have occurred in any event. If so, only nominal damages for false imprisonment would be available at common law.[18]

(2) Detention vitiated by material public law error

Where detention is unlawful as a result of a public law error, substantial damages **20.12** will be payable unless detention could and would have occurred in any event.[19] In *Lumba*, the appellants' detention was 'inevitable'[20] even if the published policy had lawfully been applied. The appellant in *OM (Nigeria)* argued that 'inevitability' was the test.[21] Richards LJ rejected this proposition. He noted that in *Kambadzi* Lord Hope had said that 'an award of damages for false imprisonment is based on normal compensatory principles',[22] and that on such principles 'it would be for a claimant to prove his loss on the balance of probabilities'. He continued:

> It well may be that in circumstances such as these the burden shifts to the [Secretary of State] to prove that the claimant *would and could* have been detained if the power of detention had been exercised lawfully, but . . . I see no reason why the standard of proof should be anything other than the balance of probabilities.[23]

On this approach, whether a person *would* have been detained is a question of **20.13** fact to be proven by the defendant on the balance of probabilities.[24] Whether the appellant *could* have been detained is 'a matter of legal assessment in relation to which the burden and standard of proof are of no materiality', which gives rise to two sub-questions:

(1) 'The first, concerning the policy itself, depends on normal *Wednesbury* principles: would it have been open to a reasonable decision-maker, directing himself correctly in relation to the policy, to detain the appellant in the circumstances of the case?'[25]

(2) 'The second requires the lawfulness of continued detention to be assessed by reference to *Hardial Singh* principles.'[26]

---

[17] See Chapter 8, paragraph 8.34.

[18] In this example, a claim for exemplary damages might arise.

[19] See *Lumba per* Lord Dyson at [71], [90]–[96], Lord Collins at [237], Lord Kerr at [252]–[256].

[20] At [95]. N.B.: the *Hardial Singh* issues in Mr Lumba's case were remitted for further consideration.

[21] [2011] EWCA Civ 909 at [22].

[22] At [23], referring to *Kambadzi* at [56].

[23] At [23], our emphasis.

[24] In *R (EO & Ors) v Secretary of State for the Home Department* [2013] EWHC 1236 (Admin) the Secretary of State argued unsuccessfully that Richards LJ was wrong in *OM* to suggest that the burden of proof lay on her to establish that a claimant would have been detained in any event: see *per* Burnett J at [70]–[74].

[25] At [24].

[26] At [24].

20.14 As the outcome would have been the same even if the appellant's proposed test of inevitability was adopted the point was *obiter* in *OM (Nigeria)*.[27] However, it was subsequently approved by a differently constituted Court of Appeal in *R (Abdollahi) v Secretary of State for the Home Department*.[28]

(3) No power to detain

20.15 Where a person is detained without statutory authority the same approach will apply: the court will inquire into what would have happened if the tort of false imprisonment had not been committed. If the tort of false imprisonment is made out because a procedural pre-condition for statutory detention was not complied with, the court will ask what would have happened if the pre-condition had been complied with. In *Roberts v Chief Constable of the Cheshire Constabulary*,[29] detention was unlawful as a result of a failure by a custody officer to conduct a review that was required by statute. If the review had taken place, detention would have been re-authorized. In *Lumba*, Lord Dyson held that this case was wrongly decided on the issue of damages: Mr Roberts should only have recovered nominal damages because he would have been detained even if the tort had not been committed.[30]

C. Compensatory Damages

20.16 There are three kinds of compensatory damages available at common law for false imprisonment:

(1) general damages;
(2) aggravated damages; and
(3) special damages.

(1) General damages

20.17 General damages are intended to compensate a victim of false imprisonment for loss of liberty and for the shock, humiliation, and loss of reputation (if established) which flow from the detaining authority's wrongful act and for any psychiatric or physical injury caused by the wrongful imprisonment.[31]

---

[27] At [24].
[28] [2013] EWCA Civ 366, *per* Moses LJ, with the agreement of the full Court, at [35].
[29] [1999] EWCA Civ 655; [1999] 1 WLR 662.
[30] See *Lumba, per* Lord Dyson at [93].
[31] The term 'basic damages' is often used to refer to general damages for loss of liberty, including the elements of shock, humiliation, and loss of reputation, but not including damages for personal injury.

(a) General damages for loss of liberty, shock, humiliation and loss of reputation

20.18 Guidance on the approach to be taken in false imprisonment cases was given in *Thompson*. The guidance is directed to judges giving instructions to juries, but is of general application. The guidance on basic damages is as follows (with references to the jury omitted):[32]

(1) [Where liability and an entitlement to more than nominal damages is established] the only remedy [the court has] power to grant is an award of damages. Save in exceptional situations such damages are only awarded as compensation and are intended to compensate the [claimant] for any injury or damage which he has suffered. They are not intended to punish the defendant.

(2) . . . compensatory damages are of two types. (a) Ordinary damages which we would suggest should be described as basic, and (b) aggravated damages.

(3) . . . the basic damages will depend on the circumstances and the degree of harm suffered by the [claimant]. . . .

(5) In a straightforward case of wrongful arrest and imprisonment the starting point is likely to be about £500 [Updated: £825.00] for the first hour during which the [claimant] has been deprived of his or her liberty. After the first hour an additional sum is to be awarded, but that sum should be on a reducing scale so as to keep the damages proportionate with those payable in personal injury cases and because the [claimant] is entitled to have a higher rate of compensation for the initial shock of being arrested. As a guideline we consider, for example, that a [claimant] who has been wrongly kept in custody for twenty four hours should for this alone normally be regarded as entitled to an award of about £3,000 [Updated: £4,950.00]. For subsequent days the daily rate will be on a progressively reducing scale. . . .

(7) . . . circumstances can vary dramatically from case to case and . . . these and the subsequent figures which we provide are not intended to be applied in a mechanistic manner.

20.19 Although the guidance in *Thompson* on basic damages applies directly in the context of immigration detention, it is in some respects of limited assistance. In particular:

(1) It proposes a comparatively high award for the initial detention, on the basis that there is an initial 'shock of being arrested', yet in many cases where detention under the Immigration Acts is found to be unlawful the period of false imprisonment comes after a period (often quite lengthy) of lawful detention. In such circumstances the claimant will not have suffered any 'first shock', so an inflated figure to compensate the early part of the detention will not be appropriate.[33]

---

[32] At pp 514F–516B. See paragraphs 20.28–20.29 and 20.41–20.44, respectively, for the guidance on aggravated damages and exemplary damages.

[33] *Cf. R (Lamari) v Secretary of State for the Home Department* [2013] EWHC 3130 (QB) in which HHJ Cotter QC took into account the shock for the claimant of not being released following an undertaking to the court that release would occur on or before a specified date; see at [48].

(2) The guidance on quantifying basic damages is limited to suggesting a figure for the first hour and the first 24 hours which will progressively reduce thereafter. Whilst there may be no conceptual difficulty in applying this guidance in the context of a detention of four days[34] or even 24 days,[35] the same cannot be said when the period in issue is one running into months or even years.

20.20　Lord Woolf returned to the issue of basic damages for false imprisonment in the context of the very different facts of *R (Evans) v Governor of Brockhill Prison (No. 2)*.[36] Miss Evans had been held in prison for 59 days beyond the date on which she should have been released. The error arose from a good faith and blameless misunderstanding of the law regarding the calculation of sentence end date.[37] The judge below had found there was no element of 'damage to reputation, humiliation, shock, injury to feelings and so on'.[38] Only loss of liberty fell to be compensated. Lord Woolf said the case was materially different to *Thompson* due, *inter alia*, to the prior lawful imprisonment for a serious offence, as a result of which Miss Evans 'would have already made the necessary adjustments to serving a prison sentence'.[39]

20.21　Lord Woolf further approved Collins J's approach of awarding damages on a 'global' basis rather than trying to identify an amount for each extra day imprisoned. However, his award of £2,000 (Updated: £3,249) was well below the appropriate figure for 59 extra days' imprisonment. The Court of Appeal increased the award to £5,000 (Updated: £7,830). Whilst it was possible to derive a daily, weekly, or monthly figure from the court's award, such an approach was discouraged: 'No two cases are the same. The shorter the period the larger can be the pro rata rate. The longer the period the lower the pro rata rate.' The length of sentence lawfully imposed was significant, as was Miss Evans' poor disciplinary record.[40]

20.22　Whilst the awards discussed in *Thompson* need to be considered with caution in the present context, so too does the award in *Evans* given (a) that the governor, applying the law as understood at the time, could not have acted differently, (b) Miss Evans could not have known her detention was unlawful, and (c) she was of bad character, was habituated to incarceration, and had jeopardized her prospects of release by her conduct in prison.

20.23　Appendix I sets out the awards made in a number of immigration detention and other relevant claims. The awards show a consistent recognition of the 'first shock'

---

[34] *R (J) v Secretary of State for the Home Department* [2011] EWHC 3073 (Admin) at [41].
[35] *MK (Algeria) v Secretary of State for the Home Department* [2010] EWCA Civ 980 at [12].
[36] [1998] EWCA Civ 1042; [1999] QB 1043.
[37] For details of how the error came to be made see the judgment of the House of Lords upholding the decision of the Court of Appeal on liability and quantum: [2000] UKHL 48; [2001] 2 AC 19, *per* Lord Slynn of Hadley at pp 25F–26G.
[38] At p 1060A–B.
[39] At p 1060D.
[40] At p 1060F–H.

principle emerging from *Thompson*, and there is a resultant 'tapering' of pro rata sums as the duration of the false imprisonment increases.[41] It has also been recognized that where detention becomes unlawful as a result of wilful non-cooperation by a detainee, that will be reflected in reduced damages.[42]

(b) General damages for personal injury

Where a period of false imprisonment has caused psychiatric or physical harm, **20.24** damages for personal injury can be claimed.[43] Claims for damages for personal injury suffered in detention may, of course, arise in the absence of any viable challenge to the detention itself, for example where injury results from a third party's negligence or an assault.

In valuing a claim for damages for personal injury, reference should be made to the **20.25** *Judicial College Guidelines for the Assessment of General Damages in Personal Injury Cases*[44] and to specialist personal injury practitioner resources.[45]

(c) Simmons v Castle: 10% uplift on pre-April 2013 general damages

With effect from 1 April 2013 the proper level of general damages in all civil claims **20.26** for (i) pain and suffering, (ii) loss of amenity, (iii) physical inconvenience and discomfort, (iv) social discredit, or (v) mental distress, will be 10 per cent higher than previously, unless the claim is one brought under a Conditional Fee Agreement entered into prior to 1 April 2013.[46] This will include general or basic damages in false imprisonment claims.

It follows[47] that when seeking to value a claim by reference to basic or general damages awarded in cases that were decided prior to April 2013, as well as adjusting the figure to take account of inflation it will be necessary to increase it by 10 per cent before applying it to the case at hand. **20.27**

---

[41] *Cf. R(MK (Algeria)) v Secretary of State for the Home Department* [2010] EWCA Civ 980 in which £12,500 (Updated: £14,357) was awarded for 24 days' false imprisonment and *R (B) v Secretary of State for the Home Department* [2008] EWHC 364 (Admin) in which £32,000 (Updated: £38,736) was awarded for six months' false imprisonment.

[42] *R (NAB) v Secretary of State for the Home Department* [2011] EWHC 1191 (Admin) at [17].

[43] See the analysis in *McGregor on Damages,* Harvey McGregor, Sweet & Maxwell, 18th edition, 2009 at 37-014. For two unreported examples of awards being made for psychiatric damage in immigration detention cases see *B v Home Office* and *E v Home Office* in Appendix I.

[44] *Guidelines for the Assessment for General Damages in Personal Injuries,* 12th edition, Oxford University Press, 2013.

[45] See, for example, Kemp & Kemp: *Quantum of Damages,* Sweet & Maxwell, and Lawtel's PI Quantum Reports. N.B.: Awards of £10,000 or more for pain, suffering and loss of amenity predating 23 March 2000 are subject to an uplift in accordance with the guidance in *Heil v Rankin* [2001] QB 272.

[46] See *Simmons v Castle* [2012] EWCA Civ 1288, 10 October 2012, at [50] amending the Court of Appeal's judgment in *Simmons v Castle* [2012] EWCA Civ 1039 at [20]. The two judgments are reported together at [2013] 1 WLR 1239.

[47] Save in pre-April 2013 CFA cases.

(2) Aggravated damages

20.28 Aggravated damages can only be awarded (i) where they are claimed and (ii) where there are features about a defendant's conduct justifying such an award.[48] They will be justified where there are aggravating features about the case which would result in the claimant not receiving sufficient compensation for the injury suffered if the award were restricted to a basic award.[49]

20.29 Aggravating features can include humiliating circumstances at the time of arrest or any conduct of those responsible for the detention which shows that they had behaved in a high handed, insulting, malicious, or oppressive manner. Aggravating features can also include the way the litigation and trial are conducted.[50] If aggravated damages are warranted a separate award should be made.[51] At the time of *Thompson* Lord Woolf said that an award of aggravated damages was unlikely to be less than £1,000 (Updated: £1,650), and whilst it was not possible to indicate a precise arithmetical relationship between basic damages and aggravated damages, it was unlikely that aggravated damages would be as much as twice the basic damages except perhaps where, on the particular facts, the basic damages were modest.[52] The total figure for basic and aggravated damages should not exceed what is fair compensation for the injury suffered. Such damages, though compensatory and not intended as a punishment, will in fact contain a penal element as far as the defendant is concerned.[53] Improper conduct by a claimant can reduce or even eliminate an award of aggravated damages if it 'caused or contributed to the behaviour complained of'.[54]

20.30 Whilst aggravated damages, where awarded, should be addressed separately, there is no bright line between matters which fall to be compensated as basic damages and matters which attract an award of aggravated damages. What matters in the final analysis is that the total award of compensatory (i.e. basic and aggravated) damages is appropriate in the circumstances of the case.[55]

---

[48] *Thompson, per* Lord Woolf at p 514G–H.

[49] *Thompson, per* Lord Woolf at p 516B–C.

[50] *Thompson, per* Lord Woolf at p 516C–D. Lord Woolf suggested, in the context of a claim against the police for false imprisonment, that the conduct of a prosecution might give rise to a claim for aggravated damages. It follows, in our view, that the way in which deportation or removal proceedings are conducted might also found such a claim. In *Muuse (Abdillaahi) v Secretary of State for the Home Department* [2009] EWHC 1886 (QB) aggravated damages were awarded because the claimant, a Dutch national, was put at real risk of being deported to Somalia; see at [112].

[51] *Thompson, per* Lord Woolf at p 516D–E.

[52] *Thompson, per* Lord Woolf at p 516E–F.

[53] *Thompson, per* Lord Woolf at p 516F–G.

[54] *Thompson, per* Lord Woolf at p 517D–E.

[55] In *Muuse*, referring to the matter which led him to award aggravated damages (see fn 50) the judge said (at [112]) that this was 'something which could be allowed for as part of basic damages or by way of aggravated damages'. He considered it preferable to make separate awards for each to enable the position 'to be better understood'.

(3) Special damages

Damages for financial loss ('special damages') can be recovered in a false imprison- **20.31**
ment claim where established. They must be pleaded. This might include a claim
for the value of property lost or damaged as a result of the detention[56] or an award
for loss of business or earnings.[57] In a case in which personal injury, whether physical or psychiatric, is established, there may also be a claim for the cost of future care
and/or treatment.[58]

D. Exemplary Damages

(1) General principles

The exceptional remedy of exemplary damages is intended to punish a tortfeasor's **20.32**
wrongdoing rather than compensate the victim of the tort. There are certain categories of case in which an award of exemplary damages has been held to serve a
useful purpose in vindicating the strength of the law, justifying the admission into
civil law of a principle which ought logically to belong in the criminal law.[59] Those
categories include cases of 'oppressive, arbitrary or unconstitutional action by servants of the government'[60] or 'gross misuse of power, involving tortious conduct by
agents of the government'.[61]

The availability of exemplary damages has been held to have played a significant **20.33**
role in buttressing civil liberties, in claims for false imprisonment and wrongful
arrest. On occasion 'conscious wrongdoing by a defendant is so outrageous, [its]
disregard of the [claimant's] rights so contumelious, that something more is needed
to show that the law will not tolerate such behaviour'. The remedy is one 'of last
resort' which fills 'what otherwise would be a regrettable lacuna'.[62]

A claimant can only recover exemplary damages if he or she is the victim of the **20.34**
conduct complained of. It is a 'weapon' that 'while it can be used in defence of
liberty' must be 'used with restraint'. Everything which aggravates or mitigates a
defendant's conduct is relevant.[63]

---

[56] *Cf. R (M) v Secretary of State for the Home Department* [2011] EWHC 3667 (Admin) at [33].
[57] See discussion in *McGregor on Damages,* 18th edition, at 37-015.
[58] Such claims arise rarely in this context and are beyond the scope of this work.
[59] *Rookes v Barnard* [1964] AC 1129, *per* Lord Devlin at p 1226.
[60] *Rookes v Barnard, per* Lord Devlin at p 1226; *cf.* at 1223: '... the exemplary principle ... serves
a valuable purpose in restraining the arbitrary and outrageous use of executive power'.
[61] *AB v South West Water Services Ltd* [1993] QB 507, *per* Sir Thomas Bingham MR at p 529F.
[62] *Kuddus v Chief Constable of Leicestershire Constabulary* [2001] UKHL 29; [2002] 2 AC 122 *per*
Lord Nicholls at [63].
[63] *Rookes v Barnard, per* Lord Devlin at pp. 1227–1228.

20.35 Exemplary damages should only be awarded if the sum which is awarded by way of compensation (including aggravated damages) is inadequate to punish the defendant for its outrageous conduct, to mark the court's disapproval of such conduct and to deter its repetition.[64]

20.36 Whilst the test for an award of exemplary damages is a high one, it does not need to be qualified 'by further looking for malice, fraud, insolence, cruelty or similar specific conduct'.[65]

20.37 The way in which a party conducts litigation has no bearing upon whether exemplary damages should be awarded.[66]

20.38 Where there is a potentially large number of claimants seeking redress for a single wrong and not all are before the court, an award of exemplary damages will not be appropriate.[67] In *Lumba*, where many people had been detained by reference to the same unlawful policy that had been applied in the appellants' cases, this was one of the reasons an award of exemplary damages was refused.

20.39 It was further held in *Lumba* that it would be unsatisfactory and unfair to award exemplary damages where the basis for the claim was a number of serious allegations against named officials and Ministers of arbitrary and outrageous use of executive power and those persons had not been heard and their answers to the allegations had not been tested in evidence.[68] Lord Dyson noted that in a private law action the relevant officials would almost certainly have been called to give evidence, but this was not the norm in judicial review proceedings, and had not happened in that case.[69]

20.40 As with aggravated damages,[70] a claim for exemplary damages must be pleaded.

(2) Exemplary damages in practice

20.41 Compensation for injury suffered as a result of a defendant's oppressive and insulting behaviour will be by way of aggravated damages which, although not punitive

---

[64] *Rookes v Barnard, per* Lord Devlin at p 1228.

[65] *Muuse (Abdillaahi) v Secretary of State for the Home Department* [2010] EWCA Civ 453 at [71].

[66] *Lumba*, per Lord Dyson, at [165]. It can be reflected in an award of aggravated damages and in costs.

[67] *Lumba per* Lord Dyson at [167].

[68] At [168], *per* Lord Dyson.

[69] Where it is proposed to claim exemplary damages in judicial review proceedings consideration should be given to ensuring that the officials whose conduct is the subject of criticism (if their identities are known) are given an opportunity to answer the criticisms made of them. In some cases, it may be appropriate for this to be by way of live evidence at the hearing of the claim. In others, it may be preferable for the question of exemplary damages to be transferred to the county court, or Queen's Bench Division of the High Court if liability in false imprisonment is established.

[70] See paragraph 20.28.

in nature, will inevitably include 'a measure of punishment from the defendant's point of view'.[71]

Exemplary damages should be awarded only where the awards of general or basic **20.42** damages and aggravated damages are inadequate punishment for the defendants in the circumstances of the particular case.[72] Such an award—which goes over and above that required to compensate any injury—is a 'windfall' for a claimant and, in the present context, is payable from public funds.[73]

Where an award is made, it should be sufficient to mark the court's disapproval of **20.43** the oppressive or arbitrary behaviour but should be 'no more than is required for this purpose'.[74]

As to the level of the award, as at 19 February 1997,[75] Lord Woolf said that **20.44** where such an award was justified at all, it was unlikely to be less than £5,000 (Updated: £8,254). Conduct had to be 'particularly deserving of condemnation' for an award of as much as £25,000 (Updated: £41,274). A figure of £50,000 (Updated: £82,548) should be regarded as the absolute maximum involving, in the police context, officers of at least the rank of superintendent.[76] As with aggravated damages, conduct by the claimant which 'caused or contributed to the behaviour complained of' can reduce or even eliminate an award of exemplary damages.[77] It could be a 'useful check' to bear in mind that it will be unusual for an award of exemplary damages to bring the total award of general or basic damages, aggravated damages, and exemplary damages[78] to more than three times the level of general damages alone.[79]

There is no reason in principle why a claimant who establishes liability for false **20.45** imprisonment but who fails to establish a claim for more than nominal compensatory damages would be precluded from claiming exemplary damages. Such an award might be appropriate where a decision to detain was motivated by malice or bad faith but would have occurred in any event. However, if a lawful decision could have been taken, that will inform the court's judgment on whether exemplary damages are appropriate.[80]

---

[71] *Thompson, per* Lord Woolf at pp 516H–517A.
[72] *Thompson, per* Lord Woolf at p 517A.
[73] *Cf. Thompson, per* Lord Woolf at p 517B.
[74] *Thompson, per* Lord Woolf at p 517B–C.
[75] The date of judgment in *Thompson*.
[76] *Thompson, per* Lord Woolf at p 517C–D.
[77] *Thompson, per* Lord Woolf at p 517D–E.
[78] Not including, presumably, damages for personal injury or pecuniary loss.
[79] *Thompson, per* Lord Woolf at p 518A–B. Save where the award of basic damages is modest. (N.B.: the word 'modest' appears to have been omitted in error at p 518B, but the judgment refers back to the earlier guidance in similar terms on aggravated damages).
[80] *Lumba, per* Lord Dyson at [166].

E. Damages for Breach of Convention Rights

(1) Introduction

20.46 As discussed at paragraphs 15.01–15.03, there are three Convention rights that are most likely to be engaged by immigration detention: Articles 3, 5, and 8. In this section, we consider what damages, if any, should be awarded for breaches of those Convention rights.

20.47 Section 8 HRA allows courts, which have the power to award damages or order compensation in civil proceedings (e.g. the High Court and county courts), to award damages, where a public authority has 'acted unlawfully'—i.e. acted in a way which is incompatible with a Convention right, in circumstances where that was not required by primary legislation.[81] Thus, if primary legislation required detention that was contrary to a Convention right, domestic courts would not be able to award damages, only the European Court of Human Rights ('ECtHR').

20.48 Domestic courts are not allowed to award damages for 'acting unlawfully'[82] unless, having regard to all the circumstances including any relief or remedy granted under domestic law, the court is satisfied that the award is necessary to award just satisfaction to the person in whose favour it is made.[83] Section 8(4) HRA requires domestic courts, when deciding whether such an award is necessary and, if so, how much it should be, to take into account principles applied by the ECtHR when awarding compensation. The Supreme Court has interpreted this to mean that domestic courts should be guided by 'clear and consistent practice' of the ECtHR in awarding damages.[84] The common law approach to damages in such situations should not be applied.[85] If the great majority of ECtHR judgments award substantial damages for a particular kind of Convention breach, domestic courts should also award substantial damages.[86] It matters not if there are some exceptions in the ECtHR's case-law so long as a general practice can be discerned.[87]

20.49 The Grand Chamber of the ECtHR[88] has said this about its practice in awarding damages:

> The Court recalls that it is not its role under Article 41 to function akin to a domestic tort mechanism court in apportioning fault and compensatory damages between

---

[81] Section 6(1)-(2) HRA.

[82] As defined in section 6(1)–(2) of HRA 1998.

[83] Section 8(3) HRA.

[84] *R (Greenfield) v Secretary of State for the Home Department* [2005] 1 WLR 673; *R (Faulkner) v Secretary of State for Justice* [2013] UKSC 23 at [13(3)].

[85] *R (Greenfield) v Secretary of State for the Home Department* [2005] 1 WLR 673; *R (Faulkner) v Secretary of State for Justice* [2013] UKSC 23 at [27].

[86] *R (Faulkner) v Secretary of State for Justice* [2013] UKSC 23 at [41]–[54].

[87] *R (Faulkner) v Secretary of State for Justice* [2013] UKSC 23 at [50]–[54].

[88] *Al-Jedda v United Kingdom* (2011) 53 EHRR 23 at [114].

civil parties. Its guiding principle is equity, which above all involves flexibility and an objective consideration of what is just, fair and reasonable in all the circumstances of the case, including not only the position of the applicant but the overall context in which the breach occurred. Its non-pecuniary awards serve to give recognition to the fact that moral damage occurred as a result of a breach of a fundamental human right and reflect in the broadest of terms the severity of the damage. . .

As the particular examples at paragraphs 20.57-20.68 demonstrate, the ECtHR's **20.50** approach to awarding damages for a breach of a Convention right is very different to the domestic courts' approach in awarding damages for false imprisonment. The domestic courts are concerned with whether the unlawfulness caused the detention to be longer than it would otherwise have been.[89] By contrast, the ECtHR is concerned with whether the unlawfulness led to 'moral damage', an elusive concept that only roughly approximates to 'distress' and is often presumed in light of the nature of the breach.

(2) Article 3

Where there has been a finding that immigration detention violated Article 3, **20.51** there should be an award of substantial damages. There is clear and consistent jurisprudence from the ECtHR that immigration detention which violates Article 3 gives rise to non-pecuniary damage which requires substantial monetary compensation. There have been 29 judgments where the ECtHR has found immigration detention to violate Article 3 and gone on to consider what damages should be awarded.[90] In all but one of these judgments, the ECtHR awarded

---

[89] See paragraphs 20.08-20.14.

[90] *Dougoz v Greece* Application Number 40907/98 (6 March 2001) at [69]; *Mayeka and Mitunga v Belgium* Application Number 13178/03 (12 October 2006) at [118]; *Riad and Idiab v Belgium* Application Numbers 29787/03 and 29810/03 (24 January 2008) at [117]; *Shchebet v Russia* Application Number 16074/07 (12 June 2008) at [102]; *S.D. c. Grèce* Application Number 53541/07 (11 June 2009), at [85]; *Tabesh c. Grèce* Application Number 8256/07 (26 June 2009) at [68]; *Mushkhadzhiyeva et autres c. Belgique* Application Number 41442/07 (19 January 2010) at [103]; *Muminov v Russia* Application Number 42502/06 (4 November 2010) at [18]; *Abdokhani and Karimnia v Turkey* Application Number 50213/08 (27 July 2010) at [40]; *Koktysh v Ukraine* Application Number 43707/07 (10 December 2009) at [116]; *Charahili v Turkey* Application Number 46605/07 (13 April 2010) at [84]; *Kurkaev v Turkey* Application Number 10424/05 (19 October 2010) at [39]; *Rahimi c. Grèce* Application Number 8687/08 (5 April 2011) at [125]; *R.U. c. Grèce* Application Number 2237/08 (7 June 2011) at [110]; *Kanagaratnam et autres c. Belgique* Application Number 15297/09 (13 December 2011) at [99]; *Mwanje c. Belgique* Application Number (20 December 2011) at [139]; *Stanev c. Bulgarie* Application Number 36760/06 (17 January 2012) at [264]; *Popov c. France* Application Numbers 39472/07 and 39474/07 (19 January 2012) at [152]; *Lica c. Grèce* Application Number 74279/10, at [73]; *Mahmundi et autres c. Grèce* Application Number 14902/10, at [107]; *Ahmade c. Grèce* Application Number 50520/09 (25 September 2012) at [157]; *Bygylashvili c. Grèce* Application Number 58164/10 (25 September 2012) at [83]; *Lin c. Grèce* Application Number 58158/10 (6 November 2012) at [83]; *Chkhartishvili c. Grèce* Application Number 22910/10 (2 May 2013) at [88]; *Aden Ahmed v Malta* Application Number 55352/12 (23 July 2013) at [157]; *Horshill c. Grèce* Application Number 70427/11 (1 August 2013) at [72]; *Khuroshvili c. Grèce* Application Number 58165/10 (12 December 2013) at [129]; *C.D. et autres c. Grèce* Application Number 33441/10 (19 December 2013) at [84]; *B.M. c. Grèce* Application Number 53608/11 (19 December 2013) at [129].

substantial damages. The only exception was a case where the applicant did not allege damage and did not ask for compensation.[91] In many of these 29 cases, the ECtHR found several violations. However, there are at least three judgments where damages were awarded solely because of the Article 3 violation—no other Convention rights were violated.[92] The majority of the awards of damages are not reasoned. However, on occasions the ECtHR has said that a finding of a violation was not sufficient because the applicant had suffered inhuman and degrading treatment.[93]

20.52   It follows that domestic courts should follow this 'clear and consistent' practice and award substantial damages where immigration detention violates Article 3, even if:

(1) the detention did not amount to 'false imprisonment' at common law; or

(2) only nominal damages are available at common law.

20.53   What is less clear is whether there needs to be a separate award of damages for a violation of Article 3, where there has already been an award of substantial damages for the false imprisonment. It is arguable that the common law remedy will already provide just satisfaction in such a case because in assessing the level of basic, aggravated and special damages the court will ensure that the claimant is compensated for every aspect of their loss.[94] The facts that give rise to a breach of Article 3 should be taken into account when assessing the quantum of damages for false imprisonment. For that reason, it is arguable that a separate award is not necessary to afford just satisfaction. On the other hand, the ECtHR does not regard awards of damages by domestic courts as preclusive – they may still award additional damages. At least in theory, therefore, it is open to domestic courts to make further awards for breaches of Convention rights, on top of the damages for false imprisonment, if they consider it necessary to afford just satisfaction. At the time of writing (16 June 2014), this issue had not yet been addressed in a reported judgment.[95]

20.54   There is little guidance from the case-law as to what would be the appropriate amount to award for a violation of Article 3. In each of the three Greek immigration

---

[91]   *Horshill* c. *Grèce* Application Number 70427/11, 1 August 2013, at [72].

[92]   *Bygylashvili* c. *Grèce* Application Number 58164/10 (25 September 2012) at [83]; *Chkhartishvili* c. *Grèce* Application Number 22910/10 (2 May 2013) at [88]; *B.M.* c. *Grèce* Application Number 53608/11 (19 December 2013) at [129].

[93]   See *Mayeka and Mitunga v Belgium* Application Number 13178/03 (12 October 2006) at [118]; *Mushkhadzhiyeva et autres* c. *Belgique* Application Number 41442/07 (19 January 2010) at [103]; *Stanev* c. *Bulgarie* Application Number 36760/06 (17 January 2012) at [264].

[94]   See paragraphs 20.16 to 20.31.

[95]   *Sizarev v Ukraine* Application Number 17116/04 (17 January 2013) at [204]–[210]; and *Vistins and Perepjolkins v Latvia* Application Number 71243/01 (25 October 2012) at [115]–[131]. In *Vistins*, the ECtHR made an additional award of 10,000 Euros, on top of the award made by the domestic courts, on account of the 'powerlessness and frustration' that the applicants must have felt during the proceedings—see the quantum judgment (25 March 2014).

detention cases where damages were awarded for a violation of Article 3 only, the ECtHR awarded 8,000 Euros.[96] However, awards of damages by the ECtHR reflect the cost of living in the relevant country and the cost of living in Greece is lower than in the United Kingdom. In *Popov v France*,[97] the ECtHR gave a global award of 10,000 Euros for the detention of a family in violation of Articles 3, 5, and 8. In *Aden Ahmad v Malta*,[98] the ECtHR awarded 30,000 Euros for violations of Articles 3, 5(1), and 5(4).

(3) Article 5

When considering remedies for unlawful immigration detention, domestic courts **20.55** have focussed on the remedies afforded under domestic law for the tort of false imprisonment. Domestic courts have arguably overlooked the possibility of greater damages being available for breaches of Article 5.

It is necessary to distinguish between the different ways in which Article 5 may be **20.56** breached:

(1) breach of Article 5(1) where the detention was not 'in accordance with a procedure prescribed by law' or where some or all of detention was not justified under Article 5(1)(f);
(2) breach of Article 5(2) where the detainee was not given adequate reasons for their detention; and/or
(3) breach of Article 5(4) where the detainee was not able to review the lawfulness of their detention 'speedily'.

(a) Article 5(1)

By definition, any immigration detention which is unlawful at common law will **20.57** also breach Article 5(1) because it will not be 'in accordance with a procedure prescribed by law'.[99] Damages will always be available at common law for unlawful detention. However, such damages may be substantial or nominal.

Where a claimant would not have been detained but for the unlawfulness, they **20.58** will be entitled to substantial damages for the tort of false imprisonment. In such a case, Article 5 is very unlikely to have any role to play in the assessment of damages. The level of tortious damages is usually significantly higher than the awards of damages made by the ECtHR for breaches of Article 5(1).[100] As a result, there is usually no need for domestic courts to increase the tortious award to reflect the

---

[96] *Bygylashvili c. Grèce* Application Number 58164/10 (25 September 2012) at [83]; *Chkhartishvili c. Grèce* Application Number 22910/10 (2 May 2013) at [88]; *B.M. c. Grèce* Application Number 53608/11 (19 December 2013) at [129].

[97] Application Numbers 39472/07 and 39474/07 (19 January 2012) at [152].

[98] *Aden Ahmed v Malta* Application Number 55352/12 (23 July 2013) at [157].

[99] See paragraph 15.13.

[100] Compare paragraph 20.70 and the Appendix.

breach of Article 5. The common law damages are usually sufficient to afford just satisfaction.

20.59 By contrast, if the claimant's detention was unlawful, but he would have been detained in any event, he will only be entitled to nominal damages (usually of £1) at common law. The question arises as to whether, in such a case:

(1) damages should be awarded, either by domestic courts under section 8 HRA or by the ECtHR, for the breach of Article 5; or

(2) the award of nominal damages provides 'just satisfaction'.

20.60 This question is due to be determined by the ECtHR in *VM v United Kingdom*,[101] where the ECtHR will consider whether the domestic court's award of nominal damages constituted adequate compensation for the purposes of Article 5(5). We consider that there are powerful arguments that the ECtHR's answer to this question should be 'No'. In our view, domestic courts should generally be awarding more than nominal damages for breaches of Article 5(1), even where the detainee's detention was not prolonged by the breach.

20.61 At the time of writing, there are more than 90 judgments where the ECtHR found immigration detention to violate Article 5(1). In all but four of these cases, the ECtHR awarded substantial damages. In one of these four exceptions, the applicant did not ask the ECtHR for damages.[102] The other three exceptions—*Amuur v France*,[103] *Galliani v Romania*,[104] and *Kozhayev v Russia*[105]—contain no reasoning as to why the ECtHR departed from its general rule as to damages. They were decided in 1996, 2008, and 2012 respectively and concerned cases where detention was relatively short. *Amuur* involved asylum seekers being held in an international transit zone for 20 days in circumstances which led the European Commission on Human Rights to think that there had not been a deprivation of liberty at all. *Galliani* involved only three days of detention. *Kozhayev* involved only a few hours of detention that was not 'lawful'.[106]

20.62 In many of these 90 judgments, the ECtHR found a breach of more than one provision of Article 5—e.g. Article 5(1) and 5(4). However, there have been 21 judgments, involving immigration detention, where the only violation was of Article 5(1), and the applicant has sought damages. In 19 of these 21 cases, the ECtHR made a substantial award of 'non-pecuniary' damages.[107]

---

[101] Application Number 49734/12.

[102] *Mohd c. Grèce* Application Number 11919/03 (27 April 2006) at [27]–[28].

[103] Application Number 19776/92 (25 June 1996).

[104] Application Number 69273/01 (10 June 2008).

[105] Application Number 60045/10 (5 June 2012).

[106] *Kozhayev v Russia* Application Number 60045/10 (5 June 2012) at [106].

[107] *Bozano v France* Application Number 9990/82 (2 December 1987) at [10]; *Quinn v France* Application Number 18580/91 (22 March 1995) at [64]; *Shamsa c. Poland* Application Number 45355/99 45357/99 (27 November 2003) at [65]; *John c. Grece* Application Number 199/05 (10 May 2007) at [41]; *Mikolenko v Estonia* Application Number 10664/05 (8 October 2009) at

In the majority of cases where it has found immigration detention to violate Article **20.63**
5, the ECtHR has made an award for non-pecuniary damages without explaining
why a finding of a violation was not just satisfaction.[108]

In the relatively few cases where the ECtHR has explained these awards, it has **20.64**
generally been by reference to the 'distress' which the victim must have suffered as
a result of the unlawful detention, rather than by reference to any loss of liberty.

So, for example, in *Auad v Bulgaria*, the ECtHR found a breach of Article 5(1) **20.65**
because Bulgaria had not pursued expulsion with due diligence[109] and because the
expulsion order did not set out the country to which he was to be deported. The
ECtHR did not analyse whether either of these failures caused Mr Auad to be in
detention for longer than he otherwise would have been. Nonetheless, the ECtHR
went on to find that the distress Mr Auad suffered 'cannot wholly be compensated
by the finding of violation' and awarded him 3,500 Euros.[110] There was no reference, in the judgment, to any evidence of distress.

Similarly, in *Lokpo and Toure v Hungary*, the ECtHR found a breach of Article 5(1) **20.66**
because the procedure for immigration detention did not meet the requirement for
lawfulness. The ECtHR did not examine whether these procedural flaws had any
causative effect. Even so, the ECtHR awarded the applicants 10,000 Euros on the
basis that they 'must have suffered some non-pecuniary damage'.

Abdi v the United Kingdom[111] is the only case where the ECtHR has considered **20.67**
damages from a similar perspective to the UK's courts. The UK admitted a breach
of Article 5 but argued against damages on the basis that the unlawfulness had not
prolonged detention. The ECtHR referred to 'a number of previous cases' where
it had concluded that a finding of an Article 5 violation was just satisfaction and it

---

[72]; *Garkavyy v Ukraine* Application Number 25978/07 (18 February 2010) at [81]; *Ranjbar v
Turkey* Application Number 37040/07 (13 April 2010) at [47]; *Alipour and Hosseinzadgan v
Turkey* Application Number 28960/08 (13 July 2010) at [78]; *Jusic c. Suisse* Application Number
4691/06 (2 December 2010) at [109]; *Lokpo and Toure v Hungary* Application Number 10916/10
(20 September 2011) at [29]; *Auad v Bulgaria* Application Number 46390/10 (11 October 2011)
at [144]; *Longa Yonkeu v Latvia* Application Number 57229/09 (15 November 2011) at [169]; *Al
Hamdani v Bosnia and Herzegovina* Application Number 31098/10 (7 February 2012); *Al Husin v
Bosnia and Herzegovina* Application Number 3727/08 (7 February 2012); *Al-Tayyar Abdelhakim
v Hungary* Application Number 13058/11 (23 October 2012) at [43]; *Hendrin Ali Said and Aras
Ali Said v Hungary* Application Number 13457/11 (23 October 2012) at [42]; *Bakoyev v Russia*
Application Number 30225/11 (5 February 2013) at [175]; *Abdi v United Kingdom* Application
Number 27770/08 (9 April 2013) at [91]–[93]; *Barjamaj c. Grece* Application Number 36657/11 (2
May 2013) at [52]. The only two exceptions were *Amuur v France* Application Number 19776/92
(25 June 1996) and *Kozhayev v Russia* Application Number 60045/10 (5 June 2012) referred to at
paragraph 20.61.

[108] e.g. *Louled Massoud v Malta* Application Number 24340/08 (27 July 2010) at [83].
[109] Application Number 46390/10 (11 October 2011) at [127]–[135].
[110] *Auad v Bulgaria* Application Number 46390/10 (11 October 2011) at [144].
[111] Application Number 27770/08 (9 April 2013).

gave one example.[112] However, it went on to say that it could not 'exclude the possibility that it might have found a breach of Article 5(1) even if the detention had been in accordance with domestic law'.[113] The ECtHR held that 'therefore' it could not accept that a finding of a violation was just satisfaction, although it would award a lower award than in other cases.[114]

20.68 In conclusion, there is, in our view, a 'clear and consistent practice' by the ECtHR of awarding substantial damages for immigration detention which violates Article 5(1), regardless of whether the breach prolonged detention. *Abdi v United Kingdom* hints at a different approach but does not go so far as to undermine this general practice. If that is right, it is arguable that domestic courts should be awarding damages under section 8 HRA for unlawful immigration detention where only nominal damages are available at common law. They should start with a strong, but not irrebuttable presumption, that such detention causes distress and/or 'moral damage' which requires substantial monetary compensation.[115]

20.69 The quantum of such awards should reflect the levels usually awarded by the ECtHR in comparable countries. In *Abdi v United Kingdom* damages of 1,500 Euros were awarded but this was expressed to be at a lower than usual level on the (odd and potentially unfair) basis that the ECtHR had declined to look at the merits of the applicant's Article 5 complaints as a result of the United Kingdom's concession.

20.70 The usual level of award for a breach of Article 5(1) by a Member State comparable to the United Kingdom, can be assessed by having regard to the following awards:

(1) *Suso Musa v Malta*[116]—the applicant was awarded 25,000 Euros on 23 July 2013 in light of 'multiple violations of Article 5' in two periods of detention, lasting in total 18 months, in unsatisfactory conditions;

(2) *Louled Massoud v Malta*[117]—the applicant was awarded 12,000 Euros for violations of Articles 5(1) and 5(4), as a result of flaws in Maltese procedures in relation to his immigration detention, which lasted approximately 18 months.

---

[112] *Hilda Hafsteinsdóttir v Iceland* Application Number 40905/98, 8 June 2004 at [60]. This was not a case concerning immigration detention. *Hafsteinsdóttir* concerned a woman who was detained overnight on several occasions because she was intoxicated. The ECtHR declined to award damages because the breach of Article 5(1) was 'technical' and the ECtHR did not doubt the necessity of detaining the applicant. The ECtHR made no reference to the fact that it had awarded damages for a breach of Article 5(1) far more often than it had not. *Abdi v United Kingdom* Application Number 27770/08 (9 April 2013) at [91].

[113] *Abdi v United Kingdom* Application Number 27770/08 (9 April 2013) at [92].

[114] *Abdi v United Kingdom* Application Number 27770/08 (9 April 2013) at [92].

[115] See, *mutatis mutandis*, *R (Faulkner) v Secretary of State for Justice* [2013] UKSC 23 at [13(12)].

[116] Application Number 42337/12 (23 July 2013).

[117] Application Number 24340/08 (27 July 2010).

(3) *Stephens v Malta (No. 1)*[118]—the applicant was awarded 500 Euros on the basis that he 'must have suffered' some non-pecuniary damage as a result of 10 days of detention that violated Article 5.

(b) Article 5(2)

In our view, the law requires that damages should be available for a breach of **20.71** Article 5(2) if the claimant can satisfy the court that he suffered distress as a result of not knowing the reasons for his detention.

There is only one judgment of the ECtHR where it has considered whether to **20.72** award damages for a breach of Article 5(2) on its own—*Saadi v United Kingdom*.[119] In that case, the ECtHR concluded that the finding of a violation provided just satisfaction.[120] However, this one judgment on its own does not demonstrate a 'clear and consistent' practice by the ECtHR not to award damages for a breach of Article 5(2).

In *Haynes v Secretary of State for Justice*,[121] a Deputy High Court judge awarded **20.73** £1,500 (Updated: £1,585) for a violation of Article 5(2). Mr Haynes had provided witness evidence that he had suffered distress as a result of not being told the reasons for his recall to prison.[122] The Deputy High Court judge was prepared to accept that Mr Haynes must have suffered distress as a result of being re-imprisoned without being told what he was alleged to have done wrong.[123]

In our view the approach of the Deputy High Court Judge in *Haynes* was correct **20.74** and the court should examine the evidence and circumstances to assess whether the absence of prompt and adequate reasons for detention caused any distress. If so, a modest award of damages, in line with the award in *Haynes*, will be necessary to award just satisfaction.

(c) Article 5(4)

The usual practice of the ECtHR is to award damages for a violation of Article **20.75** 5(4) on the basis that the proceedings to challenge lawfulness were not sufficiently 'speedy'.[124] By contrast, it does not usually award damages, where the only flaw that led to a violation of Article 5(4) was in the fairness, as opposed to the speediness, of the proceedings.[125]

---

[118] Application Number 11956/07 (21 April 2009).
[119] Application Number 13229/03 (29 January 2008).
[120] *Saadi v United Kingdom* Application Number 13229/03 (29 January 2008) at [89].
[121] [2012] EWHC 2481 (QB) at [58].
[122] *Haynes v Secretary of State for Justice* [2012] EWHC 2481 (QB) at [54].
[123] *Haynes v Secretary of State for Justice* [2012] EWHC 2481 (QB) at [57].
[124] *R (Faulkner) v Secretary of State for Justice* [2013] UKSC 23 at [53].
[125] *R (Faulkner) v Secretary of State for Justice* [2013] UKSC 23 at [59].

20.76 In ECtHR judgments involving immigration detention, the finding of a violation of Article 5(4) has invariably been accompanied by a finding that Article 5(1) was also violated. The damages awarded are global—there is no distinction between the damages awarded for Article 5(1) and Article 5(4). However, if there were a breach of Article 5(4) in such a context, without a breach of Article 5(1), *R (Faulkner) v Secretary of State for Justice*[126] suggests that the level of damages should be significantly lower than the level awarded for a breach of Article 5(1)—in *Faulkner*, the Supreme Court held that £300 (Updated: £307) was a reasonable award of damages for the frustration and anxiety resulting from a six month delay in a parole hearing.[127]

(4) Article 8

20.77 The ECtHR has only found immigration detention to violate Article 8 in two cases, each involving the detention of children—*Mayeka and Mitunga v Belgium*[128] and *Popov v France*.[129] In each of these cases, the ECtHR found violations of Articles 3 and 5, as well as 8. It is not clear from the judgments whether a violation of Article 8, on its own, would have resulted in an award for non-pecuniary damage.

20.78 However, there are several ECtHR judgments concerning Article 8 and other kinds of detention—e.g. imprisonment pursuant to a criminal sentence. The general practice of the ECtHR is to award non-pecuniary damages for violations of Article 8 that may have caused distress to the applicant—e.g.:

(1) *Juhnke v Turkey*[130]—the applicant was made to undergo a gynaecological examination without her informed consent while she was in detention. This was held to breach Article 8 but not Article 3 and she was awarded 4,000 Euros for non-pecuniary damage.

(2) *Dickson v United Kingdom*[131]—the Government refused a prisoner access to artificial insemination facilities without taking adequate account of the interests of the prisoner and his wife. The ECtHR awarded the applicants 5,000 Euros on the basis that the breach was 'frustrating and distressing for the applicants'.

(3) *Kurkowski v Poland*[132]—the applicant prisoner was denied family visits and not allowed direct contact with his family, without any reasons being provided. He was awarded 1,500 Euros for non-pecuniary damage.

---

[126] [2013] UKSC 23.
[127] *R (Faulkner) v Secretary of State for Justice* [2013] UKSC 23 at [96].
[128] Application Number 13178/03 (12 October 2006).
[129] Application Numbers 39472/07 and 39474/07 (19 January 2012).
[130] Application Number 52515/99 (13 May 2008) at [74]–[82] and [103].
[131] Application Number 44362/04, 4 December 2007 at [92].
[132] Application Number 36228/06, 9 April 2013 at [93]–[105] and [113].

(4) *Lindstrom and Masseli v Finland*[133]—the applicant prisoners were awarded 3,000 Euros each for having to wear 'closed overalls' when that was not authorized by law.

The exceptions to this practice are generally where the violation is relatively minor—e.g. an unlawful interference with a prisoner's correspondence.[134] **20.79**

The domestic courts provide little guidance on when monetary compensation is necessary to provide just satisfaction for a violation of Article 8. The Court of Appeal in *R (Anufrijeva & Ors) v Secretary of State for the Home Department*[135] laid down some principles that were so general as to be of limited practical assistance—e.g. that first instance courts should take a 'broad brush' approach to whether a breach of Article 8 should result in damages, including the 'scale and manner of the violation' and the 'degree of loss'. Perhaps the case that provides most assistance is *R (Bernard) v Enfield*,[136] (approved in *Anufrijeva*). The claimants, a severely disabled woman and her husband-carer, were left in unsuitable accommodation for 20 months. This was held to amount to a violation of Article 8 (but not Article 3) and the claimants were awarded £10,000 (Updated: £14,384) under section 8 HRA. **20.80**

In conclusion, in our view, where immigration detention violates Article 8, it is likely to require substantial damages in order to provide just satisfaction. The practice of the ECtHR is generally to award damages for violations of prisoners' Article 8 rights unless the violations were relatively minor. In the sort of case where immigration detention violates Article 8 (e.g. *R (D) v Secretary of State for the Home Department*),[137] the claimant is likely to have suffered distress or frustration that will require monetary compensation. Where substantial damages are not available at common law, damages should be awarded under section 8 HRA. By contrast, if substantial damages are available at common law (e.g. damages for false imprisonment), that will often be sufficient to provide just satisfaction, particularly if there has been an award of aggravated damages.[138] **20.81**

---

[133] Application Number 24630/10 (14 January 2014) at [58]–[66] and [70].
[134] e.g. *Silver v UK* [1983] 6 EHHR 62; *Enea v Italy* Application Number 74912/02, 17 September 2009 at [159].
[135] [2003] EWCA Civ 1406 at [65]–[70].
[136] [2002] EWHC 2282 (Admin).
[137] [2012] EWHC 2501 (Admin).
[138] See paragraphs 20.53 and 20.58.

APPENDIX I

Quantum Case Summaries

The updated damages figures are adjusted for inflation by reference to the May 2014 Retail Price Index.[1]

CASE	*George Lunt v Liverpool City Justices*[2]
DATE	5 March 1991 (first instance 30 November 1989)
PERIOD OF ILLEGALITY	42 days
BASIC DAMAGES	£25,000 (Updated: £48,687)
AGGRAVATED DAMAGES	n/a
EXEMPLARY DAMAGES	n/a
PI DAMAGES	n/a

L, a 57-year-old man 'of impeccable character and reputation' with no prior experience of custody was wrongly committed to prison for non-payment of domestic rates. The first instance award of £13,500 (Updated: £29,153) was increased on appeal to £25,000 (Updated: £48,687). Bingham LJ said that L's age, good character, lack of prior incarceration, and poor health were all relevant. So too were the fact that the damage to L's reputation was 'relatively minor' given the absence of widespread publicity and the fact he was not arrested in public view. Also relevant were the fact the arrest was not at night or in the early morning, the absence of any accusation of serious crime, and the absence of malice or wilful abuse of power. He accepted that 'any form of imprisonment gives rise to a stigma and that stigma is not removed until the reputation of the imprisoned party is vindicated in an appropriate manner'. He observed that 'this is not a field. . . where very much help is given by seeing what happened to other [claimants] on other occasions'.

---

[1] They have not been further increased to take account of *Simmons v Castle* [2013] 1 WLR 1239, and accordingly, a further adjustment may be necessary, as discussed at paragraphs 20.26 and 20.27.
[2] CA, unreported. Referred to in *R (Evans) v Governor of Brockhill Prison (No 2)* [1998] EWCA Civ 1042; [1999] QB 1043 at p 1060B–E.

CASE	*R (Evans) v Governor of Brockhill Prison (No. 2)*[3]
DATE	19 June 1998
PERIOD OF ILLEGALITY	59 days
BASIC DAMAGES	£5,000 (Updated: £7,830)
AGGRAVATED DAMAGES	n/a
EXEMPLARY DAMAGES	n/a
PI DAMAGES	n/a

The claimant was detained for 59 days as a result of a good faith and blameless error by the prison governor in calculating her sentence end date. She was of bad character, had misbehaved during the currency of her sentence, and could not have been aware her detention was unlawful. *Lunt* was not an appropriate comparator, and the guidance in *Thompson*[4] was of no assistance. Adopting a 'global' approach, the Court of Appeal increased damages from £2,000 (Updated: £3,249) to £5,000 (Updated: £7,830).[5]

CASE	*R (B) v Special Adjudicator and Secretary of State for the Home Department*[6]
DATE	Liability: 17 December 1997. The undated quantum judgment post-dates *Evans*.
PERIOD OF ILLEGALITY	63 days
BASIC DAMAGES	£10,000 (Updated: £15,565)
AGGRAVATED DAMAGES	n/a
EXEMPLARY DAMAGES	n/a
PI DAMAGES	£8,000 (Updated: £12,452)

B, an Algerian asylum seeker, was lawfully detained in June of 1995. His detention remained lawful during the asylum determination process and the initial part of the appeals process. However, Kay J held that the submission of further evidence on 17 April 1996, which bolstered B's asylum claim, changed the position. The evidence should have been reviewed by 8 May 1996. Had that occurred the Secretary of State would have realised that the balance had 'swung firmly in favour of release on bail'. B's detention from that date until his release on 10 July 1996 was unlawful. Damages were assessed at a separate hearing by Master Turner who awarded £10,000 (Updated: £15,565) to compensate the 63 days' loss of liberty and £8,000 (Updated: £12,452) to compensate exacerbation of a pre-existing depressive disorder. A loss of earnings claim was entertained but rejected on the facts. Master Turner noted that 'at the start of April 1996, [B] heard the horrendous news that it was likely that he was to be returned to Algeria' which would 'almost invariably' have resulted in 'torture and his death'. He held that this was relevant to the quantification of both damages for psychiatric injury and basic damages, 'as each day spent in detention was a further day in which he feared the subsequent removal to Algeria'.

[3] [1998] EWCA Civ 1042; [1999] 1 QB 1043. See Chapter 20, paragraphs 20.20–20.22.
[4] *Thompson v Commissioner of Police for the Metropolis* and *Hsu v Commissioner of Police for the Metropolis* [1997] EWCA Civ 3083; [1998] QB 498, discussed at Chapter 20, paragraphs 20.18–20.23.
[5] At p. 1060B–G.
[6] Liability: [1998] Imm AR 182; [1998] INLR 315, also referred to as *R (B) v Special Adjudicator and Secretary of State for the Home Department*. The quantum judgment of Master Turner is unreported and undated. For the purpose of updating we have assumed it dates from December 1998, a year after the liability judgment.

CASE	*R (E) v Secretary of State for the Home Department*[7]
DATE	25 July 2006
PERIOD OF ILLEGALITY	Between two and three days
BASIC DAMAGES	Interim award of £4,000 (Updated: £5,156) based upon a possible final of around £6,000 (Updated: £7,735)
AGGRAVATED DAMAGES	n/a
EXEMPLARY DAMAGES	n/a
PI DAMAGES	n/a

Whilst not making a final ruling, Mitting J held that if the issue was ever tried, E's detention for 'at least two days and less than a full three days' pending his unlawful removal would inevitably be held unlawful. Damages were to be assessed by reference to *Thompson,* not *Evans,* the claimant being 'a young man of (as far as I know) good character, [who] was detained in the early hours of the morning with his family, removed to a place of detention and then put on an aeroplane under escort'. Although there was none of the stigma attaching to an arrest for a crime, 'in every other respect the circumstances are just as upsetting for the person detained as if arrested for a crime'. The judge 'would not [have been] surprised to see [a final] award of £6,000 [(Updated: £7,735)]', and ordered the payment of interim damages of £4,000 (Updated: £5,156).

CASE	*R (B) v Secretary of State for the Home Department*[8]
DATE	4 December 2008
PERIOD OF ILLEGALITY	Six months
BASIC DAMAGES	£32,000 (Updated: £38,463)
AGGRAVATED DAMAGES	£6,000 (Updated: £7,211)
EXEMPLARY DAMAGES	n/a
PI DAMAGES	n/a

B, an asylum applicant, was unlawfully detained for six months. The Secretary of State's medical practitioner failed to conduct a medical examination under Rule 34 of the Detention Centre Rules 2001. Had this happened it would, on the balance of probabilities, have resulted in a report being made under Rule 35 which in turn would have led to B's release from detention as someone in respect of whom there was independent evidence of torture. Kenneth Parker QC awarded £32,000 (Updated: £38,463) basic damages, noting that 'significant tapering of amounts in respect of longer periods of custody is necessary, in particular to ensure proportionality with other awards. . . '.[9] The judge took into account the compromise reached in *R (Johnson) v Secretary of State for the Home Department.*[10] Aggravated damages of £6,000 (Updated: £7,211) were awarded (i) because of the failure to apply rules and policies designed to ensure that, absent special circumstances, those who may have been the victims of torture were not held in detention;[11] and (ii) because the defendant maintained an unjustified defence up until the eve of the hearing in circumstances where the true situation should, with reasonable diligence, have been discovered well before that date.

---

[7] [2006] EWHC 2500 (Admin).

[8] Judgment on liability [2008] EWHC 364 (Admin); judgment on quantum [2008] EWHC 3189 (Admin).

[9] At [11].

[10] [2004] EWHC 1550. Mr Johnson was held unlawfully in the detained fast track for 32 days after a brief period of lawful detention, and then unlawfully detained for a further 27 days (a total period of 59 days). Damages were agreed at £15,000 (Updated: £20,309).

[11] At [13]. He added that the amount of uplift 'needs to incorporate a discounting factor that reflects the possibility that the claimant, notwithstanding the independent evidence, may in fact not have been a victim of torture'.

CASE	*Muuse (Abdillaahi) v Secretary of State for the Home Department*[12]
DATE	17 July 2009
PERIOD OF ILLEGALITY	128 days
BASIC DAMAGES	£25,000 (Updated: £29,978)
AGGRAVATED DAMAGES	£7,500 (Updated: £8,993)
EXEMPLARY DAMAGES	£27,500 (Updated: £32,976)
PI DAMAGES	n/a

M, a Dutch national of Somali descent, was unlawfully detained by the Home Office for 128 days in 2006 on the mistaken basis that he was a Somali national who could be deported to Somalia. At the time of his detention M was at liberty, having previously been held on remand for 147 days. On 8 August 2006 he attended court and entered guilty pleas to three charges. He was sentenced to nine months' imprisonment but time spent on remand meant he was entitled to immediate release. He was then detained by the Secretary of State. Numerous errors were made in authorizing and maintaining his detention, the most significant of which were serious failures to check M's claims to Dutch nationality before setting in play the process to deport him to Somalia.[13] The judge accepted M 'would have suffered considerable anxiety about whether or not he would be deported to Somalia' which would have increased the longer his detention continued.[14] Although M was at liberty prior to his detention, the judge held that 'having already had considerable experience of custody, [he] would not have been subject to the initial shock and experience that first time custody can bring'.[15]

Basic damages for loss of liberty were assessed at £25,000 (Updated: £29,978).[16] The judge considered the fact that M was 'wrongly put at real risk of deportation, with the fears and anxiety that such brought' to be a factor justifying aggravated damages, which were assessed at £7,500 (Updated: £8,993).[17] He said this could have been included within basic damages but it was 'preferable that there be separate awards of basic and aggravated damages to enable the award to be better understood'.[18] The approach to basic and aggravated damages was not challenged on appeal.

The judge also awarded M exemplary damages of £27,500 (Updated: £32,976), observing that 'what makes [M's] imprisonment far more serious than the more usual case. . . is the high handed and oppressive way in which it was not only initiated but maintained for such a long time in complete disregard of laid down procedures. The decision to imprison him, keeping him in custody without good cause and adequate explanation, disregard of the concerns. . . he expressed to prison officers, acceleration of his deportation. . . when his nationality could easily have been confirmed from the outset, not publicly acknowledging his nationality until [late in the day] and then not ensuring his immediate release were individually and cumulatively "high handed" and "oppressive".' He considered that they justified a 'significant punitive award'.[19]

On appeal[20] Thomas LJ observed that M's detention 'was not merely unconstitutional but an arbitrary exercise of executive power which was outrageous. It called for the award of exemplary damages by way of punishment, to deter and to vindicate the strength of the law.'[21] He criticised both the numerous discrete failings and the systemic failures which allowed these to occur.[22] The Court of Appeal declined to interfere with the level of exemplary damages awarded, Thomas LJ suggesting that, if anything, the circumstances could have merited a slightly higher figure.[23]

---

[12] [2009] EWHC 1886 (QB).
[13] See at [71].
[14] At [107].
[15] At [111].
[16] At [113].
[17] At [112]–[113].
[18] At [112].
[19] At [117].
[20] [2010] EWCA Civ 453.
[21] At [72].
[22] At [73]–[74].
[23] At [84].

CASE	*R (S, C & D) v Secretary of State for the Home Department*[24]
DATE	9 October 2009
PERIOD OF ILLEGALITY	105 days
BASIC DAMAGES	S: £25,000 (Updated: £29,618)
	C: £20,000 (Updated: £23,694)
AGGRAVATED DAMAGES	S: £5,000 (Updated: £5,923)
	C: £5,000 (Updated: £5,923)
EXEMPLARY DAMAGES	S: £5,000 (Updated: £5,923)
	C: £7,500 (Updated: £8,885)
PI DAMAGES	n/a

S, who had been temporarily admitted to the United Kingdom in 2002, lost contact with the Home Office. Following an arrest for shoplifting in July 2005 she was released and told to report to the Home Office. She reported with her two children, C (aged 4) and D (aged 9 months) on 2 August 2005 and claimed asylum. They were detained. The asylum application was refused as unfounded on 15 August 2005. They were held thereafter until 1 December 2005 for removal, and then released. Detention was ruled unlawful by the Administrative Court from 15 August 2005, a period of 105 days. The matter was then transferred to a Master for damages to be assessed. D's case was compromised in the meantime.

General damages of £25,000 (Updated: £29,618) were awarded to S, taking into account the distress she experienced as a result of witnessing the effect of detention on her children (in D's case he developed rickets and anaemia; in C's case she began to wet the bed, soil herself, and became disruptive and angry in the presence of other children). C recovered £20,000 (Updated: £23,694) general damages, a figure which took into account the effect of detention on her.[25]

Aggravated damages of £5,000 (Updated: £5,923) were awarded to each claimant, having regard in particular to the inadequate support facilities provided, the unfounded allegation that S posed a risk of absconding, misstating the time it would take to obtain documentation from the Jamaican authorities, the delay in releasing the claimants after the decision to release was taken, the unsuccessful defence before the Administrative Court, and the failure to comply with orders once the matter had been transferred to the Master.[26]

Exemplary damages were awarded in the sum of £5,000 (Updated: £5,923) to S and £7,500 (Updated: £8,885) to C. Such an award was appropriate *inter alia* because officials misled the Minister and misled bail hearings, and failed to respond appropriately to serious concerns being raised by S about her children's welfare. In particular the failure to investigate and detect the fact D was suffering from rickets and anaemia when on notice that his health and welfare were suffering was arbitrary and oppressive conduct warranting exemplary damages. The Secretary of State's breach of policy, and the decision to maintain detention when it was known S, C and D could not be removed for two months were further aggravating features. A higher award was made to C because of the deficiencies in the provision for and safeguards of children detained by the Secretary of State.[27]

[24] Unreported quantum decision following judgment of Wyn Williams J in *S, C and D v Secretary of State for the Home Department* [2007] EWHC 1654 (Admin).

[25] At [8]–[9].

[26] At [10]–[13].

[27] At [14]–[18].

CASE	R (Mehari) v Secretary of State for the Home Department[28]
DATE	22 February 2010
PERIOD OF ILLEGALITY	Eight days
BASIC DAMAGES	£4,000 (Updated: £4,669)
AGGRAVATED DAMAGES	n/a
EXEMPLARY DAMAGES	n/a
PI DAMAGES	n/a

M, a failed asylum seeker, held Eritrean and Ethiopian passports. It was accepted she was at real risk of persecution in Eritrea, so could not be removed there. However, there was no legal barrier to her being removed to Ethiopia. She was detained on 22 May 2008 and directions set for her removal to Eritrea. These were maintained until 29 May 2008 when the Court stayed her removal. She was detained thereafter with a view to removal to Ethiopia. It was common ground that M was entitled to compensation for unlawful detention between 22 and 29 May 2008. The judge awarded £4,000 (Updated: £4,669), which she referred to as a global figure that took account of M's good character and the distress the detention must have caused.

CASE	R (MK (Algeria)) v Secretary of State for the Home Department[29]
DATE	29 April 2010
PERIOD OF ILLEGALITY	24 days
BASIC DAMAGES	£12,500 (Updated: £14,357)
AGGRAVATED DAMAGES	£5,000 (Updated: £5,742)
EXEMPLARY DAMAGES	n/a
PI DAMAGES	n/a

MK was an Algerian national with a right to reside in the United Kingdom as the spouse of an EEA national. The Secretary of State wrongly concluded this right had ceased to exist and detained him for 24 days with a view to removal. Detention was unlawful from the outset.[30] Laws LJ took into account the guidance in *Thompson* and *Evans* and concluded that the appropriate figure for basic damages was £12,500 (Updated: £14,357). He further held that the case was 'pre-eminently' one for aggravated damages, given the 'blinkered and high-handed' conduct of the Home Office. Relevant factors included (i) that the claimant was entitled to rely on his EEA rights throughout his detention; (ii) administrative errors regarding MK's correct address; (iii) the defendant's failure to respond when the claimant's solicitors sought to clarify matters; (iv) the fact bail was opposed; (v) the fact the claim was initially resisted on 'extremely fragile' grounds; and (vi) the fact that liability was eventually conceded 'in grudging and not wholly appropriate terms'. The appropriate sum was £5,000 (Updated: £5,742).

[28] [2010] EWHC 636 (Admin).
[29] [2010] EWCA Civ 980.
[30] N.B.: See at [10], [12], and [13].

CASE	*E v HomeOffice*[31]
DATE	10 June 2010
PERIOD OF ILLEGALITY	30 days
BASIC DAMAGES	£12,500 (Updated: £14,273)
AGGRAVATED DAMAGES	£10,000 (Updated: £11,419)
EXEMPLARY DAMAGES	£25,000 (Updated: £28,547)
PI DAMAGES	£10,000 (Updated: £11,419)

E was unlawfully detained for 30 days in the Detained Fast Track. Detention was unlawful, *inter alia*, as a result of (i) a failure to take account of E's assertion that she had been raped in prison in Cameroon when concluding there were 'no compelling or compassionate circumstances'; (ii) failings in relation to the application of Rule 34 and 35 of the Detention Centre Rules 2001, the proper application of which would have led to E's release; and (iii) a failure to apply the policy of putting fast track cases 'on hold' when a case was accepted for pre-assessment by the Medical Foundation for the Care of Victims of Torture.[32]

General damages of £22,500 (Updated: £25,692) were awarded comprising £12,500 (Updated: £14,273) basic damages for loss of liberty and £10,000 (Updated: £11,419) for psychiatric injury (two to three years' exacerbation of a pre-existing post-traumatic stress disorder).[33]

Aggravated damages of £10,000 (Updated: £11,419) were also awarded, having regard to (i) the fact detention was unlawful for four different reasons arising at four points during the course of E's detention; (ii) the failure to conduct a medical examination under Rule 34; (iii) the fact E was not given a change of clothes when detained, betraying a lack of respect for her personal dignity; (iv) the failure to offer counselling despite this being recommended by a doctor; (v) the failure of the defendant to call evidence from any of the decision makers involved in the case; and (vi) the defendant's conduct of the proceedings generally.[34]

The judge also awarded exemplary damages of £25,000 (Updated: £28,547). The conduct which reached the threshold for a punitive award of this order was the failure of the Home Office to conduct a Rule 34 examination and have in place an adequate system for dealing with Rule 35 cases. In particular, it was relevant that the arrangements for such cases at Yarl's Wood 'remained dysfunctional notwithstanding [a] recommendation made in May 2005 by Her Majesty's Inspector of Prisons to remedy the situation'. This was 'as grave a failure on the part of the Home Office and its contractors as can be imagined in the context of this sort of case'.[35]

---

[31] Unreported, Central London County Court, Claim 9CL01651.
[32] Liability judgment at [21], [41], [51]–[55], [57].
[33] Quantum judgment at [6]–[8].
[34] Quantum judgment at [9]–[16].
[35] Quantum judgment at [17]–[21].

CASE	*R (NAB) v Secretary of State for the Home Department*[36]
DATE	13 May 2011
PERIOD OF ILLEGALITY	82 days
BASIC DAMAGES	£6,150 (£75 per day) (Updated: £6,691) (Updated: £81 per day)
AGGRAVATED DAMAGES	n/a
EXEMPLARY DAMAGES	n/a
PI DAMAGES	n/a

NAB's detention became unlawful because of inactivity on the part of the defendant and because there was no realistic prospect of removal. However, he had 'persistently and in a determined fashion' refused to cooperate with his return to Iran, rendering his removal impossible.[37] The period found to be unlawful was 82 days, following two earlier lengthy periods of lawful detention. Irwin J concluded that the appropriate award was £75 (Updated: £81) per day, or £6,150 (Updated: £6,691) in total. The 'critical factors' were (i) the absence of any 'first shock'; and (ii) the 'unusual situation' that NAB 'chose detention in the United Kingdom over freedom in Iran'.[38] These factors meant that the appropriate level of damages 'must be very much lower than in most of the reported authorities', including *Evans*.[39] Although the judge purported to apply a daily rate we would suggest that this must be read as having been assessed having regard both to NAB's particular circumstances and to the period of detention in issue. Were the position otherwise, the judge's approach would be inconsistent with the clear guidance in *Evans* that a rigid daily rate should be avoided.[40]

CASE	*R (J) v Secretary of State for the Home Department*[41]
DATE	24 November 2011
PERIOD OF ILLEGALITY	Four days
BASIC DAMAGES	£7,500 (Updated: £8,047)
AGGRAVATED DAMAGES	£2,500 (Updated: £2,682)
EXEMPLARY DAMAGES	n/a
PI DAMAGES	n/a

J, an unaccompanied child from Afghanistan, was unlawfully detained for four days. In breach of policy, reliance was placed upon a local authority age assessment which was not '*Merton*-compliant'. Detention was also unlawful owing to a failure to take into account clear and strong fresh claim representations.[42] The judge awarded £7,500 (Updated: £8,047) basic damages[43] and £2,500 (Updated: £2,682) aggravated damages. The fact J was a child who had been detained as an adult went to the unlawfulness of his detention so was held not to be an aggravating factor.[44] However, the manner of his arrest, which involved the 'painful' use of handcuffs on a young person who was 'obviously upset and who manifestly did not pose a risk either to the officers or of escape' betrayed an element of high-handedness.[45]

---

[36] [2011] EWHC 1191 (Admin). Judgment on liability: [2010] EWHC 3137 (Admin).
[37] At [2].
[38] At [17].
[39] See Chapter 20, paragraphs 20.20 and 20.21, and case summary in Appendix I.
[40] See Chapter 20, paragraph 20.20.
[41] [2011] EWHC 3073.
[42] At [17]–[18], [23]–[26], [37].
[43] At [41].
[44] At [44].
[45] At [46].

CASE	*R (M) v Secretary of State for the Home Department*[46]
DATE	6 December 2011
PERIOD OF ILLEGALITY	Eight and a half hours during the course of an unlawful removal
BASIC DAMAGES	Father: £2,500 (Updated: £2,672) Mother: £3,000 (Updated: £3,206) Son: £2,500 (Updated: £2,672) Daughter 1: £3,000 (Updated: £3,206) Daughter 2: £3,000 (Updated: £3,206)
AGGRAVATED DAMAGES	Father: £2,000 (Updated: £2,137) Mother: £3,000 (Updated: £3,206) Son: £2,000 (Updated: £2,137) Daughter 1: £3,000 (Updated: £3,206) Daughter 2: £3,000 (Updated: £3,206)
EXEMPLARY DAMAGES	n/a
PI DAMAGES	n/a

It was conceded that the claimant family had been unlawfully removed from the United Kingdom and their detention for the purpose of that removal from 2.20 am until 10.50 am was unlawful. The claimants contended their detention was especially traumatic given the hour and the manner in which it was conducted, and that this was particularly so for the mother, who suffered from mental health problems, and for the family's two daughters, who were then aged eight and fourteen. The family's son was just over eighteen. The judge awarded the father and the son £2,500 (Updated: £2,672) basic damages and £2,000 (Updated: £2,137) aggravated damages each and the mother and two daughters £3,000 (Updated: £3,206) basic damages and £3,000 (Updated: £3,206) aggravated damages each.[47]

Special damages for the value of property lost during the removal were also awarded in the sum of £10,000 (subject to the defendant being given 28 days in which to raise a challenge that award).[48]

CASE	*R (Bent) v Secretary of State for the Home Department*[49]
DATE	28 September 2012
PERIOD OF ILLEGALITY	23 days
BASIC DAMAGES	£12,500 (Updated: £13,098)
AGGRAVATED DAMAGES	n/a
EXEMPLARY DAMAGES	n/a
PI DAMAGES	n/a

B, a Jamaican overstayer, was detained for 37 days in 2011. His initial detention to effect removal was lawful, given the factors pointing to a risk of absconding. However, by the time 15 days had passed there were representations before the defendant disclosing at least a prima facie case for leave to remain, it was apparent that risk of absconding was not as high as previously thought, and proceedings were underway, meaning matters would not be resolved quickly. Detention thereafter was 'a disproportionate and unnecessary response to the concerns which initially led to the decision to detain'.[50] The claimant was unlawfully detained for 23 days. The judge awarded £12,500 (Updated: £13,098) basic damages.[51]

---

[46] [2011] EWHC 3667 (Admin).
[47] At [31].
[48] At [33].
[49] [2012] EWHC 4036 (Admin).
[50] At [109].
[51] At [113]–[116].

CASE	*R (Shaw & Anor) v Secretary of State for the Home Department*[52]
DATE	18 January 2013
PERIOD OF ILLEGALITY	Ten hours during the course of an unlawful removal
BASIC DAMAGES	£2,000 (Updated: £2,082) for each claimant
AGGRAVATED DAMAGES	n/a
EXEMPLARY DAMAGES	n/a
PI DAMAGES	n/a

The claimants (a mother and son) were unlawfully removed from the United Kingdom to Jamaica. The period of detention in issue was the 10 hours from the point they were told they were to be removed until they were able to leave the aircraft in Jamaica. It was common ground that this period amounted to detention. The judge awarded each claimant £2,000 (Updated: £2,082).

CASE	*NS (Palestine) v Secretary of State for the Home Department*[53]
DATE	21 August 2013
PERIOD OF ILLEGALITY	12 months
BASIC DAMAGES	£36,000 (Updated: £36,702)
AGGRAVATED DAMAGES	n/a
EXEMPLARY DAMAGES	n/a
PI DAMAGES	n/a

The final 12 months of the claimant's 32 and a half month detention were unlawful. Following a change in circumstances there ceased to be a reasonable prospect of removal within a reasonable time.[54] He had failed to cooperate but the Court considered that even with cooperation it was unlikely removal could be effected[55] and declined to follow *NAB* in assessing damages. NS recovered basic damages of £36,000 (Updated: £36,702).[56] This was the full sum claimed.

---

[52] [2013] EWHC 42 (Admin).
[53] [2013] CSOH 139 (Outer House of the Court of Session).
[54] At [28].
[55] At [26]–[28].
[56] At [33].

CASE	*R (Mallick) v Secretary of State for the Home Department*[57]
DATE	8 October 2013
PERIOD OF ILLEGALITY	Three days
BASIC DAMAGES	£5,000 (Updated: £5,079)
AGGRAVATED DAMAGES	n/a
EXEMPLARY DAMAGES	n/a
PI DAMAGES	n/a

M, who had been present in the United Kingdom on a student visa, was unlawfully detained for three days prior to his removal. The decision to detain had been premised in significant part upon an allegation of deception which an Immigration Judge subsequently found to be 'wholly flawed'. The Secretary of State had 'failed to point to a proper evidential foundation. . . for the centrally important conclusion as to deception on which she relied',[58] and as such M was unlawfully detained for the three days in issue. Basic damages of £5,000 (Updated: £5,079), the sum sought by the claimant, were awarded.

---

[57] [2013] EWHC 3220 (Admin).
[58] At [46].

CASE	*R (Lamari) v Secretary of State for the Home Department*[59]
DATE	16 October 2013
PERIOD OF ILLEGALITY	23 days
BASIC DAMAGES	£10,000 (Updated: £10,158)
AGGRAVATED DAMAGES	£5,000 (Updated: £5,079)
EXEMPLARY DAMAGES	£10,000 (Updated: £10,158)
PI DAMAGES	n/a

L challenged the legality of his detention by reference to the mental health provisions in EIG 55.10 and on *Hardial Singh* grounds. He had been detained on 21 December 2010 following a 12-month prison sentence. HHJ Cotter QC found L to have been unlawfully detained for 23 days.[60] He also found the Secretary of State to be in contempt of court for failing to honour an undertaking that had been given regarding the claimant's release.[61] Her officials' conduct was, he said, 'a direct snub to the court without any justification'.[62] By ignoring the undertaking the Secretary of State had caused a deterioration in L's condition 'and created a serious and significant extra risk of suicide'.[63]

The failure to release by the agreed deadline, or in the two days thereafter, was an aggravating feature.[64] A decision to re-authorize detention on the third day after the agreed release date was 'even more serious', being 'an outrageous flouting of an undertaking and order'.[65] The position was further exacerbated by the defendant applying to a different judge to be released from her undertaking, in the course of which she advanced 'incomplete and misleading information'.[66] Her conduct amounted to an 'astonishing, wilful and highhanded disregard of the court and the rights of the Claimant'. L's eventual release was mismanaged, resulting in him having to sleep on the street without money for food or water.[67] The Secretary of State's conduct was 'little short of shameful'.[68]

Basic damages of £10,000 (Updated: £10,158) were awarded.[69] Aggravated damages of £5,000 (Updated: £5,079) were awarded[70] having regard in particular to (i) the fact that the continuation of the claimant's detention beyond the date agreed for his release impacted upon his mental health; (ii) the conduct of the litigation; and (iii) the defendant's conduct when releasing the claimant.[71] Exemplary damages of £10,000 (Updated: £10,158) were awarded.[72] The judge had 'little hesitation in finding that the relevant conduct in this case was indeed outrageous'. There was, 'an extraordinary, wilful and highhanded disregard of the court and the Claimant's rights flowing from his success at court. The disregard of the court was arbitrary and unconstitutional and taken against the background of the Claimant's mental health. . . it was most obviously oppressive.' There had been a 'gross misuse of power' in continuing to detain the claimant despite the undertaking and an order of the court that required his release.[73]

[59] [2013] EWHC 3130 (QB).
[60] At [1].
[61] See separate judgment on this issue: [2012] EWHC 1895 (Admin) at [42].
[62] [2013] EWHC 3130 (QB) at [10].
[63] At [21].
[64] [28].
[65] At [29]–[30].
[66] At [31].
[67] At [34].
[68] At [37].
[69] At [50].
[70] At [65].
[71] At [58]–[60].
[72] At [90].
[73] At [74]–[75].

INDEX